C000254029

YORKSHIRE

A

VISITOR'S

GUIDE

by

Stuart W. Quin

sheffield

—A Visitor Guide To Yorkshire—

CONTENTS

published by Stuart W Quin   December 2012   -ISBN- 978-0-9574979-0-0

Leeds-Liverpool canal
Bingley five rise locks

USING THIS GUIDE

This is a travel companion for residents and visitors.
Increasing leisure time now makes it feasible for Yorkshire folk to enjoy a day out to any one or more of the county's 40 to 50 main towns and cities, two national parks, two areas of outstanding natural beauty and the many stately homes, abbeys and castles. For the visitor from further afield, it should provide a useful reference manual to decide where to go, how to get there, and then to inform the visit. Each chapter about a town or city provides the reader with a brief history, advice as to how to get there, what to do and see when there, and information on restaurants hotels and car parking.

Listing of places Not everywhere is covered; to do so would be impractical. Small towns and villages are generally not included nor are those towns and cities formerly part of the county, and equally Yorkshires many stately homes castles and abbeys are only included if they are normally open to visit.

Restaurants and Hotels The information provided on restaurants and hotels cannot be fully comprehensive; the listings tending to be those with positive user reviews. Of course, life moves on, and changing economic conditions may mean that some of those listed in the guide will be different or simply not be there.

Restaurants (maps show restaurants etc in green : ●) are classified according to cost and type of food. For cost, a typical a la carte two course meal with half bottle of mid priced wine and coffee has been taken as the benchmark.

£ less than £20 per head	££ £20-£30 per head
£££ £30-£40 per head	££££ more than £40 per head

Hotels (maps show hotels in purple : ●) are classified by their star rating as far as possible. Presently, there is much use of a self classification system and many hotels now rely on their reputation with no formal star or diamond designation. There are some guest houses included, almost exclusively in relation to the smaller towns, but regrettably space limitations prevent any information on self catering accommodation or camp sites.

Public transport information is given on regular services as far as possible. Plainly, these may be subject to change. Occasional and seasonal services are generally not included. This affects particularly some bus routes into the Dales and Moors that only run on some days in the summer months.

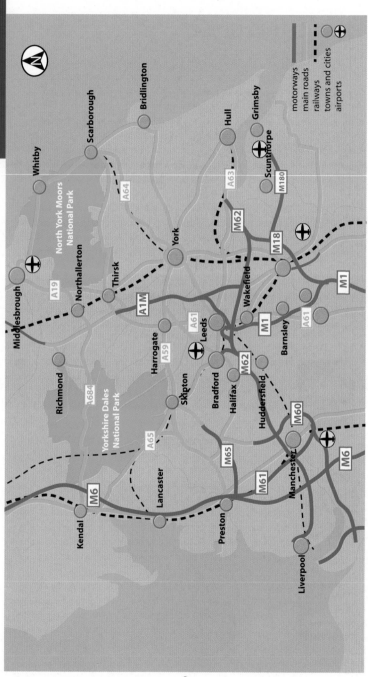

motorways
main roads
railways
towns and cities
airports

INTRODUCING YORKSHIRE

Scarborough North Bay

"Gods own county" is the phrase often quoted about Yorkshire, and it is alleged-ly said that Yorkshire folk have as strong a sense of loyalty to their county as to their country. The sense of identity and belonging is more evident here than in most other parts of England. Yorkshire men and women celebrate their heritage and are quick to defend both their countrymen and the place of their birth or resi-dence. The county cricket club was one of the last cricket bastions to drop a re-quirement of having been born in the county as a requirement to play for the club.

What is certain is the county's size. By some margin, it is the largest in the UK; and larger than some sovereign states like Luxembourg. Stretching from Low Bentham near Lancaster in the west, across to Flamborough Head in the east is a distance of over 100 miles; and from the south of Sheffield to Staithes in the north, again a distance of over 100 miles. The county's population, at around 5million, is larger than that of the Republic of Ireland or of New Zealand. Although often described as the north of England, in terms of the UK, it is centrally placed. It is as far to Edinburgh from Leeds as it is to London and modern communications make it a comfortable days return journey from each.

Yorkshire's 6000 square miles are a rich blend of landscape and culture. They embrace widely differing experiences; from the cosmopolitan bustle of Leeds to the isolation and tranquillity of the North Yorkshire Moors; from the steep paths and high dry stone walled green lanes of the Pennine hills to the wide safe sandy beaches of the coastal resorts, and from the dark and moody towering cliffs on the north part of the coast to the narrow flat sand spit on the south. Yorkshire's environment is widely varied and always interesting.

Rich diversity of the physical environment matches a richly diverse culture. The West Riding towns and cities, with their 24hr culture and vibrant hedonistic nightlife, strike a vivid contrast with the relaxed, gentle pace of life in places like the Vale of York and the Yorkshire Dales. Such distinguishing distinc-tive features create a strong magnet both for visitors from outside the county, and equally for residents of the county – Yorkshire folk visit their own coun-ty's attractions more than residents of any other English county visit theirs.

History

Prehistoric 7000-1000BC Archaeological excavation and research shows that the county was inhabited in prehistoric times. Remains of human settlement from the Mesolithic era (7-8000BC) have been found on the east coast and traces of hunting encampments are also evident in the Pennines.

Neolithic 1000BC- 100AD Neolithic settlers left their mark across the county, and in particular there are monuments like Thornborough Henge (near Masham) which can be regarded as comparable in impor-tance to Salisbury plain and Stonehenge as a Neolithic ritual landscape.

INTRODUCTION

the Roman multangular tower in York

The Iron Age from about 700BC has left a legacy of hill forts such as at Sutton bank (see page 278) and at Castle Hill near Huddersfield (see page 223), together with a settlement pattern, much of which survives today. The Iron Age brought to the area the Brigantes. Probably of Celtic origin, this warlike tribe established the Yorkshire area as their kingdom and, over time, controlled much of northern England. Although adapted by the Romans, the Brigantes established forts in Aldborough (see page 385) and at Ilkley (see page 105).

Romans 55AD-450AD It was with the Brigantes the Romans had to contend when they ventured north into the county. There are remains of the Roman fort at Templeborough (see page 250) which was probably established about 55AD, but by 71AD Roman rule had been achieved across the county, and York, called Eboracum (see page 25) created as the Roman capital of the north. Eboracum became a miniature Rome; Roman emperors lived here- Constantine, the emperor who espoused Christianity, was crowned here in 306 and, within its walls, at least two emperors died and one is said to have been born, and from it, the whole of Britain was governed. The advanced civilising ability of the colonisers is very evident today in the remains of York as a walled city; and across the county in the lead and tin mines and the efficient roads, which connected the principal camps and centres. The Romans built their roads straight; rather than diverting around, they would go straight over a hill and evidence of this abounds both in the Vale of York- Dere Street linking York with Aldborough, and in the Dales, the Roman road from Bainbridge climbs straight up over Fleet Moss. Roman occupation continued for nearly 400 years, and gradually ceased as the Empire declined in about 400-500AD.

INTRODUCTION

Thornborough Henge from the air

Anglo-Saxons 450AD-850AD German invaders from Schleswig Holstein came ashore in the 5thC and 6thC and quickly spread; Yorkshire becoming the Kingdom of Deira. It was during this time that Christianity became widely practiced, first as an adaption of Celtic tradition, then after the Synod of Whitby in 663, (see page 298) in conformity with Rome. The remains of religious buildings from this period include the crypt at Ripon cathedral (see page 135) and Whitby Abbey.

The Viking Era 850AD-1066AD The invasion of the Danish Vikings was a time of plunder and destruction. These bellicose tribes destroyed churches and monasteries built by the Anglo-Saxons and demolished York's walls, although they based much of their administration here and renamed the city Jorvik. It was under Danish rule that the now traditional administrative areas of the county known as Ridings (East, West, and North) were first established; the boundaries being drawn in a manner so that they met at Jorvik. Riding -in Danish *projungr*- means a third. The Vikings did not capture all of England; indeed it was only Yorkshire and parts of the Midlands and North East which came completely under their control. Fierce battles with the Anglo-Saxons were frequent, some for control of York itself, until the battle of Stamford Bridge in 1066 when the English king Harold Godwinson (who would perish at the Battle of Hastings some three weeks after) finally routed the Danes under Harold Hardrada. A number of common Yorkshire words derive from this period : gate (gata) Norse for street; beck means stream; thwaite meaning a village or small settlement.

The Normans 1066-1154 William the Conqueror's bloody victory at Hastings was not immediately followed by hegemony over England, and there was much resistance to Norman rule. Yorkshire proved particularly troublesome; the indigenous Anglo Saxons laying siege to and eventually slaughter ing the Norman garrison in York. William was forced to quell rebellions here in a campaign between 1068 and 1071 known as the Harrying of the North, where Yorkshire was laid waste through a scorched earth policy.   The rebellion put down, much of the county was given by William to powerful Norman barons such as Ilbert de Lacy, and Robert de Romille, who had lent support to his military interventions. These nobles built castles for both defensive and domestic purposes (such as those at Middleham and Pontefract), and sponsored the founding of great Abbeys. Selby Abbey is said to have been sponsored by William the Conqueror not only to mark the birth of his son Henry (later Henry I) but also as a penance to atone for his bloodthirsty activity in the Harrying of the North.   The Normans founded 14 large abbeys, with remains of at least 9 still evident.   The barons pursued ambitions to extend their new found landed wealth by developing towns and villages and so the likes of Richmond and Pontefract became prominent towns, and the establishment of a system for the awarding of a charter to hold a market began, with many 12th and 13th century charters surviving.

Later middle ages   The 12th and 13thC also saw the rise of small scale farming as well as the emergence of iron, lead and coal industries. Beverley and York were pre-eminent in the cloth industry, although by the early 14thC this had been eroded with the development of cottage industries in the West Riding area. The Black Death spread to the county in about 1345 decimating the population, but in its wake came the better availability of land and the rise of the wealthy farmers and minor gentlefolk, and many of the large landed estates, such as Ripley, and Duncombe Park date from this period.

The 15th-17thC   Disputes over land and right to inherit were rife in royal circles in the late 14thC and led, some fifty years later, to the Wars of The Roses, a civil war between the Royal Houses of York and Lancaster. This took place, sporadically, between about 1455 and 1485 and culminated in the ascension to the throne of Henry Tudor, of the House of Lancaster, who successfully fought the Yorkist King Richard III at Bosworth (in Leicestershire) in 1485. Although ostensibly a war between two northern families, it was fought across the country. There were battles in the county. The Battle of Wakefield, fought near Sandal Castle in 1460, which claimed the life of Richard Duke of York, and the bloody Battle of Towton (near Tadcaster) in 1461 where the Yorkist Edward roundly defeated the Lancastrian King Henry VI, temporarily assuming the throne before Henry briefly reclaimed it in 1470.   The mid 16thC saw the county in disarray from Henry VIII's dissolution of the Monasteries. There were many important abbeys in the county, whose abbots had become all powerful, and not always religious.   Reaction to the dissolution in Yorkshire was the Pilgrimage of Grace. Centred in York, it was a rebellion, by both religious leaders and some senior landed barons, to Henry's proposals, but it was bloodily put down; one of the leading exponents, the Abbot of Jervaulx Abbey (see page 393) being hunted down and executed for treason. Henry proceeded to sell of many of the lands and properties of the Abbeys. In a county the size of Yorkshire the sale of all of 120 abbeys that had been developed over the centuries created many more

11

large privately owned estates. The latter part of the 16thC, under Elizabeth I, saw a rise in wealth and prosperity from new industrial processes and farming improvements. The steady increase in population created demand to enclose agricultural land and there was a noticeable development of cottage industries, particularly in the cloth trade in the western part of the county. The start of the 17thC saw the rise of Sheffield as England's preeminent centre for cutlery production and Leeds rise as a centre for cloth and associated industries; indeed, the Pennine towns and villages were now exerting increased influence in trade and commerce, sometimes at the expense of hitherto dominant towns further east such as Ripon and Beverley.

Roundheads and Cavaliers were however the headline story of this era, as the English civil war was played out in full in the county. Some towns and cities such as York were inextricably Royalist and cavalier; some, like Hull, implacably Parliamentarian and roundhead; indeed when the governor of Hull, Sir John Hotham, refused entry to King Charles I in 1642, it is said that this act was the catalyst sparking onset of the full scale English civil war, an event which tore Yorkshire apart with divided royalties. It included the Battle of Marston Moor which took place in 1644, the largest battle of the war with over 45,000 men assembled on the flat fields between York and Tadcaster.

18thC to Modern Day Large country houses and toll roads were features of the 18thC, with many of the great houses such as Castle Howard and Wentworth Woodhouse stemming from this period. In the urban areas the continued rise of industrial and commercial classes saw West Riding towns expand; York

Richmond castle: built by Norman barons

Pontefract market still going strong after 700 years

became a prominent city of middle and upper class gentility, and Hull's importance grew as it exploited burgeoning marine commerce such as the whaling industry. The start of the 1800's witnessed inexorable growth of West Riding towns and cities as industrialisation took hold; population mushroomed in cities like Bradford, Sheffield and Leeds and created the fortunes of ironmasters and other self made men; fortunes which some spent wisely in philanthropic and civic projects. People like Titus Salt (see page 159), John Barran (see page 166), and Thomas Ferens (see page 360) stamped an indelible mark on Yorkshire to the benefit of thousands of people, both then and now. Some developments, such as Salts Mill, and inventions such as the Bessemer converter, were the most advanced in the world of their time and underlined Britain's claim to be the world's foremost power.

Accompanying great wealth was great poverty and often inhumane working and living conditions with resultant spread of disease and early death. Some publicly spirited entrepreneurs such as Titus Salt, Joseph Rowntree (see page 42) and Edward Aykroyd (see page 218) sought to improve the conditions of their workers and so model settlements of Saltaire, Copley and New Earswick were created.

Railways came to the county in the early 19thC and revolutionised transport, becoming a staple means of communication and efficient conveyor of goods and commerce. Innovators and entrepreneurs such as George Hudson (see page 30) were responsible for establishing the comprehensive networks of railway lines and iconic station buildings such as Huddersfield and York that are an integral part of today's life. The rise of the industrial classes and the availability of railway travel produced much demand for holidays on the east coast, and most of Yorkshire's resorts can trace their growth and prosperity back to this time when lavish plans, not always followed through, envisaged the creation of holiday paradises. The Grand Hotel at Scarborough is testimony to that (see page 312), as is the West Cliff development at Whitby. The 19thC left Yorkshire folk with a legacy of great parks and town halls, theatres, concert halls and other monuments ensuring today's residents and visitors can enjoy the rich heritage created by far sighted, ambitious but philanthropic Victorian spirit and now given a new lease of life in many the county's towns and cities.

The 20th century has been a curate's egg for the county where, although communications and living standards have improved beyond the wildest dreams of Yorkshire folk's 19thC forebears, much of the erstwhile industrial dominance has faded, and Yorkshire people, like most in Britain, have endured the ravages and heartache of two world wars. As the century came to a close, new modern industry began to emerge, and together with a re-energised focus on arts, culture, heritage, and access to the great outdoors, the county's prospects for the 21st century in the longer term look very positive.

Leeds Town Hall   icon of Victorian municipal grandeur

Getting here

Yorkshires position, in the centre of the UK, makes it easily accessible from all parts of the country, as well as from Europe, by land, by air and by sea. Journey times from London by train can be as little as 1 hour 45 minutes to York, whilst a flight to Leeds Bradford Airport from Paris or Amsterdam is little over an hour.

By Air

Leeds/Bradford Airport 8 miles north west of Leeds. The airport has an increasing range of flights from European cities with regular flights from Amsterdam, Paris, Dusseldorf, Dublin, Brussels, Milan and Rome. There are also domestic connections with London (Heathrow) Edinburgh, Aberdeen, Glasgow, Belfast, Bristol, Southampton, Exeter.   0871 288 2288   www.lbia.co.uk

Robin Hood Airport (Doncaster) 0871 220 2210 www.robinhoodairport.com
Humberside Airport (Kirmington) 0844 8877747 www.humbersideairport.com
Teesside Airport   08712 242426 www.durhamteesvalleyairport.com
All have more limited connections, but offer regular services with Amsterdam and other UK destinations.

Manchester Airport lies about 50 miles west of Leeds in Lancashire but is the nearest fully international airport with regular flights from all parts of the world. Access from Manchester airport is by train or by motorway. The airport has a regular train service to Leeds, Huddersfield, Sheffield, Doncaster, York, and Scarborough. The M56, M60 and M62 motorways provide a motorway connection with Leeds and Hull. Journey time from the airport to Leeds is about 60—75 mins dependent on traffic.   08712 710711 www.manchesterairport.co.uk

By Rail

Yorkshire benefits from comprehensive national and local services. There are frequent trains from London (King's Cross) to Doncaster, Wakefield, Leeds, York Hull, and from London (St Pancras) to Sheffield. Frequent services from Manchester, Liverpool, Newcastle, Birmingham, Bristol, Aberdeen, Glasgow, and Edinburgh call at Leeds and York.

INTRODUCTION

By sea
access from Northern and Western Europe is convenient and comfortable with regular overnight ferry crossings to Hull from both Rotterdam and Zeebrugge (Belgium)   08716 642020 www.poferries.com

By coach
Coach services to the county's main towns and cities go from London (Victoria) in addition to comprehensive cross country services from Birmingham, Plymouth, Newcastle and other cities. 08717 818178 www.nationalexpress.com

By road
The county is very well served by the extensive UK motorway network, the M1 and A1 passing north - south through the middle of the county. The M62 passes east - west between Liverpool and Hull, part of the trans-european route   E20 from   N Ireland to   St Petersburg.

Getting around the county

For those visitors and residents who do not use or do not wish to use a car, getting around Yorkshire can be achieved in a wide variety of ways.

Public Transport The comprehensive network of rail and bus services services makes most places accessible. Bus services cover most of the county. Most towns and cities now have dedicated bus stations, many adjoining the principal rail station. Details of these services are set out in each chapter.

Cycling There is a growing network of long distance cycleways, some using tracks and bridleways exclusively, some using generally minor roads. The main signposted long distance national routes are:

  1 : Humber Bridge through Hull and Scarborough to Whitby
  62: Woodhead Pass via Doncaster to Selby
  65: Middlesbrough to Hull via York and Selby
  66: Hull to York
  67: Leeds to Sheffield
  68: Holmfirth through the Dales National Park to Appleby in Cumbria

There are also some regional cycle routes, the most notable being a 130 mile circumnavigation of the Dales, starting or finishing in Ilkley or Skipton. More information on cycle routes can be found on www.sustrans.org

Walking There are well established popular long distance footpaths which bring the walker into or through Yorkshire.

The Pennine Way perhaps the first long distance footpath established after the second world war, this 268 mile trail, from the Peak District to the Scottish border, enters the county south west of Huddersfield, and follows the high hills as far as Tan Hill near the head of Swaledale.

www.thepennineway.co.uk

The Dales Way from Ilkley to Windermere, this 80 mile route wends through Wharfedale and Ribblehead before descending into Cumbria at Dentdale.

www.dalesway.org.uk

The Cleveland Way a semi circular route of about 106 miles, it starts in Helmsley and loops around the top of the North York Moors before following the spectacular east coast down to Filey.

www.nationaltrail.co.uk/clevelandway/

Coast to Coast a strenuous walk of 190 miles from St Bees head in Cumbria to Ravenscar, it enters the county by Tan Hill at the top of Swaledale and crosses the county to the east coast. www.coast2coast.co.uk

There is an established company who provide a courier service for walking and cycling holidays in the county, ferrying bags from one overnight accommodation to the next night. www.brigantesenglishwalks.com 01756 770402

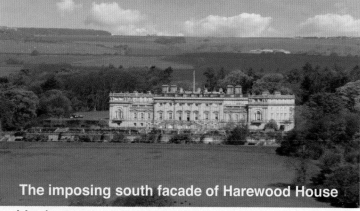

The imposing south facade of Harewood House

Heritage

Yorkshire's diversity as a county and long history as a prominent region of Great Britain has endowed a rich heritage. From the ancient abbeys, Edwardian theatres and museums, tranquil villages, to the natural beauty of the Moors and the Dales, Yorkshire offers something for everyone. Museums and art galleries form popular family attractions and nearly every town boasts at least one museum or art gallery; Leeds, Sheffield and other cities lay claim to several, some of international standard.

The National Media Museum in Bradford (see page154) is designated a world class facility, as is the National Railway Museum in York (see page 33). Preservation of the County's once all powerful abbeys, and its historic and romantic castles provides a valuable educational resource and historical experience. No visit to Richmond would be complete without venturing into the castle and enjoying the dramatic panoramic views over its walls facing the River Swale to appreciate the sheer dominance and defensive strengths of this Norman edifice. Likewise, the city of York offers seemingly unlimited heritage; its Roman and Viking pedigree well documented, with its walls and historic street pattern creating a unique experience; a place where a week's stay is probably insufficient for a realistic appreciation of its instrumental role in the making of Yorkshire; indeed its wider influence on British history.

Contrast York with Heptonstall on the shoulders of the high Pennines where this tiny settlement, with its largely unaltered streets and buildings, take the visitor back to the 17thC and the then prosperous cottage industry of cloth weaving. Yorkshire's broad expanse of countryside is home to iconic country houses whose survival is testimony to their unique historical importance. The imposing yet graceful outlines of Castle Howard dominate the northern edge of the Howardian Hills; its history and the characters associated with it provide the visitor with a who's who of 18thC and 19thC Britain. Such a rich vein of history echoes through other stately edifices and include Harewood House, Wentworth Woodhouse and Brodsworth Hall.

Culture, sport and the great outdoors

Yorkshire enjoys a rich variety of cultural activity and a wide range of sporting activity. Internationally renowned artists and sculptors have their work displayed across the county; the Hockney gallery in Saltaire containing much of the prolific output of Bradford born artist David Hockney; The Yorkshire Sculpture Park near Wakefield with many pieces of Castleford born Henry Moores work, as well as a panoply of the work of other internationally distinguished sculptors, whilst in the nearby Hepworth Gallery in Wakefield are many of the sculptures of local girl Dame Barbara Hepworth.

Theatres and entertainment venues have seen a revival; many Victorian and Edwardian buildings have been restored, some with the benefit of lottery grants, to enable authentic re-creation of their original aura and atmosphere. The Royal Hall in Harrogate; the Spa complex in Scarborough, as well as places such as the Grand Theatre in Leeds all provide a regular entertainment programme and allow patrons to experience the "Good Old Days". But culture and entertainment are not confined to historic theatres and concert halls; Yorkshire peoples' organisational spirit produces many other events, such as the Bramham Festival, held in the grounds of Bramham Park near Wetherby, where over 70,000 pop music fans gather for a three day cornucopia of pop music performed by top bands and artists every August, or Castle Howard, Van Brughs masterpiece country house near Malton, which plays host to an annual outdoor prom concert. At a smaller scale, the streets of Haworth and other nearby villages are regularly filled with Morris dancers during the summer period, while in July the country's biggest agricultural show, the Yorkshire Show is held in Harrogate. Yorkshire sporting prowess is ably demonstrated across the county. World class athletics and swimming facilities allows Sheffield to host high profile swimming and athletic events, whilst the county has 10 football clubs playing in the top British leagues, and 7 Super League rugby clubs.

For hundreds of years the county has been a centre of excellence for the horseracing fraternity, and the sport remains a staple offering for racegoers from all over the country. There are no fewer than 9 courses offering a high frequency of racedays throughout the year, and some icon races to see, such as Doncaster's St Leger, the oldest and longest of the British racing classics which has been held at the course every year since 1776.

The county's extensive rural areas include two long established national parks – the Moors and the Dales - as well as the Areas of Outstanding Natural Beauty of Nidderdale and the Howardian Hills. Additionally, there are vast tracts of peaceful countryside, dotted with country pubs and inns, as well as a well used network of footpaths and bridleways. The many routes that can be taken from York across to the east coast offer quiet byways and attractive scenery, particularly when crossing the Wolds to the west of Driffield; or if travelling west towards Lancashire, a traveller can get a taste of the wild countryside and moorland with its ever changing and panoramic long distance views.

The Yorkshire coast stretches for over 100 miles from the dark brooding high cliffs at Boulby, down to the flat erosion torn headland of Spurn Point on the northern estuary of the Humber, encompassing on the way quaint fishing villages like Staithes, historic towns like Whitby, and the pirate coves of Robin Hoods Bay and Boggle hole, before reaching the family resorts of Scarborough, Filey and Bridlington.

Yorkshire hospitality

Yorkshire people are renowned for their pride, straight-talking honesty and refusal to "beat around the bush"; some would say Yorkshire folk do not always ascribe to the well worn Wykehamist epithet "Manners Makyth Man", but however blunt and straightforward they may be, it is a fact that Yorkshire folk are famed for their warm and generous hospitality. For whatever reason, they seem to have an innate ability to make visitors feel at home and to provide a friendly quality of service that inspires many return visits.

Boulby high cliffs

There are over 215 million visits to Yorkshire annually and the visitor economy is now one of the county's biggest industries. The county boasts a plethora of restaurants, bars, and country pubs to satisfy every taste and pocket, as well as a growing number of fine dining and Michelin starred establishments. There are traditional, and long established, curry houses in Bradford that serve delicious authentic currys - it is not for nothing that the city has won the Curry Capital of Great Britain award on a number of occasions. There are innumerable chain restaurants in most towns across the county, as well as an increasing number of pubs who have widened their offering to include lunch time and evening meals, often with outstanding success in providing good home cooked value for money meals. The big cities have a constantly changing and evolving range of bistros and bars aimed at disciples of a metropolitan way of life, and the offers available to the visitor for fine dining are growing, both in the cities and in the countryside. The Pipe and Glass, a small pub near Beverley, has gained a nationwide reputation for innovative home cooked fine food and has achieved a Michelin star rating; the Box Tree at Ilkley, long an established gourmet eatery has also held a Michelin rating. The increase in the range and quality of eating establishments is mirrored by hotels and other overnight accommodation.

It wasn't too long ago that a visitor's choice of places to stay in some parts of the county was relatively constrained, but the visitor is now confronted with a wide selection of overnight accommodation, most of good quality. Not only is there choice in the traditional 3/4 star accommodation, such as Marriott hotels and Holiday Inns, but for one night stays, or for visitors on a tight budget, there is a wide choice of accommodation in Travelodges and Ibis hotels and similar brands. For those seeking something different,  the boutique hotel is gaining in popularity. Small boutique hotels such as the Traddock in Austwick near Settle, or the Feversham Arms in Helmsley offer a comfortable night in individually designed rooms and food of very high quality.

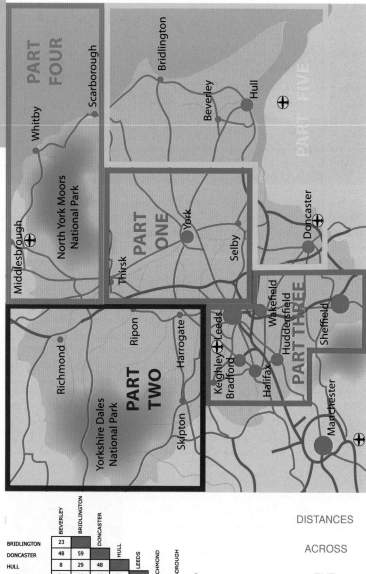

DISTANCES

ACROSS

THE

COUNTY

(in miles)

	BEVERLEY	BRIDLINGTON	DONCASTER	HULL	LEEDS	RICHMOND	SCARBOROUGH	SHEFFIELD	SKIPTON	WHITBY
BRIDLINGTON	23									
DONCASTER	48	59								
HULL	8	29	48							
LEEDS	51	68	35	56						
RICHMOND	82	94	72	90	55					
SCARBOROUGH	41	18	77	47	69	75				
SHEFFIELD	59	85	27	72	38	96	108			
SKIPTON	75	89	62	86	26	59	96	67		
WHITBY	61	38	82	67	73	64	20	113	98	
YORK	31	44	36	41	25	52	44	64	48	49

PART ONE
THE VALE OF YORK

THE VALE OF YORK

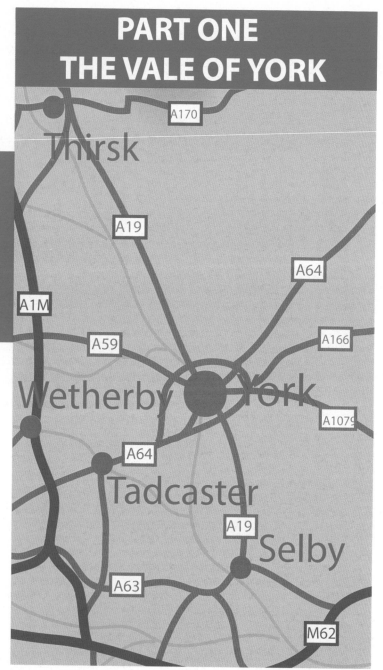

YORK

York Minster at night

*"**The history of York is the History of England**"* was a very prescient comment by King George VI – who was Duke of York before ascending to the throne. Perhaps the best-known city in Britain after London and Edinburgh, York lies in the very heart of the county. Popular particularly with American tourists, the city of New York is named after Britain's Duke of York. No fewer than six Dukes of York- generally the second son of the Royal family- have ended up as King. Despite economic changes as the city's traditional industries have withered and new ones emerged, particularly around the University, the historic core of the city retains its reputation as a popular destination for visitors worldwide. This book cannot do justice to all of York's character, its rich historical provenance and its universally compelling attraction to visitors; but as part of the county to which it gives it name, it must figure as one of the most important places to visit.

History

York was generally acknowledged to have been founded by the Romans, about 71AD as Eboracum. The name is thought to derive from the ancient British tribes then living in the area or from Eboros - the Celtic name for a yew tree. Eboracum became a key city for the Roman Empire, assuming military and administrative importance as the northern capital of Rome's British territories; a role sustained until the last vestiges of Roman rule. Remains of the Roman fortress were found under the Minster in the 1960s, and a relic from that excavation -a 22ft high column- now stands imperiously opposite the south door. During the Roman occupation, three emperors of the Holy Roman Empire – Hadrian, Septimus Severius and Constantine all held court in York, such was the significance of the city. As the Roman Empire disintegrated, the city was occupied by the Angles, a tribe from north west Germany, and later became the royal city of the Kingdom of Northumbria.

In the 7thC the first Minster –a wooden structure – was built, probably on the site of the current building.   In the 9thC the Vikings took control, renaming the city Jorvik, that name gradually evolving into the present name of York. Viking hegemony over the city and its hinterland lasted less than 100 years when King Edred drove Eric Bloodaxe - the King of Norway and the last Viking governor - from the city as part of his successful unification of England.

Following the Norman invasion in 1066, the city proved a thorn in William the Conqueror's efforts to extend control over all England, and the storming of the Norman garrison by disaffected Saxons led to his rapacious campaign known as the Harrying of the North where much of the county was laid waste and many thousands of Anglo Saxons slaughtered. By the 12thC, the city had become prosperous as it lay at a crossroads of communications- the Roman Roads (Dere Street and Ermine Street) and the River Ouse. The river, which remains navigable, became a Hanseatic port and so an important destination for shipping to and from Europe- exporting grain and wool to France and the Low Countries and importing cloth and other raw materials.

Henry I granted the city a charter in the early part of the 12thC. York also became a prominent and important religious centre. Economic decline came in the following centuries, particularly in the wake of the dissolution of the monasteries, when many monastic houses along with hospitals were lost. A revival in fortunes under Elizabeth 1st was followed by a difficult time during the English civil war when the City sided with the Royalists and was put under siege by the Parliamentarians in 1644. The growth of Leeds and Hull in the latter part of the 17thC saw York's diminution as a trading centre, but was counterbalanced in the 18thC by a rise in social and cultural fortunes, with many of the city's finest houses dating from this period. With the 19thC came the railways, and growth both as a centre for rail engineering and for administration. Such communications brought other industry; notably the development of the confectionery trade and the creation of the industrial village of New Earswick through the beliefs and funding of the Rowntree family who were devout Quakers. Continuing development in the 20thC has seen the city assume a place as an icon tourist attraction (winning the European tourism city of the year in 2007), and new industry on the back of the creation of York University in the 1960's.   Today York is a city both of the past and of the future. Its historic legacy and culture provide the visitor with much to see and do.

Getting here

Centrally positioned in the county, York is easily reached by rail and road with good linkages to northern airports.

Rail The city is well served by frequent, fast trains from London and Edinburgh. London is less than 2 hours. There are also regular services to most other parts of the UK, including Manchester and Newcastle airports.

Road York lies close to the A1M -the main road between London and Edinburgh- being only some 20 minutes drive from A1(M) motorway junction No 45.

Bus local and national services run into York; to a number of points in the city, but mainly the railway station (RS), Exhibition Square (EX) and Piccadilly (PC).

destination	service(s)	frequency	bus stop
Leeds	743/840/843/844	15 min	RS
Tadcaster	743/840/843/844	15 min	RS
Malton	840/843/845	30 min	RS
Pickering	840	hourly	RS
Scarborough	843	hourly	RS
Filey	743	3x per day	RS
Whitby	840	5x per day	RS
Helmsley	31X	every 2 hrs	EX
Thirsk	30	hourly	RS
Ripon	142/143	hourly	PC
Wetherby	412/413	hourly	PC
Selby	42	hourly	PC
Hull	746/X46	hourly	PC
Bridlington	744	3x per day	PC
London	421/426/561	3x per day	RS
Glasgow	534	1x per day	RS
Birmingham	53	1x per day	RS
Manchester	380	1x per day	RS

RS : Rougier St   EX:Exhibition Sq   PC : Piccadilly

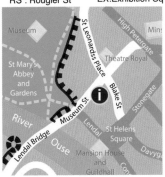

York Visitor Information Centre

Museum Street
01904 550099
www.visityork.org

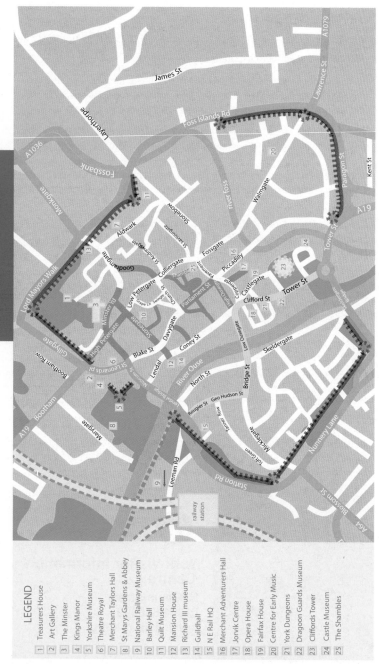

YORK

LEGEND

1. Treasurers House
2. Art Gallery
3. The Minster
4. Kings Manor
5. Yorkshire Museum
6. Theatre Royal
7. Merchant Taylors Hall
8. St Marys Gardens & Abbey
9. National Railway Museum
10. Barley Hall
11. Quilt Museum
12. Mansion House
13. Richard III museum
14. Guildhall
15. N E Rail HQ
16. Merchant Adventurers Hall
17. Jorvik Centre
18. Opera House
19. Fairfax House
20. Centre for Early Music
21. York Dungeons
22. Dragoon Guards Museum
23. Cliffords Tower
24. Castle Museum
25. The Shambles

What To See And Do

Steeped in history, in architecture, in culture and in commerce, there is plenty to see and do in York. There are a multitude of attractions, most within walking distance of each other inside or close to the city walls. York's ambience and charisma are widespread and infectious. Visitors should spend time here if they are to absorb a full picture of this historic city.

Railway station   Station Road

The advent of the railway transformed York. The city was an early beneficiary of rail travel – having a service as far back as 1839. The larger than life figure of George Hudson, a prosperous York draper, was responsible for this. His vision and initiative saw the railway connecting the city to towns in the West Riding. Hudson then persuaded George Stephenson (of Stephenson's rocket fame) to build his proposed London to Newcastle line through York rather than through Leeds. In 1840 the first train ran direct from York to London. By the 1850s, there were 13 trains a day between the two cities, carrying 341,000 passengers a year. The original station was built inside the walls between the northern western walls and Tanner Row and parts of the building still survive. Growth in popularity of rail travel and the importance of York in the railway network meant the original station quickly became too small. So, in 1877, a new station, then the largest in the country, opened to accommodate the burgeoning passenger numbers. The 800ft long roof, held 42ft above the platforms by iron columns was widely admired and development included a new hotel, now The Royal York Hotel. The whole station is built on a curve, making the architecture all the more impressive and described at the time as 'a monument to extravagence'. Even today, York station must rank amongst the   busiest in the country outside London; an accolade it seems set to keep as   visitor numbers grow and rail travel makes a resurgence in popularity.

YORK

George Hudson *The Railway King* 1800-1871

was born to a farming family in Howsham-near Malton. After early schooling he became apprenticed to a York drapers quickly impressing his employers, and becoming a partner in what was one of the largest retail businesses in the city (although he also married one of the partners daughters!). In 1827 a distant relative left him £30,000 in his will (about £3M at today's values).   The birth of commercial railways was then evident and Hudson used the money to buy shares in the North Midland railway. This proved successful and having met George Stephenson (inventor of the Rocket and the Stockton to Darlington railway), Hudson extended his ambitions to form his own railway company to link the city with towns in the West Riding. In doing this he persuaded Stephenson to route his own London to Newcastle railway proposal through York not Leeds, as Stephenson had originally intended. If it were not for George Hudson, York might be a radically different place from what it is today, since the city's position as an important railway hub brought trade and industry, as well as visitors, and established York as the second most important railway destination after London.   This successful venture led to further investment elsewhere in England. Such ventures entailed generous bribes to MPs to ensure appropriate Acts of Parliament were passed. He personally guaranteed payment of a 6% dividend- having already borrowed £5m (about £500m today) to help finance construction. He was also active in politics, becoming Lord Mayor in 1837 and MP for Sunderland in 1845. By then he was known as the Railway King and continued to acquire shares in railway companies but his share dealing involved manipulating share prices. When the bubble burst, investors lost heavily and Hudson was forced to resign as chairman of all the companies under his control. An investigation quickly showed malpractice and systemic bribery. He had also sold shares at inflated prices as well as land that he did not own. He agreed to refund money he had swindled from shareholders. Despite this corruption, he continued as an MP until 1859, but failed to pay back the money he owed and, in 1865, was imprisoned in York Castle for debt. After friends had raised a substantial sum of money to pay these debts, Hudson was released in October 1866 and lived out his last years on the continent.

North Eastern Rail Headquarters [15]   Station Rise

This substantial building, by the city walls near the station is now the Cedar Court Hotel. Built in 1906, at the time it was described by the Yorkshire Herald as "a huge palace of business". It reflected the prosperity of the railways, with generous use of expensive materials like handmade bricks and Portland stone, with an interior of Belgian white marble and parquet wooden flooring.The shields and badges carved above the entrance and on the Station Road side of the building tell the story of the many early railway companies which amalgamated in 1854 to form the NER. A smaller replica of this building was built in Cowley Street, Westminster as the NER's London office and is now the Liberal Democrat Party HQ.

St Mary's Abbey [8]   Marygate/Lendal

The romantic and idyllic atmosphere created in romanesque style by the abbey grounds provide a glimpse of how powerful this Benedictine monastery was prior to the dissolution. As well as the ruins of the Abbey, the grounds contain a long established museum and remains of Roman walls. Opened in 1830 by the Yorkshire Philosophical society as part of the Yorkshire Museum, the garden contains many native and exotic trees. The Abbey itself was built in 1088 and became so influential that its Abbot, at the time of the Dissolution, rivalled the power of the Archbishop of York. The stone walls surrounding the abbey were built in the 1260's. The gate on Marygate, adjoining St Olave's Church, was the main entrance. It was here that the poor came to claim alms.   Also in the grounds is the hospitium. A medieval building, it was used to house the frequent visitors to the abbey. Now restored, it is used as a small conference and meetings venue. The York Observatory, in the Gardens, contains the museum's Astronomy Collection. Built in 1833, it is the oldest working observatory in Yorkshire. It has a refractor telescope by Thomas Cooke, a York instrument maker who pioneered the use of refractor telescopes and who went on to make the then largest telescope in the world.   The Observatory also contains a clock dating from 1811 which tells the time based on observations of the positions of stars. It is always four minutes, 20 seconds, behind Greenwich Mean Time.

The Yorkshire Museum [5]

Also set in the gardens, and built in 1830 by the Yorkshire Philosophical Society,   the Museum contains many artefacts and antiquities.   The building, Greek revival in style, was designed by William Wilkins, a classical scholar turned architect who is perhaps best known for his design of the National Gallery in Trafalgar Square. Three core collections are exhibited in the main building: biology; geology, and archaeology. A fourth collection, astronomy, is housed in the observatory. The artefacts include an Anglo Saxon helmet

Middleham Jewel

YORK

discovered during excavation work for the Jorvik centre, the Cawood Sword, probably the best preserved Anglo Saxon sword in the UK, and the Middleham Jewel.   The museum is open most days. There is an admission charge.

01904 687687   www.yorkshiremuseum.org.uk

Kings Manor 4   Exhibition Square

This cluster of 15thC medieval buildings is tucked away behind St Leonards Place. It originally housed the Abbot of St Marys and after the dissolution of the monasteries, became the home of the Council of the North (set up by Richard III to improve governance of the north of England). Much of the present buildings were erected during the reign of Elizabeth I and regularly used by the Royal family. The 17thC Council Chamber is now the refectory whilst the decorative main entrance doorway is Jacobean. The Council of the North was abolished in 1641 and over the next two centuries the buildings fell into disrepair. Revival came with the establishment of the Yorkshire School for the Blind in 1833 and, from the 1870s, the Manor was gradually restored and enlarged. The Principal's house, now the Centre for Medieval Studies, was built in 1900. In 1958, the Manor was acquired by the City Council, and occupied by York University's Institute for Advanced Architectural Studies. It now houses the Department of Archeology and Medieval studies.

The restaurant/café is open to the public, Monday to Friday 9.30 to 3.30.

York Art Gallery 2   Exhibition Square

Built for the second Yorkshire Fine Art and Industrial Exhibition in 1879, it became the City Art Gallery in 1892. The main gallery was refurbished in 2005, and is used for special and visiting exhibitions. It houses collections of paintings and ceramics. The statue on the forecourt is that of William Etty, a well known 18thC York artist and architect. The gallery is open most days. Admission is free.   01904 687687 www.yorkartgallery.org.uk

YORK

Theatre Royal 6   St Leonards Place

Prominently sited in St Leonards place, this is a long established theatre with its own productions as well as touring shows and whose programme caters for a wide range of residents and visitors. The building dates from 1744, and seats over 800 although the frontage is Victorian and is decorated with carved heads representing characters in Shakespeare plays. The modern foyer opened in 1967.   01904 623568   www.yorktheatreroyal.co.uk

National Railway Museum (NRM) 9   Leeman Road

Just outside the city walls on Leeman road is the NRM which ranks as one of the world's foremost railway museums. Part of the National Science Museum, it opened in 1975 in one of the vast locomotive sheds that accompanied the city's long reign as Englands railway capital.   There is a permanent display of over 100 locomotives, a large part of the national collection. Included in the displays are the world famous steam locomotives *Mallard* and *Flying Scotsman* as well as other historically important exhibits such as the collection of Royal Trains, Chinese and Japanese locomotives and a host of other railway artefacts and memorabilia.   The museum is open most days. Admission is free.   0844 815313   www.nrm.co.uk

YORK

Mansion House 12   St Helens Square

The official home of the Lord Mayor. Formal visits and delegations are received here.   It was built following a debate by the Council in 1725 which resolved that the first citizen of the City required a place where he could *"keep up the grandeur and dignity of the city by holding at least two public dining days in every week at the least"*   There is a comprehensive collection of silver, antique furniture, and paintings in the building. Included is the Great Sword of State, dating from 1416, which once belonged to the Holy Roman Emperor Sigismund.   The city's coat of arms - the red cross of St George and five lions - can be seen in the Stateroom.   The building is open Thu, Fri, Sat.

YORK

The Guildhall 14

Completed in 1455, the Guildhall lies behind the Mansion House, facing onto the river. It originally served as the meeting place for representatives of all the guilds in the city. The west window, part of a post war restoration, contains richly decorated stained glass depicting varied spheres of York life. On the upper floor is the City Council chamber. Dating from 1889, it is finely panelled and still houses the original furniture. The City council still use the building for council meetings and committees. The hall is open most days. Admission is free.

York Minster 3

A church has stood on the site of the present Minster since the 7thC. A succession of buildings were erected and then either rebuilt following battle or fire. The present building was begun in 1230 and completed 1472. One of the largest Gothic cathedrals in Northern Europe, it is easily visible on the horizon when approaching the city, its three main towers each standing over 200ft high. The oldest parts of the Minster are the north and south transepts. They contain lancet and rose windows; the *five sisters* lancet window of plain grey stained glass in the north transept, is unusual in lacking the decorative story or motifs usually found in such windows. The more decorative *rose window* in the south transept portrays the union of the Royal houses of York and Lancaster in 1486. The Chapter House is off the north transept. It is octagonal in shape and its high level windows, which form much of the upper level elevations, fill the space with light. There are many and varied statues in the form of human heads which sit above the canopies; no two are alike. The nave is the widest of any cathedral in England, and at its west end is the window known as the Heart of Yorkshire. The east end of the cathedral is a later addition, being built between 1361 and 1405. Despite the later period, by which time architectural tastes had moved on, it still preserves the pattern of the nave. There is a four bay choir; a second set of transepts, and the Lady Chapel. The transepts are in line with the altar and serve to throw light onto it. Behind the high altar is the magnificent East Window, the largest expanse of medieval stained glass in the world. The two west towers contain the clock bells which chime every 15 minutes, together with a concert carillon. The carillon is played most evenings just before evensong, although not always with a tune that might be expected; the sounds of the Beatles and other modern musicians having sometimes been heard.

YORK

The Minster is the city's most popular tourist attaction and there are a range of activities and tours for the visitor:

Glass conservation There are guided tours around the glazing workshops. The extent of stained glass in the Minster means a full time team working on maintenance and repair, utilising traditional artisan skills now rarely found. The Bedern studio offers an opportunity to go behind the scenes. **Climbing the towers** negotiating the 275 steps to the top of the central tower is rewarded with panoramic views over the city and surrounding countryside as well as being able to appreciate at close hand the extensive sculpturing of medieval gargoyles and pinnacles. **Exploring The undercroft** structural work in the 1960's to shore up the foundations under the central tower uncovered remains of buildings which once occupied the site; some of which are Roman.

There are also guided tours of other parts of the Minster which can be pre booked. The Minster is open daily, outside of service times. There is an admission charge.

0844 939 0015   www.yorkminster.org

THE CARILLON

An instrument of bronze cup-shaped bells, the carillon is played by striking a key board, with the fists and by pressing the keys of a pedal keyboard with the feet. These activate metal clappers that strike the bells allowing the performer to adjust the sound of the notes.

Treasurer's House [1] Minster Yard

Owned by the National Trust, this was the home of the treasurer to York Minster. Although dating from medieval times, and built over a roman road (the Via Decumana) it has been much altered and changed over the centuries and the present structure bears little resemblance to that which would have been the home to the last Treasurer to occupy it in 1547, after which it was in private ownership until bequeathed to the National Trust in 1930. It is said to be haunted and visitors can expect to be regaled with eerie tales of ghosts. Ghost related tours to selected rooms can be pre arranged with the house custodians. The house and garden are open Sat to Thu. There is an admission charge.   01904 624247 www.nationaltrust.org.uk

Merchant Adventurers Hall [16] Fossgate

Dating from 1357, the Hall was built by an influential religious fraternity called the Guild of Our Lord Jesus and the Blessed Virgin Mary. It grew in influence and power under Henry VI, and Elizabeth I granted it the status of Company of Merchant Adventurers of York. The Hall is still owned and managed by the Merchant Adventurers, and has substantial historic records charting life across the centuries. It also houses extensive collections of silver furniture and paintings. Above the Fossgate entrance is the coat of arms of the Merchant Adventurers of England. The Hall is open most days during the summer when not in use for functions. There is an admission charge. 01904 654818   www.theyorkcompany.co.uk

Merchant Taylors Hall [7] Aldwark

As its name implies, this guildhall was built for the city's tailoring trades. It was built by the Fraternity of St John the Baptists between in 1361 and substantially altered in the 17thC. At its height, the guild had over 130 master tailors who traded in the city and surrounding area. The Hall has two main rooms together with adjoining almshouses and gardens. It is frequently used for functions such as weddings and conferences but can be viewed by prior arrangement when not otherwise in use.   www.merchant-taylors-york.org

St Anthony's Hall (Quilt Museum) [11] Peasholme Green

The hall dates from the mid 15thC when King Henry VI granted a charter to the guild of St Martin, who built the hall and a chapel on the site which had previously been a chapel for St Anthony. In the 16thC it became a workhouse for the poor - with weaving being a staple chore of the inmates. Later, part was converted into a house of correction for minor criminals. Acquired and restored by the York Civic Trust in the 1950's, for many years it was the home of the Borthwick Institute, an historical research arm of the University. In 2008, it became a quilt museum and is open Tue to Sat. There is an admission charge.   01904 613242   www.quiltmuseum.org.uk

Fairfax House 19   Castlegate

Built in 1762, as a dowry for Anne Fairfax, (a descendant of Sir Thomas Fairfax Parliamentarian general and confidant of Thomas Cromwell) this grand 18thC mansion typifies the lavish lifestyle of wealthy socialites of that era. The house interior was designed by John Carr the well known York Georgian architect. It ceased to be a private residence in the mid 19thC, and fell into disrepair before being fully restored by the York Civic Trust in the 1980s and now described by some commentators as one of the *"finest houses of its era in Britain"*. The main staircase is an outstanding feature with its finely designed and crafted Venetian Window, wrought iron and decorative plasterwork. The house portrays how the interior might have looked in the 18thC. Interior decoration and fittings are complemented by the furniture, collected by the late Noel Terry, doyen of the York chocolate making firm, and includes a comprehensive collection of English clocks and several pieces made by renowned Otley cabinet maker Thomas Chippendale. The house is open most days (closed January and early February). Fridays are reserved for guided tours which may be pre-booked. There is an admission charge.   01904 655543   www.fairfaxhouse.co.uk

YORK

37

YORK

Cliffords Tower ⚟ 23 Tower Street

One of two castles built here by William the Conqueror, this one occupied the site bounded by the rivers Foss and Ouse on two sides, with the north side protected by the construction of a motte and bailey, on which the current Cliffords Tower now stands. The name Clifford's Tower derives from the family who became the hereditary constables of the castle; the Clifford family were originally from France and came to England with William the Conqueror. It is the only surviving relic of the original castle and the structure -a quatrefoil shaped keep- itself dates from the mid 13thC, built during the reign of Henry III. The quatrefoil design is thought to be unique in Britain, and was devised as a consequence of an experiment in improving flanking fire from the keep to ward off attackers. Over the centuries, the castle has been the scene of many epic events which shaped the fortunes both of the city and more widely. The role of the castle, outside the keep, greatly expanded during the 14th and 15thC as administrative buildings, and functions increased with the establishment of some mills, the arrival of a mint making gold and silver coins in 1344 and soon after, a prison - a function retained for 500 years. There is now little trace of the other parts of the castle, as in the early part of the 18thC all but Cliffords Tower were demolished or sold. In their stead was built a new jail, and later a new assize court building, and female prison; the latter now part of York Castle Museum. Fragments of the bailey wall, south gatehouse and one of the corner towers survive but it is the tower which remains the only intact structure of any size. The tower is open most days. There is an admission charge. 01904 646940 www.english-heritage.org.uk

York Castle Museum 24 Eye of York

The Museum is a recreation of everyday life in past times. It opened in the 1930's utilising the former prison built on the site of the castle. Displays include a recreated Victorian street, Jacobean and Georgian rooms, and a Victorian kitchen. There is a display about life in the prison in the cells of the old Debtors Prison. There is also has a children's Gallery as well as military and costume displays. The old prison buildings have been put to good use and displays here include the former condemned prisoners cell, once occupied by Dick Turpin. The museum is open most days. There is an admission charge.

01904 687687   www.yorkcastlemuseum.org.uk

Jorvik Viking Centre 17   Coppergate

This interactive attraction, in the heart of the Coppergate shopping centre, recreates a slice of Viking life. The attraction stems from archeological excavations prior to building the centre's foundations.   Visitors journey back through time to the 10thC in time cars, through 30 or so generations until the year 948, exploring streets, workshops and houses of this period.   The attraction is open daily. There is an admission charge.

01904 615505   www.jorvik-viking-centre.co.uk

Royal Dragoon Guards Museum 22   Tower Street

The Dragoon Guards were formed in 1685 from Troops of Horse raised by James II to defend London from the invasion threatened by William of Orange. Amongst its decorated officers is William Baden Powell who went on to found the Scout movement. There is a wide array of memorabilia and artefacts demonstrating how the regiment has performed over 300 years of history.   It is open Mon to Sat. There is an admission charge.

01904 642036   www.rdgmuseum.org.uk

York Dungeon 21   Clifford Street

An attraction which will both scare and excite the visitor. The Dungeon brings you face to face with ghosts, with Dick Turpin and other less than wholesome individuals and experiences of eras long past. The attraction is open daily (times may vary according to season). There is an admission charge.

01904 632599   www.the-dungeons.co.uk/york

YORK

Kings Staith, a popular riverside haunt for visitors

YORK

York Opera House 18   Cumberland Street

This Theatre was originally built as York's Corn Exchange in 1868 and occasionally used as a concert hall. The Corn Exchange failed and in 1902 the buildings were converted into the Grand Opera House. The auditorium is still substantially intact and reflects the style and ambience of the Edwardian era with ornately decorated balconies and ceiling. The theatre has gone through a number of life changes since 1902, being a roller skating rink for a number of years before restoration in the late 1980's.   0844 847 2322 www.grandoperahouseyork.org.uk

National Centre for Early Music 20   Walmgate

The National Centre for Early Music is in the 11thC St Margaret's Church. The Centre promotes the conservation of early music and organises concerts of early music, whether folk, jazz, choral or chamber. Not all events are in the centre; others take place elsewhere in the city- the Minster for example - but the Centre provides booking facilities for all the concerts it sponsors or organises. The church is of architectural interest, and although rebuilt several times over the centuries it retains its most distinguishing features, including an ornate Romanesque porch from the 12th century with carvings of mythological beasts and an unusual brick bell tower.   01904 632220   www.ncem.co.uk

Barley Hall   10   Coffee Yard

This restored medieval townhouse is in a small ginnel off Stonegate in the heart of the shopping centre.   Dating from the mid 14thC, it was originally built to serve the administrative needs of Nostell Priory near Wakefield as that institution needed to liaise with the many and influential churchmen resident in York in this period.   The re-creation of the hall reflects the life and times of William Snawsell a prominent York businessman and leading citizen of the late 15thC, a goldsmith and sometime Lord Mayor. The Hall is open daily.   There is an admission charge.   01904 615505   www.barleyhall.org.uk

Stonegate

printers devil
by No33

The Shambles 25

A must see for any visitor to the city, and voted Britain's "most picturesque street", The Shambles is a bustling centre piece of historic York.   The street is one of the UK's most visited and now consists of a wide variety of shops, tourist attractions, and restaurants.   Many of the buildings are14thC and lean into the middle of the cobbled street with roofs almost touching. The street is mentioned in the Domesday Book, suggesting it had been a place for butchers and slaughterhouses at the time of the Norman conquest. Its earlier name had been The Great Flesh Shambles, probably from the Anglo- Saxon word *"fles-hammels"* which literally means 'flesh-shelves'- the word for the shelves that butchers used to display their meat. As recently as 1872 there were twenty-five butchers' shops in the street, but now there are none. Until the 19thC there were no public health laws, so the by products of butchery such as offal and blood were simply thrown into a gutter (known as a runnel) down the middle of the street or open space where the butchering was carried out. By extension, any scene of total disorganisation and mess is now referred to as "a shambles".

Richard III museum 13 Monk Bar

Occupying part of the Monk Bar, this small museum provides an overview into the controversial life and death of Richard III. It includes a re-creation of his trial into the death of the princes in the tower as well as a rare example of a medieval portcullis, said to be original and whose mechanism can be operated by visitors. The Museum is open daily. There is an admission charge.

01904 634191 www.richardiiimuseum.co.uk

New Earswick

The Rowntree family were responsible for the construction of this model village community in the early 20thC, 2 miles north of the city centre, and close to the factory, this was a project to provide homes and welfare for a mixed community, many of whom worked in the Rowntree factory and was dear to the heart of the Rowntree family community ambitions. As practising Quakers, they considered it a moral obligation to better the lives of their staff, and creating healthy and civilised working and living environments was an important component in fulfillment of that obligation. The style and format of the village resembled those to be found elsewhere in the country around that period (Port Sunlight, Bourneville being contemporaneous examples). Joseph Rowntree is quoted as saying that *"I do not want to establish communities bearing the stamp of charity but rather of rightly ordered and self governing communities"*   There was housing for both workers and managers, all in a green setting with gardens for each home, each with its own fruit tree.   The village remains largely intact today and although tenure of many of the properties has passed on, there is still sufficient original character to give the visitor a feeling of a previous, quieter and more peaceful age. Bus services 1 and 12 link the village with the city centre.

YORK

Joseph Rowntree   Philanthropist   *1834-1925*

Joseph Rowntree's father was a grocer and a devout Quaker. When Joseph was 14 he started work as an apprentice. During this time visited Ireland, where he witnessed first hand the effects of the potato famine, which instilled in him the drive and commitment for social justice he was to demonstrate for the rest of his life. He joined his elder brother Henry in his chocolate factory business in 1869. The company only employed thirty workers at the time, but under Joseph's guidance and ambition it grew rapidly, a new factory opening in 1881 to produce fruit pastilles and by 1900 it was one of Britain's largest food manufacturing business employing over 4,000 staff. Josephs progressive ideas manifested themselves in his introduction of one of the country's first occupational pension schemes. After Henry's death in 1883, Joseph became the sole owner of the company. His commitment to social justice resulted in more and more public work. He served on committees for two Quaker schools (The Mount, a high school for girls and Bootham school, a high school for boys) and taught in an Adult School on Sunday. He was also instrumental in the establishment of the York Public Library and provided a park as a memorial to those killed during World War 1. He created a caring environment for his employees, the factory paying for the services of a welfare officer, doctor and dentist. Perhaps his most enduring social initiative was the development of New Earswick, where in 1901 he acquired land to build homes for low income families. He was a long time supporter of the former Liberal party and for most of his life a leading member of the Temperance Society, whilst being continually critical of the Anglican church for what he saw as its failure to deal with social injustice. He is buried in a Quaker cemetery in the grounds of The Retreat on Heslington Road on the South side of the city.

peaceful New Earswick

The Knavesmire

The Knavesmire is a low lying extensive stretch of open space off the Tadcaster road about 3/4mile from Micklegate Bar. Once known as the Tyburn, it is where the infamous highwayman, Dick Turpin, was hanged. A small plaque marks the spot, opposite Pulleyn Drive.   The land is now used for a wide variety of formal and informal recreational purposes,   but is also the home of one of the UK's premier racecourses. Horse racing has been a feature of York since Roman times, but it was not until 1731 that the present course was established. Race meetings take place here every month from May to October. The Knavesmire also serves simply as an informal common, and is much used as an area for picnics, football and other family recreational activities. Other notable events on the Knavesmire include the annual York Cycle Show, and hot air ballooning launches.   The Knavesmire is one of four natural and extensive stretches of open land in the city; the others being Monk Stray, on the eastern fringes of the city; Bootham stray in the north and Walmgate Stray in the south east. The Strays are characterised by being open common land. Historically, the freemen of the city enjoyed the right to graze cattle on these areas, but the city council has, over the past 100 years and utilising the benefit of an Act of Parliament, bought out the rights of the freemen and these areas are now common land for the benefit of the enjoyment of the city's residents.

Horse Racing

One of Yorkshires nine courses, the races takes place at the Knavesmire regularly between May and October.   York races are a prominent diary fixture for serious racegoers from all over the country and race days are characterised by fashionable hats tops and tails and a buoyant lively crowd; the Ebor Festival in August being one of the most important dates in the UK's flat racing calendar.

01904 620911   www.yorkracecourse.co.uk

YORK

The Knavesmire

The walking tours

Whilst most attractions are within easy reach of one another, to get a full appreciation of the character of the city, just wandering around within the city walls is recommended. Three walking routes are suggested. These go past or close to many of the attractions referred to above. In the city the medieval street pattern gave rise to tiny pedestrian linkages from the streets to small courtyards or just linking streets. These alleys are called snickelways and they abound in the city centre.

YORK

● ● ● ● ● ● **Walk 1   Around The walls**

York's medieval walls probably represent the most complete city walls of any city in the UK, and are certainly the longest, totalling over 2.75 miles. The present walls, although much modified in the 19th and early 20thC, mainly date from between 1250 and 1380.   Defensive walls have been a feature of the city since Roman times. The present line follows, in part, that of the original Roman construction when the fort was built in AD 71. There are four bars (entry points into the city), at Bootham, Monk Bar, Walmgate and Micklegate. Only limited sections of the Roman walls are now visible - the most notable is the **Multangular tower** and Anglian tower with a short stretch of walling in Museum Gardens.

Dick Turpin   Highwayman

was an 18thC Essex butcher who quickly turned to a life of crime. He was a member of a gang of deer thieves, and later a horse thief and murderer. After his death, his life and exploits were romanticised in a book by the Victorian novelist William Harrison Ainsworth, which had him making a fictional overnight ride from London to York on his steed Black Bess. Turpin was most known however for his exploits as a highway robber but after the arrest of the other members of his gang in 1735 he disappeared from public view, resurfacing in 1737 with two new accomplices, one of whom he may have accidentally shot and killed. Turpin fled the scene of the killing and shortly afterwards killed another man attempting his capture, He moved to Yorkshire and changed his name to John Palmer. Local magistrates became suspicious of "Palmer", and having enquired how he earned his living, he became suspected of being a horse thief. He was imprisoned in York Castle where his true identity as Turpin became known following a letter he wrote to his brother which was intercepted by the authorities. He was brought to trial, and found guilty of horse theft, was executed in April 1739 by hanging on the Tyburn, now part of the Knavesmire.

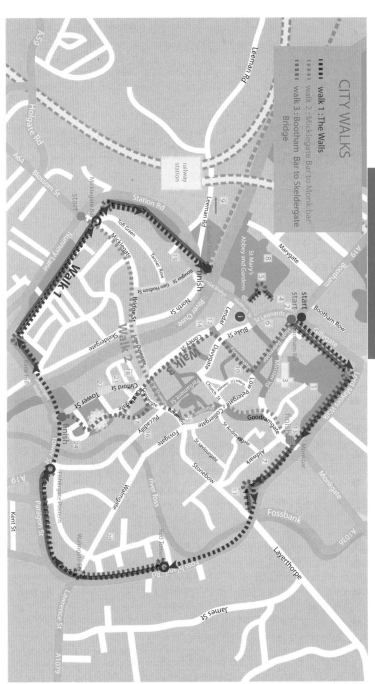

CITY WALKS

walk 1 : The Walls
walk 2 : Micklegate Bar to Monk bar
walk 3 : Bootham Bar to Skeldergate Bridge

YORK

YORK

This was built during the reign of Emperor Severius, who resided in York from 209-211 AD. It has 10 sides, and stands almost 30 ft. high.   Following the cessation of Roman rule, the walls fell into disrepair. The Vikings demolished all the towers save the Multangular Tower but restored the walls. Walking the walls should take between 2 and 4 hours, using a clockwise route starting at Bootham Bar. This is the only medieval gate on the site of the Roman walls, and was named for the market which would have been held here in medieval times (the name literally means bar at the booths). The structure holds a portcullis although it is now fixed, and three statues can be seen on top which date from the late 19thC. The statues, which replaced medieval ones, represent:

* *A stone mason who holds a model of the Bar.*
* *14thC Mayor of York Nicholas Langton, who holds a scroll.*
* *A knight in medieval armour with a sword and shield.*

The walk runs behind Gillygate, and turns south east towards Monk Bar, adjoining Lord Mayors Walk. There are good views of the Minster from this part as well as those of the courtyards and buildings associated with the Minster, such as the Treasurers House.   At Monk Bar, there is a museum to Richard III and it is thought that Richard added a storey to the Bar itself. It is a more complex structure than the other Bars with four storeys; each storey designed to be defended independently. Continuing south east along the walls, some modest remains of the Roman section can be seen shortly before the 14thC building known as the Merchant Taylors Hall. A

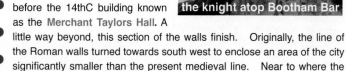
the knight atop Bootham Bar

little way beyond, this section of the walls finish.   Originally, the line of the Roman walls turned towards south west to enclose an area of the city significantly smaller than the present medieval line.   Near to where the walls finish, on Peasholme Green, is St Anthony's Hall.   Also by this spot is St Cuthberts church, dating from the 15thC.   The walls resume again at the Red Tower, along Foss Islands Road. This was originally built to guard the King's Fishpool, a flooded stretch of the River Foss created by the Normans damming of the river where the city had no defensive wall. The building was later used as a stable, and a factory for making gunpowder, when it became known as "Brimstone House".   The medieval walls continue south and west to Walmgate. Most of Walmgate Bar was built during the 14thC, although the inner gateway dates from the 12th C.

The Bar retains its barbican, reputed to be the only one surviving on a town gate in England. Like Monk Bar and Bootham Bar, it retains its portcullis. On the inner side, a house dating from the reign of Elizabeth 1, and supported on stone pillars, extends out over the gateway. The Bar has seen its fair share of turmoil -notably in the civil war when it was bombarded by cannon fire, it was also the scene of riots in the late 15thC when there was a popular protest over tax rises.   The walls continue west of Walmgate Bar as far as Fishergate Postern, just to the east of the River Foss before it joins the Ouse. The Postern –the only one to survive around the walls- dates from the early 16thC (a postern is a side gate or back entrance into a fort or castle).   Nearby, in the graveyard of St Georges Church, is the grave of Dick Turpin, the notorious highwayman. Between the Foss and the Ouse rivers, there are no surviving walls. This area would have been part of the Castle, the promontory between the two rivers providing a natural defensive line.   West of the Ouse - having crossed the river on Skeldergate Bridge - the walls begin again at Skeldergate by Baile Hill, once the site of a small secondary Norman castle (and from where the city was besieged by the Parliamentarians during the 1644 Civil War). They then follow the east side of Nunnery Lane to Micklegate Bar. This is the main entrance into the city from the west. The name Micklegate is a derivation of the word Micklelith, meaning great gate. This is both the Bar where royalty traditionally enter the city, as well as that used to display the heads of those executed for treason. Micklegate Bar has four storeys. North of Micklegate, the walls pass by the station and at the riverside is the North Street Postern Tower (sometimes known as the Barker Tower) the more original of the two riverside towers. The steps beside it once led to a ferry which predated the construction of Lendal Bridge in 1833. The tower was once linked by a chain across the river to Lendal tower on the east side with the aim of preventing enemy ships from breaching the city!!

Walk 2 Micklegate Bar to Monk Bar

From the start at Micklegate Bar, Micklegate curves gracefully towards the river, and offers a rewarding architectural vista. Many of the buildings date from 18C, as it was here that many of York's wealthier classes established their homes. The timber framed building just to the far side of Priory Street, dates from c.1500, and although much modified is probably amongst the older buildings surviving in this part of the city.   Just beyond is the church of Holy Trinity, whose tower and some internal parts of the nave date from the mid 16thC. On the north side of the street stand Micklegate House and Bathurst house, gentlemens residences both dating from the mid 18thC and perhaps typical of the style in which the more wealthy gentry of York became accustomed to in that era. Another similar building further on toward the river is No 54, most recently a girls school, but whose original purpose was as a fine town house. Opposite is St Martin-cum-Gregory, now used for offices but which

WALK 2

YORK

gets a mention in the Domesday Book, and although the majority of the present building is much later, parts of the interior are thought to date from the 13thC. Micklegate leads on to the **Ouse Bridge** (early 19thC). On the east side of the river is the heart of York's retail centre. Spurriergate and Coney Street - probably the prime shopping streets in the city- lie to the north. The church of St Michaels is on the corner, and although no longer used as such, records suggest a church existed here well before the Norman Conquest. Continuing along High Ousegate, leads into Pavement where can be found the **Church of All Saints**, sometime described as the stateliest of all York parish churches. The west tower has, at its top, a distinctive open octagonal lantern dating from the early 15thC and whose light used to guide travellers into the city but which nowadays is a memorial to the fallen of the two world wars. The west window is richly decorated with stained glass which dates from the late 14thC. The eastern end of the church was shortened in the late 18thC to enlarge York's burgeoning market place. Continuing across the lower end of Parliament Street, Pavement forms part of the core of the old market place. **The Shambles** and Whip-Ma-Whop-Ma gate (so called after the medieval custom of whipping small yelping dogs) lie beyond. Continue through the Shambles and into Kings Square, a small open area at the meeting of several streets- notably Low Petergate and Colliergate (Yorks outdoor market fills the snickelways and narrow streets to the immediate west). The Square, where street performers can be seen on summer days, is probably built on the site of one of the main entrances into the roman fort- the porta principalis sinistra- and Petergate is built over this original roman street. Turn right into Goodramgate, still a vibrant shopping street and whose architecture spans some 700 years. On the north side is Lady Row, the oldest surviving timber framed buildings in the city dating from the early 14thC and built on the churchyard of **Holy Trinity Church**. This religious building is in a tranquilly set, away from the hustle and bustle of the street and is reached through a small archway adjoining Lady Row. Its interior is notable for its box pews and "double decker "pulpit. The church is open Tue to Sun. A little further on is the junction with Deansgate which affords views over the Minster and College Street. **St Williams College**, long associated with the Minster, lies on the east side. Built around 1465, and named for a 12thC Archbishop of York, the college is laid out in a way that reflects the older Oxford and Cambridge colleges with a central courtyard. It is currently used as a small conference centre, with a small restaurant and tearooms.

Towards Monkbar, the buildings on the right hand side of the street are predominantly 16thC timber framed.   Tucked away behind them, and accessed through a snickelway is **Bedern Hall**; a restored 14thC refectory, now used as a small meeting house and conference facility, but which originally formed a small part of a more extensive college known as Vicars Choral- dedicated to housing and educating 36 vicars who formed the choir for the Minster prior to the dissolution.   Bedern is the Anglo Saxon word for house of prayer. Goodramgate (an adaption from the Danish *Gutherumgate*) was probably formed during the Viking's occupation of the city, as a street to connect the former eastern Roman gateway in Kings Square with the former northern Roman gateway (close to the current MonkBar gateway). The walk finishes at Monkbar.

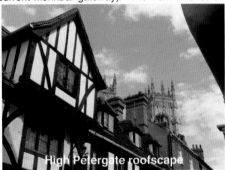

High Petergate roofscape

Walk 3 Bootham Bar to Skeldergate Bridge

Start by passing under Bootham Bar, into High Petergate. This is the route of the Roman Via Principalis. Bootham Bar is on the site of one of the main north gates into the Roman fort. Its Roman name was Porta Principalis Dextra. High Petergate is a rich mix of pubs, shops, restaurants and offices, and opens out in front of the Minster with its excellent views of the west end of the cathedral and where the nighttime illumination of the Minster can be seen to dramatic effect.   To the left of the Minster is the gate that leads to the informal park and grounds   Crossing Duncombe Place and Minster Yard, the **Church of St Michael-le Belfry** is on the east side of the street. Dating from c.1530, the church is perhaps best known as the place where Guy Fawkes was christened in 1570. The church is open to the public Tue to Sun. High Petergate continues with distinctive 16thC to 18thC buildings lining both sides of the street and finishes at the junction with **Stonegate**. Turn right into one of the oldest commercial streets in the city, and crowded with timber framed buildings, most in use as shops or restaurants. Built over the Roman road, the Via Praetoria, which connected the centre of the fort with the crossing over the Ouse, the name Stonegate is said to derive from the stone laid along its length to support the movement of materials to the minster during its construction.

WALK 2

YORK

WALK 3

YORK

The Petergate end of the street was, in earlier times, controlled by the Minster authorities and home to crafts such as goldsmiths, printers and glass painters. Some of the buildings still show evidence of this, such as the stained glass in the windows of No35 and the red devil -the traditional symbol of a printer -outside No33. The entrance to the Barley Hall is off Stonegate. At the far end is St Helens Square. Here is the Mansion House and the entrance to the Guildhall as well as Betty's Tea rooms. Continue by turning left on the far side of the square into Coney Street, probably York's main shopping street with a host of well known brands lining its frontage, some housed in 16thC timber framed buildings. On the right hand side of the street is St Martin Le Grand church, distinguished by a large clock overhanging the street and which is topped by an 18thC figure of a naval officer. The Church has been here for over 1000 years, although little remains of earlier construction. The tower is 15thC and the building was sympathetically restored in1968, although a part remains as ruins, deliberately left as a memorial following its destruction in an air raid in the second world war.   The southern end of Coney Street becomes Spurriergate, and after crossing Ousegate into Nessgate, there is a choice of routes. Turn-

ing left into Coppergate will give access to the Coppergate shopping centre, where the Jorvik Viking centre is situated, and thence to Castle Street- and Fairfax House, Tower Street and on to Cliffords Tower and the Castle Museum. An alternative is to keep ahead along Clifford Street, which is lined with redbrick and terracotta buildings built as part of an 1881 city development scheme. Turn west down King Street to the river. Here is Kings Staith, a cobbled quay which was the city's main landing place for boats navigating the Ouse. On the Staith is a stone wall with buttresses which was the original river wall of a 13thC Franciscan friary.   Return along Cumberland Street, past the Grand Opera House, and turn south along Clifford Street which becomes Tower Street Before reaching Skeldergate Bridge. Cliffords Tower and Castle Museum are visible to the east.

River tours

The river is no longer used by commercial traffic, but does provide a visitor attraction. River tours take place daily. Boats leave Lendal Bridge (St Mary's gardens side) or Kings Staith for trips on the river.   www.yorkboat.co.uk

Ghost walks

The city is allegedly one of the most haunted in England. A number of different guided tours around the cities darker alleys and haunts take place on most nights. The start points vary and full details can be found in the tourist information centre and in many hotels.

50

Festivals

February	Jorvik festival- various venues	www.yorvik-viking-centre.co.uk
March	Festival of Science and Technology University	www.scy.co.uk
April	Open Studios various venues	www.yorkopenstudios.co.uk
May	York Races Knavesmire	www.yorkracecourse.co.uk
June	York Races Knavesmire	
	Cycle Rally and show Knavesmire	www.ctc.org.uk
July	Early Music Festival various venues	www.ncem.co.uk
	York Races Knavesmire	
August	York Races Knavesmire	
September	York Races Knavesmire	
	Food festival various venues	www.yorkfoodfestival.com
	Antiquarian book fair Knavesmire	www.yorkbookfair.com
October	York Races Knavesmire	
	Illuminating York various locations	www.illuminatingyork.org.uk
	Ghost Festival various venues	www.yorkghostfestival.co.uk
November	St Nicholas Xmas Market city centre	www.yorkfestivals.com
December	Early Music Xmas Festival Minster Walmgate	www.ncem.co.uk

YORK

York Mystery plays

The York Mystery Plays, more properly called the York Corpus Christi Plays, were performed in the city between the mid 14thC and mid 16thC. They were revived in the 1950's. The cycle of plays, which are held either every other year, or every four years, comprise some 48 pageants, which were originally presented upon carts and wagons, dressed for the occasion. They told stories from both the old and new testaments from the Creation to the Last Judgement. The majority of the plays are now held in St Mary's Abbey.

01904 715450

www.yorkmysteryplays.com

The revived 1954 mystery plays. A young Judi Dench is on the right

51

Restaurants (see map page 55)

££

European **31 Castlegate**   Castlegate
01904 621404 www.31castlegate.co.uk   ①

Indian **Akbars**   6-8 George Hudson Street,
01904 679888 www.akbars.co.uk   ②

Italian **Bari** 15 Shambles   01904 633 807   ③

English **Betty's Tea Rooms cafe** 6-8 St. Helen's Square
01904 659142   www.bettys.co.uk/bettys_york   ④

English/French **Biltmore** 76 Swinegate
01904 610075 www.thebiltmorebarandgrill.com   ⑤

Italian **Caesars** 27-29 Goodramgate
01904 670914 www.caesars-restaurants.co.uk   ⑥

Mexican **Fiesta Mehicana** 14 Clifford St
01904 610243   www.fiestamehicana.com   ⑦

English **Gert&Henry's** 4 Jubbergate 01904 621 445   ⑧

American **Henry J Beans** 1 Tower St
01904 464727 www.henryjbeans.co.uk   ⑨

Italian **La Vecchia-Scuola** 62 Low Petergate   01904 644600   ⑩

Indian **The Mogul**   39 Tanner Row
01904 659622   www.themogulyork.co.uk   ⑪

£££

Mediterranean **Ate O'Clock** 13A High Ousegate
01904 644080 www.ateoclock.co.uk   ⑫

English **Café Concerto** 21 High Petergate
01904 610478 www.cafeconcerto.biz   ⑬

vegan **El Piano** 17 Grape Lane 01904 610676   www.el-piano.com   ⑭

English **J Bakers** 7 Fossgate 01904 622688   www.jbakers.co.uk   ⑮

Eclectic **Masons Bar and Bistro** 13 Fossgate
01904 611919   www.masonsbarbistro.co.uk   ⑯

Tex-Mex **Plunkets** 9 High Petergate
01904 637722   www.plunkets.co.uk   ⑰

English **Russells** 26 Coppergate
01904 644330   www.russells-restaurants.com   ⑱

French **Rustique** 28 Castlegate
01904 612744 www.rustiqueyork.co.uk   ⑲

YORK

English **The Living Room** 2 Bridge St — 20
01904 461000 www.thelivingroom.co.uk

Mediterranean **The Olive Tree** 10 Tower St — 21
01904 624433 www.theolivetreeyork.co.uk

English **The Waterfront** 5 King's Staith — 22
01904 671108 www.thewaterfronthotelyork.co.uk

Italian **Tuscany** 3-7 Coney St   01904 733880 — 23

English **The LimeHouse** 55 Goodramgate — 24
01904 632734 www.limehouserestaurant-york.co.uk

££££

English **Meltons** 7 Scarcroft Road — 25
01904 634341 www.meltonsrestaurant.co.uk

English **Nineteen** 19 Grape Ln — 26
01904 636366 www.nineteenyork.com

English **The Blue Bicycle** 34 Fossgate — 27
01904 673990 www.thebluebicycle.com

YORK

Hotels (see map page 55)
★★

Ibis Hotel 77 The Mount 91 Bedrooms — 28
01904 658301 www.ibishotel.com

Travelodge York Central 90 Piccadilly 104 Bedrooms — 29
0871 984 6187 www.travelodge.co.uk

Holgate Hill Hotel 124 Holgate Road 33 Bedrooms — 30
01904 653786 www.holgatehillhotel.co.uk

Knavesmire Manor Hotel 302, Tadcaster Road 21 Bedrooms — 31
01904 702941 www.knavesmire.co.uk

Travel Lodge Micklegate 104 Bedrooms — 32
0871 9846443 www.travelodge.co.uk

Jorvik Hotel 50-52 Marygate 22 Bedrooms — 33
01904 653511 www.jorvikhotel.co.uk

Lady Anne Middletons 55-57 Skeldergate 54 Bedrooms — 34
01904 611570 www.ladyannes.co.uk

The Queens Skeldergate 78 Bedrooms — 35
0845 080 5104 www.queenshotel-york.com

YORK

The Alhambra Court 31, St.Marys, Bootham   24 Bedrooms   ③⑥
01904 628474   www.alhambracourthotel.co.uk

Wheatlands Lodge 75/85 Scarcroft Road   60 Bedrooms   ③⑦
01904 654318   www.wheatlandslodge.co.uk

★★★

Premier Inn 20 Blossom Street   107 bedrooms   ③⑧
0871 5279196 www.premierinn.com

Churchills 65 Bootham   32 Bedrooms   ③⑨
01904 644456 www.churchillhotel.com

Monkbar Monkbar 99 Bedrooms   ④⓪
01904 638086   www.monkbarhotel.co.uk

Elmbank The Mount   63 Bedrooms   ④①
01904 610653   www.elmbankhotel.com

Holiday Inn Tadcaster Road   142 Bedrooms   ④②
0871 4234917 www.holidayinn.com

The Kilima 129, Holgate Road   26 Bedrooms   ④③
01904 625787   www.bw-kilimahotel.co.uk

York Pavilion 45 Main Street, Fulford 57 Bedrooms   ④④
01904 622099 www.yorkpavilionhotel.com

★★★★

The Judges Lodgings 9 Lendal   14 bedrooms   ④⑤
01904 638733   www.judgeslodgings.com

Dean Court Duncombe Place   37 bedrooms   ④⑥
01904 625082   www.deancourt-york.co.uk

Hotel du Vin 88 The Mount   44 bedrooms   ④⑦
01904 557350   www.hotelduvin.com/hotels/york

Mount Royal Hotel 117/119 The Mount 24 bedrooms   ④⑧
01904 628856   www.mountroyale.co.uk

The Grange 1, Clifton 36 Bedrooms   ④⑨
01904 644744 www.grangehotel.co.uk

Marriott Tadcaster Road   151 Bedrooms   ⑤⓪
01904 701000   www.marriott.co.uk

Hilton 1 Tower Street, 130 Bedrooms   ⑤①
01904 648111 www.hilton.com/york

Park Inn North Street 200 Bedrooms   ⑤②
01904 459988   www.parkinn.co.uk/hotel-york

Royal York Station Parade   170 Bedrooms   ⑤③
0844 824 6171   www.royalhotelyork.co.uk

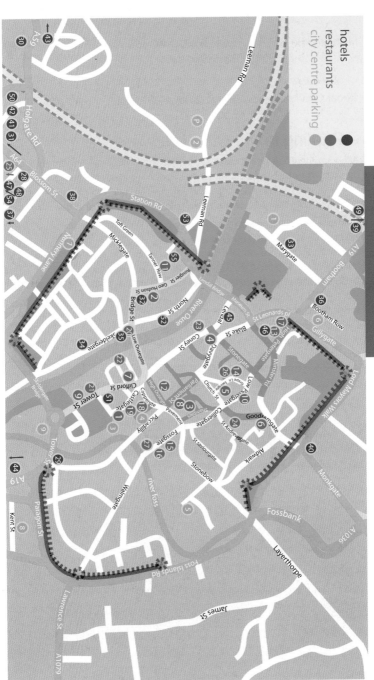

YORK

hotels
restaurants
city centre parking

YORK

Middlethorpe Hall Middlethorpe Road   29 Bedrooms   54
01904 641241   www.middlethorpe.com

★★★★★

Cedar Court Station Rise York   107 bedrooms   55
01904 380038   www.cedarcourtgrand.co.uk

Parking in the City ⓟ

Although there are many car parks in the city centre, day visitors may best be advised to use the park and ride scheme. Parking at these sites is free of charge with a modestly priced return bus fare into the city and frequent services   between 6.00am and 7.45 pm.   The park and ride sites are:

Askham Bar: approach from the south west (A1M and Leeds direction) by the Tesco superstore.   No 3 bus.

Grimston Bar: approach from the south east (Hull direction). The park and ride site is close to the A1079 junction with the A64. No 8 bus.

Designer Outlet: approach from the south (Selby direction). The park and ride site adjoins a retail park close to the A63 junction with the A64. No 7 bus.

Rawcliffe Bar: approach from the north (Thirsk direction). The park and ride site is close to the junction of the outer ring road and the A19. No 2 bus.

Monks Cross: approach from the east (Scarborough direction). The park and ride site adjoins the retail park near the outer ring road and the A64. No 9 bus.

The main city centre public car parks are identified on the accompanying map

1 St Mary's	352 spaces		6 Bootham Row	100 spaces
2 Leeman Road	498 spaces		7 Nunnery Lane	193 spaces
3 Castle-Tower St	318 spaces		8 Kent Street	370 spaces
4 Piccadilly	287 spaces		9 St George Field	270 spaces
5 Haymarket	102 spaces			

part of the city's comprehensive Park and Ride system

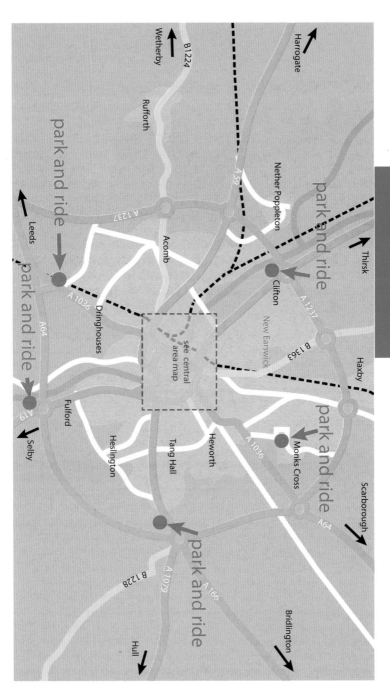

SELBY

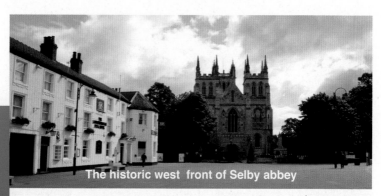

The historic west front of Selby abbey

The market town of Selby is best known for its Abbey and as the birthplace of Henry I. Sited astride the River Ouse, in a low lying area of Yorkshire known as the Humberhead levels, it is 13 miles south of York and 18 miles north of Doncaster.

History

The town is thought to be of Viking origin, named *Seletun*, and archaeological excavations have revealed some remains which support this, but there is no visual evidence in the town. Henry I, William the Conqueror's fourth son, was born here in 1068 during his father's direction of the "harrying of the north" (the ruthless crushing of the rebellion against Norman rule in the north of England). It may be no co-incidence that Selby Abbey was established around the same time. The town's early growth was largely as a consequence of the Abbey, and in the later medieval period it assumed a role for shipbuilding, and other mercantile trade as passage of ships in the River Ouse to York and other ports inland increased. A market charter was granted in 1310, and a market is still held on a Monday. It was the site of the Battle of Selby during the English civil war, when Parliamentarians under Fairfax surrounded the town and overcame the Royalists. This victory allowed them to press on to besiege York. The 18thC saw the construction of the Selby Canal linking the Ouse with the River Aire, and improving the town's trading position by capturing the rapidly growing trade to and from the West Riding. Railways came early to the town; the Leeds to Selby line opening in 1834, and the continuation on to Hull by 1840. The East Coast Main Line passed through the town until the emergence of the Selby coalfield demanded a diversion as coal became a key attribute in the 1980's; the deep mines in and around the town were the last new mines in Britain and the deepest anywhere in the world. The shift away from coal as a fossil fuel spelt the end of the industry and the last mine closed in 2004. Selby is still a bustling centre, serving a hinterland of the lower reaches of the Humber, and its historic Abbey draws visitors from far and wide.

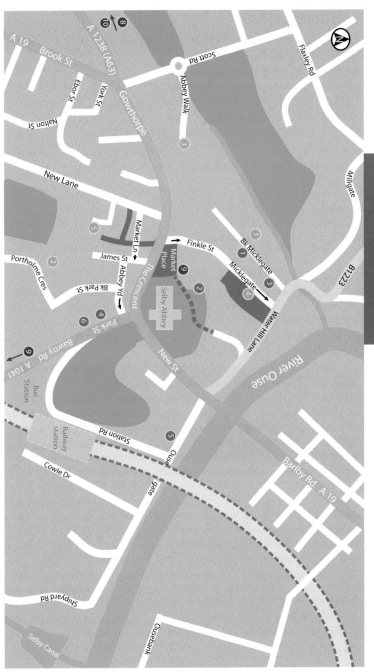

SELBY

SELBY

Getting Here

Rail Selby station lies just to the east of the town centre close to the swing bridge over the Ouse. There are regular services to Hull, Leeds, Manchester, Doncaster and London.

Road Although by-passed, Selby is located on the cross roads of the A19 (Teesside to Doncaster), and the A63 (Leeds to Hull). It is 10 miles north of the M62 (J34). London is 4hrs away; Leeds and Hull 45 mins. York is 30 mins.

Bus the bus station adjoins the railway station. Most services arrive at and depart from here.

destination	service	frequency
Leeds	402	hourly
York	42/415/416	hourly/20 min
Doncaster	405/407	hourly
Wakefield	150	hourly
Goole	400/401	30 min

Things to see and do

Selby's long established market held on a Monday often includes an open air auction. Centred around the market place, about 100 stalls trade their wares in the shadow of the Abbey. It is supplemented by a farmers market held on the 1st Wednesday of each month.

Selby Abbey

Selby Abbey sits majestically at the eastern end of James Street; a striking west front of cathedral like proportions testifying to the importance of the original abbey. It was founded by Benedict of Auxerre in 1069, to celebrate the birth of Henry 1 the year before, and William the Conqueror's own desire to provide a means of commemorating the Norman conquest, in much the same way that Battle Abbey had been established following the Battle of Hastings.   It is one of the few surviving abbey churches in the UK.   The tower dates from the Norman era and the nave from the 13thC, although other parts of the building have been altered over time with Sir George Gilbert Scott, the prolific Victorian arhitect, masterminding a 19thC restoration.   The abbey itself was lost during the Dissolution of the Monasteries, although the church survived intact and becaming the parish church during James 1 reign.   It is said the church survived because the Abbot of the monastery refused to support the Pilgrimage of Grace, the ill fated religious rebellion of the Abbots against Henry VIII's Dissolution of the Monasteries. The interior bears a strong resemblance to Durham cathedral, and includes some fine stained glass windows; notable being the George Washington window, named for the ancestors of the first US president, John Wessington, Prior of Durham, and the Jesse window, said to be only surpassed by the west window of York Minster.   The Abbey is open Monday to Saturday.   Admission is free.   01757 703123   www.selbyabbey.org.uk

Henry 1
Norman King   1069-1135

The youngest of nine children and the fourth son of William the Conqueror and Matilda, Henry was born in Selby in about 1068 whilst his father was directing the so called harrying of the north, a rebellion by the northern Anglo-Saxons against Norman rule. He ascended to the throne in 1100, and proceeded to create a stable social and economic environment, in contrast to the turbulent reign of his older brother William Rufus. He married the daughter of the King of Scotland, and sought to combine the Norman and Anglo Saxon cultures. He initiated the Treasury and a number of other financial reforms.

SELBY

Drax power station

About 4 miles to the south east of Selby lies one of Britain's most iconic power stations with a visitor centre that, by prior arrangement, conducts guided tours around the station, and also boasts a nature reserve, which provides a complete contrast to the industrial workings of the power station. Drax power station is the UK's largest, providing over 7% of the nation's electricity power capacity. It was built in 1974 as a coal fired station, but has diversified to produce power through gas desulphurisation, and biomass as well as other forms of energy generation.   01757 612933 www.draxpower.com

Drax power station can be seen from a long distance

TADCASTER

Restaurants (see map page 59)

££

Thai Thai Sunshine 3 Abbey Walk
01757 428081 www.thaisunshineselby.co.uk ①

Italian Capri 4 Abbey Place
01757 706856 www.caprirestaurantselby.co.uk ②

Italian Osteria 23 Back Micklegate
01757 704011 www.osteria23.co.uk ③

Italian Caesars@The Abbey 12 Park Street
01757 706660 www.caesars-restaurants.co.uk/selby/ ④

Indian Le Raj 64 Ousegate 01757 210124 ⑤

£££

English Number 8 8 Park Street
01757 291188 www.number8restaurant.co.uk ⑥

Hotels (see map page 59)
★★★

The Wishing Well Oakney Wood Road 40 bedrooms
08712 003363 www.newcountryinns.com ⑦

Monk Fryston Hall Monk Fryston 29 bedrooms
01977 682369 www.monkfrystonhallhotel.co.uk ⑧

not rated

The Londesborough 3 Market Place 24 Bedrooms 01757 707355 ⑨

The Owl Main street Hambleton 22 bedrooms
01757 228374 www.owlhotelpub.co.uk ⑩

Parking Ⓟ

① Back Micklegate	198 spaces	④ Micklegate	52 spaces
② Portholme Road	146 spaces	⑤ South Parade	54 spaces
③ Market Cross	48 spaces		

TADCASTER

St Marys Church

Lying 4 miles east of the A1, and 10 miles from York, Tadcaster is a small town best known for its association with brewing beer; no less than three major breweries brew beer here.

History

The Roman name for Tadcaster is *Calcaria (latin for limekilns)*, on account of the quarrying undertaken by the Romans to provide limestone for buildings and for roads. Roman buildings and roads in York were frequently made from stone hewn from the warm creamy Magnesian Limestone which is visible in and around the town. Tadcaster was also an important staging post on the alternative Ermine Street between Lincoln and York as this was where the crossing of the River Wharfe took place. Historians believe the town is where King Harold assembled his forces for a march on York and then onto the Battle of Stamford Bridge in 1066. The Domesday book refers to the town as *Tatecastre* and its new Norman landlords, the De Percy's, established a timber and earthwork motte and bailey castle on the west side of the river; some outline remains of which are still visible. Henry III granted the rights to a market- still held on a Tuesday- in about 1270, and the brewing industry had firmly established itself in the town by the mid 14thC. Tadcaster lies close to two of the bloodiest battles fought in English history - the Battle of Towton, 4 miles south on the Sherburn-in Elmet road (A162), fought in 1461 during the Wars of the Roses and where some 28,000 soldiers on both sides perished, and the Battle of Marston Moor, 6 miles to the north between the villages of Tockwith and Long Marston, which took place in 1644 during the English Civil War and was a pivotal point in that bloodiest of english conflicts. The town has relied on brewing beer for its economy and this continues to the present day; despite its small size, it is the second most important brewing location in the country.

Getting Here

Rail the nearest station is at York with services to all parts of the country.

Road the town lies just off the A64 linking Leeds with Scarborough. York is 20 min; Leeds 45 min, and London 4hrs.

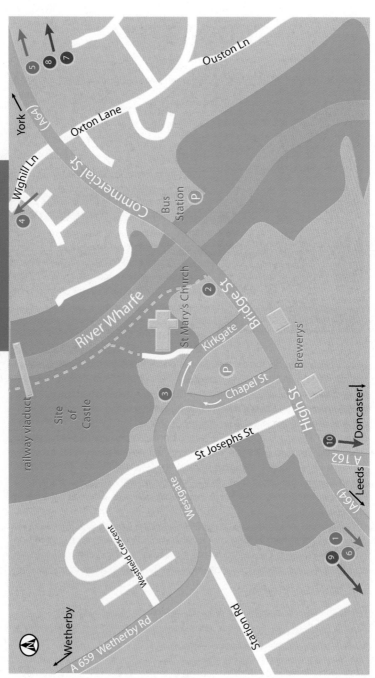

TADCASTER

Ouston Ln

York (A64)

Oxton Lane

Wighill Ln

Commercial St

Bus Station

P

River Wharfe

St Mary's Church

Bridge St

Kirkgate

railway viaduct

Site of Castle

P

Chapel St

Brewerys'

High St

St Josephs St

Doncaster

A 162

Leeds (A64)

Westgate

Westfield Crescent

Station Rd

Wetherby

A 659 Wetherby Rd

Bus all bus services arrive at and depart from the bus station which is on the east side of the river close to the Wharfe bridge.

destination	service(s)	frequency
York	37/743/844	3xper day/2x hour
Leeds	743/844	2x hour
Pontefract	492/493	hourly
Scarborough	843	hourly
Wetherby	923	6x per day
Otley	923	6x per day

Things to see and do

The core of the town, west of the 18thC road bridge, is largely Georgian in character, along the High St, Bridge St, and Kirkgate with some imposing buildings; notably Samuel Smiths brewery offices and the White horse pub on the south side of Bridge St; the Duke of Somerset's house in Kirkgate. The oldest secular buildings in the town are The Ark, on Kirkgate which is a timber framed hall built around late 15thC, and behind it, the Old Vicarage, dating from around the same period.

St Marys Church

Notable for remains of a Saxon cross and some surviving Norman sections of the nave, a 19thC restoration to prevent flooding nevertheless faithfully reproduces the churches perpendicular 12thC style. The font is 15thC, and the east window has some distinctive stained glass. The church is open Mon to Sat.

www.stmarytadcaster.co.uk

Castle

Remains of the Norman motte and bailey castle are visible on the west bank of the River Wharfe. It was built in about 1090 by the de Percy family, followers of William the Conqueror, who bestowed upon them vast tracts of land in Yorkshire and Lincolnshire. The site is thought to be close to the original Roman crossing of the river. It had became derelict by late 12thC when the family ceased to live in the area; they later purchased the castle at Alnwick in Northumberland, where descendants still live. Today, parts of the motte, the inner bailey and north part of the outer bailey are visible. A riverside footpath running from the west side of the road bridge provides access both to the castle and the church.

Railway viaduct

This imposing magnesian limestone railway viaduct was built about 1848. as part of a Leeds to York railway line proposed by George Hudson, but which failed to materialise. The only time the viaduct had a railway on it was as an extension of the branch line to Wetherby to serve a paper mill that was operated on the east side of the river between about 1882 and 1950.

Breweries

The soft water quality, rich in lime sulphate, gives the town a natural advantage for brewing beer, and it has exploited such natural assets for over 600 years.

TADCASTER

Today there are three breweries here; two owned by large multi- national corporations and one independent (Samuel Smiths). Two are located on the south side of Bridge Street/ High Street, and one, owned by the CoorsBrewing group on the road to Boston Spa. The buildings on the south side of the main street representing Samuel Smith's and John Smiths date as far as 1758, and Samuel Smiths still use shire horses to deliver to local pubs. The horses are stabled behind the White Horse pub.

breweries dominate the High Street

Restaurants (see map page 64)

££

Indian **The Aagrah** York Road 01937 530888 www.aagrah.com ①

Indian **Sonali** 20 Bridge Street
01937 530607 www.sonali-indianrestaurant.co.uk ②

£££

English **Singers** 16 Westgate 01937 835121 www.singersrestaurant.com ③

pub food **The White Swan** Main Street Wighill
01937 832217   www.whiteswanwighill.com ④

pub food **The Sun Inn** Main Street Colton
01904 744261 www.yeoldsuninn.co.uk ⑤

££££

English **The Vavasour** Hazlewood Castle Paradise Lane
01937 535353   www.hazlewood-castle.co.uk ⑥

Hotels (see map page 64)

★★

Travelodge York Road Bilbrough 62 Bedrooms
0871 9846186 www.travelodge.co.uk ⑦

★★★

Premier Inn York Road Bilbrough Top Colton 59 Bedrooms
01937 5279202 www.premierinn.com ⑧

★★★★

Hazelwood Castle Paradise Lane 25 Bedrooms
01937 535353 www.hazlewood-castle.co.uk ⑨

not rated

Old Presbytery London Road Barkston Ash 4 bedrooms
01937 557708 www.presbyteryguesthouse.co.uk ⑩

THIRSK

Thirsk is a small market town in the Vale of York, east of the A1 great north road and west of the North York Moors. It is best known for it's association with James Herriot, the famous vet, and for its long established racecourse.

History

The settlement is first recorded in the Domesday Book as *"Tresche"*, a Viking name for marsh. It developed as a centre for the surrounding fertile agricultural lands of the Vale of York; a twice weekly market has been held in the Market Place since medieval times, and the town was the home to woollen, flax and linen weaving until the industrial dominance of the West Riding saw the industry die out in the 19thC. Like its near neighbour, Northallerton, Thirsk became a coaching stop for travellers on the great north road and the coming of the railways strengthened its role as a place to stay.   It also boasted a castle but there is scant evidence of any remains.   Today, Thirsk is a characterful market town with its markets and wide range of independent shops.

Getting Here

Rail   Thirsk is on the east coast main line, with fast frequent trains to York (20 min), Leeds(50 min), Newcastle(1hr), Manchester(1hr 45min), and London (2hrs 20 min). The station is 1 mile from the centre, on the A61 Ripon Road.

Road   well connected by road, Thirsk adjoins the A19 road to Middlesbrough(40 min) and the north east, and is 10 min   from the A1. There are also good roads to York (A19 40 min), Scarborough (A170 1 hr), and Ripon (A61 20 min).

Bus   most services arrive at and depart from the Market Place.

destination	service(s)	frequency
York	30/58	hourly/3x per day
Northallerton	70/153	2 hourly/3x per day
Ripon	70	two hourly

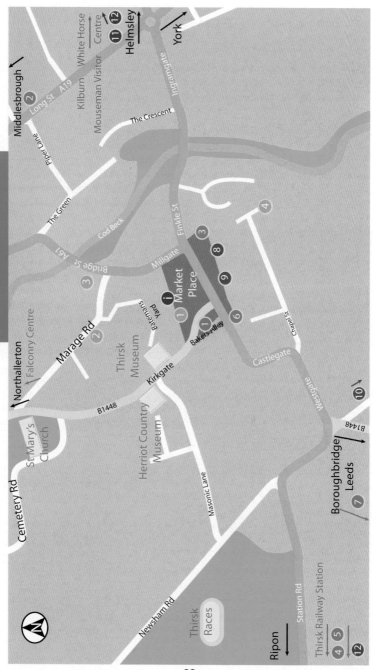

THIRSK

Things to see and do

Thirsk is centred around the **Market Place**; a large bustling, part cobbled square with a twice weekly market (Mon and Sat).   Most of the frontage buildings are Victorian or Georgian, and of note are the clock tower and the coaching inns - The Three Tuns, once the town's Manor house; the Golden Fleece and The Crown. All bear witness to the towns function as a staging post in centuries past. Off the north west corner of the Market Place runs Kirkgate with it's largely unaltered 18thC buildings, including the former surgery of Alf Wight, better known as **James Herriot**, and now a museum to his life and work, and the small but informative **Thirsk Museum**.   At the top of the street, just before the church, is **Thirsk Hall,** an imposing early 18thC manor house.

St Mary's Church

Kirkgate leads to St Mary's parish church, described by the architectural historian Niklaus Pevsner as "the most spectacular perpendicular church in the North Riding". It was built in the 15thC following the foundation of a chantry on the site of an earlier Saxon Minster.   The present church is remarkable not only for its size, but also because it has remained largely unaltered since its construction. The 80ft high tower contains eight bells, which are still rung regularly, with the oldest- the "Jesus Bell"- predating the church, having an inscription dated 1410. In the nave are some faded 17thC wall paintings of the Apostles, and a 15thC 21ft high font cover.   The church is open daily from Easter to the end of October.

Herriot Country museum

Thirsk is perhaps best known for the TV vet, James Herriot, whose life and works are celebrated in the museum on Kirkgate. James Herriot was the pen name of Alf Wight, who lived in the town for over 50 years and whose stories of life as a country vet have entertained millions all over the world, and whose books were made into several TV series (All Creatures Great and Small). The Museum is open daily through the year. There is an admission charge.   01845 524234   www.worldofjamersherriot.org

THIRSK

Thirsk Museum

A small museum in Kirkgate opposite the James Herriot museum, this is the house of Thomas Lord (1755-1832), founder of Lords cricket ground in London. The museum is a celebration of local life – of the history and customs of Thirsk folk. The museum is open from Easter to October five days per week. There is an admission charge. 01845 527707 www.thirskmuseum.org

Thirsk Races

There has been regular horse racing at Thirsk since 1855 when the present course was created. It lies alongside the A61 Ripon road just west of the town centre. It hosts about 13 meetings, all for flat racing, every year between April and September. 01845 522276 www.thirskracecourse.net

The Mouseman Visitor Centre

At Kilburn, 4 miles to the east of the town, nestling under the lee of Sutton Bank, is the workshop and museum of Robert Thomson, an early 20thC carpenter best known as The Mouseman for the mouse carvings he sculpted on every piece of furniture he made. The visitor centre is a celebration of his life and work and contains his own personal domestic furniture. It is open daily from Easter to September and Wed to Sun in the winter. There is an admission charge. Bus service 59 runs 4x per day on Mondays and Fridays from Thirsk market place. 01347 869102 www.robertthompsons.co.uk

White Horse of Kilburn

On the south west facing escarpment of the North Yorks Moors at Kilburn, some 4 miles east, is an iconic white horse cut into the limestone hillside. 318 ft long and 220 ft high, it can be seen on a clear day from as far away as north Leeds, over 40 miles away. The horse was carved out of the hillside in 1857 by a local merchant who had seen the Uffington white horse in Sussex and thought to repeat it in his home village. The practice of carving white horses is known as leucippotomy and is more prevalent in southern England. There is a car park below with a footpath leading to it up the escarpment. Bus service 59 4x per day Mon to Fri from Thirsk market place.

Falconry Centre

The centre at Sion Hill Hall, 4 miles north of Thirsk was set up to provide a means of ensuring the survival and protection of these birds, and at the same time providing visitors with an opportunity to experience them close at hand. The centre is open daily March to October. There is an admission charge. 01845 587522 www.falconrycentre.co.uk

Thirsk Visitor Information Centre
93A Market Place   01845 522755
www.thirsk.org.uk/thirsk-visit.php

Restaurants (see map page 68)

££

Italian **Charles Bistro**   Bakers Alley Market Place   01845 527444   ①

Indian **The Raj of India** 42 Long Street   01845 526917 www.rajofindia.net   ②

Chinese **Hung Moey** 60 Market Place   01845 522363   ③

English **The Dog and Gun** Carlton Miniott 01845 522150   ④

£££

pub food **The Black Lion** 8 Market Place   ⑤
01845 574302   www.blacklionthirsk.co.uk

££££

Fish **The Crab and Lobster** Dishforth Road Asenby   ⑥
01845 577286   www.crabandlobster.co.uk

Hotels (see map page 68)

★★★

The Three Tuns Market Place 12 Bedrooms   ⑦
01845 521370 www.jdwetherspoon.co.uk/home/hotels/the-three-tuns

The Golden Fleece Market Place 23 Bedrooms   ⑧
01845 523108   www.goldenfleecehotel.com

★★★★(GA)

Oswalds Front Street Sowerby 16 Bedrooms   01845 523655   ⑨

not rated

White Horse Lodge Hotel Sutton Road 12 Bedrooms   ⑩
01845 522293 www.whitehorselodgehotel.co.uk

The Old Red House Station Road 10 Bedrooms   ⑪
01845 524383 www.oldredhouse.com

The Carpenters Arms Felixkirk 10 Bedrooms   ⑫
01845 537369 www.thecarpentersarmsfelixkirk.com

Parking

① Market Place	174 spaces	③ Millgate	86 spaces
(not available on market days)			
② Marage	71 spaces	④ Nursery	41 spaces

THIRSK

WETHERBY

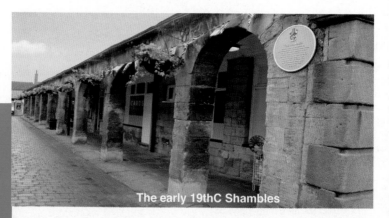

The early 19thC Shambles

Wetherby is a small prosperous market town on the north bank of the River Wharfe, characterised by warm and creamy magnesian limestone buildings. Historically it has made its living from the Great North Road. It is equidistant between London and Edinburgh (198 miles in each direction).

History

Although there may have been a roman settlement here, the first real evidence of settlement is in the Domesday book, called "*Wedrebi*" which means settlement on the bend of a river.   It was a market town as early as the 13thC when Henry III awarded it a charter. The controlling lords at the time were the Knights Templar and there may well have been a castle here (some evidence has been uncovered in Scotts Lane). The first bridge across the Wharfe was built in 1233, and there has been a bridge across the river at this point ever since - the current one dating from 1769.   The town grew substantially in the 17th and 18thC's with the advent of regular coaches along the Great North Road, and at one time there were 40 inns and alehouses here. Many of the former coaching inns can be seen today.   One of the wealthiest of English aristocratic families- the Cavendishes – the Dukes of Devonshire, acquired the Wetherby Manor in the late 16thC and by the time they sold it, in 1824, they owned virtually all of the town. The sale was caused by the expense of building alterations to the family seat, Chatsworth House in Derbyshire.   Wetherby's role as a stop for travellers increased with the advent of the motor car, and even though the by passing of the town had an adverse effect, it still provides for travellers, in new and old accommodation.

Getting here

Rail the nearest rail stations are at Leeds and York, with direct access onto the national intercity rail network.

Road the town lies on the Great North Road at the point just north of where the M1 and the A1 merge and where the A58 Leeds road joins the A1. Leeds is a 30 min journey; Manchester 90 mins and London 3 hrs 30 mins.

Bus all services depart from the bus station in the Market Place.

destination	service(s)	frequency
Leeds	98/99	every 30 min
York	412/413	hourly
Harrogate	77/770	4x hour
Knaresborough	780	hourly
Wakefield	173/174/175	hourly

Things to see and do

The core of the town is in the Market Place, a wide street fronted with 18th and 19thC buildings.   Of particular note are the **Town Hall** of 1847 and opposite, **The Shambles** erected by the Devonshire estate in about 1811.   There is a weekly market on a Thursday, and a farmers market on the second Sunday of each month.   The town has an historic trail, with buildings and points of interest marked by blue plaques.   Trail leaflets are available in most shops. Around the market place, small narrow streets are filled with independent shops in whose windows to browse, and the High St, (the old Great North Road) where the evidence of former coaching inns is still prevalent in hostelries such as the Angel Inn or the Swan and Talbot. The town has a small restored cinema, on Crossley St, and which puts on the latest films in a 1950's atmosphere.

coaching inns still feature in the town

Wetherby Races

A leading Yorkshire venue, Wetherby racecourse lies   east of the town, with its modern stands and pavilions, promotes a year round calendar of fixtures, and is renowned as the county's premier National Hunt course.   01937 582035   www.wetherbyracing.co.uk

Spofforth Castle ⛫

Some 3 miles NW of the town on the Harrogate road, lies the ruins of an 11thC fortified Manor house, the original base of the powerful de Percy family and where, it is reputed, the Magna Carta was originally devised. Ruined in the English civil war, it is open as a monument between April and September. There is no admission charge.   0870 333 1181 www.english-heritage.org.uk

WETHERBY

WETHERBY

Restaurants (see map page 75)

£

Fish **Wetherby Whaler** 18 Market Place
01937 582968 www.wetherbywhaler.co.uk ①

English **The Gourmet** 9 The Shambles 01937 58603 ②

££

Italian **Ask** 1 Market Place 01937 589831 www.askitalian.co.uk ③
French **Le Bon Appetit** 6-8 Bank Street 01937 587897 ④
Italian **Sant Angelo** High Street 01937 581422 www.santangelo.co.uk ⑤
Thai **Yum Yum Thai** 9 Bank Street 01937 918081 ⑥

£££

English **Scotts Arms** Sicklinghall 01937 582100 www.scottsarms.com ⑦

Hotels (see map page 75)

★★

Days Inn J46 A1M Wetherby Service 129 Bedrooms
01937 547557 www.daysinnwetherby.co.uk ⑧

★★★

Mercure Leeds Road 103 bedrooms 0844 8159067 www.mercurewetherby.co.uk ⑨

★★★★(GA)

Swan Guest House 38 North Street 01937 582381
www.swanguesthouse.co.uk ⑩

★★★★

Wood Hall Trip Lane Linton 44 Bedrooms
01937 587271 www.handpickedhotels.co.uk ⑪

The Bridge Walshford 30 Bedrooms
01937 580115 www.thebridgewetherby.co.uk ⑫

Parking Ⓟ

① Crossley Street   82 spaces   ③ Wilderness Riverside   231 spaces
② North Street   39 spaces

ⓘ **Wetherby Visitor Information Centre**
Council Offices Westgate
01937 582151 www.wetherby.co.uk

74

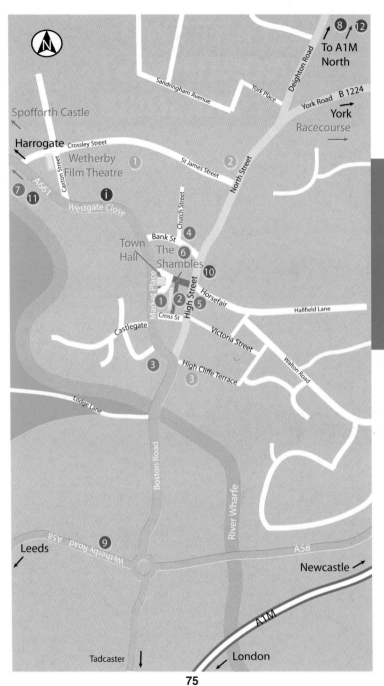

WETHERBY

PART TWO
NORTH WEST
YORKSHIRE

YORKSHIRE DALES

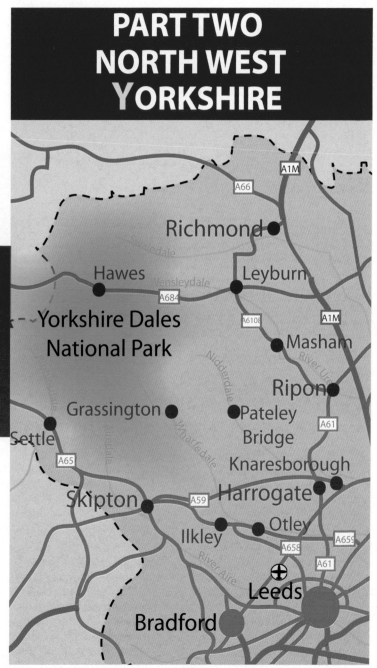

Richmond

Hawes   Leyburn

A684

**Yorkshire Dales
National Park**

Masham

Ripon

Grassington   Pateley
Bridge

Settle

Knaresborough

Skipton   Harrogate

Ilkley   Otley

Leeds

Bradford

THE YORKSHIRE DALES

tranquil Burnsall nestling in Wharfedale

YORKSHIRE DALES

The Yorkshire Dales probably need no introduction. Famous for a number of TV series, such as "It Shouldn't Happen to a Vet", and "Emmerdale Farm" and for its popular Wensleydale Cheese, the Dales rank amongst the best known destinations in the country. Much of the area is a National Park, one of the first established after the second world war, and where there is an obligation to balance commercial and tourism activity with landscape and ecology conservation.

The boundaries of the Dales are somewhat fuzzy, but they cover an area stretching from about 15 miles east of Lancaster, to the Vale of York, and from about 5 miles south of Barnard Castle (Co Durham) to Skipton; an area of about 1000 sq Miles, but with a population of less than 60,000 people; indeed a local farmer will proudly tell you that there are far more sheep than people in the Dales. Visitors cannot help but admire the deep broad valleys, with their often steep sides, green upland pastures divided by dry stone walls and dotted throughout with small stone barns, and brown heather moorland tops. Nestling in the valley bottoms are villages and small towns, making much of their living from tourism and from farming, although recent years have seen the hill farms particularly suffer economically and turn their hand to other activities.

The Dales are a mecca for walkers and hikers, for cyclists - on and off road -and rising popularity has been accompanied by a rise in the number of places to stay, whether campsites or hotels. The weather here is, like much of Britain, unpredictable, although rainfall tends to be lower than average as much of the area lies in the rain shadow of the high Pennines. Winter, when snow falls, can be an exceedingly attractive time of year to explore the area, although venturing on foot away from the roads and the settlements can be hazardous unless well prepared.

Ribblesdale

The only Dale where the river runs west, flowing into the Irish Sea through Preston in Lancashire.   Upper Ribblesdale, north of Settle, to the source of the river Ribble above Ribblehead is dominated by the Yorkshire Three Peaks- **Pen-y- ghent**, **Whernside**, and **Ingleborough**. Pen-y-ghent is an unusual name and stems from the ancient Britons, many of whom emigrated from Wales, and the name is considered to mean "hill of the border country". The hills are the highest in the county, at around 2,350ft (hills above 2000ft are often known as Marilyns to compare those in Scotland above 3000 ft which are known as Monroes).   Walking the three peaks is a popular pastime, with many visitors attracted to the arduous challenge of a 24 mile walk, over these three high hills. Walkers contemplating this need to be experienced and fit, for there is nearly 6,000ft of climbing, with much of the route over uneven terrain. However, those who have done it describe the walk as fulfilling and completing it is certainly a feather in your cap. The walk starts and finishes in the little village of **Horton–in Ribblesdale**, where there is the all day Pen-y-Ghent café to fuel up at the start of the walk, and to quench thirst and rest weary limbs at the end. Those hardy souls completing the task within 12hours are entitled to become members of the Three Peaks Club. At the head of the valley is the **Ribblehead viaduct**, one of the triumphs of 19thC railway civil engineering and just one of the 22 viaducts along the famous Settle- Carlisle railway (see page 97). The curved viaduct with its 24 arches is over 1300 ft long and 100ft high. It took 1000 navvies, who lived in shanty towns by the route (often with their families) four years to build, opening in 1874. Much of the countryside is covered with limestone outcrops, called pavements with their peculiar striations known as clints and grykes. (clints and grykes are a peculiar feature of this area where rainfall and wind has eroded weak fissures in the limestone to create a patterned effect) Further down, is the picturesque waterfall of **Stainforth Force**.

Ribblehead Viaduct

Just away from the Ribble valley, on the south side of Ingleborough, lying by the A65 trunk road, are the villages of Austwick, Clapham, and Ingleton with accommodation and food providers. Above Clapham, on the slopes of Ingleborough lies **Gaping Gill** where the Fell Beck, rising on the higher slopes, plunges 300ft down through the limestone plateau to Britains largest known underground cavern and which leads into the country's most complex cave system and the holy grail for all potholers and cavers. Access into the cavern for visitors must be by prior arrangement with a potholing club, but there are several meets in the summer months where, weather permitting, visitors can be winched down onto the floor of Gaping Gill. The system emerges above ground through Ingleborough Cave, about a 2 mile walk from Clapham, and which is a show cave, and open daily from March to the end of October. There is an admission charge. 01524 251242 www.ingleboroughcave.co.uk

Bus service 581 from Settle to Kirkby Lonsdale passes through Clapham 4x per day. During the summer there are additional services between Settle and Hawes.

On the west side of the hill, above Ingleton, on the B6255 road to Hawes, is **White Scar Cave**, which contains distinctive stalactite and stalagmite formations and waterfalls as it burrows deep under Ingleborough. There are regular bus services to Ingleton from Settle (service 581), and in the summer service 831 from Settle to Hawes passes the site The cave is open daily from February to October. There is an admission charge. 01524 242244 www.whitescarcave.co.uk

Ribblesdale Restaurants and Hotels

The Traddock Austwick hotel/restaurant 12 bedrooms traditional English
01524 251224 www.thetraddock.co.uk ①

The Crown Horton in Ribblesdale pub/accommodation 10 bedrooms pub food
01729 860209 www.crown-hotel.co.uk ②

Austwick Hall Austwick hotel and restaurant 5 bedrooms English food
01524 251794 www.austwickhall.co.uk ③

La Tavernetta Ingleton Italian restaurant 01524 242465 ④

The Craven Heifer Ingleton pub and accommodation 4 bedrooms pub food
01524 242515 www.cravenheiferingleton.co.uk ⑤

Brookhouse Clapham   guesthouse and restaurant 4 bedrooms English food
01524 251580 www. brookhouse-clapham.co.uk ⑥

Upper Airedale

The River Aire, a primary source of water and power for the West Riding mills in earlier times, rises in limestone country above picturesque Malham village. It is a peaceful dale, dominated by the mighty **Malham Cove** towering above the village. Shaped like a natural amphiteatre, the cove is some 250 ft high, and 1000ft wide, and was a waterfall after the last ice age.

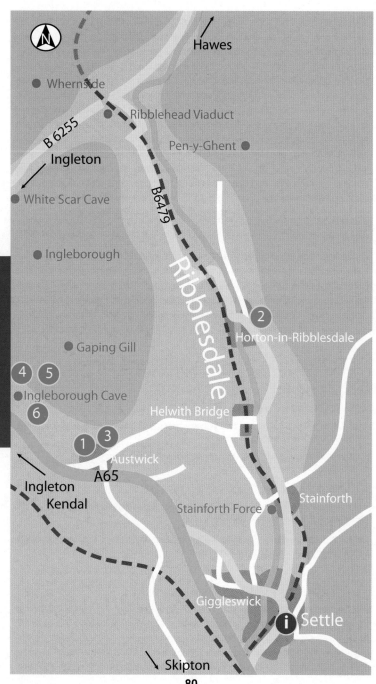

YORKSHIRE DALES

The permeable nature of the carboniferous limestone has caused the water to find its way underground, and it now emerges from the foot of the cove. The water is not, however, that of the River Aire, as many think, but from sinks about 3/4m north west of the cove. The real source of the Aire, which rises above ground south of the village, is Malham Tarn. The cove can be reached by footpath from the village with a path which climbs to the top, where there is an expansive section of limestone pavement, with a clint and gryke pattern.

The mighty Malham Cove

YORKSHIRE DALES

To the east is Gordale Scar. This is a short but deep gorge created from erosion of the limestone by the Gordale beck; it's overhanging sides suggesting this was once a cavern. The beck tumbles over a number of small but spectacular waterfalls as it makes its way down to join the River Aire. It is possible to clamber up the rocks on the side of the Scar, but it is a trek which requires considerable exertion and care. Malham Tarn lies about two miles beyond the cove. This glacial lake is the source of the River Aire. It is the highest lake in England at 1200ft above sea level, and was the inspiration for Charles Kingsley's book, the Water Babies. There is a nature trail around the tarn, where visitors can view the wide range of wildlife from hides on its north side.

Wharfedale

The River Wharfe which flows into the Ouse near York, rises in remote Langstrothdale to the north of Pen-y-Ghent, and flows down through the steep sided valley, forming the southern edge of the Dales as it turns eastwards at Bolton Abbey. Many of the small farm hamlets at the very northern end of the dale above Buckden were created in the10thC by Norse settlers, and in medieval times much of the land in Upper Wharfedale was owned and managed by the great Abbeys of Bolton and Fountains.

The Abbeys' monks and lay brothers working the land were responsible for creating today's patterns of country roads and green lanes on the upper pastures and moorland. The Enclosure Acts of the 18th/19thC have endowed a pattern of fields and meadows in the lower slopes of the valley which remain today, the fields being marked by dry stone walls. Along the way the river passes through small, inescapably Yorkshire, villages. Hubberholme, the smallest and most northerly has a distinctive church, parts of which are thought to be 12thC, and in whose graveyard the author and critic J.B. Priestley is buried (see p.161). Below Hubberholme, as the valley widens, are the archetypal villages of Buckden, Kettlewell and Conistone, together with Kilnsey Crag, an imposing overhanging cliff much favoured by rock climbers. Also here is Kilnsey Park, where can be seen a trout farm and one of the few places in the country to boast presence of the red squirrel. A few miles further down the dale is its main "metropolis", Grassington. This small attractive town is a touring base for many visitors to the Dales and boasts a range of hotels and guesthouses. The small cobbled market square leads onto the narrow rising main street. With a range of shops selling both everyday goods and gifts, Grassington has a compelling aura as a place to browse and rest a while. A farmers market is held in the Square the third Sunday of each month and annually, the last two weeks in June, sees the Grassington festival, a popular arts and culture event featuring music, dance drama, and street theatre. (www.grassington-festival.org.uk) The Upper Wharfedale Folk Museum in the Square recounts Dales life over the centuries including lead mining, craft tools, and costumes. It is open Tues to Sun, April to October. There is an admission charge. (www.grassingtonfolkmuseum.org.uk) Buses serve the town from Ilkley, (services 74 5x per day and 874 2xper day), Skipton (service 72 hourly), and during the April to October period, the Dalesbus service provides links with York, Leeds and Bradford on certain days of the week.

Below Grassington the Wharfe passes through the small pretty village of Burnsall, often quoted by locals as England's prettiest village, before reaching Barden Bridge, and the 15thC Barden Tower and a little further down, the turbulent rapids known as The Strid and then Bolton Abbey.

Burnsall

Wharfedale Restaurants and hotels (map page 84)

Black Horse Grassington   pub food   ①
01756 752770 www.blackhorsehotelgrassington.co.uk

Grassington Lodge Grassington   guest house   10 bedrooms   ②
01756 752518 www.grasssingtonlodge.co.uk

The Red Lion Burnsall   coaching inn   25 bedrooms   traditional English food   ③
01756 720204   www.redlion.co.uk

The Devonshire Fell Burnsall   small hotel/restaurant   12 bedrooms   ④
modern English food. 01756 729000   www.devonshirefell.co.uk

The Fountaine Inn Linton   gastropub   ⑤
01756 752210   www.fountaineinnatlinton.co.uk

Grassington House Grassington hotel/restaurant 8 bedrooms; English food   ⑥
01756 752406 www.grassingtonhousehotel.co.uk

Ashfield House Grassington   hotel/restaurant   7 bedrooms English food   ⑦
01756 752584 www.ashfieldhouse.co.uk

The Racehorses Kettlewell   pub and accommodation 10 bedrooms   pub food   ⑧
01756 760233 www.racehorseshotel.co.uk

The Craven Arms Appletreewick gastropub   ⑨
01756 720270   www.craven-cruckbarn.co.uk

The Buck Inn Buckden coaching inn 14 bedrooms   English food   ⑩
01756 761401 www.thebuckinnbuckden.co.uk

The Priests House Barden Tower restaurant   traditional English food   ⑪
01756 720616 www.thepriesthouse.co.uk

Nidderdale

Nidderdale lies outside the National Park, but most of this Dale is designated an Area of Outstanding Natural Beauty. The river Nidd rises just below Great Whernside, the hill dividing Nidderdale from Wharfedale.   At its head are two large reservoirs, Angram and Scar House, both built in the early 20thC to provide Bradford with a reliable source of clean water, to supplement the earlier construction of Gouthwaite reservoir, further down the Dale. The remains of a shanty town which housed the mainly Irish navvies working on the project, and included a hospital, cinema and concert hall, can be seen on the south side of Scar House near the dam. There is public access to the reservoirs, where there is a picnic area and footpaths, including a circuit of Scar House reservoir. Below the reservoirs, are the tiny villages of Middlesmoor, Lofthouse, and Ramsgill. A small road leads from just below Middlesmoor to How Stean Gorge. This is a steep sided chasm some 2/3 mile long, 250ft deep in places with an intricate network of footpaths, caves and tunnels, supplemented by a web of rope walks, aerial beams ladders and cables.   Instructors provide courses in canoeing caving and rock climbing.   01423 755666 www.howstean.co.uk

YORKSHIRE DALES

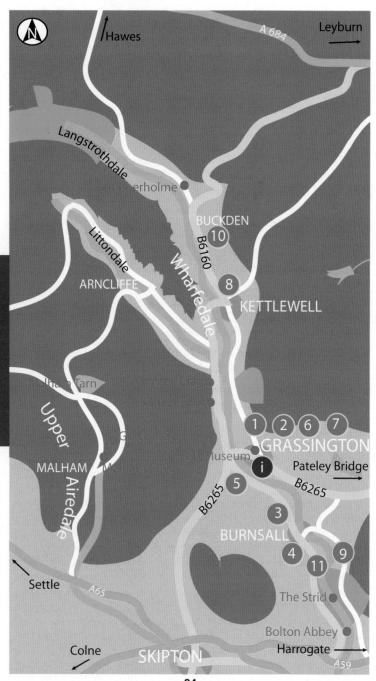

YORKSHIRE DALES

Scar House reservoir

At **Lofthouse**, a sharp climb out of the village gives way to a spectacular winding road with superb long distance views as it passes over the watershed of Pott Moor and down alongside Leighton Reservoir to Masham on the shoulders of Wensleydale. **Pateley Bridge** is Upper Nidderdale's main commecial centre. A small attractive market town whose charter was granted in the early 14thC is, with the adjoining village of Bewerley on the west side of the 17thC bridge, a place to stop and explore. The small winding High Street with a number of small ginnels off contain cafes and gift shops. Next to the Church is the **Nidderdale Museum**. A conversion of a former workhouse, the Museum recounts the history of the people of Nidderdale and their way of life. The museum is open afternoons, daily from Easter to the end of October. There is an admission charge.   01423 711225 www.nidderdalemuseum.com The meadow by the bridge is the scene for the annual Nidderdale Show**.** Taking place in September, it is generally Yorkshire's last big agricultural show of the year, and a true agricultural affair featuring sheep dog trials and dry stone walling competitions.   01969 650129 www.nidderdaleshow.co.uk. To the west of the town, on the B6265 road to Grassington lie two worthwhile attractions.   **Stump Cross Caverns** is a well known cave complex, found in 1860 by miners searching for sources of lead. The caverns are decorated with colourful and intricate stalactite and stalagmite formations, and extend for 4 miles below the surface. Open daily from mid Feb to the end of Nov. There is an admission charge.   01756 752780 www.stumpcrosscaverns.co.uk

Coldstones Cut, adjoining a large quarry, near the top of Greenhow Hill, is a stunning piece of public sculpture on a grand scale. Visitors can walk through the sculpture, to a viewing platform which affords fabulous long distance views to the Vale of York and beyond, as well as views over the massive limestone quarry. The cut is open everyday. There is no admission charge.

www.thecoldstonescut.org

Coldstones Cut

YORKSHIRE DALES

85

Brimham rocks

Brimham Rocks 🔲 lies 3 miles east of the town, a collection of weird and wonderful rock formations, scattered over 50 acres. The distinctively shaped rocks reflect animals and other objects and provide a iconic place for a picnic or short stroll. A visitor centre provides clues as to the origin of these strange geological formations. The site is open all year. The visitor centre is open daily between June and September and weekends the rest of the year. 01423780688 www.nationaltrust.org.uk

Below Brimham Rocks, the Dale extends down to Ripley and Knaresborough, before emerging into the Vale of York and joining the river Ouse just upstream of York at Nun Monkton.

The Washburn Valley

Immediately south west of Nidderdale is the Washburn valley. Not normally recognised as the Yorkshire Dales but a popular haunt for residents of Leeds and Bradford, Harrogate and further afield. The Washburn river rises south of Coldstones Cut, and flows down a narrow valley, much of it flooded with reservoirs, before joining the River Wharfe to the east of Otley. The water company who constructed the reservoirs to provide water for Leeds historically owned much of the Valley. There is evidence of Neolithic and Roman occupation here, as well as remains of a large flax mill at Blubberhouses. Nowadays, the valley is a tranquil rural retreat enjoyed by visitors for its calm, its stunning views, and its recreational activities.

Thruscross reservoir, near the head of the valley, was built in the 1960's, flooding the small village of West End, which had become largely derelict following the decline of the flax industry, but locals claim that when the reservoir is low, the church bell tower and remains of the flax mill can be clearly seen. The stream below Thruscross dam is used for competition wildwater canoeing, and the outlets from the reservoir are turned up to create a strong challenging flow of water, which in use creates one of the most important sites for this sport in the country. www.yorcie.co.uk/washburn

YORKSHIRE DALES

the thrill of whitewater canoeing

The hamlet of Blubberhouses on the A59 road is sometimes called Little Switzerland for the area around its small but prominent church which sits above Fewston, the next reservoir. Surrounded by managed woodland this reservoir, together with Swinsty and Lindley, a little further down the valley towards Otley were built earlier, in the 19thC. There is a well defined and popular walk around Swinsty and Fewston reservoirs, parts of which enjoy an almost Mediterranean micro climate allowing early flowering of colourful gorse and other shrubs. The former 18thC church in Fewston village is a recently established heritage centre; open weekends April to October, it contains information about the valley, its history, its people and identifies activities and places to visit as well as walking trails.   01943 880794   www.washburnvalley.org

YORKSHIRE DALES

Nidderdale Restaurants and Hotels (map page 88)

The Crown Middlesmoor pub and accommodation 7 bedrooms pub food   ❶
01423 755204

The Crown Lofthouse pub and accommodation pub food 01423 755206   ❷

Yorke Arms Ramsgill hotel and restaurant 12 bedrooms; gourmet food   ❸
01423 755243 www.yorke-arms.co.uk

Sportsmans Arms Wath hotel and restaurant 11 bedrooms   ❹
traditional english food 01423 711306 www.sportsman-arms.co.uk

Olleys Pizzeria Pateley BridgeItalian restaurant   ❺
01423 712200 www.olleyspizzeria.co.uk

Roslyn House Pateley Bridge guest house 6 bedrooms   ❻
01423 711374 www.roslynhouse.co.uk

New Inn Burnt Yates pub with accommodation 8 bedrooms pub food   ❼
01423 771070   www.thenewinnburntyates.co.uk

Boars Head Ripley hotel and restaurant 25 bedrooms traditional English food   ❽
01423 771888 www.boarsheadripley.co.uk

Apothecary's House Pateley Bridge Japanese restaurant 01423 711767   ❾

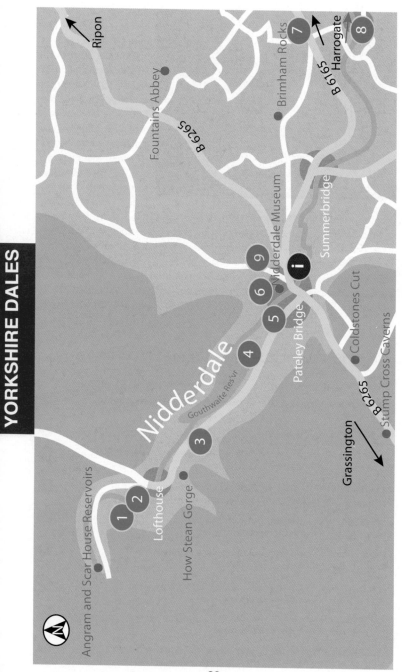

YORKSHIRE DALES

Ripon

Fountains Abbey

Brimham Rocks

B 6165 Harrogate

B 6265

Nidderdale Museum

Summerbridge

Nidderdale

Gouthwaite Resvr

Pateley Bridge

Coldstones Cut

Stump Cross Caverns

B 6265

Grassington

Angram and Scar House Reservoirs

Lofthouse

How Stean Gorge

Wensleydale

The longest of all the Yorkshire Dales, it stretches from near Masham up to the source of the River Ure on Lunds Fell near Kirkby Stephen in Cumbria, a distance of over 30 miles. It is the only dale not named for its river, the river Ure which changes names downstream, becoming the River Ouse above York. The dale is named for the small village of Wensley, 2 miles west of Leyburn, which until virtually wiped out by a plague in 1563, was the main settlement, with a long standing market charter. Garsdale Head, near the source marks the watershed between East and West; the Ure flowing east, and the smaller Clough river, flowing into the River Lune west into the Irish Sea. The Settle - Carlisle railway passes through here with a station below Garsdale common. To the north of Hawes is Hardraw Force, England's largest single drop overground waterfall at over 100 ft. The waterfall is in the grounds of the Green Dragon pub in the small village of Hardraw. (admission charge payable at the pub.) Hawes is the main settlement in Upper Wensleydale. The names derives from the Norse name "*hause*" meaning narrow neck of land or pass between mountains. Very much the honeypot for Upper Wensleydale, a bustling market takes place here every Tuesday to supplement the towns range of colourful shops, cafes and other attractions. These include the Wensleydale Creamery which makes the famous Wensleydale cheese and is open daily, (01969 667664 www.wensleydale.co.uk)

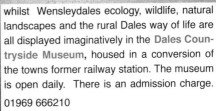

whilst Wensleydales ecology, wildlife, natural landscapes and the rural Dales way of life are all displayed imaginatively in the Dales Countryside Museum, housed in a conversion of the towns former railway station. The museum is open daily. There is an admission charge.

01969 666210

www.yorkshiredales.org.uk

Hawes also boasts a ropemakers, who manufacture a variety of ropes for sale all over the world, and who are open Monday to Friday for visitors to see how ropes are made. 01969 667487 www.ropemakers.co.uk

Hardraw Force

YORKSHIRE DALES

Further down the dale is Bainbridge, a small village centred around a village green complete with medieval stocks, and the site of *Virosidum*, a Roman fort. Situated on the top of a small hill overlooking the village, the fort is thought to have been constructed in the 1stC AD during one of the Roman emperor Agricola's campaigns against the Brigantes, as Bainbridge was an important cross roads in Roman Britain. The fort is largely unexcavated. Aysgarth Falls is set amidst woods where the River Ure tumbles furiously over a succession of limestone pavements. A pleasant riverside footpath links the three main falls. On the north side of the Dale is the village of Castle Bolton and its romantic ruined castle (see page 401), and in the adjoining village of Redmire is the western terminus for the Wensleydale railway. This is a heritage line, running 17 miles east to Leeming Bar on the A1 Great North road and provides the Dales community – visitor and resident alike - with a service throughout the year, although more restricted in the winter months. The route passes through the lower dale and the stations have been restored to their earlier decorations and appearance. A trip on the line is a good way to see the countryside here. (0845 4505474 www. wensleydalerailway.com) At Leyburn, the main settlement of the lower dale, is a variety of local shops and eating places, a central square with a Friday market and a traditional auction mart where livestock are bought and sold in the traditional way. Middleham, 3 miles further east, is best known for its medieval castle (see page 402), where Richard III was brought up, as well as the large number of horse racing stables around the village. There is a gallop on the moors above where, on most days, thoroughbred horses, normally busy racing at Epsom, Doncaster or other well known race venues, can be seen being put through their paces. Nearby is the Forbidden Corner, a private folly which has been adapted and extended to create an atmospheric, if eerie, experience; full of interesting things which are sometimes difficult to find! Centred around Tupgill Park, it is open daily between April and October. There is an admission charge. 01969 640638 www.theforbiddencorner.co.uk The small town of Masham effectively marks the eastern end of the dale.

Here is the home of two traditional breweries, Theakstons and Black Sheep. Both offer guided tours and have their own visitor centres where the tasty range of ales being brewed here can be sampled. The Masham steam rally is held at the end of July. A high spot in the traction engine enthusiasts calendar, it fills a field full of colour, noise and atmosphere. The annual Masham Sheep Fair takes place at the end of September and fills the town square with sheep, some 70,000 animals being sold during the course of the fair, recreating the appearance and atmosphere more typical of Victorian and earlier times.

YORKSHIRE DALES

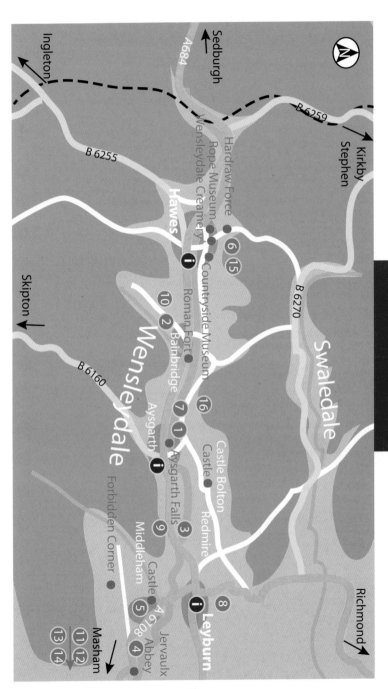

YORKSHIRE DALES

Wensleydale Restaurants and Hotels (map page 91)

Stow House Aysgarth guest house 9 bedrooms ❶
01969 663635 www.stowhouse.co.uk

Rose and Crown Bainbridge coaching inn 11 bedrooms pub food ❷
01969 650225 www.theprideofwensleydale.co.uk

Wensleydale Heifer West Witton hotel and restaurant 13 bedrooms ❸
English food 01969 622322 www.wensleydaleheifer.co.uk

Blue Lion East Witton coaching inn 15 bedrooms English food ❹
01969 624373 www.thebluelion.co.uk

White Swan Middleham coaching inn 17 bedrooms English food ❺
01969 622093 www.whiteswanhotel.co.uk

Stone House Hawes hotel 9 bedrooms ❻
01969 667571 www.stonehousehotel.co.uk

Black Swan Leyburn coaching inn 9 bedrooms pub food 01969 622221 ❼

Thornton Lodge Aysgarth hotel 9 bedrooms ❽
01969 663375 www.thorntonlodgenorthyorkshire.co.uk

The Old Star West Witton guest house 7 bedrooms 01969 622949 ❾

Yorebridge House Bainbridge 11 bedrooms English food ❿
01969 652060 www.yorebridgehouse.co.uk

Black Swan Fearby nr Masham coaching inn 12 bedrooms pub food ⓫
01765 689477 www.blackswan-masham.co.uk

The White Bear Masham coaching inn 14 bedrooms pub food ⓬
01765 689319 www.thewhitebearhotel.co.uk

Kings Head Masham coaching inn 23 bedrooms pub food ⓭
01765 618025 www.chefandbrewer.com

Swinton Park Masham hotel 30 bedrooms English food ⓮
01765 680900 www.swintonpark.com

Simonstone Hall Hawes hotel 18 rooms English food ⓯
01969 667255 www.simonstonehall.com

The Wheatsheaf Carperby coaching inn 13 rooms pub food ⓰
01969 663216 www.wheatsheafinwensleydale.co.uk

YORKSHIRE DALES

Swaledale

The "quiet dale". Swaledale is the most northerly of the Yorkshire Dales, and completely unspoilt. The fast flowing Swale rises in the hills of Nine Standards Rigg, on Yorkshires border with Cumbria, and threads its way down a steep sided valley amidst ancient field patterns, dry stone walls and stone barns, to Richmond where it emerges onto the Vale of York and turns south to join the River Ure near Boroughbridge. The Dale is famous for its sheep, its wild flowers found in many of the fields, and in the 19thC was a major lead mining area. At the head of Arkengarthdale lies the

Tan Hill, renowned for being the highest pub in England at 1750ft and a good refreshment point for those hardy souls tackling the Pennine way which crosses the county boundary nearby. Evidence of lead mining in Arkengarthdale can be seen above Langthwaite, and in Swaledale above Gunnerside where there are a number of smelt mines and associated artefacts, together with interpretive boards recounting the history of lead mining. Reeth is the main settlement in the Dale. At the confluence with Arkengarthdale, it has a range of small gift shops and eating establishments. The Swaledale folk museum contains a record of rural life in the Dale. It is open daily from Easter to October. There is an admission charge. 01748 884118 www.swaledalemuseum.org Further down the Dale is Marrick Priory. This was built as a Benedictine nunnery in the 12thC, and is now an outdoor pursuits centre which adjoins the parish church.

Swaledale Restaurants and Hotels (map page 94)

Keld Lodge Keld hotel 11 bedrooms ❶
01748 886259 www.keldlodge.com

Kearton Country Hotel Thwaite hotel 12 bedrooms ❷
01748 886277 www.keartoncountryhotel.co.uk

The Kings Arms Reeth coaching inn pub food 01748 884259 ❸

The Buck Reeth coaching inn 10 bedrooms pub food ❹
01748 884210 www.buckhotel.co.uk¨

Rowleth End Long Row guest house 5 bedrooms ❺
01748 886327 www.upperswale.co.uk

The Burgoyne Hotel Reeth hotel 8 bedrooms ❻
01748 884292 www.theburgoyne.co.uk

Cambridge House Reeth guest house 5 bedrooms ❼
01748 884633 www.cambridgehousereeth.co.uk

Charles Bathurst Inn Longthwaite coaching inn 19 bedrooms pub food ❽
01748 884567 www.cbinn.co.uk

YORKSHIRE DALES

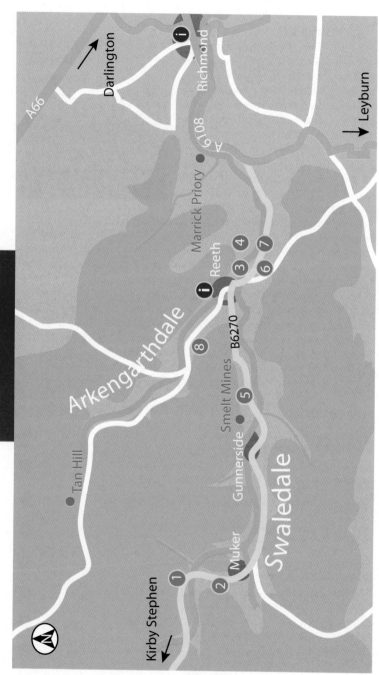

SETTLE

Best known as the starting place of Britain's most iconic railway journey- the Settle - Carlisle line, Settle is a small market town on the edge of the Dales National Park and an ideal touring base. It sits under the shadow of the Yorkshire three peaks and is closely associated with the world of speleology and caving. It is also close to the Area of Outstanding Natural Beauty, the Trough of Bowland. Although well ensconced within Yorkshire, it lies on the River Ribble which flows westwards through Lancashire. Adjoining is Giggleswick, a small village inherently intertwined with the town and best known for its public school - Giggleswick Grammar- founded in 1509 and one of the oldest in the country.

History

There is evidence of the area being a settlement as far back as the 7thC- its name being Anglo-Saxon for settlement. The entry in the Domesday book simply refers to it as waste ground. It was in the mid 13thC that Henry II granted a charter for a market which has run ever since. The early communications were over the moors- east to west- with Victoria Street, High Street and Kirkgate forming the original route. Development of the Keighley to Kendal turnpike in the mid 18thC boosted the towns fortunes as a stopping off place to rest, and it is this route (the A65) that still exists today. Arrival of the railway in 1875 failed to produce the kind of economic boost engendered by the turnpike although cotton mills and tanning became staple industries for the town in the 19thC.

Getting Here

Rail the town lies on the Leeds-Carlisle line, just north of the junction with the line to Morecambe. There are regular services to both Leeds (1 hour) and Carlisle (90 mins). Trains to Morecambe and Lancaster from Skipton and Leeds pass through Giggleswick station 2 miles to the west of the town. The journey to Morecambe takes about an hour; there are 4 trains per day.

Settles busy market place

Road the A65 trunk road between Kendal and Leeds by-passes the town. Leeds is about 1hr drive; Kendal about 45 mins.

Bus all services arrive at and depart from the Market Place.

destination	service(s)	frequency
Skipton	580	hourly
Kirby Lonsdale	581	7x per day
Leeds	580/X84	hourly

Things to see and do

The town is built at the foot of a limestone outcrop, which gives rise to a characteristic stone built collection of buildings with a steep and intricate network of streets and lanes, particular in Upper Settle.   A walk around the town is a rewarding experience; soaking up the ambience of a relatively untouched Dales market town. Much in and around the Market Place is of 18thC or early 19thC vintage. In Victoria Street is the building known as **The Folly** which dates from 1679; so named because its style might be determined extravagantly eclectic. The building currently houses the **Museum of North Craven Life**. In the Market Place is the **Shambles** built as a kind of Market Hall in the 18thC with, strangely, a row of cottages built on top.   The **Town Hall** on the south side of the Market Place is late Georgian with neo Jacobean facades, and is the venue for a number of events through the year. Opposite is the Naked Man Café, a well known landmark in the town, this 1660 building formerly possessed a relief of a fully unclothed male figure on the front façade.   A weekly market takes place in the Market Place on Tuesdays.   On the west side of the River Ribble, the vista to Giggleswick is dominated by the dome of the Chapel to Giggleswick school, a building of 1901, whose dome is consciously based on the Dome of the Rock in Jerusalem.

St Alkelda Church

The main church here is in Giggleswick, St Alkelda, which dates from the mid 15thC, although there has been a church on this site since Norman times, and there are traces of Norman construction in the piers on the south side of the nave. There are only two churches dedicated to St Alkelda; this and one at Middleham According to legend, St Alkelda may have been a Saxon princess. This church was responsible for establishment of the Grammar School, and until the 19thC, when a new church was built in the town itself, Settle folk had to use St Akeldas as the parish church.

Falconry Centre   Crows Nest road

On the A65, three miles north of the town, the Falconry centre provides both a glimpse into the sport of falconry as well as acting as an educational centre and a centre of excellence for assisting with the re-population of falcons across the world. The centre is open daily. There is an admission charge. 01729 822832   www.hawkexperience.co.uk

SETTLE

Settle Carlisle railway line

The notional start of the famous line, regular trains between Leeds and Carlisle stop at Settle. The line is steeped in history and passengers enjoy unrivalled views of some of the finest scenery in Britain. From Settle, the 72 mile route to Carlisle weaves between the Three Peaks, over the 24 arches of the Ribblehead Viaduct, plunges into the longest tunnel on the line at Blea Moor and then into Dentdale, Garsdale and through the rolling hills surrounding the Eden Valley, before arriving at the border city of Carlisle.   Train staff are knowledgeable about the route, the sights and its history and are happy to explain this to passengers.   Constructed in the 1870's it is a triumph of Victorian enterprise and engineering and derived from the intense rivalry between railway companies to establish viable routes into Scotland. The engineering project involved some 6000 navvies, mainly Irish, who lived in camps alongside the line and who built, to express train standards, the 14 tunnels and 22 viaducts along the route.   Regular services from run through the year between Leeds and Carlisle, and there are a number of special steam train trips from Settle during the Summer months

www.settle-carlisle.co.uk

Museum of North Craven Life

The Folly, Victoria Street

The museum tells the story of the life and times of the folk and environment of the North Craven area as well as the chequered history of The Folly itself. The museum is open 5 days a week (closed Mon and Wed) from Easter to October. There is an admission charge.   01729 822361   www.ncbpt.org.uk

SETTLE

Restaurants (see map page 98)

££

English **Craven Arms** Brackenber Lane Giggleswick   01729 825627   **1**
www.craven-arms-giggleswick.co.uk (also provides accommodation)

English **Ravenous** Market Place 01729 822277   **2**

Italian **Gusto** The Shambles 01729 824929   **3**

£££

English **Little House** 17, Duke Street   **4**
01729 823963 www.littlehouserestaurant.co.uk

Hotels (see map below)

★★★

The Falcon Manor Skipton Road 19 Bedrooms **5**
01729 823814 www.thefalconmanor.com

★★★★

The Maypole Inn Long Preston 6 Bedrooms **6**
01729 840219 www.maypole.co.uk

not rated

The Golden Lion Duke Street 12 Bedrooms **7**
01729 822203 www.thelionsettle.co.uk

The Eldon Church Street Long Preston 8 Bedrooms 01729 840246 **8**

Settle Visitor Information Centre
Town Hall Cheapside
01729 825192
www.settle.org.uk

Parking Ⓟ

① Lower Greenfoot 106 spaces ③ Whitefriars Court 60 spaces
② Settle Railway station 40 spaces ④ Ashfield 105 spaces

SKIPTON

"The Gateway to the Dales" - Skipton is a long established lively market town in the upper reaches of the Aire Valley equidistant from the heart of the West Riding and the core of the Yorkshire Dales National Park. Served by road, rail, and canal, it forms an ideal touring base for both areas, as well as having its own bustling atmosphere, with a variety of shopping, markets and other local attractions.

Skipton Parish Church

History

Sheeptown is the Anglo Saxon translation of Skipton, which was settled by sheep farmers as far back as the 7thC. The towns importance derived from its position commanding the Aire Gap, then the main route for crossing the Pennines. The De Romille family, supporters of William the Conqueror, were granted the lands after the Norman conquest, and built both the castle and the church. A charter was granted in 1204 by King John and Skipton continued to consolidate its position as a trading centre for the surrounding countryside. The present High Street was, and remains, the busy hub of the town with its vibrant market and burgage plots still in evidence. Stoutly royalist during the English civil war, the castle was under siege for much of the war. The arrival of the Leeds-Liverpool canal in 1777 helped develop the cotton and wool mills; industries which were enhanced following the arrival of the railway in 1847. Today, the town is a strong commercial centre with its market and comprehensive array of shops and other commercial businesses, as well as being a touring base for much of this part of Yorkshire.

Getting Here

Rail Skipton railway station, dating from 1877 and still largely showing its unaltered Victorian architecture, lies west of the town centre. There is a regular and fast service to Leeds and Bradford, and the station serves the famous Settle Carlisle route with regular services crossing the Ribblehead viaduct. Leeds is 40 mins, Bradford 35 mins, Carlisle 1hr 50 mins and Morecambe 1hr 20 mins. Connections onto the national intercity network are at Leeds and Carlisle.

SKIPTON

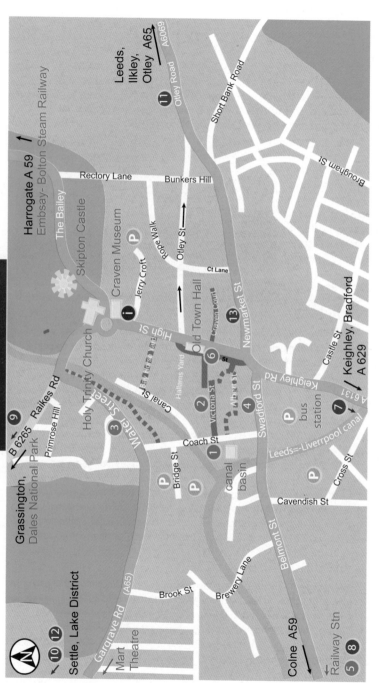

SKIPTON

Road the town lies at the crossroads of the A65 trunk road between Leeds/ Bradford and Kendal (with connections onto the M6 northwards to Glasgow), and the A59 road between Preston and Hull (via Harrogate and York). Leeds is about a 1hr drive; London about 4hrs 30 mins, and Glasgow about 3 hours.

Bus all bus services arrive and depart from the Bus Station, which is on Keighley Road, just south of the High Street.

destination	service(s)	frequency
Leeds	X84	hourly
Bradford	X84	hourly
Keighley	66/67	30 mins
Harrogate	X59	2 hourly
Burnley	215	hourly
Preston	X28/280	hourly
London	561	1x per day

Things to see and do

The core of the town centre revolves around the Market Place/High Street. The lively large outdoor market is four days a week (Mon, Wed, Fri, Sat). This wide, open space, visible when the market is not in session, is dominated at the north end by the war memorial and Church, with the spectre of the Castle looming behind. Evidence of the burgage plots is perhaps best demonstrated by ginnels off the High Street such as Craven Yard, or Bay Horse Yard. In the group of buildings between Sheep Street and the High Street is the Old Town Hall (previously the Tollbooth which dates from 1789). Cobbled Sheep Street and many of the High Street buildings date from the 17thC although 19thC front facades are now prevalent. On the east side is the covered Craven Court Arcade with its interesting mix of independent shops - well worth a diversion from the attractions of the market place. On the west side of the High Street, a number of yards and ginnels- like Bay horse yard or Victoria Street- lead down to the canal and canal basin where there are a range of pubs and restaurants, as well as the location for the hire of canal boats (see page 103). The canal towpath on the canal spur (the Springs Branch) leads up to the main road by the Church. The Springs Branch extends for about ½ mile to the back of the Castle and was formerly used to transport limestone from a nearby quarry.

Skipton Market

SKIPTON

Skipton Castle

Originally a Norman motte and bailey earth construction, with timber buildings, built by the Robert De Romille on land granted by William the Conqueror, the castle was substantially rebuilt in stone in the 12thC, and still ranks as one of the most complete preserved castles in England. It occupies a natural defensive position, with its northern perimeter having a sheer drop down to the beck. The earliest surviving parts are the inner gatehouse and the inner bailey defences, built between 1190 and 1240; much of the visible building is 16thC.

Ownership of the castle was granted to the de Clifford family by Edward II in 1310, and succeeding generations occupied it for over 300 years, and although the last Clifford to occupy was Lady Anne Clifford (d.1676), the family still own it, their flag flying proudly above. It was a fiercely royalist stronghold in the English civil war, and despite Cromwell instructing the removal of the roofs as a consequence, Lady Anne Clifford did much rebuilding and restoration following the civil war to restore the castle. The entrance is via the Outer Gatehouse, which was built between the14th and 16thC. Much of the castle is open daily. There is an admission charge.   01756 792442   www.skiptoncastle.co.uk

Holy Trinity Church

There has been a church on this site since the 12thC, originally established with help from the monks at Bolton Priory and possibly before. The present building dates mainly from the 14th to 16thC, and much can be ascribed to the energy and generosity of Lady Anne Clifford.   There are a number of tombs in the interior in which members of the Clifford family are buried.   The church is open daily.   01756 793622   www.holytrinityskipton.org.uk

Embsay and Bolton Steam Railway

Originally part of the 1885 line between Ilkley and Skipton, and built to take traffic from the north east of England via Knaresborough. It closed in 1965 but re-opened as a heritage line running between Embsay and Bolton Abbey. The line is an attraction in itself but also enables access to Bolton Abbey and the range of short walks which start from the Abbey. Services run on Sundays for much of the year, but   daily during peak holiday periods.
       01756 710614   www.embsayboltonabbeyrailway.org.uk

SKIPTON

Leeds-Liverpool Canal

At 127 miles, this is the longest inland waterway in Britain, and was built between 1773 and 1816 enabling exports of cloth from Yorkshire through Liverpool docks, and equally imports of raw materials in to the county. It remains navigable today, and Skipton is one of the main locations on the canal from which to hire boats, as well as acting as a popular overnight or lunch stop for those travelling by boat or barge on the canal. There are many locks and swing bridges (including the famous five locks rise at nearby Bingley (see page 160), and the plethora of attractive mooring stops on the way, make it a rewarding if not unique experience.   www.waterscape.com

The Canal Basin

SKIPTON

Museum

Located in the Town Hall on High St, the museum contains collections relating to local history archaeology and modern art. It is open Mon Wed Thu Fri Sat between April and September, and afternoons on Mon Wed Thu Fri during the rest of the year. Admission is free.   01756 706407   www.cravenmuseum.org

The Mart Theatre

An unusual venue, located in the local auction mart, the theatre provides a mix of plays, concert and films.   01756 708011   www.themarttheatre.org.uk

Festivals

May	Waterways Festival Canal basin	www.penninecruisers.com
	Beer Festival Town Hall	www.keighleyandcravencamra.org.uk
July	Sheepday	www.sheepday.co.uk
December	Yuletide market	www.skiptononline.co.uk/yuletide

SKIPTON

Restaurants (see map page 100)

££

english **Canalside** Waterside Court, Coach Street   01756 795678   **1**

english **The Narrow Boat** 38 Victoria Street
01756 797922 www.markettowntaverns.co.uk   **2**

tex-mex **Sam Houstons** 36 Water Street 01756 794747   **3**

english **Verdes** 34 Swadford Street 01756 700822   **4**

£££

english **The Rhubarb** Broughton Road
01756 792781 www.herriotsforleisure.co.uk   **5**

french **Le Caveau** 86 High St 01756 794274 www.lecaveau.co.uk   **6**

Hotels (see map page 100)
★★★

The Rendezvous Keighley Road 80 Bedrooms 01756 700100   **7**

Herriots Broughton Rd 7rooms 01756 792781 www.herriotsforleisure.co.uk   **8**

Craven Heifer Grassington Rd 19 Bedrooms 01756 792521
www.cravenheifer.co.uk   **9**

★★★★

The Coniston Coniston Cold 77 bedrooms
01756 748080 www.theconistonhotel.com   **10**

★★★★★(GA)

Chinthurst Guest House Otley Road 10 bedrooms
01756 799264 www.chinthurst.co.uk   **11**

Premier Inn Hellifield Road Gargrave 21 Bedrooms
0871 5278980 www.premierinn.com   **12**

not rated

Boutique 25 25 Newmarket St 5 Bedrooms 01756 793676   **13**

Parking Ⓟ

1 East of High Street	340 spaces	**4** Coach Street	243 spaces
2 Keighley Road	60 spaces	**5** Bridge Street	160 spaces
3 Cavendish Street	180 spaces		

Skipton Visitor Information Centre
 Town Hall
01765 792809
www.cravendc.gov.uk

ILKLEY

"On Ilkla Moor Baht 'at" (*on Ilkley Moor without a hat*) so goes the famous song, often regarded as the Yorkshire Anthem.   Ilkley is a small town in the Wharfe Valley famous for its 19thC spa which, although shortlived, was frequented by amongst others, Charles Darwin. It lies on the A65 12 miles east of Skipton, 15 miles west of Leeds.

History

There was a settlement here in the Bronze Age; demonstrated by artefacts of flint arrowheads as well as carvings on Ilkley Moor. The Romans found Ilkley suitable for a fort, at the crossroads of two roman roads, one from York to Lancaster; the other from Aldborough (see page 385) to Manchester. The fort was called *Oliciana* or *Olenacum*, (people from Ilkley are known as Olicians) and founded in A.D.79 - some exposed walling can be seen at the Manor House - and whose foundations run beneath the nearby parish church.   After Roman occupation, Ilkley became a small village until the mid 19thC when the scientific effects of hydrotherapy, as practiced in nearby Harrogate and in Bath, began to draw large numbers of visitors.   A "hydro" was built at Ben Rhydding, just to the east of the town in 1843, quickly followed by a number of others. The palatial Wells House was built as a hydro in 1855 and still stands (off Wells Road and now converted to flats).   However, spa activities did not last very long here, and the advent of the railway from Leeds in 1865 coupled with some strategic land sales by the main local landowners, the Middleton family, combined to see rapid population growth as a dormitory town for Leeds and Bradford; a role it continues today.

Getting Here

Rail   the town is the terminus of a line which serves both Leeds and Bradford.

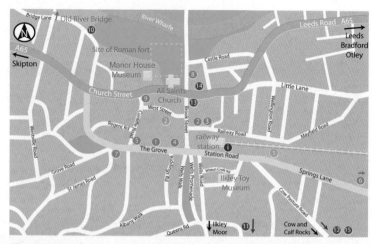

Road Ilkley lies on the A65 trunk road from Leeds to Kendal in Cumbria. Leeds is a 40 min journey; Manchester 90 mins. London is 4 hours.

Bus all bus services arrive at and depart from the bus station which adjoins the railway station.

destination	service(s)	frequency
Otley	962/X52/X84	hourly/2hourly/30 min
Leeds	X84	30 min
Bradford	963	hourly
Skipton	X84	hourly
Keighley	762/765	30 min
Harrogate	X52	2hourly

Things to See and Do

Starting by the bus and railway station, to the west is The Grove, the main shopping street with its parades, on both sides of the road, of chic independent shops and ornate Victorian canopies; to the north lies Brook Street which leads down to the crossroads with the A65, and where, on the north west corner is the parish Church of All Saints with Roman and Anglo- Saxon origins. Behind is the Manor House, a 17thC building where the museum of Ilkley's history can be found. To the north of the Manor House are the tranquil Riverside Gardens edged by the River Wharfe. To the west is the Old Bridge, with its steep narrow path dating from 1676. Retracing steps to the core of the town centre, it is worth taking the somewhat strenuous climb on Wells Walk which leads up to Ilkley Moor and the White Wells. On the way, worthy of note is the Art Noveau style Methodist Assembly Hall style and Wells House which was the largest and most palatial hydro built in the town and designed by Yorkshire architect Cuthbert Brodrick. For the more hardy, a trek onto the moor will yield magnificent views as well as a visit to the White Wells baths, the Tarn and the neolithic circle.

From Wells Road, it is possible to cut across to Cowpasture Road and the Craiglands hotel, also formerly a hydro. Cowpasture Road continues up to the Moor and Cow and Calf Crags and its nearby hotel. The residential area of Victorian villas around the west side of the town, with their leafy streets and luxuriant gardens are worth a stroll. Of particular interest is Heathcote, on Kings Road, designed by the well known Edwardian architect Edward Lutyens.

All Saints Church

In a prominent position by the main cross roads, the parish church is on a site first occupied by a church around 627 A.D, and probably built from the remains of the roman fort. Inside the church are remains of 9thC Saxon crosses which originally would have been outside the church. The church was substantially rebuilt and enlarged in the 19thC to cope with the towns burgeoning population, but the core of the church is medieval. The church is open daily.   www.ilkleypc.co.uk

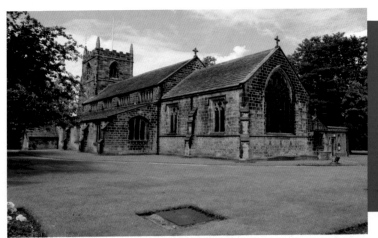

ILKLEY

The Manor House   Castle Yard

The house was the seat of the Lords of the Manor when built in the15thC, on top of the remains of the Roman fort. Probably re-built in the early 17thC, it became a museum in 1892, largely to conserve and protect the evident Roman ruins which by then were being removed from the site. Updated and extended, it remains a museum. The ground floor is devoted to the history of the town, including a substantial number of roman remains whilst the first floor hosts temporary art and cultural exhibitions. The Museum is open Wed to Sat and Tues and Sun afternoons.   Admission is free.   01943 600066   www.bradfordmuseums.org

Ilkley Toy Museum   Whitton Croft Road

A small museum, near the station, dedicated to celebrating the history and diversity of childrens' toys.   It is open weekends. Admission is free.
                     01943 603855   www.ilkleytoymuseum.co.uk

Ilkley Moor

The inspiration for the infamous Yorkshire anthem "On Ilkla Moor Baht 'at" is part of Rombalds Moor, a round topped high plateau between the Wharfe and Aire Valleys. Ilkley moor is the north facing part of this overlooking the town and the Wharfe Valley. Made popular in the 19thC as a stretch of accessible and safe moorland for the towns growing population to roam and take exercise, it also provided stone to build rapidly developing new housing. There are two millstone grit climbing areas: Rocky Valley and Ilkley Quarry. The latter is the site of the famous "Cow and Calf", a large millstone grit rock formation consisting of an outcrop and boulder, (also known as Hangingstone Rocks) and named because of the resemblence to a cow sitting with a calf. According to local legend, the Calf was split from the Cow when the giant Rombald was fleeing an enemy -his angry wife- and stamped on the rock as he leapt across the valley. The wife dropped the stones held in her skirt to form the local rock formation The Skirtful of Stones. There are a large number of neolithic engraved stones on the Moor, including the Swastika Stone, the Badger Stone and St Margaret's Stones. There are also carvings on the Hanging Stones and Panorama Rocks. A small Neolithic stone circle, the Twelve Apostles can be found near the top of the Moor. Lying above Wells Road on the edge of the Moor is White Wells. This is a former bath house, now a café, and dates originally from 1791, although the site had been used for bathing for nearly 100 years prior to that. It was probably the first hydropathic centre in the town. One of the baths is still visible and can be used by visitors. There is an extensive network of well signposted footpaths on the moor and walking over the Moor to Baildon in the Aire Valley and back is a good days hike.

The Cow and Calf rocks

Festivals

October Literature Festival various venues www.ilkleyliteraturefestival.org.uk

ILKLEY

Restaurants (see map page 106)

££

English **Betty's** 32 The Grove 01943 608029 www.bettys.co.uk ①

Vietnamese **Bistro Saigon** Railway Rd 01943 817999 ②

Italian **Emporio Italia** 7 Railway Rd 01943 430005 www.emporio-italia.co.uk ③

Italian **La Sila** 7 The Grove 01943 601908 ④

£££

English **Monkmans** 3-5 Cunliffe Rd ⑤
01943 817485 www.monkmans-ilkley.co.uk

pub food **Wheatley Arms** Wheatley Lane Ben Rhydding ⑥
01943 816496 www.wheatleyarms.co.uk

££££

English **Martha and Vincent's** The Grove ⑦
01943 602444 www.marthaandvincent.com

English **The Farsyde** New Brook St 01943 602030 www.thefarsyde.co.uk ⑧

£££££

English **Box Tree** 35-37 Church St 01943 608484 www.theboxtree.co.uk ⑨

Hotels (see map page 106)

★★

Riverside Bridge Lane 10 Bedrooms 01943 607338 www.ilkley-riversidehotel.com ⑩

★★★(GA)

Rombalds West View 15 Bedrooms 01943 603201 www.rombalds.co.uk ⑪

★★★

Craiglands Cowpasture Rd 60 Bedrooms 01943 430001 www.craiglands.co.uk ⑫

not rated

The Crescent Inn Brook St 11 Bedrooms ⑬
01943 811250 www.thecrescentinn.co.uk

Dalesway 1 Leeds Rd 9 Bedrooms 01943 605438 www.hotelilkley.co.uk ⑭

Cow and Calf Hangingstone Rd 13 Bedrooms ⑮
01943 607335 www.vintageinn.co.uk

Parking ℗

① Railway Station   36 spaces   ② South Hawksworth Street   195 spaces

ILKLEY

Visitor Information Centre
Station Road
01943 602319   www.visitbradford.com/ilkley

109

OTLEY

Otley is a small market town which sits by the river Wharfe below the looming wooded escarpment known as The Chevin. Close to Leeds, this market town is also close to the Yorkshire Dales and the Dales National Park.

History

The first references to Otley go back to the 8thC, when *Otta* (a Saxon personal name) made his *leah* here; leah being an Anglo Saxon term for clearing. The town was an important centre for the Archbishops of York around the 10thC. The Archbishops palace became the Manor House and excavations close to the west side of the river bridge have revealed traces of a chapel. A market charter was granted in the 13thC and a street market continues today. Allied to this, the Archbishops sought to attract merchants and tradespeople to the town by granting burgage plots- mainly on Boroughgate, Kirkgate, and Walkergate, a settlement pattern which is still evident. With the decline of the influence of the church, so the town declined until the industrial revolution witnessed the advent of a broad and prosperous economic base with textiles, paper making, and machinery manufacture. The *Wharfedale print machine* which revolutionised printing techniques in the 19thC was devised and manufactured here. The town provided accommodation and subsistence to both Royalists and Parliamentarians during the course of the English Civil War, and legend has it that the Parliamentarians drank the Black Bull dry prior to the battle of Marston Moor whilst the Royalists stationed their horses just outside the town! The well known 18thC cabinet maker, Thomas Chippendale was born in the town, and the artist JMW Turner was a frequent visitor. Today the town retains a popular market and much of its centre built in the 18th and 19thC remains intact.

Otley visitor Information centre
Nelson Street
01943 466572
www.leeds.gov.uk/otley_library

Otley from the Chevin south of the town

110

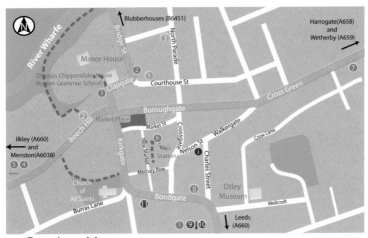

Getting Here

Rail the nearest rail station is Burley in Wharfedale (2 miles west) with feeder services into Leeds city station and access to the intercity rail network.

Road the town lies on the A658 which runs in the Wharfe Valley from Ilkey to Wetherby, and on the A661 to Leeds. London is 4 hrs, Manchester 90 mins.

Bus all buses arrive at and depart from the bus station on Crossgate.

destination	services(s)	frequency
Leeds	33/33A/X84	30 min
Bradford	653	2 hourly
Harrogate	X52/X53	hourly
Ilkley	962/X52	hourly/2 hourly
Skipton	X84	6x per day
Airport	967	30 min

Things to see and do

The centre has been described as 'pleasingly intricate' with its dog legged crossroads, ginnels and cobbled squares. It is reputed to have one of the highest density of pubs of any town in England.   **The Market Place** is the scene of a lively street market on Tue/Fri/Sat, with stalls surrounding the jubilee clock and *Butter Cross* shelter. Fronting Kirkgate is the Old Hall, a building dating back to the late 1600's. To the north is **Manor Square**, dominated by the aptly named former pubs, The Black Horse and the Royal White Horse. On the north side of the square is the old **Grammar School**, a dark stone building of 1840, although the grammar school was founded in 1611. Adjoining is the statue of Thomas Chippendale, the master cabinet maker, whose furniture pieces are hotly sought after today. Further north along Bridgegate is the River Wharfe. The bridge over the river is 17thC. On both sides of the river is a public park. To the south of the Market Place, at the end of Kirkgate, is the parish Church.

OTLEY

Church of All Saints

The site may have been consecrated as early as the 2ndC when Christianity first came to Britain. The church contains remnants of Anglian crosses, the oldest dating from c.750 AD. Such crosses provided focal points for Christian gatherings before church buildings were erected. The foundations of the church are Anglo Saxon, and parts of the chancel and doorway are Norman. It was enlarged in about 1240 by the addition of a wide nave together with the south transept and the tower, and the sumptuous stained glass east window was made in 1851. The church also contains the tomb of Thomas, Lord Fairfax and his wife- the parents of Cromwell's parliamentarian general in the English Civil war.

OTLEY

Otley Museum   Crow Lane

This small museum contains a number of collections relating to the development of the town, including the artefacts excavated from the site of the Archbishops Palace and the story of the development of the Wharfedale printing press. The museum is open Mon Tues and Fri mornings. Admission is free.

01943 468181   www.otleymuseum.org

The Chevin

The Chevin is a steep sided area of woodland and rocky gritstone outcrops dominating the south side of the town, much of it a country park very popular with local residents. There are walking and horse and mountain bike trails, and orienteering courses.   By the Royalty public house on Yorkgate is Surprise View, a dramatic viewing spot over the town and the Wharfe valley.   The former quarries scattered around provided the stone for the Houses of Parliament. The park is open daily.   Admission is free.   www.chevinforest.co.uk

Thomas Chippendale Cabinet Maker *1718-1778*

This well known craftsman was born and educated in Otley He came from a line of local cabinet makers and joiners.   After apprenticeship he moved to London and set up a cabinet making business which quickly flourished and he became hotly sought after in London society for his furniture pieces. He wrote a popular book of his designs   which provided the basis for the styles of furniture common in the late 18th/early 19thC.   His talents extended to interior design for wealthy aristocratic clients and his works are still evident in many great houses across the country including Harewood House.

Festivals

May	Otley Show	Bridge Street	www.otleyshow.org.uk
June	Otley Cycle races	town centre	www.otleycycleraces.co.uk
September	Folk festival	various venues	www.otleyfolkfestival.com
November	Beer festival		www.otleybeerfestival.co.uk
December	Victorian Fayre	town centre	www.victorianfayre.co.uk

Restaurants (see map page 111)

££

Veg   Cheerful Chilli   East Chevin Road   **1**
01943 466567 www.thecheerfulchilli.co.uk

Indian   Jewel of India 1 Bridge Street   **2**
01943 467138   www.thejewelofindia.co.uk

Thai   Nan Jai Thai   13 Manor Square   01943 465734   **3**

Indian   Westbourne Spice   Bradford Road   01943 462464   **4**

£££

Italian   Buon Apps   Wharfedale Business Centre   **5**
01943 468458   www.buonappsotley.co.uk

Greek   The Dales Café   Orchard Gate   01943 850980   www.dalescafe.com   **6**

pub food   The White Hart   Main Street   Pool in Wharfedale   **7**
0113 2037862   www.thewhitehartpool.co.uk

££££

English   Korks   40 Bondgate   01943 462020   www.korks.co.uk   **8**

Hotels (see map page 111)

★★★

Chevin Lodge   Yorkgate 49 bedrooms   **9**
01943 467818 www.chevincountrypark-hotel.co.uk

Britannia Bramhope   Leeds Road Bramhope   137 bedrooms   **10**
0871 2210191 www.britanniahotels.com

not rated

Dowgill House   5-7 Bondgate   4 bedrooms   **11**
01943 850836 www.dowgillhouse.co.uk

OTLEY

Parking   **P**

1 Courthouse Street   56 spaces   **2** Beech Hill   86 spaces
3 North Parade   100 spaces

HARROGATE

Two questions often asked by visitors to this elegant and stylish North Yorkshire town are "*Are we in Yorkshire*? and "*Where's the sea*?" The questions derive from Harrogate's radically different environment, quite unlike anywhere else in the county. Its expansive open spaces and decorative tree lights give the impression that this could be the south coast or leafy Surrey. It lies 17 miles north of Leeds, close to the regional airport and is best known for being probably the foremost British spa, and now an international conference and exhibition destination, as well as bosting a unique record as an internationally renowned floral town. Historic roots have endowed Harrogate with an enviable range of hotels and restaurants, making it an ideal place both to visit for its own qualities and an excellent touring base for the more metropolitan attractions of West Yorkshire, for the city of York, as well as the more peaceful atmosphere of the Dales.

The Stray- part of Harrogate's 200 acres of open space

History

Unlike its near neighbours, Harrogate is a creature of more recent times. Although there is reference to it as early as the 14thC, it is largely as a place name (the name derives from the Anglo- Norse *Here-gatte*, which means the way to the hill of the soldier where *Herre* is Harlow and *Gatte* means the way). It was part of the Royal Forest of Knaresborough, in the custodianship of the Duchy of Lancaster, and did not emerge as a settlement until the latter half of the17thC when its waters were found to have curative properties. The Tewit Well, now clearly marked on the Stray, began attracting increasing numbers of visitors seeking medicinal benefit from its waters. Amongst these was Dr Timothy Bright, a respected Elizabethan medical scholar who, after a visit, christened it the "English Spaw". Harrogate thus became England's first spa resort. Subsequently a town grew up dedicated to servicing the needs of the visitor, most coming to take the curative waters, and the dominant professions were either doctors or innkeepers!!

The number of wells increased - and with it a staggering variety of water quality; some drinkable; some most certainly not, but all were regarded as curative. As the wells expanded, so did commercial activity. By the early 19thC, a number of spa baths and pump rooms were being built, as well as formal gardens. Advent of the railway made the town universally popular as a spa resort with

spa water tap

the local paper publishing a weekly list of the "great and good" who were staying to take a curative rest in its balmy air and medicinally beneficial waters.   From about 1840 through to the end of the Edwardian period much of the town centre visible today was created, and the turn of the 20thC probably saw Harrogate's apotheosis as a spa of European importance with, allegedly, as many as six crowned European heads staying in the town all at the same time.   Around 1900, a number of key buildings to support the towns booming spa business were built including the Majestic Hotel, the Grand Opera House (now Harrogate Theatre), the Royal Baths, and the Royal Hall. All survive today, largely unchanged.   In the post war period, advent of the NHS heralded demise of the spa, and the town adjusted by utilising the hotels and public buildings for the promotion and staging of conferences; an industry which has seen the town become one of the main destinations in the UK conference and exhibition business, and led to the development of the conference centre complex on KIngs Road, with the Royal Hall at one end and the conference centre at the other, interlinked with exhibition halls.   Today, the town is very much a stylish cosmopolitan centre with specialist shopping, a wide choice of accommodation and dining, and an internationally renowned centre of floral excellence.

Getting Here

The towns train station and bus station adjoin on Station Parade, and all bus services arrive at and depart from the bus station.

Rail rail links to London (1 per day) plus regular local services to both Leeds (30 mins) and York (40 mins) connect with intercity services. London is a 3 hr journey; Manchester 1 hr 30 min.

Road Harrogate lies on the A61 Chesterfield – Thirsk road and the A59 Preston to Hull road. It is 15 mins from the A1;   London is 4 hrs; Manchester 1hr.

Bus all services arrive and depart from the bus station adjoining the station.

destination	service(s)	frequency
Leeds	36	15 min
Ripon	36	15 min
Knareborough	1A/1B	30 min
Pateley Bridge	24	2 hourly
Skipton	X59	2 hourly
Airport	767	90 min
Newcastle	381	1x per day
London	561	1x per day

HARROGATE

Things to see and do

● ● ● ● ● ● **Walk 1**

A stroll around the centre of the town and the Valley Gardens, and for those wishing to venture a little further, out towards Harlow Carr Gardens, can capture the essence of this cosmopolitan elegant spa town. In most of the town centre, the balmy air and atmosphere of gentility is enhanced with the presence of many eye catching floral displays and fastidiously maintained green open spaces. Start at the Station, and walk past the 1887 memorial to Queen Victoria, along James Street with its Italianate 1860's façade on the north side of the street and its up market shops, and come into Prospect Square with the war memorial. Opposite, adjacent to the Pierhead, is the renowned Betty's Tea Rooms where, even with queuing- which is the norm here- the experience is one that should be sampled. The northern edge of the town's famous Stray is here, an expanse of open space amounting to over 200 acres, protected by Act of Parliament, and wrapping around the south and west of the town centre it is well used for recreation by visitors and residents alike. Montpellier Hill is the specialist shopping area of the town with a host of independent shops, including antiques and confectionery nd stylish boutiques. At the bottom is the Crown Hotel. The original building of 1740 is one of the earliest hotels in town with many well known names having stayed over the years, from Byron to the Beatles. Adjoining is the Pump Room Museum with a tap from its sulphur well on the north side; allegedly having the strongest water in Europe- but not to drink!! Immediately across the road is the entrance to the Valley Gardens. Walk through the gardens, with the Sun Pavilion on the north side and, in the centre, the Magnesia Well café. Further up, the footpath enters the Pine Woods, where having crossed Harlow Moor Road, the path through the woods emerges by Harlow Carr Gardens. Retracing steps back through the woods and the gardens, back in the town centre on Swan Road is the Mercer Gallery and beyond that can be seen the Old Swan hotel, dating from c.1700. Its fame derives from the curious story of the novelist Agatha Christie who, having gone missing, turned up as a resident of the hotel. An internationally popular annual crime writing festival has developed on the back of this association attracting visitors from all over the world.

Harlow Carr Gardens

On Crescent Road is the well known **Royal Baths**. Now a series of bars and restaurants, the 1897 Baths provided visitors during the spa heyday with the ultimate in spa experience. The central part is now a Chinese restaurant but until the late 1970's was a tea room complete with resident pianist. Within the Baths complex (entrance on Parliament St), are the **Turkish Baths** and Wetherspoons pub a coversion of the former Lounge Hall, and whose entry is down imposing curved stairs known as the Merry Wives of Windsor stairs. Across the road, is the conference and exhibition centre with the **Royal Hall** prominent on the frontage opposite the George Hotel, one of the towns earlier coaching inns built in 1778.

Turkish Baths

Sitting prominently behind and above the Royal Hall is the Majestic Hotel. Dating from the turn of the last century, it reflects the fine grandeur of the Edwardian era with the gents wc's in the basement being well worth a visit !!. Further along Kings Road is the modern conference centre, one of the largest centres in Europe whose 2000 seat auditorium occasionally hosts public concerts and shows.

Walk 2

The second walk takes in the **Stray** and High Harrogate. Starting from Betty's, walk across the Stray with the Victorian facades of West Park on the left and, crossing York Place at the Prince of Wales roundabout, follow the cherry tree lined footpath to the **Tewit Well**. Although the open domed rotunda is of a later date (c.1840), the well was amongst the early discoveries in the late 17thC, and was the first of the chalybeate wells (chalybeate refers to water rich in iron). Further east the stray often hosts a circus and a bonfire night. The Cedar Court hotel on the left originally the Queens hotel and the town's first inn, opened in 1687 (although rebuilt in the 19thC). Forming a small island in the green expanse is the 19thC **Christ Church**, replacing an earlier chapel of 1749 and built to allow increasing numbers of visitors a means of worship. On the Wetherby Road is **St Johns Well**, the first well of 1631, with a small octagonal shaped pump room. Turning north the Stray narrows until, at the junction with East Parade in what was the centre of High Harrogate it disappears altogether and a return to the town centre is along East Parade.

The Tewit Well

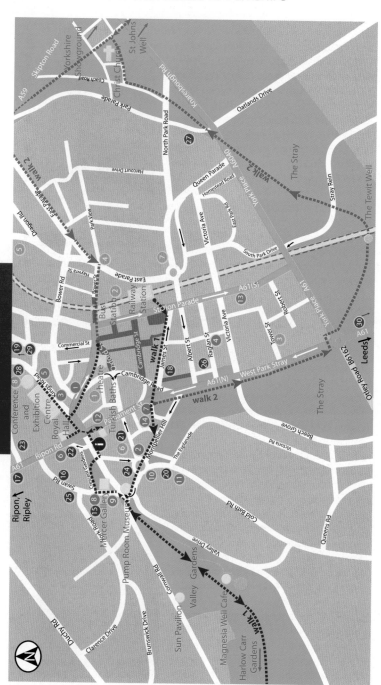

HARROGATE

Harlow Carr Gardens   Cragg Lane

This is an extensive garden, managed by the Royal Horticultural Society, and the society's northern showpiece garden (the southern one being at Wisley in Surrey). Built in the grounds of a small 19thC spa (the adjoining pub was originally the hotel and the bathhouse is now the RHS Study centre), the 70 acres of gardens offers a wide variety of species and ever changing displays, including roses, alpines, bonsai's and ferns. There is even a Betty's tea room here !!   01423 565418   www.rhs.org.uk

Valley Gardens

The Valley Gardens and Pinewoods reach down like a giant green finger into the town centre, covering 17 acres with a variety of displays of shrubs and flowers including alpines, rhododendrons, and dahlias. Part of the Valley Gardens is known as Bogs field where many mineral springs come to the surface – some 36 of Harrogate's 88 mineral wells are found here, with no two being alike.   Developed in the Victorian era as a romantic glen, the first pump room for the Magnesia Well (now a café) was built in 1895. The Sun Pavilion and Colonnades were added in the inter war period. Later, a wide variety of botanical specimens were planted including the New Zealand Garden - a gift of the people of Christchurch in New Zealand.   In the woods at the western end of the Gardens is Harlow Hill tower. Built in 1829, it has a camera obscura at the top, and it is said that, looking due east from here, the next highest ground is in the Russian Urals!! The tower is not normally open although it can be viewed by prior arrangement (www.harlowhilltower.org.uk).   The gardens are a public park and open throughout the year; there is no admission charge.

Royal Pump Room Museum Crown Place

The pump room of 1845 is now a museum that focuses on the development of Harrogate as a spa town. It contains many artefacts and displays particularly from the Victorian era. The museum is open daily. There is an admission charge.

01423 556188   www.harrogate.gov.uk

Mercer Gallery   Swan Road

Utilising the former 1874 assembly rooms, the Mercer Art Gallery houses a fine art collection with over 2000 pieces mainly from 19th/20thC. The whole collection is not on permanent display but paintings, prints and drawings from it are featured in a diverse annual exhibition programme. The gallery is open Tue to Sun through   the year. 01423 556188   www.harrogate.gov.uk

Entrance to the Pump Room Museum

HARROGATE

HARROGATE

Turkish Baths   Parliament Street

Built as an integral part of the Royal Baths in 1897, the facility has remained open ever since. When opened by the Duke of Cambridge, it was said to be the most advanced facility for hydrotherapy in the world.   The Baths, one of very few 19thC Turkish Baths still operating in the UK, were faithfully restored in 2003, and this steamy warren of richly decorated Moorish décor provides the visitor with a wide range of treatment, for both men and women. The baths are open through the year. Admission charges depend on the treatment specified.

01423 556746   www.harrogate.gov.uk

Royal Hall   Ripon Road

The sole surviving British Kursaal, the Royal Hall was built in 1903 to enhance the town's high profile reputation as a leading European spa, its functions being to provide a wide variety of daytime and nighttime entertainment for those visiting the town to take the waters.   Largely unaltered from its 1903 inception, the Hall was fully restored in 2008 and is open to view on days when there is no event on.   Although designed by an unknown architect called Robert Beale, the lavish opulent interior was the work of illustrious Victorian theatre architect Frank Matcham whose influence on the project grew over the period of the construction until it was he who dictated the appearance and

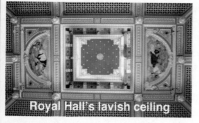

Royal Hall's lavish ceiling

facilities, rather than the sponsors, the local Council. Over the years many famous artists have played here, from Dame Nellie Melba to the Beatles and the Hall provided the towns first conference facility. It hosts a varied programme of entertainment and community events.

01423 500500   www.harrogateinternationalcentre.co.uk

Samson Fox   Inventor   1838-1903

Born into poverty in Bradford, Samson Fox was a self made man. He started up an engineering business in Leeds and was the inventor of a steam boiler which greatly enhanced the speed of ocean going ships, of the pressed steel railway bogie and other engineering items we take for granted today. He came to the town in the 1870's, and greatly influenced its development and prosperity.   He was Mayor three times.   He built and paid for an advanced form of street lighting in the town, quietly funded the construction of social housing, and was a leading figure in promoting the enhancement of the spa, by championing the Royal Hall project. Perhaps he is best known for his sponsorship of the arts, for he was the sponsor for the construction of the Royal College of Music in London- his statue is in the entrance hall there. His great grandson is the well known stage and screen actor, Edward Fox.

Harrogate Theatre   Oxford Street

Originally the Grand Opera House, it opened in 1900 with a charity gala in aid of British troops fighting in the Boer War. The theatre which, like the Royal Hall, is sumptuously decorated, has sustained a role as a theatre for most of its life. Today, it puts on a varied programme throughout the year, including comedy nights and a pantomime.   01423 502116 www.harrogatetheatre.co.uk

Yorkshire Showground (*Yorkshire Show*)   Wetherby Road

One of the UK's largest showgrounds, it is home to a large number of public events, but is mainly known for the country's largest agricultural show held each July and attracting over 100,000 visitors across the three days. It showcases the best of Yorkshire's thriving agricultural industry as well as fiercely competitive showjumping and a variety of other exhibitions and attractions. The event provides a full day out for all the family with a range of attractions for children.   Adjoining the Showground is a "green" business called *Fodder* which sells local organically produced food in a fully green self sustaining building and which also contains a cafe.
                     01423 544544   www.eventscentre.co.uk

Ripley

Lying 3 miles north of the town, Ripley is a model village, the centre of a large estate owned by the Ingilby family for nearly 700 years.   The village itself was demolished in the early 19thC by Sir William Amcotts Ingilby who, after a visit to France, had it rebuilt along the lines of a village he had seen in Alsace, including a Hotel de Ville. Ripley Castle, the gatehouse of which dates from the 15thC, is open for tours by prior arrangement.   Ripley is served by the 36 bus route.

HARROGATE

the idyllic srroundings of **Ripley Castle**

HARROGATE

Festivals

April and September Flower Show Yorkshire Showground
www.flowershow.org.uk

July Crimewriting festival Old Swan Hotel and other venues
www.harrogate-festival.org.uk/crime

Harrogate International Festival variety of venues
www.harrogate-festival.org.uk/crime

Yorkshire Show showground www.greatyorkshireshow.co.uk

Restaurants (see map page 118)

££

Indian Jinnah Spice 34 Cheltenham Parade
01423 563333 www.jinnah-restaurants.com **1**

£££

Fish Drum and Monkey 5 Montpellier Gardens
01423 502650 www.drumandmonkey.com **2**

English B.E.D. 24 Kings Rd 01423 568600 www.bedltd.uk **3**

English The Tannin Level 5 Raglan St 01423 560595 www.tanninlevel.co.uk **4**

Italian Brios 40 Kings Rd 01423 553953 www.brios.co.uk **5**

Italian Joe Rigatoni's 3 Ripon Rd 01423 500071 www.joerigatoni.com **6**

English Betty's Tea Rooms 1 Parliament St 01423 814070 www.bettys.co.uk **7**

Oriental Orchid 28 Swan Rd 01423 560425 www.orchidrestaurant.co.uk **8**

French Mirabelle 28a Swan Road 01423 565551 www.mirabellerestaurant.co.uk **9**

English Quantro's 3 Royal Parade 01423 503034 www.quantro.co.uk **10**

££££

English William and Victoria 6, Cold Bath Rd **11**
01423 521510 www.williamandvictoria.com

English Restaurant Bar and Grill 46-48 Parliament St **12**
01423 705777 www.therestaurantbarandgrill.co.uk/harrogate

French Chez la Vie 92-94 station Parade 01423 568018 www.chelavie.com **13**

£££££

English Van Zellers Montpellier St 01423 508762 www.vanzellerrestaurants.co.uk **14**

Hotels (see map page 118)

★★★

Studley 28 Swan Rd 36 bedrooms 01423 560425 www.studleyhotel.co.uk **15**

Grants Swan Rd 41 bedrooms 01423 560666 www.grantshotel-harrogate.co.uk **16**

Cairn Ripon Rd 135 bedrooms 01423 504005 www.strathmorehotels.com **17**

Yorkshire Prospect Place 80 bedrooms 0844 8559141 www.akkeronhotels.com **18**

Balmoral 16-18 Franklin Mount 23 bedrooms **19**
01423 508208 www.balmoralhotel.co.uk

White Hart 2 Cold Bath Rd 53 bedrooms 01423 505681 www.whitehart.net **20**

Travelodge The Ginnel 48 bedrooms 0871 9846238 www.travelodge.co.uk **21**

St George Ripon Rd 90 bedrooms 01423 561431 www.shearings.com **22**

★★★★

Majestic Ripon Rd 60 bedrooms 01423 700300 www.barcelohotels.co.uk **23**

Crown Crown Place 116 bedrooms 01423 567755 www.crownhotelharrogate.com **24**

Old Swan Swan Road 136 bedrooms 01423 500055 www.classiclodges.co.uk **25**

Du Vin 1 Prospect Place 48 bedrooms 01423 856800 www.hotelduvin.com **26**

Cedar Court ParkParade 100 rooms 01423 858585 www.cedarcourthotels.co.uk **27**

Holiday Inn Kings Rd 214 bedrooms 0844 4431761 www.holidayinn.com **28**

Kimberley 11-19 Kings Rd 93 bedrooms 01423 505613 www.thekimberley.co.uk **29**

Rudding Park Follifoot 90 bedrooms 01423 871350 www.ruddingpark.co.uk **30**

HARROGATE

Parking

1 Jubilee	440 spaces	**5** Dragon Road	187 spaces
2 Victoria	786 spaces	**6** Montpellier Square	65 spaces
3 Tower Street	331 spaces	**7** Odeon	88 spaces
4 Park View	78 spaces	**8** Conference centre	210 spaces

**Harrogate Visitor Information Centre
Crescent Road
01423 537300 www.harrogate.gov.uk**

The Magnesia Well Cafe in Valley Gardens

KNARESBOROUGH

As the River Nidd wends its way towards the Ouse, it carves a channel through a deep gorge where Knaresborough occupies a spectacular setting, with views dominated by the castle and the railway viaduct, and a jumble of houses perched precariously on the steep slopes of the gorge.   It is a market town dating from the Norman period, and lies close to Harrogate, and the A1 Great North Road. In the 19thC and first part of the 20thC it was Yorkshire's main inland resort, attracting visitors from both the industrial West Riding and Teesside.

History

The Domesday book refers to the town as *Chenaresburg* (the name means Cenheards fortification), but the first evidence of real settlement is the castle, of c.1130, with St Johns church (see page 127) established not long after.   The town grew as a market centre – records show a market place by the castle gates as early as 1206- and was later granted a charter by King Edward II. King John in 1210 chose Knaresborough as the location for the very first issue of Maundy money.   Earlier, the castle acquired infamy when the knights responsible for assassinating Thomas a Becket (on Henry II's instructions) and led by the constable of Knaresborough, Sir Hugh de Morville, took refuge in the castle following Becket's murder in 1170. The town was affected by the English Civil war when, after the nearby battle of Marston Moor, the castle was besieged by parliamentary forces and eventually fell. Much of it was destroyed on parliamentary orders after the civil war, and the towns citizens looted the stone. A considerable number of older local houses are built of "castle stone". The town developed a prosperous linen manufacturing industry in the late 17thC which would last for 200 years, and led to the construction of mills by the river on Waterside. Advent of the railways in 1848 sparked Knaresborough's tourism

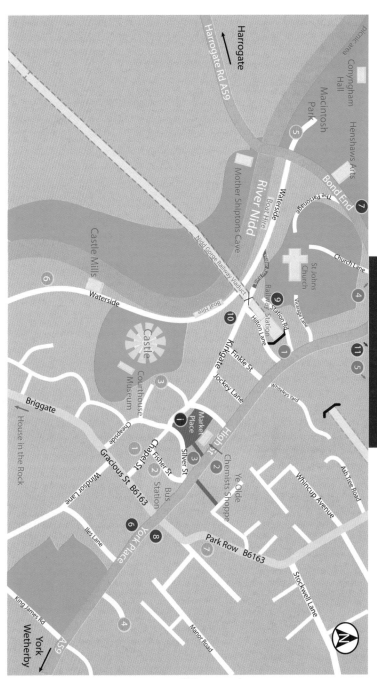

industry attracting visitors from the West Riding and Teesside, and created a number of attractions, including a zoo which finally closed in the 1980s. Knaresborough is also home to the 17thC seer Mother Shipton, whose cave is still a popular tourist attraction, and to the well known 18thC road builder Blind Jack.

Getting Here

Rail the station lies just off the High St, nestling between the gorge and a tunnel. Services are to Harrogate and Leeds (half hourly) and York (hourly). London is c.3 hours away via York, and Manchester c.2 hours via Leeds.

Road the town is served by the A59 Preston to Hull road, and is 5 mins west of the A1. York is c. 45 mins, Leeds c.45 mins and London c.4hrs.

Bus all buses arrive and depart from the bus station in the High Street.

destination	service(s)	frequency
Harrogate	1A/1B	30 mins
Ripon	56/56A	2 hourly
Wetherby	780	hourly
Leeds	561	1x per day
London	561	1x per day

Things to see and do

The setting above a steep gorge can make getting around a strenuous exercise, but a stroll around is rewarding in showing the varying character of this historic settlement. In the early 13thC market place, the group of buildings on the south side originally adjoined the castle gates. The market cross signals the existence of the market held here every Wednesday. On the north side, is "Ye Oldest Chemist Shoppe" reputedly the oldest in England. The shop dates from 1720, although the building is over 100 years older. The shop was famous for it's old drawers and shelves which held lotions, crystals and powders, as well as preparations for animals like *Colic Drink for Horses*. A dog-spit mortar stood in the corner next to the *'bleeding couch'* where leeches were used to draw infection from open wounds. The chemist or apothecary traditionally acted as a dentist, pulling teeth from sufferers sitting on the couch- a practice which only faded out in the post war period. Walk down Kirkgate towards the church, going under the railway by the station, and thence into the expansive treelined church yard and the Norman church of St John (see below). Retrace steps back to the railway, and continue down towards the river via the steeply cobbled Water Bag Bank and the 16thC thatched roof cottage. At the riverside, walking towards

ye old chemists shoppe

the High Bridge, there is a jetty where boats can be hired for a gentle row on the river. On the other side is the famous Mother Shiptons Dropping Well.

On the far side of High Bridge is Macintosh Park named after the Macintosh family, sweet manufacturers from Halifax, who lived in Conyngham Hall, the main house to the park. This 18thC building is now a business centre, but the park is open all year and provides access to the riverside for picnicking, and offers tennis courts and a mini golf course. On the site of the former zoo is Henshaws, a school for the blind, which has established an impressive arts and crafts centre here. Returning along Waterside affords a dramatic view of the viaduct and castle with the variety of different buildings seemingly clinging on precariously to the steep slope. Further down, beyond the viaduct is Castle Mills. Now private residences the mill, of 1791, originally manufactured cotton, but quickly converted to flax spinning and then linen manufacture. The mill owners, Walton&Co, were appointed linen manufacturers to the Royal Household. Waterside leads to the Low Bridge and beyond, Abbey Road. Here, high up on the cliff face is the 18thC House in the Rock and the nearby Chapel of Our Lady of the Crag. This is a cave converted into a small chapel and used as a small shrine, hewn out of the rock in the early 15thC. A carving of a knights templar adjoins the entrance; said to guard the chapel. Return up the steep hill, Briggate, and turn into Cheapside and thence to the Castle and finish at the Courthouse Museum.

St Johns Church

This spacious church is set in an expansive tree-lined churchyard. Parts of the tower and chancel are 13thC. The interior contains effigies of the Slingsby family, owners of extensive tracts of Yorkshire and the Lords of the Manor of the nearby village of Scriven from the 14th to 19thC. Several members of the family served as MPs for the town in the 16th and 17thCs. The church is open daily.

Knaresborough Castle

The castle, as might be expected, occupies the highest part of the bluff overlooking the Nidd Gorge. It was begun in 1130 and completed c.1300. Substantially demolished after the civil war as a penalty for supporting the Royalists, the remains are now confined to a small section of walls, the east gateway, Kings tower, and the courthouse, all set in landscaped park grounds. There are two sallyports still in existence, and there is a guided tour of one of these as it cuts through the bedrock under the castle itself. Castle and grounds are open daily.

01423 556188   www.harrogate.gov.uk

Courthouse Museum

Lying within the Castle grounds, this small museum is the former courthouse; the ground floor is 14thC, the upper 17thC. The museum focuses on the life and times of the castle. It is open daily from April to the end of September. There is an admission charge.   01423 556188 www.harrogate.gov.uk

Mother Shiptons Cave

This well known attraction has been a magnet for tourists for nearly 400 years.   It is the home of Mother Shipton, born Ursula Southeil, a16thC prophetess who allegedly predicted the 1666 Great Fire of London. The park consists of the cave in which she was born, the petrifying well and dropping well, together with picnic areas and woodland walks.   Open February to October. There is an admission charge. 01423 864600   www.mothershiptonscave.com

Henshaws Arts and Craft Centre   Bond End

The centre is adjoins Macintosh Park and is built on the site of the old zoo. It exhibits and sells arts and craft products made by pupils at Henshaws school for the blind, as well putting on a variety of entertainment and other local events. Open Mon to Sat. Admission is free.   01423 541888   www.henshaws.org.uk

KNARESBOROUGH

The Nidd Gorge Walk

The natural beauty of the Nidd Gorge can be intimately experienced from this 4 mile walk which starts in Lands Lane, off the Ripley Road, and descends to the floor of the gorge to follow the river as far as Bilton in north west Harrogate.

A good days walk is to start off from the town, and go as far the Gardeners Arms in Bilton, take a much deserved drink and a bite to eat before returning. The densely wooded gorge is home to much wildlife and provides a peaceful tranquil place in which to explore the natural environment.

Festivals

June	The Bed Race a race through the town using home constructed beds on wheels, pushed by a team of five or six	
	www.knaresborough.co.uk/bedrace	
August	FEVA (Festival of Entertainment and Arts)	various venues www.feva.info
December	Edwardian market Market Square and surrounding streets	
	www.knaresboroughchristmasmarket.co.uk	

Restaurants (see map page 125)

££

Spanish   Carriages   89 High St   01423 867041   **1**

Indian   Zolsha's   38 High St   01423 866555   www.zolsha.com   **2**

Tex-Mex   So Bar   1 Silver St   01423 863202   www.sobarandeats.co.uk   **3**

£££

English   Restaurant 48   Bond End   01423 863302   **4**

English   General Tarleton   Ferrensby   01423 340284   www.generaltarleton.co.uk   **5**

Hotels (see map page 125)

★★★(GA)

Ebor Mount   18 York Place 8 Bedrooms 01423 863315 www.ebormount.co.uk   **6**

★★★

Dower House   Bond End   31 Bedrooms   **7**
01423 863302 www.dowerhouse-hotel.co.uk

★★★★(GA)

Newton House   5-7 York Place 11 Bedrooms   **8**
01423 863539 www.newtonhouseyorkshire.com

★★★★★(GA)

The Mitre   4 Station Road   01423 868948   www.themitreinn.co.uk   **9**

Gallon House   Kirkgate   3 Bedrooms   01423 862102   www.gallon-house.co.uk   **10**

General Tarleton   Ferrensby   14 Bedrooms   **11**
01423 340284 www.generaltarleton.co.uk

KNARESBOROUGH

Parking 🅿

1 Chapel Street	60 spaces	**5** Conyngham Hall	483 spaces
2 Fisher Street	51 spaces	**6** Waterside	96 spaces
3 Castle Yard	80 spaces	**7** Park Row	28 spaces
4 York Place	370 spaces		

Knaresborough Visitor Information Centre
Castle Courtyard
01423 866886
www.harrogate.gov.uk

RIPON

'Except ye Lord Keep ye Cittie ye Wakeman waketh in vain'. So says the inscription on the front façade of Ripon Town Hall. The saying reflects the presence of a wakeman who was responsible for keeping the curfew and law and order in this small city for several hundred years until the early 17thC. England's third smallest city (only Ely in Cambridgeshire and Wells in Somerset are smaller), Ripon sits astride the River Ure on the fringes of the Yorkshire Dales 4 miles west of the A1 and close to the World Heritage site of Fountains Abbey (see page 390). It also boasts one of the oldest of the 39 English cathedrals, the crypt dates from the late 7thC; only Ely Cathedral can claim similar provenance.

History

Although the Celtic tribe -the Brigantes- and the Romans would have been in the area, and there was a Celtic name for the area in which the city is built- *Iphryum*- the earliest evidence of a settlement at Ripon is the 7thC when St Wilfrid, later to become Bishop of York, built a monastery on the site of the present cathedral. King Alfred the Great made the city a royal borough in the 10thC. The first settlement would have been around the cathedral and in the area of High St Agnesgate and St Marygate, although the modern day city centre was established in the 12thC with a fair in what is now the Market Place, and a weekly market has taken place here ever since. After overcoming persistent raids by the Scots in the 12thC - from which time the role of the Wakeman assumed long standing importance - the city developed a booming wool trade, attracting overseas - particularly Florentine- merchants, much aided by effective sheep farming practices of the Cistercian monks of nearby Fountains Abbey. The city continued to prosper as it widened its industry to other cloths and was, during the 14thC, one of the most important producers of cloth in Yorkshire.

Kirkgate

The city was a rebel stronghold in the northern rebellion of 1569 – where the nobles unsuccessfully attempted to depose Queen Elizabeth I - and 300 rebels were hanged at Gallows Hill (now a residential area to the south of the city centre). There was also an attempt to make Ripon a university city at this time, to equal Oxford and Cambridge, but despite the efforts of the Queens chief advisor, Lord Burghley, she vetoed the proposal, possibly in reprisal for Ripon's part in the uprising.   The rise of West Riding towns such as Leeds and Halifax led to demise of the city's cloth industry in the 16thC and the following two hundred years saw it become renowned for the manufacture of spurs - an essential part of horse riding equipment - and during the 17thC, an item of high fashion. The proverb *"as true as Ripon Rowells"* is a testimony to the quality of manufacture, and the city regularly supplied spurs to the monarch of the day.   It's MP in the late 17thC, John Aislabie, was responsible for developing the gardens at Studley Royal, but perhaps better known as the unfortunate Chancellor of the Exchequer who supported the South Sea company and the resultant south sea bubble affair, being incarcerated in the Tower of London as a consequence.   In the late 18thC, Ripon's communications improved with the construction of the canal, intended to connect with the River Ouse to transport goods through York and Hull- coal inward to Ripon; lead and agricultural produce out to Hull. Only a limited commercial success, the canal closed in 1906, but has now been restored and links to the UK canal network.   City status was granted in 1836 and the railway opened in 1848, finally closing in 1969. During World War I the city became a training camp for the army, an association it has since retained.

RIPON

Getting Here

Rail   the nearest stations are at Harrogate, (connections by bus service 36) or Thirsk (connection by bus service 70).

Road Ripon lies at the northern end of the A61 linking Chesterfield through Sheffield Leeds and Harrogate to Thirsk, and about 4 miles west of the A1. Leeds is c.1hrs drive; Newcastle c.1hr 30 mins and London is c.4 hours drive.

Bus services arrive and depart from the bus station east of the market place.

destination	service(s)	frequency
Harrogate	36	15 min
Thirsk	70	2 hourly
Knaresborough	56	2 hourly
Richmond	36	15 min
Leeds	159	hourly
London	561	2x per day

Things to see and do

Any tour of the city should start in the medieval Market place. Not quite square, the market place has been the centre of the city for nearly 700 years.   The buildings fronting it are however nearly all 18th or 19thC, but the really notable features are the **obelisk** and the **town hall**.   The obelisk was probably the first monumental obelisk built in England and promoted by John Aislabie. Its design, by Nicholas Hawksmoor, was based on the main obelisk in the Vatican. Hawksmoor, a pupil of Sir Christopher Wren, was a well known architect of the baroque era responsible for, inter alia, the West towers of Westminster Abbey. It is 90 ft high and at its peak are two emblems; a Ripon horn, and a star. It was originally built in 1702, although substantially rebuilt and altered 80 years later. At its foot, every Thursday morning, the Bellman rings his bell to mark the opening of the market; a practice which has endured since the 13thC. The town hall on the south side dates from 1799, originally built as assembly rooms for formal community functions, with a couple of rooms set aside for civic purposes. Its inscription on the frieze *'Except ye Lord Keep ye Cittie ye Wakeman waketh in vain'* was added in 1886 to commemorate the wakeman function. On the first floor the main assembly room, used as a council chamber, has a musicians gallery. Also on the south side of the market place is the Wakemans House. This well known

local building, restored in the 1990's, is the parlour wing of a now demolished 16thC hall which lay behind it. The original hall was the home of Hugh Ripley, the city's last wakeman and first Mayor. There is a large Thursday market, probably one of the busiest in the region, for the city fills up with shoppers and visitors very early and obtaining a car park place can often prove difficult.

The Wakeman - policeman extraordinaire

The city administered its own justice system and policed its own streets for over a thousand years; the practice only finishing in the late 19thC. A key feature in this was the Wakeman. He was responsible to the Archbishop for the town's safety and security. The Wakeman could exact fines and was required to make compensation in the event of burglary during the hours of his watch. By the end of the 16thC, these arrangements had become ineffective and major changes were introduced, which saw the demise of the wakeman and his responsibilities assumed by the Lord Mayor, as well as levying taxes on residents to pay for security, and later to fund the employment of constables and a Hornblower. Even today, every night at 9pm, the Ripon Hornblower still 'sets the night watch' at the four corners of the obelisk in the Market Square. The last Wakeman, and first Mayor, was Hugh Ripley whose house, known as the Wakemans House, stands on the SW corner of the square.

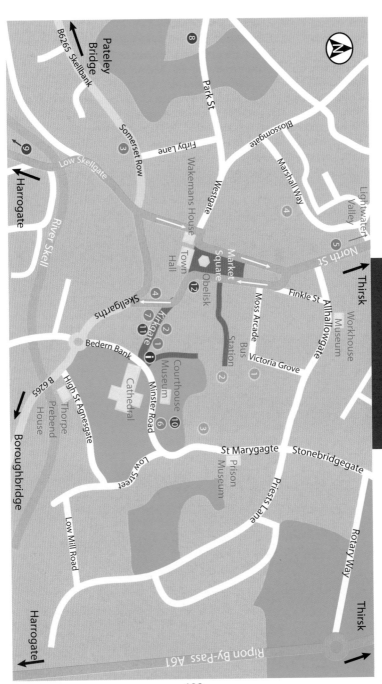

RIPON

The Cathedral lies to the east of the market place and is reached through Kirkgate, a cobbled medieval street whose end is dominated by its great west towers. To the east of the cathedral is the original settlement of Ripon, although nothing now remains of it. The steps down from the cathedral precinct on the south side connect with High St Agnesgate, where there are ecclesiastical and other associated buildings dating from the 14th to 18thC. The most notable is Thorpe Prebend house. Other buildings include the remains of St Annes hospital the Old Hall, and the 17th C St Agnes house. To the north of the cathedral, Minster Road is dotted with former ecclesiastic buildings. The Old Courthouse, behind a high garden wall, was probably an outlying remnant of the Archbishops palace.

St Wilfrid - Religious Reformer (633-709)

Born a Northumbrian noble, Wilfrid studied religion at Lindisfarne and at Rome.   He was made Abbot of the nascent monastery in Ripon about 660, and was influential in persuading the church to adopt the Roman version of Christianity at the Synod of Whitby.   Internal wrangles in the Kingdom of Northumbria caused Wilfrid's banishment on a number of occasions, but during his life he was made Bishop of York. He was instrumental in developing monastic life and influence in Northumbria and elsewhere, building more abbeys, and monasteries- notably those at Hexham and at Selsey in Sussex. He spent his final years in Ripon and is buried under the Cathedral. For many years after his death, Ripon became a place of pilgrimage.   His great claims to fame are his success in imposing the Rome version of Christianity at the Synod of Whitby, and his legacy of a number of monastic institutions- Ripon for example would be unlikely to have the religious importance it had and has without him.

Studley Water Garden

RIPON

In the 18th and 19thC it served as a jail. The courthouse to the east, now a museum is mid 19thC. The Old Deanery, now a hotel and restaurant, dates from 1625, although much altered in the 18thC, and is built on the site of the Bedern (the college for canons and vicars pre-reformation). A high brickwall marks the boundary of the Bedern and stretches around into St Marygate. Some way north of the market place at the junction of the road to Masham is the distinctive clock tower. This was privately funded and built to commemorate Queen Victoria's jubilee in 1897. The streets around the market place to the south and west create an ambience of the medieval city although most buildings are 18th or 19thC.

Cathedral

One of the oldest of England's cathedral buildings (although not awarded cathedral status until 1836 when Ripon became a city), the Minster of St Peter and St Wilfrid can be traced back to the 7thC, when first built as part of a monastery by St Wilfrid, a prominent English religious figure who had been mentored by St

RIPON

Hilda of Whitby and was instrumental in the re-orientation of the English church towards Rome. Although only the crypt survives from this period, this is in remarkable condition. It is thought Wilfrid intended the crypt to represent Christ's tomb, and it is possible that the large recess on the east wall contains relics of saints, brought back from Rome. This recess now contains a 14thC alabaster carving of the resurrection, part of a collection found in the 19thC which had lain hidden following the Reformation. The remainder of the building dates primarily from between the 12thC to the 14thC. Particular points of interest are the west front with its magnificent 13thC Early English styled twin towers, built of warm light brown sandstone; the ornately carved misericords - mercy seats designed to allow clergy to lean against when standing in long services; and the library, above the chapter house off the south choir annex, containing the cathedral's treasury which has a valuable collection of gold and silver artefacts, including the Ripon Jewel, a Saxon gold roundel. The cathedral is open most days. There is no admission charge. 01765 603462 www.riponcathedral.org.uk

Thorpe Prebend House   High St Agnesgate

The house dates from the mid16thC, although substantially altered in later years.   The term "prebend" means an ecclesiastic estate whose income goes towards supporting the clergy.   The restored house is a museum recounting the story of the cathedral and the city with reference to the writer Lewis Carroll (whose father was dean of the cathedral) and how the cathedral inspired the writing of Alice in Wonderland.   There is also a room devoted to the poet Wilfred Owen who was stationed in the city during the first world war.

Law and Order trail

Ripon enjoyed wide powers to control law and order - including its own police force - dating from Saxon times; powers only withdrawn in late 19thC. Reflecting this particular piece of history, there are museums devoted to the theme of law and order, which visitors can easily cover in a short stroll around the city.

• **Old Court House Museum**   opposite the Minster; this early 19thC building was a courthouse in regular use until 1998. The original dock, bench and public gallery are all intact. The museum traces the path of some of those convicted here.

• **Prison and Police Museum** on St Marygate north east of the minster; the building dates from the late 17thC and has been a house of correction, a prison and a police station. The exhibits inside give a vivid impression of life as a prisoner and as a policeman in bygone eras.

• **Workhouse Museum** in Allhallowgate, north of Market Place, is the original 19thC workhouse.   It reconstructs what life was like for Victorian paupers.

The opening times are from Thu to Sun afternoons April to October. There is an admission charge.   01765 690799 www.riponmuseums.co.uk

Lightwater Valley

Lying 4 miles north of the city on the Masham road, Lightwater Valley is both a leading UK theme park and an out of town shopping complex. The theme park has over thirty thrill rides to suit all ages. It is open daily from April to October. There is an admission charge.   0871 7200011   www.lightwatervalley.co.uk

Ripon Races

One of the county's racecourses, in an area steeped in equine history with the first records showing races on Bondgate Green in 1664. The present site on Boroughbridge Road has held regular events since 1900. Ripon is believed to have promoted the first ever race for lady riders in 1723. Known as the 'Garden Racecourse' there are thirteen race meetings between April and September.

RIPON

the motto to the Wakeman on the facade of the Town Hall

Restaurants (see map page 133)

£

English Dish's 25 Kirkgate 01765 602722

££

Italian Marios 27 Kirkgate 01765 608688 www.mariosrestaurant27.co.uk

Mediterranean The Terrace 2-4 Skellbank 01765 606815

Indian The Spice Zone Duck Hill 01765 690885

£££

English Lockwoods 84 North St 01765 607555 www.lockwoodsrestaurant.co.uk

English The Old Deanery Minster Rd 01765 600003 www.theolddeanery.co.uk

Italian Prima Pizzeria 33 Kirkgate 01765 602034 www.prima-ripon.co.uk

Hotels (see map page 133)

★★★

Ripon Spa Park St 40 Bedrooms 01765 602172 www.riponspa.com

Hob Green Markington 11 Bedrooms 01423 770031 www.hobgreen.com

The Old Deanery Minster Rd 11 bedrooms 01765 600003
www.theolddeanery.co.uk

★★★★(GA)

The Royal Oak 36 Kirkgate 6 Bedrooms 01765 602284 www.royaloakripon.co.uk

not rated

The Unicorn Market Place 30 Bedrooms 0844 288 7348

RIPON

Parking Ⓟ

1 Victoria Grove 187 spaces   2 Lower Victoria Grove   32 spaces

3 St Marygate   132 spaces   4 Marshall Way   177 spaces

**Ripon Visitor Information Centre
Minster Road
01765 604625
www.harrogate.gov.uk**

RICHMOND

Positioned west of the A1, at the edge of the Yorkshire Dales, Richmond is an atmospheric market town built in a dramatic setting around a large castle on the northern bank of the River Swale as it cuts through the limestone strata marking the edge of the Dales.   Daniel Defoe describes the town, in 1727, in his book *"A Tour through this Whole Island of Great Britain"* : *This town of Richmond (Cambden calls it a city) is wall'd, and had a strong castle; but as those things are now all slighted, so really the account of them is of small consequence, and needless; old fortifications being, if fortification was wanted, of very little signification; the River Swale runs under the wall of this castle, and has some unevenness at its bottom, by reason of rocks which intercept its passage, so that it falls like a cataract, but not with so great a noise"*

History

RICHMOND

There was probably a settlement in this area in Saxon times, although there is no direct evidence, but the area was called *Hindrelac,* Norse for clearing for deer. Richmond really begins in 1071, when Alan the Red, a French Count and favourite of William the Conqueror, was granted the rights to land in this part of Yorkshire and built the castle which can be seen today.   The name Richmond derives from Riche-Mont, French for "Strong Hill" and Alan the Red became the Lord of Richmondshire. A later Lord, King Henry VII, built a palace at Sheen in Surrey which was later renamed Richmond on Thames, and so a large London suburb takes it's name from a market town in Yorkshire.   The 14th and 15thC saw the town prosper, being granted a royal charter in 1441 by Henry IV, and there was at one time as many as 13 craft guilds in the town.   It developed as a commercial centre for the Swaledale woollen industry and later, in the 17th and 18thC, for the lead mining industry in nearby Arkengarthdale. Burgeoning prosperity in this period is amply evidenced by some of the grand Georgian houses in Frenchgate and Newbiggin.   Richmond traditionally has strong military links, and although the Castle had fallen into a state of disrepair by the 15thC, the early 19th saw it in use again for military purposes. Although Richmond is no longer a garrison town, nearby Catterick Camp is one of the largest army barracks in the UK, and there is a museum in the town to the Green Howards.   The railways came to the town in 1848, although only as a branch line, always regarded as marginal,   it finally closed in 1968. The Tudor style station building survives and, following restoration, is now in use as a workspace and community centre.

Getting here

Rail   the closest railway station is Darlington, with regular services to York, Leeds, Newcastle and London. Bus service (X27) links with Darlington station

Road   the town lies just to the west of the A1, through links with the A 6136 and A 6108; to the west the A6108 and B6270 leads up Swaledale.

Bus   Most buses arrive at and depart from the Market Place.

destination	service(s)	frequency
Ripon	159	2hourly
Northallerton	54/55/73	hourly
swaledale	30/36	2hourly
Darlington	X26/X27/X28/29	15 min
Barnard Castle	79	2hourly

Things to see and do

Richmonds heart is its Market Place- a spacious, sloping cobbled square- around which the original castle walls were built. The middle of the square is an "island' with a former church (now the Green Howards museum). The prominent 1771 obelisk is the market cross, and a market is still held every Saturday. Georgian period properties grace the frontages which, with the ob- elisk and cobbles, produce an atmospheric environment often featuring in film and TV production.   On the south side are the old 1756 Town Hall, which re- places an earlier guildhall on the site, and the 19thC market hall.   On the north side is the stately Kings Head hotel, built 1717 as a gentleman's townhouse, but which has been a hotel for nearly 200 years and has hosted the likes of the composer Franz Lizst and the artist JMW Turner.   The Castle lies immediately south of the Market Place with its walls providing a domineering presence. Leading off the Market Place are historic streets emphasising the towns dis- tinctive historic character. Of particular note is Newbiggin, an elegant 18thC wide tree lined boulevard.   At its western end is Cravengate, where turning toward the river and arriving at The Green will gives glimpses of the Culloden Tower, a folly erected in 1746 by the local MP John Yorke to mark the final

defeat of the Jacobites and the establishment of Hanoverian rule.   It is now used as a holiday home and let out to visitors by the Landmark Trust. (www.landmarktrust.org.uk) The bridge over the Swale just below The Green dates from 1789.   Returning towards the Market Place up the strenuous climb of Bridge Street, turning right into Cornforth Hill leads to one of the remaining two bargates which marked the original outer walls of the castle and town. Return through the Market Place and cross- ing into Friars Wynd leads to the other surviv- ing entrance in the town walls.   At the other side is Victoria Road is one of the UK's old- est surviving Georgian theatres, The Theatre Royal.   Just off Frenchgate, to the east of the Market Place, is the Richmond Museum, whilst along Station road is St Marys Church.

Culloden Tower

RICHMOND

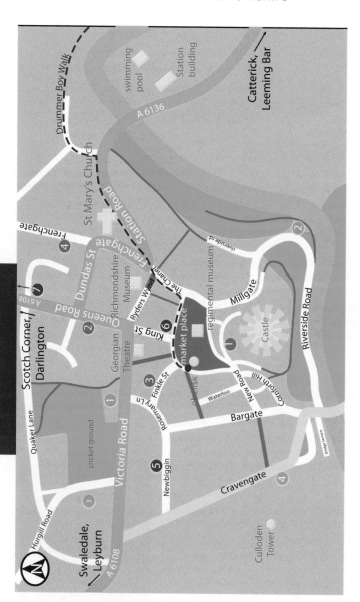

RICHMOND

Parking Ⓟ

① Victoria Road

② The Fosse

③ Hurgill Road

④ Cravengate

The Castle ⚏

One of the oldest surviving castles (those at Durham and Colchester can claim equal age), the keep towers above the town and walls tower over the River Swale. It was built 1071-86 by Alan the Red on land granted to him by William the Conqueror. It became the headquarters of the Honour of Richmond, an extensive collection of lands and estates across northern England, and which became so powerful, it presented challenges to some kings so that they eventually confiscated the Honour. The castle itself was extensive, with its outer bailey walls being by the outer edges of the present Market Place. The keep, still substantially intact, was built over the original gatehouse in the late 12thC by Henry II. A climb to its battlements affords dramatic views over the town, as well as panoramic views over the surrounding countryside, and emphasises the strong defensive position originally selected by Alan the Red. It had fallen out of use by the end of the 15thC, but became the headquarters of the North Yorkshire militia in the mid 19thC. Within the grounds are the remains of the Scolland Hall which formed an early keep and was the main residence, and the Gold Hole tower, the latter still possessing the latrines of the castle. The castle is open daily March to October, with more limited opening in the winter. There is an admission charge.   01748 822493   www.english-heritage.org.uk

RICHMOND

St Mary's Church

Built outside the original town walls, this parish church is probably late 14thC, although there is evidence in the interior –the west arcades - of 12thC construction. The church was however comprehensively altered as part of a 19thC restoration. The organ is considered to be one of the finest of any English parish church and has recently been restored. The building is open during the week and there are interpretive boards relating to points of interest inside.

Richmond Visitor Information Centre
Friary Gardens
01748 828742
www.richmondshire.gov.uk

The Green Howards Museum   (former Holy Trinity church)

The building is described by Niklaus Pevsner, the architectural historian, as "the queerest ecclesiastical building one can imagine"   Made redundant as a church after the second world war, it was acquired by the Green Howards to house their museum and archive collection. The Museum tells the story of the regiment, created in the late 17thC, known as "*The 19th (First Yorkshire North Riding regiment) of Foot*", Richmond became the regiments home town in 1873. The Museum is open Mon to Sat February to November. There is an admission charge.

01748 826561 www.greenhowards.org.uk

Theatre Royal Victoria Road

Richmond's Georgian theatre dates from 1788, one of the oldest and best preserved English theatres. Part of a small collection developed and managed by the Georgian impresario Samuel Butler, it ceased being a theatre in the 1840's but was resurrected in the 1960s and recently fully restored.   It seats 214 in an authentically recreated Georgian atmosphere. There is also a museum charting the buildings history. A full programme is provided throughout the year.

01748   825252   www.georgiantheatre.com

Richmondshire Museum   Ryders Wynd

This small museum is housed in a former joiners workshop just off Frenchgate. It tells the story of the life and times of Richmondshire folk.   The Museum is open daily from April to October. There is an admission charge.

01748 825611   www.richmondshiremuseum.org.uk

The Drummer Boy Walk

This is a 3 mile return walk starting and finishing in the Market Place and follows footpaths eastwards from the town to Easby Abbey and back. Legend has it that the walk relates to the discovery, in the late 18thC, of a tunnel under the Castle sufficiently small in size to permit only a boy to explore it, beating his drum as he went. Soldiers following the sound traced a path to Easby Abbey where the sound of the drumming stopped; the drummer boy was never seen again. A stone stands to mark the spot and is called the 'Drummer Boy Stone'.

Easby Abbey

Yorkshire is full of monastic ruins, but the Abbey of St Agatha at Easby must rank amongst the most picturesque.   It was founded c.1155 for the Premonstratensian canons –an order which had no monks, and who became known as the white canons. Their way of life and religious practices bore much similarity to the Cistercians. The Abbey was abandoned with the dissolution of the monasteries, and is now an idyllic ruin. However, Easby's parish church lies in the middle of the ruins and still in use. It contains 13thC wall paintings, and a replica

142

of the Easby Cross, a 7thC Anglo-Saxon sculpture, the original of which is in the Victoria and Albert Museum in London.   The Abbey can be reached either by walking from the town using the Drummer boy walk or from Easby village. The ruins and church are open daily. Admission is free.

Richmond Station

The former station building, built in 1846, lies by the River Swale on the south side of the Mercury Bridge. Its Tudor style is described by commentators as "exuberant" but was a conscious choice to reflect the high status of a railway journey experience. Although closed in 1968, it was fully restored in 2003 and now forms a visitor and resident icon attraction. There are two cinema screens, an art gallery, a café, a heritage centre, and the buildings are also home to six artisan food makers. The station lies near the route of the Drummer boy walk, and is open every day, although the food makers are normally closed on Mondays.

01748 850123 www.richmondstation.com

Catterick Races

The village of Catterick, 4 miles east of the town is best known for its vast military camp, but is also the home to a well known and busy racecourse which hosts 17 flat racing fixtures and 10 National hunt racing fixtures annually.   01748 811478   www.catterickbridge.co.uk

Restaurants (see map page 140)

££

Chinese **New Treasure Garden** 7 Castle Hill   ❶
01748 826085 www.newtreasuregarden.co.uk

Indian **Amontola** 8-10 Queens Rd 01748 826070 www.amontola-restaurant.co.uk ❷

£££

French **Rustique** Chantry Wynd Finkle St 01748 821565 www.rustiqueyork.co.uk ❸

££££

English **The Frenchgate** 59 Frenchgate 01748 822087 www.thefrenchgate.co.uk ❹
(also a 9 bedroom hotel)

Hotels (see map page 140)

★★★(GA)

The Buck hotel Newbiggin 6 bedrooms 01748 822259   ❺
www.thebuckhotelrichmond.co.uk

★★★

Kings Head   Market Place 30 Bedrooms 01748 850220   ❻
www.kingsheadrichmond.com

★★★★(GA)

Rosedale Guest House 2 Pottergate 6 bedrooms 01748 823926   ❼
www.richmondbedandbreakfast.co.uk

RICHMOND

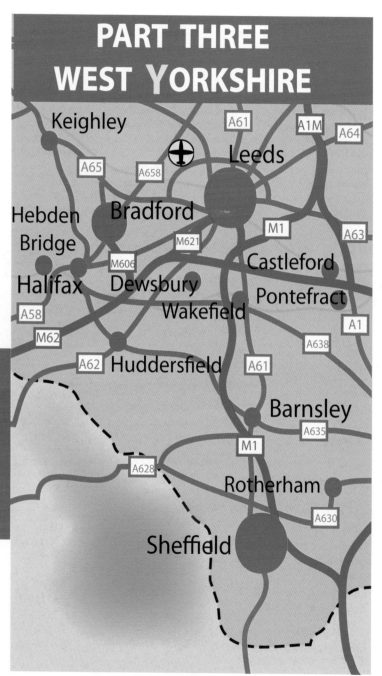

PART THREE
WEST YORKSHIRE

Keighley

A61

A1M

A64

Leeds

A65

A658

Hebden
Bridge

Bradford

M1

A63

M621

Castleford

M606

Halifax

Dewsbury

Pontefract

A58

Wakefield

A1

M62

A638

A62

Huddersfield

A61

Barnsley

A635

M1

A628

Rotherham

A630

Sheffield

WEST YORKSHIRE

KEIGHLEY

Keighley is a long established town in the Aire valley between Bradford and Skipton which has traditionally made it's living from textiles and associated engineering. Today it is perhaps best known for its association - in the nearby village of Haworth – with the Bronte sisters and the Worth Valley Railway.

History

Keighley is mentioned in the Domesday book as *Chicehlai*, which means the field belonging to Chyya.   King Edward 1 granted a charter in 1304 to hold a market, although the current daily market is held indoors.   The textile industry has long been its mainstay, and it was one of the few Yorkshire towns to be an early location for cotton spinning, normally associated with Lancashire.

Getting Here

Rail   the station is to the east of the town centre and has half hourly services to Leeds and Skipton, as well as links into Bradford, Lancaster and Morecambe. Leeds is 30 mins away; London is 3 hrs via Leeds.

Road   the A65 Aire valley route passes through the town. Substantially improved, it offers a rapid route into Bradford (20 mins), and to Skipton (15 mins). London is a 4hr 30 min;   Manchester is 1hr.

Bus   all buses arrive at and depart from Keighley Bus Station in Bow Street.

destination	service(s)	frequency
Leeds	760	30 mins
Bradford	662/697	10mins/30mins
Skipton	66/78A	30 mins
Ilkley	762/765	30 mins
Haworth	500/664/665	20 mins
Burnley	25	hourly

Things to see and do

What remains of the towns Victorian heritage is best experienced by a walk along North Street and Church Street where the late Victorian stone buildings are still largely intact.   The indoor market is in Lowe Street near the parish church adjoining the modern Airedale Shopping centre, a mall with over 60 shops including major multiple brands.

Haworth

A classic Pennine village, Haworth is on the southern edge of the town. Its steep main street has the church at the top, and the mills at the bottom. Many of the buildings are 18th or early 19thC. The street is lined with tea shops and restaurants, pubs, souvenir and antique shops. On several occasions through the year, Morris dancers perform in the main street.

KEIGHLEY

Haworth is perhaps best known for its association with the Bronte sisters and the novels they wrote, many of which are based on Haworth and surrounding area.

Bronte Museum set amongst trees behind the church, and the rather forbidding graveyard, the former Bronte family home is the Parsonage. It is now a museum recording the family's life. It is run by the Bronte Society whose main purpose is to advance the knowledge and understanding of the Bronte family and literary work. The Museum is open daily. There is an admission charge.
01535 642323   www.bronte.org.uk

Worth Valley Railway

Built in 1867, the railway linked Keighley with the prosperous woollen mills then evident throughout the valley to Oxenhope and beyond. The railway closed in 1962, but local protests produced a private line, run by volunteers, which re-opened in 1968. It has run ever since and provides both a local service for residents into Keighley - and connection with the Leeds to Skipton line - and a tourist attraction with the steam locomotives that haul heritage coaches 4 miles between Keighley and Oxenhope through Haworth.   The line is frequently used for filming and the critically acclaimed British film The Railway Children (1970) was largely filmed in and around Haworth and the railway line. Regular services are run from Easter to October between Keighley Station and Oxenhope.   01535 645214   www.kwvr.co.uk

KEIGHLEY

Keighley and Worth Valley Railway

The Bronte Sisters - Novelists

Charlotte (1816-1855)   Emily (1818-1848),   Anne (1820-1849)
The three sisters were a part of literary family who produced between them
an outstanding number of novels and poetry, many of which are now considered to rank amongst the best in English literature. They were the children of Patrick Bronte, the perpetual curate of Haworth, who outlived them
all.   Amongst their best known works are Jane Eyre (Charlotte), Wuthering
Heights (Emily), and The Tenant of Wildfowl Hall (Anne). Many of their works
were based on their life and experiences in Haworth. Their early deaths were
due in part to the poor sanitation and living conditions whic prevalent in places
like Haworth in the 19thC, although they enjoyed a middle class existence.

East Riddlesden Hall

Perhaps one of the best known 17thC Pennine houses, it lies on the banks
of the River Aire just north of the town. It was built in 1648 by James Murga-
troyd, a wealthy woollen mill owner from Halifax (and who is reputed to be the
role model for the main character in the Gilbert and Sullivan opera Ruddigore).
Noteworthy features include restored living accommodation, magnificent rose
windows, a walled garden and tithe barn. House and grounds are open Feb to
Oct. There is an admission charge.   01535 607075 www.nationaltrust.org.uk

Cliffe Castle Museum   Spring Gardens Lane

Originally the house of a wealthy textile manufacturer (J H Butterfield), and a
museum since 1959, it houses extensive, if eclectic, collections. They include
geological artefacts, William Morris stained glass, and some original furnished
rooms. The landscaped grounds contain aviaries, a children's play area and
a garden centre. The museum and grounds are open Tue to Sat and Sun pm
year round. Admission is free.   01535 618231 www.bradfordmuseums.org

Museum of Rail Travel   Ingrow

Owned and run by the Vintage Carriages Trust, the museum is based in workshops adjoining Ingrow station on the Worth Valley railway. It has a collection
of carriages, locomotives and railway miscellania many of which emanate from
the Worth Valley railway in its earlier days.   It is open all year. There is an admission charge (some tickets purchased for travel on the Worth Valley Railway
include entry to the museum). 01535 680425   www.vintagecarriagestrust.org

Keighley Bus Museum   Dalton Mills

This collection of vintage and modern buses comprises over 50 vehicles, many
in full running order. The museum is run and staffed by volunteers and is open
Tue evenings and Sat.   01282 413179 www.kbmt.org.uk

KEIGHLEY

Haworth Visitor information Centre
West Lane Howarth
01535 642329 www.visitbradford.com

Restaurants (see map page 149)

££

English **Haworth Old Hall** Sun Street Haworth 01535 642709 ①
www.hawortholdhall.co.uk

Indian **Shimla Spice** 14, South Street 01535 602040 www.shimlaspice.co.uk ②

Indian **Moghuls** 114-166 North Street 01535 604423 www.moghuls.info ③

Italian **Amici** 105-107 East Parade 01535 610699 www.amici.uk.com ④

£££

English **The Stirrup** 103, Main St Haworth 01535 642007 www.thestirrup.co.uk ⑤

English **Chaplins Bistro** Fall Wood St Haworth 01535 648090 ⑥
www.chaplinsbistro.co.uk

Australasian **Wharenui** 25-27 Main Street 01535 644511 www.wharenui.co.uk ⑦

££££

English **Weavers** West Lane Haworth 01535 643822 www.weaversmallhotel.co.uk ⑧

Hotels (see map page 149)

★★

Travelodge Bradford Road 43 Bedrooms 0871 5591824 www.travelodge.co.uk ⑨

Dalesgate Skipton Road Utley 20 Bedrooms 01535 664930 www.dalesgate.co.uk ⑩

★★★★(GA)

The Old White Lion Main Street Haworth 14 Bedrooms 01535 642313 ⑪
www.oldwhitelionhotel.com

The Old Registry 2-4 Main Street Haworth 9 Bedrooms 01535 646503 ⑫
www.theoldregistryhaworth.co.uk

★★★★★(GA)

Ashmount Country House Mytholmes Lane 12 Bedrooms 01535 645726 ⑬
www.ashmounthaworth.co.uk

not rated

The Leeming Wells Long Causeway 5 Bedrooms 01535 646757 ⑭
www.leemingwells.co.uk

Steeton Hall Station Road Steeton 9 Bedrooms 01535 655676 ⑮
www.steetonhallhotel.co.uk

KEIGHLEY

Parking ℗

① Church Green 70 spaces ② Airedale Centre 450 spaces
③ Scott Street 130 spaces ④ Cliffe Castle 42 spaces

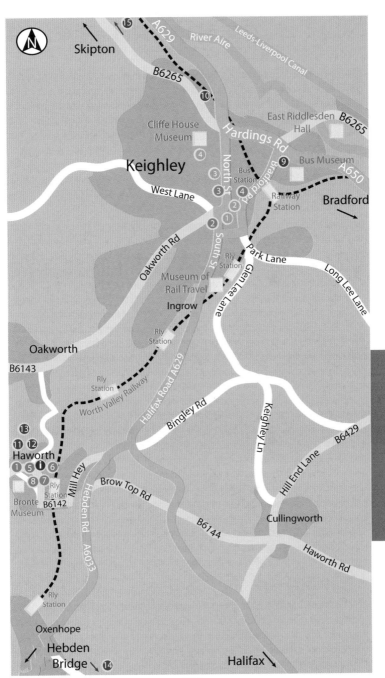

Skipton

River Aire

Leeds-Liverpool Canal

A629

B6265

East Riddlesden Hall

B6265

Cliffe House Museum

Hardings Rd

Keighley

Bus Museum

Bus Station

Bradford

West Lane

North St

Railway Station

Oakworth Rd

South St

Park Lane

Long Lee Lane

Rly Station

Glen Lee Lane

Museum of Rail Travel

Ingrow

Oakworth

Rly Station

Rly Station

Halifax Road A629

Bingley Rd

Keighley Ln

Hill End Lane

B6429

B6143

Worth Valley Railway

Haworth

Mill Hey

Brow Top Rd

Cullingworth

Bronte Museum

Rly Station

B6142

Hebden Rd

A6033

B6144

Haworth Rd

Rly Station

Oxenhope

Hebden Bridge

Halifax

KEIGHLEY

BRADFORD

The "Great Goddess of Getting On" was how John Ruskin, the eminent Victorian critic and social thinker, described Bradford to its own prominent citizens in 1864; as the city reached the height of its prosperity. Although since experiencing more challenging times, it remains one of the county's largest cities, and this Victorian heritage, combined with more modern iconic features makes this melting pot well worth a visit. Sited south of the River Aire, 10 miles west of Leeds, it draws very much on its Pennine roots for its industrial heritage, its buildings and architecture. It is the worlds first UNESCO designated city of film.

History

Bradford was first settled in Saxon times as a small village centred around what is now Ivegate, Kirkgate, and Westgate, although the Norman conquest destroyed much of this. The name derives from the Saxon for broad *(Brad)* and a river crossing *(Ford)*. The woollen and tanning trades formed the foundation of the town in the middle ages, with a market charter being granted in 1251. However, the woollen trade was common over much of Yorkshire and, in the 15thC, Bradford's had little prominence as a woollen centre of any importance; ranking well behind several other places in the county such as Ripon. Its growth in the 19thC, as industrialisation took root, was spectacular. In a hundred years, the population increased from 13,000 to 280,000. The discovery of iron ore deposits, radical improvements to transport – railways (in 1847), a link into the Leeds –Liverpool canal (in 1779)- and the immigration of European- mainly German- merchants, created the environment for the city to become a leading world centre of wool production and a mercantile centre with influential institutions such as the International Wool Exchange. By 1850 it is claimed the 38 woollen mills in the city accounted for two thirds of the country's wool production. The period after the first world war saw a rapid decline of woollen and other industries and, after the second world war, substantial immigration, mainly from the Indian sub continent. There was however some industrial diversification with other engineering industries, such as car making (the unusually engineered Jowett cars were manufactured in the city between 1906 and 1954) and machinery. The city has adjusted to its changed circumstances with new industries and a focus on media and education. Much has also been invested in restoring the heritage and the fruits of this are visible in a range of facilities and attractions.

Getting Here

Rail the city has two central railway stations,as well as suburban ones and good access to most UK destinations. Exchange station, on the south side of the centre (adj bus station) provides regular services to Leeds, York, Manchester, Blackpool, Halifax, Huddersfield and London. Forster Square Station, on the north side of the provides services to Leeds, Keighley, Skipton and London.

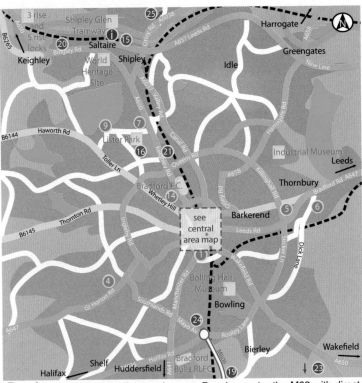

Road the city lies just off the main cross Pennine route, the M62 with direct linkages to Hull (1hr), Manchester, (45 mins) Leeds (15mins) and London (4 hrs). To the North, the city connects to the A65 road to Skipton and on to Kendal and to Scotland.

Bus Most services arrive at and depart from the Interchange on Bridge Street adjoining the railway station.

destination	service(s)	frequency
city circular	freebus	10 mins
Leeds	72	7 mins
Dewsbury	253/283	2x per hour
Wakefield	253/425/427	hourly/30 mins
Huddersfield	363	20 mins
Halifax	570/571/576	2x per hour/ 12 mins
Otley	653	2 hourly
Keighley	662	10 mins
Manchester	381	1x per day
Newcastle	280	1x per day
London	561	4x per day
Heathrow/Gatwick	240	4x per day

BRADFORD

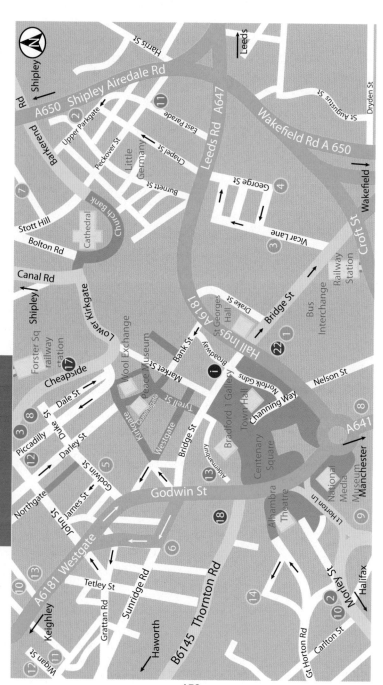

Things to See and do

The core of Victorian Bradford is still visible despite wholesale redevelopment around the city centre, and gives a powerful insight into the prosperity and ambience of the mid 19thC. City Hall is a building constructed in 1873 to a design by Lockwood and Mawson (responsible for many of Bradford's iconic 19thC buildings), although subsequently substantially altered. It dominates Centenary Square and surrounding spaces. It is designed in 13thC gothic style, with the clock tower resembling a Tuscan campanile. The interior is much altered but the Courtroom is still original.   The core of the Victorian quarter lies to the east.   Market Street, Tyrell Street leading into Hustlergate and the Wool Exchange. This building typifies the city's dominant mercantile trading stature in the19thC. Designed by Lockwood and Mawson, in Venetian Gothic style, it opened in 1867. Above the arcade there are medallion portraits of well known figures, including Titus Salt, William Gladstone and Lord Palmerston - the latter, then Prime Minister - laying the foundation stone.   Wool was traded on the floor of the exchange for a hundred years, business ceasing in the mid 1960s as the last vestiges of Bradford's once dominant wool industry faded. Being a Member of the

Captain James Cook's medallion portrait on the side of the Wool Exchange

Wool Exchange was a matter of great social distinction in Victorian Bradford. Today the Exchange ground floor is a shop although the architectural detail has been faithfully retained. Piece Hall Yard next to the Wool Exchange is worth exploring. The now demolished Piece Hall was where the cloths were traded and, like the Wool exchange, was a place not only of commerce, but of social recognition.   Still surviving is the Bradford Club, a "gentlemans club" of 1891 and another bastion of social standing in the Victorian city.   Further up the hill is Queensgate, whose Victorian character is in sharp contrast to the street at the top, Kirkgate, dominated by the modern Kirkgate centre. Kirkgate is now the main shopping area of the city centre, and most major brands in Bradford are in or close to the Kirkgate Centre. Adjoining is the Rawson Market; again by Lockwood and Mawson, and which provided the " provisions" element of Bradford's market in the late 19thC, and was the place where the large superstore operator, Wm Morrisons Ltd, first began life in 1899. Beyond Rawson Market is the Oastler Centre, Bradford's meat and fish market and which also contains other permanent market stalls. Named for Richard Oastler, a 19thC social reformer who tried to improve the lot of factory workers and particularly working children. His statue is in Northgate. The eastern side of the city centre is currently the subject of a major redevelopment which has not yet borne fruit.

BRADFORD

The Post office and Cathedral lie the other side of the development, as does Little Germany; that part of the city which became the home of the many German and Polish merchants who arrived in the city in the 19thC to make their fortunes. The west side of the city centre contains the Alhambra theatre, and the Media Museum, together with University, Peace Museum, and Bradford 1 Gallery.

Bradford Cathedral

St Peters Cathedral is built on a Saxon place of worship. Fragments of a Saxon preaching cross have been found on the site. The current building is 14thC, but much modified since and designated a cathedral in 1919. The stained glass in the east window has a design and construction orchestrated by the pre- Raphaelite designer, William Morris in 1864. Amongst the artists contributing to this homage to popular Christian figures were Rosetti and Webb, both well known arts and crafts movement designers. The interior contains a spectacular font cover with elegant spire, buttresses and tracery. The cathedral is open Mon to Sat.   01274 777720
www.bradfordcathedral.co.uk

Bradford Cathedral

Little Germany

To the immediate west of the Airedale- Shipley inner ring road, lies Little Germany. It was home to German merchants who came to Bradford in the late 1850's for the prosperous textile industry. Wandering round the area, centred on centred around Peckover Street and Vicar Lane, conveys a real impression of what commerical life may have been like in the 19thC. Today these unique buildings, primarily warehouses, form a collection constructed between 1855 and 1890, with many designed by ubiquitous Victorian architects Lockwood and Mawson.

National Media Museum

The UK's centre of excellence for film, television and photography, this museum, opened in 1983, is a veritable cornucopia of historic and contemporary iconic images and has helped the city gain the accolade of a UNESCO world rating as city of film. The Museum houses over 3.5 million images of historical importance, as well as containing an IMAX theatre, research centre interactive exhibitions and media performances. It organises a number of film festivals each year. It is open Tues to Sun year round. Admission charges apply to some galleries.   0844 8563797 www.nationalmediamuseum.org.uk

BRADFORD

Alhambra Theatre   Morley Street

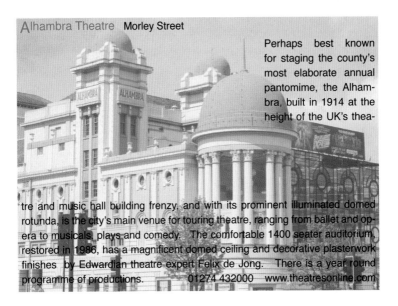

Perhaps best known for staging the county's most elaborate annual pantomime, the Alhambra, built in 1914 at the height of the UK's theatre and music hall building frenzy, and with its prominent illuminated domed rotunda, is the city's main venue for touring theatre, ranging from ballet and opera to musicals, plays and comedy. The comfortable 1400 seater auditorium, restored in 1986, has a magnificent domed ceiling and decorative plasterwork finishes by Edwardian theatre expert Felix de Jong. There is a year round programme of productions.   01274 432000   www.theatresonline.com

St Georges Hall   Bridge Street

Designed by Lockwood and Mawson in the form of a Corinthian Temple, the building opened in 1853 as a place for public assembly, cultural and entertainment events. Its promoters were Bradford philanthropists of the time including Sir Titus Salt. Nowadays, it is a popular entertainment venue; its 1500 seat capacity attracting touring bands, comedians as well as orchestral ensembles such as the Halle.   01274 432000   www.bradford-theatres.co.uk

Saltaire

3 miles north of the city centre, the Victorian industrial village of Saltaire is now a UNESCO designated world heritage site. It lies west of Shipley town centre between the A650 and the River Aire. Its promoter was the Bradford industrialist Titus Salt, who built a large woollen mill, using the river for a water source, and the Leeds – Liverpool canal to transport raw materials and finished cloth. Because of his philanthropic beliefs, he built not only the Mill, but also houses, schools and a hospital for his workers. When built, the Mill was the largest and most advanced in the world. All the buildings survive intact. The Mill now houses engineering companies, art gallery and other visitor facilities. The art gallery is known as the Hockney gallery and shows primarily art works from Bradford born artist David Hockney. The scale of Titus's project was immense. It began in 1850 with the Mill - which remarkably remained in production until 1986. There were also 820 houses, public buildings, church and hospital. Some 4,300 people lived here when it was finally completed in 1871, and this was the largest such social engineering project of its age. The architects were the well known local firm Lockwood and Mawson.

BRADFORD

155

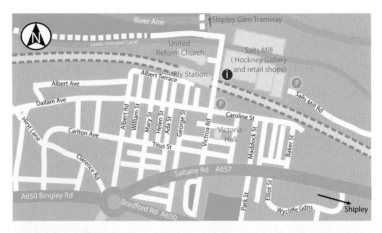

As well as the Mill, prominent buildings include the Victoria Hall (originally the Mechanics Institute) with its delicately carved bas-relief over the entrance and now home to the Museum of Victorian Reed Organs and Harmoniums; the hospital and almshouses, the School and a non conformist church. Titus Salt was a non-conformist and not surprisingly the church is perhaps the most sumptuous of all such churches with its imposing portico, round tower and elegantly decorated interior. The Salt family mausoleum, where Titus, his wife and children are buried, adjoins the church. Access to the village by road is via Shipley and the A650, but there are also good public transport links; Saltaire is on the Leeds/Bradford to Skipton railway line with regular services. The 662 Bradford to Keighley bus and the 760 Keighley to Leeds service pass close by.

Salts Mill

Saltaire Visitor Information Centre
Salts Mill
01274 437942
www.visitbradford.com

Saltaire

Shipley Glen Tramway

The tramway runs up the north slope of the Aire Valley from a point close to Saltaire.   It is Britain's oldest working cable operated tramway, built in 1895, for   local residents   to enjoy the local beauty spot of Shipley Glen. The short ride provides a more relaxing alternative to the steep wood-land path alongside. The tramway is open most weekend afternoons.

01274 589010   www.glentramway.co.uk

Cartwright Hall/Lister Park

Lister Park was voted Britain's Best Park in 2006. It was sold to the city by the Victorian wool baron Samuel Cunliffe-Lister, who built and operated the nearby city landmark building Lister Mills. The park contains botanical gardens, a boating lake, and a bandstand and is open daily.   Cartwright Hall is a city art gallery.   Set in the park's formal surroundings, it has a large collection of art exhibitions in four galleries, including 19th and 20th British Art , South Asian Art and contemporary prints.   The gallery is open Tues to Sat and Sun pm Admission is free. Bus services 622,623,625,627,662 pass the park frequently.

01274 431212   www.bradfordmuseums.org

Industrial Museum   Moorside Mills

This museum displays Bradford's   Victorian industrial heritage, housed in former mills 2 miles north east of the centre.   There are permanent dis-plays of industrial textile machinery, including some inventions   pioneered by textile magnates such as Samuel Cunliffe-Lister.   There are also dis-plays of printing machinery, motor vehicles and development of steam pow-er.   Some terraced houses have been restored to represent living condi-tions of mill workers in the 19thC, and the museum keeps a team of working horses in the Victorian Job Masters stables.   The museum is open Tues to Sun through the year. Admission is free. Bus service 645 passes the end of Moorside Road.   01274 435900   www.bradfordmuseums.org

BRADFORD

Cartwright Hall

Peace Museum   10, Piece Hall Yard

This is the only museum in the UK devoted to material relating to initiatives on the creation of conflict resolution by non violent means.   The initial idea of creating a peace museum arose in the mid-1980s from the Give Peace a Chance Trust. It is open on Wed and Fri 11.00 to 3.00pm. Admission is free.
01274 434009   www.peacemuseum.org.uk

Bolling Hall Museum   Bowling Hall Road
One of the oldest buildings in the city, this museum, 1mile south of the centre, recounts the history of the city through the lives of the families who occupied it. It became a royalist stronghold in the English Civil war, when Bradford strongly rallied to the Parliamentarian cause.   There are some important 16thC armorial stained glass windows in the hall as well as period furniture, some by Thomas Chippendale, and Oliver Cromwell's death mask.   The museum is open Wed to Sun through the year. Admission is free. Bus services 624/634 pass the Museum.   01274 431814   www.bradfordmuseums.org

Bradford 1 Gallery   Centenary Square
This modern innovative gallery puts on 4 exhibitions a year, bringing the work of national and international artists to the city. It also contains permanent exhibits.

Within the building is the Impressions gallery, containing a wide range of photographic exhibits.   Both galleries are open Tues to Sat through the year. Admission to both is free.   01274 437800   www.bradfordmuseums.org

BRADFORD

Titus Salt- Cloth Baron and Philanthropist 1803-1876

Titus Salt was born in Morley, near Leeds in 1803. His father, Daniel, was a successful woolstapler, and able to pay for a good education for Titus. He joined the family firm in 1824 following apprenticeship as a woolstapler and quickly became the firm's woolbuyer. Daniel Salt & Son took advantage of Bradford's booming economy and became one of the city's most sucessful textile companies. Titus took control of the company in 1833 and it grew to become the city's largest employer. He was an innovator, and declines in the fortunes of the worsted textile industry because of a shortage of cotton, led him to experiment with alpaca, which proved a resounding success. Poor living and working conditions then rife together with unregulated industrialisation produced pollution and much ill health leading to the city having one of the lowest levels of life expectancy in the country. Titus Salt, now owning five textile mills, was one of the few employers in the town who showed any concern for this problem. He became Bradford's mayor in 1848 and tried, unsuccessfully, to bring in by-laws to force factory owners in the town to use new safer smoke burners to reduce pollution. As a consequence he moved his businesses onto one site away from the city, and where he could create good living and working conditions. Saltaire was chosen and in 1853 the new mill was completed. It was then the largest woollen mill in the world, and one with the best working conditions; much attention being paid to low noise levels and effective removal of dust and dirt. At first his 3,500 staff travelled to work at the mill, most from the city. However, he quickly built over 800 houses for his workers, together with a park, church, school, hospital, library and shops. The houses in Saltaire were superior to those found in Bradford and elsewhere. They enjoyed fresh water and gas provided lighting and heating. Every house had its own outside lavatory. To encourage people to keep themselves clean, Salt also built public baths and wash-houses. His non conformist religious convictions were reflected by the building of

a sumptuous Congregationalist church in Saltaire. He briefly served as an MP between 1859 and 1861 but was also an active political reformer, supporting adult suffrage, and campaigning to reduce working hours- his own workers enjoyed a 10 hour day, then much shorter than the norm, but he was opposed to trade unions. He died in December 1876. He had been a wealthy man, but his social initiatives eroded his fortune, and much to the dismay of his family, it is reported he died penniless.

BRADFORD

Three Rise and Five Rise Locks   Bingley

A little way out of the city, in Bingley, the Leeds- Liverpool canal rises through a series of locks known as the Three Rise and Five Rise Locks. The locks opened in 1774 and were, at the time, major feats of engineering and a showpiece of British ingenuity and innovation.   The passage of canal boats through the locks is a major draw to sightseers on weekends.

BRADFORD

Festivals

March   Film Festival National Media Museum
                                      www.nationalmediamuseum.org.uk

June   Bradford Mela variety of venues   www.bradfordmela.org.uk
September Saltaire Festival   www.saltairefestival.co.uk
              Bite the Mango National Media Museum
              Bingley Music Live Myrtle Park   www.bingleymusiclive.com

Sporting Life

Bradford City FC   "The Bantams"

Bradford City FC play their home games at a modern stadium on Valley Parade. The team have at various times played at the top and bottom of English league football and regularly draw a crowd of   11,000-12,000 for home games.   01274 770012   www.bradfordcityfc.co.uk

Bradford Rugby League FC "The Bulls"

Bradford Bulls are a leading British rugby league football team and consistent winners of league and cup championships. Their home matches are played at Odsal Stadium, on the south west side of the city, where the average crowd is in excess of 9,000.   08448 711490   www.bradfordbulls.co.uk

J.B. Priestley- Novelist and Playwright 1894-1984

Born into an academic family in Heaton, a northern suburb of the city, John Priestley went on to become a prolific novelist and playwright. He worked as a clerk in the city centre, although moonlighted by writing pieces for local journals, until volunteering to fight in the 1st world war, where he was wounded by mortar fire. After gaining a degree at Cambridge, he set to work as freelance writer. He had established a reputation as a humourous and perceptive author by the mid 1920's. After publication of one of his best known works, The Good Companions, in 1929, he was able to branch out into stage and screen writing, and his most famous work was "An Inspector Calls". He was active in politics, and was a founder Member of the Campaign For Nuclear Disarmament. After his death in 1984, his ashes were buried in Hubberholme in the Yorkshire Dales.

Restaurants (see map pages 151 and 152)

£

Asian Karachi 15-17 Neal Street 01274 732015 ①

Kashmiri Kashmir 27 Morley Street 01274 726513 ②

Oriental Fusia Noodle Bar Centenary Square 01274 723388 ③

££

Kashmiri Mumtaz Great Horton Road 01274 571861 www.mumtaz.co.uk ④

Indian Akbars 1276 Leeds Road 01274 773311 www.akbars.co.uk ⑤

Indian Aagrah Midpoint Suite Thornbury Road 01274 668818 www.aagrah.com ⑥

Italian Orlando 204 Keighley Rd 01274 542182 www.orlandositalianbradford.co.uk ⑦

Russian The Russian 15 Manor Row, 01274 733121 www.rurest.co.uk ⑧

English Bradleys 46 Highgate Heaton 01274 499890 www.bradleyscatering.co.uk ⑨

Mediterranean Cyrus Morley Street 01274 728728 www.cyrusbradford.com ⑩

Chinese Blue Sky 18 East Parade 01274 788333 ⑪

Italian Mamma Mia Up'r Piccadilly 01274 733834 www.mammamiabradford.co.uk ⑫

£££

Thai Dragon Thai 20 Aldermanbury 01274 723388 www.chinothai.co.uk ⑬

Tex Mex El Mexicana Cocina 64-70 Manningham Lane 01274 727625 ⑭

Hotels (see map pages 151 and 152)

★★

Ibis Salts Mill Road 78 bedrooms 01274 589333 www.ibishotel.com ⑮

★★★(GA)

The Lister 22 NorthPark Rd 14 rooms 01274 492292 www.listerhotelbradford.co.uk ⑯

BRADFORD

★★★

The Midland Forster Square 90 bedrooms 01274 735735 www.peelhotels.co.uk **17**

Jurys Inn 2 Thornton Road 200 bedrooms 01274 848500 www.jurysinns.com **18**

Campanile Roydsdale Way, 127 bedrooms
01274 683683 www.campanile-bradford.co.uk **19**

Mercure Bradford Road Bingley 103 bedrooms 0844 8159004 www.mercure.com **20**

Dubrovnik Oak Avenue 01274 543511 www.dubrovnikhotelbradford.co.uk **21**

Hilton Hall Ings 120 bedrooms 01274 734734 www.hilton.co.uk/bradford **22**

Gomersal Park Moor Lane 100 bedrooms
01274 869386 www.gomersalparkhotel.com **23**

★★★★

Cedar Court Mayo Avenue Rooley Lane 130 bedrooms
01274 406606 www.cedarcourthotels.co.uk **24**

Hollins Hall Hollins Hill Baildon 122 bedrooms 01274 530053 www.marriott.co.uk **25**

Parking Ⓟ

1 Hall Ings	526 spaces	**8** Jacobs Well	198 spaces
2 Burnett street	116 spaces	**9** Sharpe Street	98 spaces
3 Crown court	180 spaces	**10** Simes Street	77 spaces
4 Leisure Exchange	996 spaces	**11** St Thomas	132 spaces
5 Kirkgate Centre	650 spaces	**12** Wigan Street	43 spaces
6 New Southgate	432 spaces	**13** Oastler Centre	404 spaces
7 Pine Street	60 spaces	**14** Randall Well St	80 spaces

BRADFORD

**ⓘ Bradford Visitor Information Centre
Britannia House, Broadway
01274 433678 www.visitbradford.com**

water features are an integral part of the city's new Centenary Square

LEEDS

Generally acknowledged as Yorkshires "capital city", Leeds is centrally placed within the region, and roughly equidistant between London and Glasgow. Like many European cities, the last twenty years have witnessed a sea change in character and attractiveness.   Regeneration schemes, commercial investment and a growing focus on arts, culture and tourism have sparked a revival in Leeds fortunes as a "must see" place to visit.   Nowhere visible is the stereotype of the grimy north: Victorian slums; back to back housing; cloth caps and whippets - not that this was ever an accurate portrayal of Leeds - and what there is in this vibrant city now is characterised by a valuable built heritage; chic retail offerings, a wealth of choice in dining, a comprehensive range of hotels, and a variety of attractions and activities for the visitor, whether from Bradford or Brisbane, Tadcaster or Timbuktu. In all these changes, Leeds retains much of its heritage and character, and is easily worth a few days of anyone's time.

History

Leeds early roots can be traced back to the 8thC AD. The Venerable Bede's Ecclesiastical History refers to Loidis as a place where the kings of the first half of the 7th century allegedly built themselves a "country seat". The name Loidis probably referred to the area now occupied by two villages to the east of the present city: Ledsham and Ledston. Over time Loidis became Leodis, then Ledes, then Leeds.   Those born in the city are sometimes referred to as Loiners, a term thought to derive from Loidis although an alternative explanation is that a Loiner is someone born within the sound of the church bells of Briggate. Leeds' mushrooming growth in the 19thC resulted in a plethora of yards and closes around Briggate whose back entrances were known as "Low Inns" or "Loins" hence "Loiner". Like many settlements, Leeds early growth – probably around the 13thC - centred around the parish church and river crossing. The crossing - Leeds Bridge - is still in place, although the present cast iron structure dates from 1730.   The city's commercial life developed along the road to the bridge, known as Briggate, and was centred around the woollen industry. Briggate became a flourishing commercial centre and from being a relatively insignificant town, by the 17thC Leeds ranked among the more important centres in Yorkshire. Growth continued unabated through the 18th and 19thC, giving prominence to the city as one of the foremost in northern England.   The population had reached 150,000 by 1840 and the economy broadened to

LEEDS

Granary Wharf at night

LEEDS

encompass transport - including development of the canal network - particularly the Leeds Liverpool canal.   But beyond the realms of the woollen trade and transport, the city developed multiple strands of economic activity including the manufacture of machinery for spinning, steam engines and gears as well as chemicals leather and pottery. Coal mining developed and the still operational Middleton Railway became the first commercial railway in the world, transporting coal into the centre of Leeds.   City status was achieved in 1893. With striking and expensive new public buildings like the Public Library and the General Post Office and with the opulent arcades threading through the blocks on either side of the main streets, the city consolidated its role as Yorkshire's first city and one of the most important in the UK outside London.   In modern times the city has continued to evolve. Widespread slum clearance took place in the 50's and 60's and the city centre in particular has undergone a comprehensive transformation over the last twenty years making it an exciting and entertaining place to be – day or night.

Getting here

Leeds is easily reached from most parts of the UK and much of Europe.

Rail Leeds City station is in the heart of the centre and one of the busiest in the UK with connections to most places. London is about 2.5 hours on the intercity service (from Kings Cross), a similar time from Edinburgh, and for those already resident in the county, most towns have rail connections into the city.

Road Leeds lies at the head of the UK's main spine motorway, the M1. This also links into the cross Pennine M62 (running from Liverpool to Hull).

Bus Most services arrive at and depart from the bus station at the far side of the market, although some more local services can be boarded on Eastgate, Park Row, South Parade or Infimary Street.

destination	services	frequency
Birmingham	310/360	3x per day
Bradford	72	7 mins
Bridlington	845	3x per day
Castleford	163/166/167/168	15 mins
Edinburgh	381	1x per day
Filey	845	3x per day
Halifax	508	30 mins
Harrogate	36	15 mins
Huddersfield	202/203/220/229	20 mins/2hr/30 min
Hull	390	1x per day
Ilkley	X84	hourly
Keighley	760	30 mins
Liverpool	60	hourly
London	561/M12	4x per day
Heathrow/Gatwick	240	4x per day
Malton	840/843/844/845	20 mins
Manchester	60/380/390	hourly
Otley	33/33A/X84	30 mins
Pontefract	410	30 mins
Ripon	36	15 mins
Scarborough	843	hourly
Selby	402	30 mins
Sheffield	310/320/321/324	7x per day
Skipton	X84	hourly
Tadcaster	840/843/844/845	20 mins
Wakefield	110/117/189/444	20 mins/hourly
Wetherby	98/99	30 mins
Whitby	840	7x per day
York	840/843/844/845	20 mins

What to see and do

Large cities now offer much to the visitor and Leeds is no exception. The city centre is a compact, vibrant area with a wide range of modern and classic hotels, innumerable restaurants, bars and a pulsating nightlife.   One way to experience what the city has to offer the visitor is by walking through it.

● ● ● ● **Walk 1 The Historic core** (map page 167)

● This starts in City Square, and finishes at the Royal Armouries. **Boar Lane** originally linked Briggate, the heart of the cloth industry, with the manor house sited where City Square now is, and later with the 4th cloth hall

● on the site of the Metropole hotel. With growth in the 19thC, Boar Lane became an important commercial thoroughfare, and most of the buildings

● on the south side from this period survive. Foremost amongst these was the development of what is now Leeds City Station between 1869 to 1876.

● Much of this development was enabled by John Barran, a clothing manu-facturer and property developer who was also a Lord Mayor of Leeds.

● On the corner of Boar Lane with City Square is the 1899 original York

LEEDS

John Barran Entrepreneur and Philanthropist 1821-1905

John Barran was a successful Victorian businessman born into a well to do London family. He moved to Leeds in 1842 and founded a clothing manufacturing company, which pioneered ready to wear clothing. He was Lord Mayor of Leeds in 1870-71. His architectural legacy is prolific as he was the sponsor of buildings which line much of Boar Lane and the west side of Lower Briggate, as well as the warehouse he had built in Moroccan style in St Pauls Street. He was the driving force behind the Councils acquisition of Roundhay Park and its creation as one of Europe's foremost public urban parks. His public responsibilities extended to acting as a Liberal Member of parliament for nearly twenty years before being made a Baronet in 1895.

WALK 1

LEEDS

shire District Bank, which remained so until the 1980's. Now a bar, it's distinctive copper domed rotunda and elegantly decorated granite elevations testify to the richness and eloquence of Victorian architecture. Griffin Hotel ① built to coincide with the opening of Leeds City station in the 1850s. The clock, high up on the corner elevation with Mill Hill, uses the letters of the Griffin Hotel instead of numerals.
Holy Trinity Church ② Redevelopment has replaced most of the original buildings on the north side, and this is the sole surviving building west of Briggate and built in the 1720's, from a design by William Etty, a York architect. The design and decoration reflects the wealth and generosity of 18thC Leeds merchants and bears a striking resemblance to the church of St Martins in the Fields in London, which was built about the same time. The Church is still in use, and also promotes arts events and has a food kitchen for the homeless.

The Griffin Clock

Continue east on Boar Lane, to the junction with Briggate; one of the cities oldest and busiest thoroughfares. To the north is the pedestrianised shopping street. The building on the north east corner of Briggate is notable for its use of local (Burmantofts) terracotta tiles. This ornate highly decorated building of 1904 was originally occupied by the renowned gents outfitters, Hepworths.   Lower Briggate forms the core of old Leeds. Time Ball Building ③ Originally built in the early 19thC, the building was occupied until the 1970's by John Dyson and Sons, jewellers and watchmakers. There are two clocks on the frontage; one dating from the 1860s, (with the inscription "Tempus Fugit") and one from 1910, together with the original front facade.   Although the ground floor is now a restaurant, most original interior fittings survive including ornate chandeliers

1. Griffin Hotel
2. Trinity Church
3. Dysons Time Ball
4. Queens Court
5. Leeds Bridge
6. Corn Exchange
7. White Cloth Hall
8. St Peter's Minster
9. Brewery Wharf
10. Crown Point Bridge
11. The Armouries

CITY WALK 1
THE HISTORIC
CORE

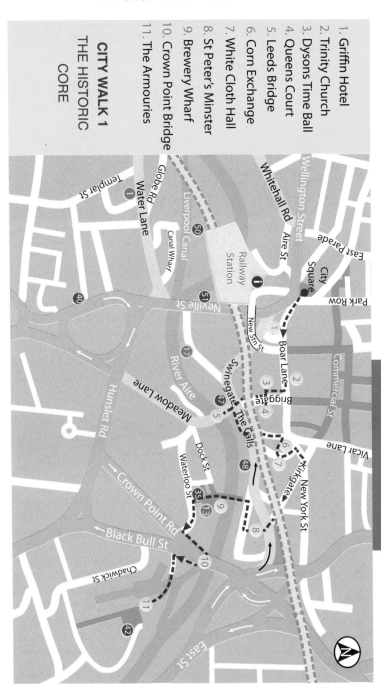

LEEDS

Time Balls : *The word time ball refers to the practice originally adopted by mariners to ensure chronometers were accurate and involved timing the drop of a large wooden or metal ball to allow synchronisation of clocks. The practice became redundant in the 1920s with the emergence of radio signals [the pips]. Time balls were erected near major railway stations as it became evident in the earlier part of the 19thC that local time varied widely across the country by as much as 15 minutes and railway companies had a commercial interest in ensuring times were accurate and synchronised. John Dyson's became the providers of this service in Leeds.*

WALK 1

acquired from the Paris Exhibition of 1890. Also of note is the mechanism which raised and lowered the window displays into a basement vault. Queens Court ④ on the other side of Briggate, dates from 1714. The frontage building was a woollen cloth merchants house; with business premises to the rear; now a courtyard populated with gay bars. These buildings sit on one of the medieval burgage plots on which the city's land holdings developed and grew.

A burgage plot was a town rental property (to use modern terms) owned by a king or lord. The property ("burgage tenement") usually consisted of a house on a long narrow plot of land, with the narrow end facing the street. Rental payment ("tenure") was usually in the form of money, but each "burgage tenure" arrangement was unique, and could include services. As population grew, "burgage plots" could be split into smaller additional units. Owners of burgage plots were generally freemen called burgesses, and formed the backbone of the local commercial activity.

On the other side of Briggate beyond the railway, on the corner with Swinegate stands the Cosmopolitan Hotel. This was built in 1879 for John Barran on the site of his first ready made clothing workshop. Opposite is the Malmaison Hotel, a restoration of the former headquarters of Leeds City tramways. The Baroque style building dates from 1915 and is built from distinctive red bricks and terracotta. The site would have been previously occupied by a woollen mill.

Leeds Bridge ⑤ This is the city's historic river crossing; a bridge having been here since 1207. The current bridge is an early ironworks structure of 1730 and substantially rebuilt in 1871. The single span arch is embellished with vine scrolls and a perforated balustrade decorated with embossed flower heads. The east side has the arms of Leeds City corporation, and on the opposite side the names of the "great and the good" of the time. The bridge is notable on three counts. Firstly, it is the site of the original river crossing with previous medieval bridges housing the original woollen trade market; second, it marks the western end of the Aire and Calder Navigation, an engineering feat which, completed in the early 18thC, enabled boats to navigate the river to Leeds (River Aire) and Wakefield (River Calder). Thirdly, the bridge was the site chosen, in 1888, by the inventor of moving pictures, Louis de Prince, to make his first film – a plaque on the bridge records this fact. (there is more about this in the Armley Mills Museum see page 184)

Corn Exchange ⑥ This distinctive building, one of only three original corn exchanges surviving in the UK (the others are in Cambridge and Edinburgh), was designed by Cuthbert Brodrick, renowned architect of Leeds Town Hall, in the early 1860's and held by many to represent the apotheosis of his prolific work output. The rare oval floor plan is probably based on the Halle au Ble in Paris. The interior is light and airy with oval galleries looking down into the central hall. Built for trading of corn, it has undergone at least two restorations to become a centre of boutique shops and a restaurant.

spectacular interior of the Corn Exchange

The White Cloth Hall ⑦ Behind this impressive building lies one of Leeds earliest cloth markets. Built around 1775 it was the third such facility in Leeds, although only part - probably less than 20% of the original floor plan - survives. The term white cloth was used to denote undyed wool. Much of the undyed woollen cloth manufactured in West Riding during this period was brought to Leeds and it is estimated between 4,000 and 5,000 clothiers attended the Leeds cloth halls each week. With more than 70 firms of cloth merchants in the city at that time, Leeds had the lions share of the country's woollen cloth exports. The restored building is used as restaurants and shops. At the rear of the Corn Exchange on Assembly Street is the Assembly Rooms, now a club, and which was

LEEDS

WALK 1

erected in the latter part of the 18th century by the more prominent merchants and traders, who frequented the White Cloth Hall for business, as a centre for recreation and entertainment. (Similar purpose, although grander, buildings were erected in other Yorkshire cities; notably in York).

Leeds Minster ⑧ To get to the church, which stands on a site occupied by successive parish church buildings since the 7thC, turn into Crown Street, and then right into Kirkgate. This somewhat down at heel thoroughfare is however one of Leeds more historic streets; originally leading from the parish church out to green fields and pastures, it predates Briggate and the buildings lining it are nearly all 18th and 19thC. The present church, St Peters, designed by Robert Chantrell, dates from c.1840 and became a Minster in 2012. Although not a cathedral it is, arguably, one of the more important churches of this early Victorian period and is largely unaltered. It was the largest and most ambitious church building erected in England since St Pauls Cathedral 140 years earlier and reflected the Victorians ambition to create churches whose size, and method of ministry appealed to the burgeoning industrial working class. The building is dominated by a tower that also provides the main entrance. The tower follows the perpendicular style common in churches in the 14th to 16thC, such retro styling being a common characteristic of Victorian church building. The interior contains some notable features. The Angel Screen at the entrance is a contemporary distinctive glass engraving of 1997. The main body of the church is a lofty but noble, well proportioned space from which can be seen the original large organ casing. Of note are the dominant pulpit and the apse, with its fan vaulted roof and stained glass windows. Some of the glass is 16thC Flemish - and windows were specifically designed to accommodate these surviving pieces.

LEEDS

There are Venetian mosaics in the apse as well as an early 10thC stone cross. The reredos (the screen behind the altar) is marble and there are many artefacts and memorials including a brass plaque commemorating the Antarctic explorer, Captain Oates. The well maintained Churchyard offers a peaceful retreat from passing traffic. The church is open everyday. It has a café serving light refreshments.

0113 2452036
www.leedsparishchurch.org.uk

Reverend Walter Hook Clergyman *1798- 1875*

Walter Hook was a prominent Victorian churchman; the driving force for rebuilding of Leeds Parish Church and its vicar from 1837-59. In a city of rapid growth and much poverty, the high church was in the minority. Hook persuaded the City Council to levy a rate towards the cost of building the new church. He was then instrumental in creating 30 parishes in the city from the single one he inherited and when successful moved to one of these smaller parishes, taking a stipend cut at the same time. He was also behind many of the churches built in the city in this period and influential in creating wholesale improvements in education standards, being largely responsible for the introduction of some 30 schools. He became Dean of Chichester in 1859. His contribution to the city is marked by a statue in City Square.

Brewery Wharf ⑨ To get here, walk along The Calls to the south of the church, and walking back briefly westwards to just before 42 The Calls (a fashionable boutique hotel and restaurant converted from an old corn mill) turn into a ginnel leading to a pedestrian bridge over the Aire. On the south side is a building originally designed as a museum and confer-ence centre but now converted to restaurants and offices. In the forecourt stands a contemporary thematic sculpture crafted in bronze and stain-less steel to record the areas former usage as wharfage and cornmills.

Crown Point Bridge ⑩ A short link from Brewery Wharf leads onto Bowman Lane and the bridge lies at the eastern end. This is one of a number of bridges built to cope with Leeds dramatic expansion in the Victorian period as Leeds Bridge became unable to accommodate in-creasing levels of traffic. The bridge is single span cast iron, 120ft wide, with an ornate fretted iron parapet and was originally a toll bridge. On the east side of Crown Point Road, Armouries Way leads to the Armouries.

The Royal Armouries Museum ⑪ has on display just part of the vast collection in the custody of the Royal Armouries; other locations include the Tower of London and Fort Nelson near Portsmouth. The Leeds mu-seum house 70,000 examples of arms, armour and artillery from antiquity to the present day. There are royal armours of the Tudor and Stuart kings; of the English Civil Wars, as well as British and foreign military weapons, hunting and sporting weapons, and an exceptional collection of oriental arms and armour. The Royal Armouries also has a significant collection of fine and decorative arts, and a special collection of material relating to the Tower of London, including antique prints and drawings and paintings. The library contains material relating to the history, development and use of arms, armour, artillery and fortifications. It has collections of original military manuals, drill books, and fencing manuals.The venue also has a tilt yard where medieval jousts are recreated as well as falconry and oth-er historical forms of entertainment are re-enacted. The Museum is open daily. There is no admission charge. Bus service 28 runs near the entrance to the centre of the city.   0113 220 1999. www.royalarmouries.org

WALK 1 ▼

LEEDS

The Royal Armouries

MEN-AT-ARMS

WALK 2   Retail Therapy and Entertainment

Befitting a city of its size, Leeds offers a wide range of shopping and entertainment. Many attractions can be experienced by walking through the centre.   Starting just east of the bus station, the cultural quarter is a rapidly growing zone offering a range of entertainment.

LEEDS

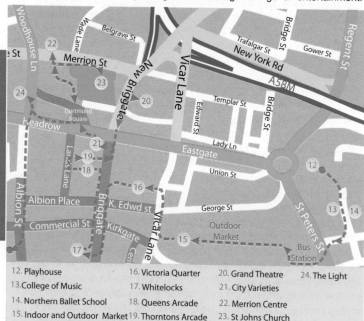

12. Playhouse	16. Victoria Quarter	20. Grand Theatre	24. The Light
13. College of Music	17. Whitelocks	21. City Varieties	
14. Northern Ballet School	18. Queens Arcade	22. Merrion Centre	
15. Indoor and Outdoor Market	19. Thorntons Arcade	23. St Johns Church	

LEEDS   CITY WALK   2
RETAIL THERAPY AND ENTERTAINMENT

WALK 2

The West Yorkshire Playhouse 12 Built on the part of the site of the old Quarry Hill flats complex, the Playhouse offers a programme of plays, concerts and comedy. Since opening in 1990, it has established an international reputation and regularly collaborates with other regional producing theatres and companies. It has a 750 seat auditorium (Quarry Theatre) and a smaller 350 seat one (Courtyard theatre). 0113 2137700 www.wyp.org.uk

Leeds College of Music 13 the largest music college in the UK with a particular specialism in jazz. Founded in 1965, it moved to the current modern buildings in 1997. There are regular performances throughout the academic year. It also hosts regular -free- lunchtime concerts on most Wednesdays through the year. 0113 223434 www.lcm.ac.uk

Northern Ballet 14 headquarters and school of dance is also nearby. A new building provides for the largest purpose-built space for dance outside London. It is unique in housing both classical ballet and contemporary dance (Phoenix Dance Theatre). It hosts a varied programme of ballet and dance across the year. 0844 848 2705 www.northernballet.com

Leeds Market 15 One of the largest such markets in Europe with over 600 stalls. The outdoor section adjoins the bus station and the indoor section links through to Vicar Lane. The western side is in an iconic building built in 1904, with a spectacular roofscape of domes and cupolas. It was here that Michael Marks, a Polish refugee, started his business in 1884, selling all items for a penny, becoming Marks and Spencers in 1894, and now one of the largest UK retailers. A commemorative clock marks the site of the original penny stall.

the delicate roofline of the market hall

LEEDS

The Victoria Quarter 16 A little further along Vicar Lane, and providing a link to Briggate, is the Victoria Quarter. Built between 1898 and 1904 it is now a collection of up market and expensive boutique stores centred around Harvey Nichols. The quarter consists of three blocks divided across two streets - Queen Victoria Street and King Edward Street - and was designed by the well known Victorian theatre architect- Frank Matcham (who was also responsible for the iconic Royal Hall in Harrogate).

173

WALK 2

LEEDS

The scheme replaced the area known as the Shambles- where all the butchers and meat traders congregated. Restored in the early 1990's with a glazed free standing roof over Queen Victoria St - to the dismay of some architectural critics - the whole complex is worthy of time spent browsing even if the merchandise is beyond many folks price range! The architecture, in true Matcham style, is rich, flamboyant and well proportioned, using exotic detailing with much use of terracotta, marbles and mosaics. The shopfronts are in mahogany and some have curved glass. The County Arcade - the northernmost of the three thoroughfares - has a richly decorated roof treatment with a central dome depicting the Leeds industries of the day. Nestling in this group of buildings is the Harvey Nichols store- one of three locations outside London - and a place where it is said if you have to ask the price, you can't afford it. Worth a visit, even just to ogle. The site originally contained the Palace Theatre- which was why Frank Matcham was appointed in the first instance - but this was demolished in 1962- the inscription of the name above Harvey Nichols rear entrance being the only trace. The western side faces Briggate - always the wide market street of the medieval town and still the core of the shopping centre containing most big brand name stores, many housed in 19thC buildings.

transforming Matchams Victorian design to the 21st century

Whitelocks 17 The existence of the burgage plots is exemplified by Turks Head Yard, a narrow ginnel leading to the famous old pub which has been serving ale since 1716, and although rebuilt in 1866, there can be seen the remains of the brewhouse and associated cottages. The interior exudes rich decoration with stained glass, engraved mirrors, marble counters and brasswork. There are similar pubs -perhaps not as iconic- on the west side of Briggate accessed through narrow ginnels (The Ship, Pack Horse Inn and The Angel). The west side of Briggate has two historic arcades leading to Lands Lane.

Queens Arcade 18 of 1889 has an unprepossessing entrance from Briggate, but a grander one from Lands Lane. The shopfronts - all brightly coloured - are divided with ornate pilasters which support the overhanging gallery on each side. The gallery gives access to a second level of shops although few are now used as such. Above is a glass roof supported on multi coloured steel trusses. Originally, the upper floor on the north side was part of the old Queens hotel.

Thorntons Arcade 19 runs parallel to the Queens arcade, constructed on a former burgage plot and dates from 1877. It's ornate gothic style was frequently favoured by the Victorians. The arcade is notable for its animated clock which contains replica figures from historic novels such as Ivanhoe and Robin Hood. Both arcades house mainly independent shops unique to the city.

Grand Theatre 20 Built in 1877/8 (the architect was George Corson responsible for many buildings in the city in the mid 19thC) in part Gothic, part Romanesque style. As with many British theatres of this era, class differences were enforced by different zones of seating for and completely separate entrances and exits in the form of a web of staircase and passages which enabled such social and economic separation. The theatre was restored in 2008; the main auditorium retains its original style with opulent decoration, a richly encrusted saucer domed ceiling, and ornate plasterfronts to the balconies. It promotes an active and comprehensive programme of events. It is also the home of Opera North who regularly host small scale events in the assembly rooms on the south side of the building.   0844 8482706 www.leedsgrandtheatre.com

The Headrow is a broad boulevard created in the 1930s as part of a civic inspired scheme to improve traffic flow in the city. It is one of Leeds principal thoroughfares, running on an east-west axis from Quarry Hill to Westgate and Park Lane. It originally formed the northern boundary of the medieval town. Along this busy thoroughfare lie many of Leeds more significant shops, as well as the Town Hall, Art Gallery, and Henry Moore Institute. The buildings on the south side are mainly 19thC but those on the north side, from the Eastgate roundabout through to the Park Row intersection were nearly all constructed in the period 1928-1932, on a design by Reginald Blomfield and reflects the "Beaux Arts" approach of his design of London's Regent Street.

City Varieties 21 on the south side is a Victorian music hall built in 1865, as an extension to the music room of the White Swan Inn (which still adjoins), for the Leeds entrepreneur George Thornton

LEEDS

Briggate the main shopping street

WALK 2

(who also built Thorntons arcade). It has a long and narrow auditorium which creates a unique atmosphere. Now restored, the interior is largely original with decorative cast iron columns supporting two tiers of bow fronted balconies, looking onto a shallow stage.
The theatre enjoyed earlier fame as home to the long running BBC
programme "The Good Old Days" which recreated the atmosphere of
a Victorian music hall in both performance and in the period dress the
audience were required to wear. The show ran for 30 years to 1983 and
played host to over 2000 performers -
including many well known celebrities.
On the north side, in the midst of the
1930's development, is **Dortmund
Square**. A small civic space created
in 1980 it was named to reflect Leeds
twinning with Dortmund in Germany.
In the square is a bronze sculpture of
a German drayman donated by the
city of Dortmund to reflect the brewery interests of both cities. The north
side leads into the St John's Centre - a shopping mall built in the 1985-6
period and named for the adjoining parish church. Walking through the
centre to Merrion Street, gives access to another, earlier shopping mall.
The Merrion Centre (22) This was an early mixed use development opening in 1964, and consisted of shops, an indoor market, nightclubs and pubs,
offices, a bowling alley, cinema, car parks and hotel. All bar the cinema exist
today. The centre marks the northerly limit of Leeds city centre retail core.
St Johns Church (23) Retracing steps towards the Headrow, this building the church pre-dates St Peters Minster having been built in 1634. It
was endowed by John Harrison, an early benefactor of the city. The exterior is typical of that period, with square mullioned windows, buttresses,
battlements and built from fine grained sandstone. Unusually, it has two
naves, divided by a central arcade. The internal arrangements and decoration include wooden corbels carved as angels, and plaster mouldings
with owl shaped motifs (the Leeds city symbol). There is much intricate
carved woodwork by the well known 17thC carpenter Francis Gunby
whose ornate woodwork fittings still grace many churches in the region.

LEEDS

John Harrison- *Cloth Merchant 1579-1656*
A cloth merchant and land owner in the city, he was active in the English civil war, although it is unclear on what side. He was instrumental in the city securing its first charter from Charles 1st in 1626 and later in acquiring all the manorial rights in the city from the Crown. Besides paying for and endowing St Johns church, he was the major benefactor in the establishment of a new purpose built home for Leeds Grammar school in 1624, and sponsored homes for the poor. His statue is in City Square.

The Light 24 Further along the Headrow, fashioned from the shell of Blomfield buildings, The Light is a new compact shopping centre containing a cinema complex, health and fitness club, and hotel. From The Light, retrace eastwards and turn south along Albion Street into the central shopping zone, and the new Leeds Shopping Plaza, before exiting out to City Square

WALK 3 Commerce Civic Pride Culture ● ● ● ●

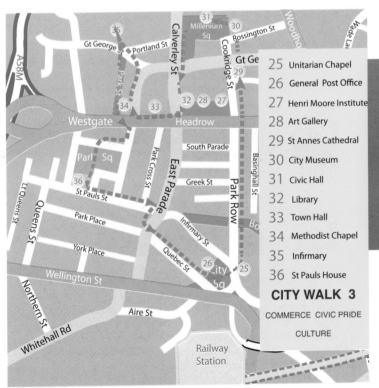

25 Unitarian Chapel
26 General Post Office
27 Henri Moore Institute
28 Art Gallery
29 St Annes Cathedral
30 City Museum
31 Civic Hall
32 Library
33 Town Hall
34 Methodist Chapel
35 Infirmary
36 St Pauls House

CITY WALK 3

COMMERCE CIVIC PRIDE
CULTURE

LEEDS

WALK 3

Starting from City Square, this walk takes in the city's main civic elements. The Square was formed in the late 19thC and marked the expansion of this side of the city. On the south side is the well known Queens Hotel. The present building, faced in Portland Stone, was built in 1937 to a design by the railway company architect. The interior is unaltered with expensive finishes in art deco style. Mill Hill Unitarian Chapel ⑮ on the east side adjoining the Park Plaza Hotel, this is the only building to predate the square's formation. It dates from 1848, and replaces a previous chapel which had, as its minister from 1767 to 1773, the well known theologian, philosopher and dissenter, Joseph Priestley –the man credited with discovering oxygen. General Post Office ㉖ now restaurants and apartments. The facade incorporates sculptures, meant to convey forms of communication. There are a number of statues in the Square. The largest, in blackened bronze, is of The Black Prince (son of King Edward III) and the smaller statues are of well known figures either with a Leeds connection or known for their scientific endeavour– James Watt (inventor of the steam engine); Joseph Priestley (theologian and discoverer of oxygen); Rev Walter Hook (Vicar of St Peters) and John Harrison. Moving onto Park Row, marks the eastern end of the financial quarter of the city, although the thoroughfare itself can be traced back to medieval times as the main route between what is now the Headrow and the Manor House (where the Post Office now stands). This was where the banks and offices were constructed in late Victorian times. Henry Moore Institute ㉗ and Leeds Art Gallery ㉘ which adjoins it lie north of the Headrow on Cookridge St. Particularly visible because of

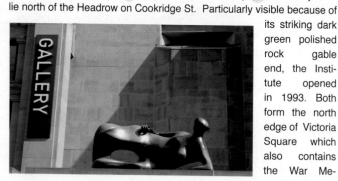

its striking dark green polished rock gable end, the Institute opened in 1993. Both form the north edge of Victoria Square which also contains the War Memorial. The Institute and Art Gallery house works of art and sculpture with, besides those of Henry Moore, pieces by famous artists such as Rodin, Jacob Kramer and Dame Barbara Hepworth, as well as work by lesser known and newly emerging artists. The collection is designated as being of national importance and only second to that of the Tate Gallery. The galleries are open all week. There is no admission charge. 0113 2478256 www.henry-moore.org www.leeds.gov.uk

LEEDS

Roman Catholic Cathedral of St Annes 29 lies further up Cookridge St.   Built in 1904 it has an striking front built in a warm limestone with carved detail relief. The interior has seen alterations over the years, but is still an impressive place particularly with a very recent (2006) enhancement. Notable is the Lady the Chapel which contains a reredos by Augustus Pugin - the architect of the tower containing Big Ben - and which was made in 1842 for the previous cathedral building.

City Museum 30 Opened in 2008 following restoration, it was originally the Mechanics Institute built in the 1860's following an architectural competition, won by the architect of the town hall, Cuthbert Brodrick. Historically, Mechanics Institutes were educational establishments that emerged in the Victorian era as the industrial revolution created a demand for adult education of working men, particularly in technical subjects. They were often sponsored by local industrialists who considered their businesses would benefit from being able to recruit and keep better skilled employees. Mechanics Institutes became 'libraries' for the adult working class, and provided alternatives to gambling and drinking. The building style shows strong Parisian influence. The imposing arched doorway includes a carved pediment with symbols representing arts and sciences. The building has a circular lecture hall (often known as the Albert Hall) surrounded by a gallery. Itwas used as a technical college into the early 1900s when it became too small for a growing educational service and it became the Leeds Civic Theatre, remaining so until conversion to a museum. The Museum has a wide variety of exhibits, revolving around the city's history and include a large map of Leeds printed on the floor, and a scale model of the former Quarry Hill Flats. Notable is the Leeds Tiger- a tigerskin rug presented to the Museum in the 19thC with a very chequered history. The Ancient Worlds gallery has archeological exhibits from this country and overseas, including a Roman floor mosaic discovered at Aldborough (nr Boro'bridge see page 385), Greek marble tomb doors, and an Egyptian mummy. Admission is free. 0113 2243732 www.leeds.gov.uk/citymuseum

Facing the Museum is Millennium Square. Created as part of the Millennium celebrations, it has become the focal point for many events; there is a skating rink in the early new year; a German Christmas market in November and December and a host of other entertainment throughout the year including outdoor concerts, civic ceremonies, and fairs.

LEEDS

The southern part of the square is Nelson Mandela gardens, a small civic garden, and The Carriageworks theatre - the successor to the civic theatre. This venue puts on a wide range of events throughout the year. It is situated on first-floor level overlooking an historic courtyard which in early Victorian times was the home of the 'West Riding Carriage Manufactory', from which the theatre takes its name. There is a main auditorium, seating 350, as well as a more intimate studio seating 65.   0113 224 3801   www.carriageworkstheatre.org.uk

Leeds Civic Hall 31 With its white portland stone facade and green slate roof, the civic hall looms majestically over the north side of the Square, and has been home to the City Council since 1933. The pediment over the portico contains the Leeds coat of arms whilst the towers on either side are reminiscent of the architectural style of Sir Christopher Wren. Two smaller freestanding pedestals either side of the front elevation are each topped by a gilded owl - for long the formal Leeds symbol.The interior of the building is what might be expected of a civic building of this age; all very formal: a grand entrance - flanked by vivid green columns and a grand black and white marble staircase, sumptuous banqueting hall, and an imposing council chamber.

The Leeds Owl

This longstanding symbol of the city originates from the coat of arms of the first Alderman, Sir John Savile, a 17thC MP and landowner and who became Alderman on the granting of the first charter by Charles 1st making Leeds a city borough.

Set around Millenium Square are bars and restaurants making this little area the focus of much of Leeds not inconsiderable nightlife.   The west side is dominated by the Brotherton Wing of the General Infirmary - one of the biggest hospitals in the country. This Wing is a 1940s addition to an extensive Victorian hospital designed by Sir George Gilbert Scott. Moving south back towards the Headrow, along Calverley Street, the buildings on both sides reflect the highlights of Leeds' Victorian expansion. On the corner of Calverley Street and Gt George Street is the Leeds Schools Board offices, whose detailing strongly reflects that of the Town Hall opposite.

Central Library 32 Fronting on to the Headrow, the library built in 1884, was originally council offices. In Franco-Italianate style, it provides an imposing facade to the civic space on the north side of The Headrow. The interior of the building is remarkable for its richly decorated fixtures and fittings. The full height inner hall -lit with a glass roof- is in renaissance style with round arch openings, some with stained glass.

The first floor is characterised by vaults carried on arches decorated in terracotta, and on the floor above the local studies library is galleried and lit by a long clerestory roof. There is much carved stone and coloured glass throughout the interior, and on the ground floor facing the Headrow is the ornately decorated hall with its tiled vaulted ceiling, formerly the reading room but now a cafe with strikingly rich decoration.

Town Hall 33 One of the city's most imposing buildings, and still one of the largest purpose built town halls in the UK, it was designed by Cuthbert Brodrick who was successful in winning a design competition sponsored by the council - the first of a number he would go on to win in the city. Rapid expansion in the19thC had rendered previous buildings unsuitable and the Council aspired to a larger building to fit growing responsibilities, and of a style and prominence to reflect a growing stature and reputation. Indeed, some prominent citizens wanted to create "a noble municipal palace", an ambition fulfilled when Queen Victoria herself opened the new building in 1858. The striking design has become a symbol of Leeds, as well as a visual icon of local government. It was built for a variety of functions including a court, police station (with bridewell) concerts and other civic events. It was subject to much criticism during construction, as with many public building projects of this ilk, original cost estimates were vastly exceeded with the council seemingly willing to pay any price in order to create a municipal building it regarded as fit for purpose. This was at a time when although the industrial growth of the city seemed limitless, great poverty abounded. The Headrow façade is set on a plinth with imposing steps up to the colonnaded entrance, flanked by statues of lions. Above the colonnade is the tower- a later addition to the design (and costed in 1855 at £5,500) - supported by a four sided colonnade. Entering from the south colonnade, there is a vestibule with a Minton tiled floor (restored in 2002 by the same firm who laid the original floor). In the east apse is a marble statue of Queen Victoria, and in the west apse, a similar statue of Prince Albert. The main space, the Victoria Hall, is a splendid basilica style space with opulent Victorian decoration- again reflecting the city fathers craving for recognition as a leading city in the land – almost every surface and moulding is gilded or painted. The other dominant feature in the Hall is the organ, one of the largest in Europe, with three manuals and pedals and 6,500 pipes.   Today, the building serves multi purposes, but in the main is used for concerts of varying kinds – notably the world famous Leeds pianoforte competition, a tri-annual musical contest to establish the best young piano player in the world.

Methodist Chapel 34 In contrast to the Town Hall, this is built from local red brick, set off with sandstone dressings, and has a distinctly Baroque feel. The original building dates from 1835, but was substantially altered at the turn of the last century, not least because of a strong desire on behalf of the Methodist hierarchy to have a frontage onto the town hall.

Leeds Town Hall-
the icon of local government

WALK 3

LEEDS

The Infirmary 35 Dating from 1869, it was one of the first hospitals to adopt a pavilion plan form with a central courtyard flanked by corridors giving access to the ward blocks. When designing the hospital, the architect, Sir George Gilbert Scott, consulted Florence Nightingale on the optimum size, equipment and layout. Built of red brick with stone dressings it has richly patterned Venetian Gothic windows. There is a striking resemblance of the facades and decorative detail toLondon's St Pancras station designed by Scott a few years later. To the west of the hospital lies St Georges Church, dating from 1838, notable for its use of the crypt as a shelter for the homeless.   Returning, pass the various modern Law courts on both sides of Park Street, cross the Headrow into Park Square. This formal public space was laid out in 1788 and most of the buildings lining its sides are 19th century, built as residences for the better off in the city. The square is formally laid out with lawns, and a popular destination for city office workers come for lunch and sunbathe on sunny summer days.

St Pauls House 36 dominating the south side of the Square, was designed for Sir John Barran as a factory and warehouse in 1878. It has a distinct Hispano –Moorish style, with much use of red and pink terra-cotta; only the facades are original, the interior having been completely rebuilt as offices in 1975. Moving eastwards along St Pauls Street, return to City Square either along Infirmary Street, or Quebec Street.

the mosque like tower
on St Pauls house

City Centre south of the river

Most of the city centre lies to the north of the river, but the Aire has always been at the heart of Leeds commercial activity and remnants of 19thC commercial activity can be seen today. Dock Street, by Brewery Wharf, is a narrow lane where most of the 18th and 19thC buildings still survive- some converted to apartments and bars, but the effect of these merchant houses and warehouse buildings close up on either side to the pavement is to create a distinctly Victorian feel. It is a popular area for nightlife with a number of restaurants and bars. Of note is the restored Flyboat warehouse at the side of the narrow basin of the Aire and Calder Dock, built in 1818. At the Leeds bridge end of Dock Street, are the former offices of the Aire and Calder Navigation Co and Bridge House, of 1875 which is a form of "flat iron" building, and although a pale resemblance of the well known New York flat iron building, built 27 years later, it may have started a trend in these type of buildings which effectively provide architectural solutions to acute angled street corners. Across Meadow Lane is a recently established river walk following the south bank of the river past the headquarters of superrmarket giant ASDA- with views across the river to the extensive restoration and rebuilding of the former warehouses on the north side of the river- many converted into apartments. Beyond the Victoria Bridge, is Water Lane where Holbeck begins. Once a separate village to Leeds until the late 19thC, a recent regeneration scheme to re-create Holbeck urban village has instilled a new and fresh identity. To the right of Water Lane opposite Bridgwater place (Leeds tallest building), is Canal Wharf, and across the canal is Granary Wharf, both with a range of restaurants and hotels operating from restored 18th and 19thC buildings, although the Doubletree Hotel and associated buildings are new and help lend a lively and vibrant atmosphere, particularly in the evening. The Doubletree Hotel has a bar on the 13th floor that affords panoramic views of the city, both day and night. On the north side of the canal is the towpath which gives pedestrian access to a number of attractions in the western part of the city. Returning to Water Lane, there are bars and restaurants on the south side created as a consequence of the resurgence of the area for modern digital commerce. These are centred around Butcher Street and Foundry Street, and a number of small but atmospheric open areas for sitting out to eat or drink and socialise. Further along Water Lane is Marshall Street. On it's west side near the junction with Water Lane is Temple Works. This is notable for its Egyptian style. Built c.1840, as a flax mill, its façade is based on the Temple of Horus with a chimney in the shape of an obelisk. The unusual design stemmed from the owners interest in Egyptology. John Marshall was a Leeds industrialist and philanthropist (he was instrumental in the creation of Leeds University) who held a patent for a flax spinning machine which ensured him a market monopoly for a number of years and made him wealthy enough to reflect his interest in Egyptology in his business. Today the building is in need of some repair, and can only be viewed from the street. Further along Water Lane on the north side of Globe Road, are distinctive features on the

LEEDS

Leeds skyline, the Italianate towers at Tower Works. This was a textile machine manufacturing works of 1866 and the three towers were erected over a 60 year period. The earliest is the chimney to the original works designed on the lines of the 13thC tower in Verona, the Torre dei Lamberti; the second and tallest (built 1899), is based on the famous campanile of the Duomo in Florence, and the third (built 1920's) reflective of the defensive towers to be found in San Gimignano in Tuscany.

Away from the City centre

Beyond the vibrant fascinating hub that is the city centre, Leeds has several attractions and points of interest which merit a mention and are equally as compelling places to visit as the city centre.

Thwaites Mill

On an island in the River Aire 2 miles south east of the city centre, this is one of the last surviving working watermills. There is also a restored mill managers house, and the working environment of the 19thC can be experienced from a visit. The Museum is open Tues to Sun. There is an admission charge. Bus service 110 from the bus station serves the site.

0113 2762887   www.leeds.gov.uk/thwaitesmill

Industrial Museum at Armley Mills

2 miles west of the city centre, the museum is in early 19thC woollen mills, although mills have been here since the 16thC. Under Benjamin Gott - a wealthy industrialist - Armley Woollen Mills were one of the largest employers in Leeds. Within the museum, there are textile exhibitions and machinery demonstrations. The change from waterwheel to steam power is narrated as well as the history of the city's clothing industry. There is also a gallery tracing the history of cinema projections, as the city was the place for the world's first attempt at cine filming. Open Tues to Sun. There is an admission charge. Bus services 5 and 67 serve the site.   0113 263 7861   www.leeds.gov.uk/armleymills

Kirkstall Abbey

Also on the west side of the city, is Kirkstall Abbey, a ruined Cistercian monastery founded c.1152 and substantially destroyed during Henry VIII's dissolution of the Monasteries. The Abbey ruins, subject of many paintings by artists, including the well known landscape painter J M W Turner, are set in a park bordering the river. Following dissolution, the abbey estate was acquired by the Brudenell family, later the Earls of Cardigan (the 7th Earl achieved infamy for his planning and leading of the disastrous Charge of the Light Brigade in the Crimean war). The Abbey was opened to the public in the late 19thC. The surviving parts of the 12thC gatehouse form part of the structure of the Abbey House museum, on the north side of the Kirkstall Road (A65). The Abbey is one of a number of surviving Cistercian buildings including those at Fountains Abbey, Rievaulx and Bylands (see pages 390-392). The Cistercian order – whose name derives from the Latin name for Citeaux, a town

184

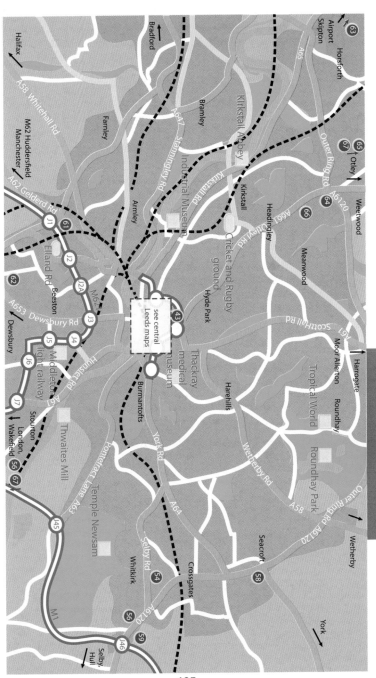

LEEDS

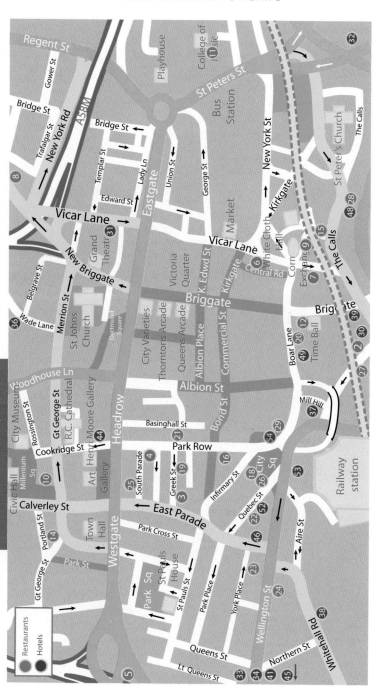

in eastern France where the original abbey started - derived from the Benedictines and focussed on manual labour and self sufficiency. Hence Kirkstall was some distance from medieval Leeds, and with the nearby river the monks produced woollen garments, as well as farming the fields on the rivers edge. During the year, there are regular events held in the abbey park, including the Shakespeare Festival which uses the dramatic setting of the cloisters for performances. There is a visitor centre in the former lay brothers w.c.s, with

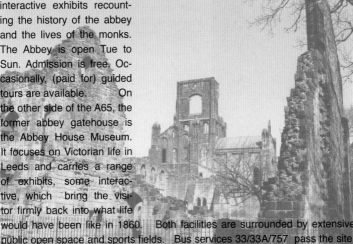

interactive exhibits recounting the history of the abbey and the lives of the monks. The Abbey is open Tue to Sun. Admission is free. Occasionally, (paid for) guided tours are available. On the other side of the A65, the former abbey gatehouse is the Abbey House Museum. It focuses on Victorian life in Leeds and carries a range of exhibits, some interactive, which bring the visitor firmly back into what life would have been like in 1860. Both facilities are surrounded by extensive public open space and sports fields. Bus services 33/33A/757 pass the site.

Headingley

Perhaps the city's best known suburb, Headingley is 2.5 miles from the city centre. A village until 1875, it was absorbed in the inexorable growth of the city. Today the area is renowned both as a student ghetto and where international cricket tests are played. Both have engendered a profusion of bars and restaurants and nightlife in the area is anything but dull. The core of the old village is around St Michaels Church. Built in 1886 on the site of a previous chapel, its style reflects the prosperity and growth of that period, with a spacious interior of dramatic height and many opulent highly crafted internal fittings and fixtures. Two icon pubs face the church; the Skyrack, named for the original medieval

Headingley Cricket Ground

name of the Headingley area and the Original Oak. The Cricket ground (also adjoins the rugby ground) is on North Lane and plays host to Test series cricket as well as county matches during the season. A new grandstand has recently been erected; and has attracted both praise and criticism.

LEEDS

Roundhay Park

On the north east side of the city, 2.5 miles from the city centre, lies one of the more significant public open spaces in Europe. Roundhay Park is over

700 acres of parkland, lakes, woodland and gardens and used by over 1 million visitors a year. In the 13thC it formed part of a hunting park for the De Lacy family; the family having been granted extensive lands in Yorkshire by William the Conqueror. By the early 19thC, ownership of the estate had passed to the Nicholson family who built the Mansion in 1826, and who carried out much landscaping of the grounds to create a formal setting. This included the construction of two lakes – a third was planned but never built on the site now occupied by the arena- as well as a castle folly. In 1871, the park was put up for sale and purchased by a group of city merchants including John Barran (see page 166) - who bought the estate in order to sell it to the City council as a public park. The size of the purchase was such that the council needed an Act of Parliament to raise the necessary funds. A tram service was introduced to connect the park with the city centre in 1892 (some tram poles still survive). On the south western edge of the park, at Oakwood Centre is an ornate clock tower. Known as the Oakwood clock this baroque structure was made by Leeds clock makers Potts in 1904 for the new Kirkgate Market, but never installed and erected on its current site in 1912. The extensive rolling parkland, woodland, landscaped gardens, and lakes provide a wide range of recreational facilities.There is a golf course, outdoor concerts in the arena, which doubles as a cricket pitch; football and rugby pitches as well as extensive walking and cycling trails; skateboarding bowling and tennis. The park contains bandstands, a visitor centre and a café by the boating house at Waterloo lake. For naturalists the park is the home to a wide variety of birds including woodpeckers warblers and swans and small mammals such as foxes and roe deer. There is a walk around Waterloo lake, of about 1hr duration. The Monet and Alhambra Gardens are recent and colourful additions to the attractions. The entrance

Monet Garden

is from the short access road leading to the Mansion. These small gardens are based on those at Giverny in France (which were planted and maintained by Monet) and of the Alhambra Palace Granada in Spain.

Canal Gardens is a further immaculately maintained garden on the west side of Street Lane. The name is misleading since there never was a canal here. The name actually refers to a linear ornamental pond surrounded by well tended gardens. Adjoining these are Coronation Gardens and Kitchen gardens.

turtles at tropical world

Tropical World is perhaps the real draw on this side of the park particularly for children. Adapted from glasshouses which once grew flowers for the park, they now house a comprehensive collection of exotic tropical plants, landscapes and wildlife. Different climates from around the world are reproduced, and the attraction has the largest collection of tropical plants in the UK outside of Kew Gardens. Wildlife include meerkats from the Kalahari desert, a host of rare butterflies, lizards and exotic fish from all over the world. The hot houses are maintained at high temperatures, with pathways winding through lush vegetation. The attraction is open most days. There is an admission charge.

0113 3957400 www.roundhaypark.org.uk

Events are regularly staged in the Park; from outdoor concerts, to firework displays and flower shows, there is a year round programme for all tastes.

0113 214 5715 www.roundhaypark.org.uk

Bus services 2 and 12 run to the park from the city centre (Vicar Lane).

LEEDS

Thackray Medical Museum

Thackrays was a long established Leeds company specialising in medical supplies, and this museum has been created from the vision of the family directors. It is housed in a former workhouse attached to St James Hospital. The museum tells the story of medicine and how it has changed lives. One of the most popular activities for visitors is taking a walk down a back street of Victorian Leeds, complete with authentic sights, sounds and smells. It is open most days. There is an admission charge. It is 1.5 miles from the city centre. Bus services 42/49/50/50A from the citycentre (Eastgate) pass the museum. 0113 2444343 www.thackraymuseum.org

Middleton Light Railway

This is the world's oldest continuously working railway. Founded in 1758 to carry coal from the plethora of small mines then common in the area, it used horse drawn wagons on wooden tracks. It was intended to provide a more efficient means of transporting coal to the wharves on the River Aire, and needed an Act of Parliament to ensure the necessary wayleaves etc could be secured. Steam powered locomotives were introduced in 1812, following the introduction of iron rails, and a railway has operated here ever since. Absorbed into the national rail network, it became the property of the Railway Trust in 1960 after the line closed. Coal mining in Middleton finally ceased in 1968. The railway is run by volunteers and operates services at weekends and on public holidays over a short track between Middleton and Hunslet. There is an engine house in which restored locomotives and rolling stock can be viewed. There is an admission charge. The railway is in Hunslet, 1.5 miles south of the city centre. Bus services 2,3,3a,12, 13,13a from the city centre (Vicar Lane) go as far as Balm Road. 0845 680 1758 www.middletonrailway.org.uk

Temple Newsam

Temple Newsam is one of the great historic estates of England. There are over 1500 acres of parkland – much of it landscaped by Capability Brown in the 18thC and, at its heart, is the main house - a Tudor–Jacobean mansion of 1628. The house is best known as the birthplace of Lord Darnley- husband of Mary Queen of Scots and father of James 1st. Following the seizure of the estate by Queen Elizabeth I, it became home to the Ingram family whose occupation spanned 300 years, culminating in ownership by Lord Halifax – Britains Foreign Secretary in the period up to World War II. Sir Arthur Ingram rebuilt the original house, retaining the central part and built two new wings. He included an inscription on the parapet:

"ALL GLORY AND PRAISE BE GIVEN TO GOD THE FATHER THE SON AND THE HOLY GHOST ON HIGH PEACE ON EARTH GOOD WILL TOWARDS MEN HONOUR AND TRUE ALLEGIANCE TO OUR GRACIOUS KING LOVING AFFECTION AMONGST HIS SUBJECTS HEALTH AND PLENTY BE WITHIN THIS HOUSE"

The interior has been much altered, but there are parts which are original or authentically restored. Notably the Great Hall (the stained glass bay windows), the Terrace Room, where the regency interior is reproduced and the dining room with its original plaster ceiling and frieze and wall panelling. The house contains extensive collections of works, particularly of decorative art. There are ceramics - including much English pottery - some continental and oriental porcelain. There are furniture collections including pieces by Thomas Chippendale - and over 400 paintings on display. Additionally, the museum houses silver and gold collections, tapestries and some original wallpapers. The house is open Tues- Sun. There is an admission charge. The gardens are extensive and renowned for the Rhododendron and Azalea walk as well as the National Plant Collections of Delphinium, Phlox and Aster novi–belgii. There is a kitchen garden with hot houses, playing fields, woodland walks and childrens play areas. Europe's largest working Rare Breeds Farm, with over 400 animals, is set within the original estate Home Farm.

Temple Newsam House

Temple Newsam hosts many events each year from music festivals to fun-fairs and there are regular family activities, demonstrations, and guided walks.

Estate and Farm 0113 264 5535   House 0113 264 7321
www.leeds.gov.uk/templenewsam/visitor

Temple Newsam lies just south of the Leeds suburb of Whitkirk 4.5 miles from the city centre.   Bus service 18/19 from the city centre (Boar Lane) passes Temple Gate, the northern entrance to the estate.

Sporting life

Football

Elland Road Stadium, some two miles south of the city centre is home to **Leeds United**. A large club with a powerful and loyal fan base, the clubs provenance belongs in the English Premier League although recent fortunes have seen it slide into lower leagues. It has a large stadium and matches regularly draw crowds in excess of 20,000.   Outside the ground is a bronze statue to Billy Bremner, a former Leeds and Scotland captain and iconic football hero.   Elland Road Stadium is 2 miles south west of the city centre.   Bus service 51 goes from the city centre (Vicar Lane).

Rugby

Leeds has a regular championship winning team in Rugby League in the form of the Leeds Rhinos, and a top Rugby Union club in the form of the Leeds Tykes. Both play at Headingley in the Carnegie stadium adjoining the cricket ground.

LEEDS

191

Significant investment has been made in the facilities over recent years and the stadium offers an attractive and comfortable environment in which to watch games.   0871 4231315 www.leedscarnegie.co.uk/tickets/index.

Carnegie stadium is in Headingley 2 miles north west of the city centre.   Trains from Leeds city station run to Burley Park, about a 10 minute walk south of the ground.   Bus services from the city centre 19,19a (Boar Lane) and 56 (Eastgate) all go past the end of the access road (St Michaels Lane). Directions also apply to the cricket ground - see below.

Cricket

The Yorkshire County cricket club is headquartered in Headingley, and has been playing cricket there since 1891. The ground is perhaps best known for its regular hosting of Test matches, including the Ashes series, and other international games   The club plays all its county championship home games here or at Scarborough.   A recent investment has been made in the ground in the form of a new grandstand which also provides educational facilities. For county championship and other league matches, it is usually sufficient to turn up at the gate on the day to gain entry; for international matches, tickets needs to be reserved in advance of the date of the match.
                    0871 971 1222 (ticket office) www.yorkshireccc.com/tickets

Festivals

Beyond the shows and performances at the multiplicity of venues in the city there are many other regular events attracting large crowds.

January	Ice Cube Outdoor Millennium Square	www.leeds.gov.uk
February	Valentine's Fair Elland Road	
March	Jazz at the Playhouse West Yorkshire Playhouse	www.wyp.org.uk
May	Yorkshire Garden Show Lotherton Hall	www.garden-festivals.com
	Leeds Hot-Air Balloon Festival Temple Newsam	www.leeds.gov.uk
	Leeds Half-Marathon	www.leeds.gov.uk
June	Bramham Horse Trials Bramham Park	www.bramham-horse.co.uk
	Yorkshire Cricket Club Matches Headingley	www.yorkshireccc.com
	Classic Car Rally Harewood House	www.harewood.org
	Historic Bike Ride Temple Newsam	www.leeds.gov.uk
July	Yorkshire Cricket Club Matches Headingley	www.yorkshireccc.com
	Teddy Bears Picnic Harewood House	www.harewood.org
	20/20 Cricket Cup Match Headingley	www.yorkshireccc.com
	Leeds Champion Dog Show Harewood House	www.harewood.org
	Party in the Park Temple Newsam	www.leeds.gov.uk
	Opera in the Park Temple Newsam	www.leeds.gov.uk
	National Archeological Days Armouries	www.royalarmouries.org
August	Mela Festival Roundhay Park	www.leedsasianfestival.co.uk
	Yorkshire Cricket Matches, Headingley	www.yorkshireccc.com
	Leeds Festival Bramham Park	leedsmusicfestival.com

LEEDS

	Steam Spectacular Harewood House	www.harewood.org
	West Indian Carnival Chapeltown	www.leedscarnival.co.uk
	Shakespeare Festival Kirkstall Abbey	www.leeds.gov.uk
	Leeds Carling Festival Temple Newsam Park	www.leeds.gov.uk
September	International Chamber Music Civic Hall	www.leeds.gov.uk
	Classic Proms Concert Harewood House	www.harewood.org
	Yorkshire Cricket Club Matches Headingley	www.yorkshireccc.com
	Leeds China Week Festival Millennium Square	www.leeds.gov.uk
October	Lunchtime Organ Music Town Hall	www.leedsconcertseason.com
	International Film Festival city centre	www.leedsfilm.com
	Autumn Glory Festival Harewood House	www.harewood.org
	Halloween Train Middleton Railway	www.middletonrailway.org.uk
November	Christmas Lights Switch On city centre	www.leeds.gov.uk
	Bonfire Night Roundhay Park	www.roundhaypark.org.uk
	Crafts Fair Harewood House	www.harewood.org
	Christmas Market - Millennium Square	www.leeds.gov.uk
December	Santa's Special Middleton Rly	www.middletonrailway.org.uk
	Leeds Abbey Dash – city centre to Kirkstall Abbey and back	
	Totally Tropical Xmas Tropical World	www.roundhaypark.org.uk
	New Year's Eve Celebrations various venues	www.leeds.gov.uk

Restaurants (see map pages 167,185 and 186)
££

Gastropub **Cross Keys** 107 Water Lane 0113 2433711 www.the-crosskeys.com ①
Thai **Chaophraya** 20 Swinegate 0113 2449339 www.chaophraya.co.uk ②
Indian **Akbars** 16, Greek St 0113 2425426 www.akbars.co.uk ③
Pan-asian **Sukothai** 15 South Parade 0113 2422795 www.sukothai.co.uk ④
Chinese **Maxi's** 6,Bingley St 0113 2440552 www.maxi-s.co.uk ⑤
Japanese **LittleTokyo** 24 Central Rd 0113 2439090 ⑥
English **Arts Café** 42 Call Lane 0113 2438243 www.artscafebar.com ⑦
Vegetarian **Hansa's** 7 North St 0113 2444408 www.hansasrestaurant.com ⑧
South American **Las Iguanas** Cloth Hall St 0113 2439533 www.iguanas.co.uk ⑨
Indian **The Spice Quarter** Gt George St 0113 2469241 www.spicequarter.co.uk ⑩
Indian **Aagrah** St Peters Sq 0113 2455667 www.aagrah.com ⑪
Oriental **AM Kitchen Bar** Lower Briggate 0113 242 2626 ⑫
South American **Azucar Bar** Brewery Place 0113 2435761 www.azucarbar.co.uk ⑬

£££

Italian **Red Chilli** Gt George St 0113 2429688 www.redchillirestaurant.co.uk ⑭
Fish **Livebait** 11-15 Wharfe St 0113 2444144 www.livebaitleeds.com ⑮
Italian **Jamies Italian** 35 Park Row 0113 3225400 www.jamieoliver.com ⑯
French **Brasserie Blanc** Sovereign St 0113 2206060 www.brasserieblanc.com ⑰
Fish **Loch Fyne** City Sq 0113 3917550 www.lochfyne-restaurants.com ⑱
English **The Living Room** 7 Greek St 0113 3800930 www.thelivingroom.co.uk ⑲

LEEDS

££££

English **Anthonys** 19 Boar Lane   0113 2455922 www.anthonysrestaurant.co.uk   ㉕

S. American **Gaucho's** 21 Park Row 0113 2461777 www.gauchorestaurants.co.uk ㉑

French **Sous Le Nez** 11 Quebec St 0113 2440108 www.souslenez.com   ㉒

English **No3York Place** 3 York Place 0113 2459922 www.no3yorkplace.co.uk   ㉓

French **La Grillade** 7 Wellington St 0113 2459707 www.lagrillade.co.uk   ㉔

Italian **San Carlo** 6 South Parade 0113 2461500 www.sancarlo.co.uk   ㉕

English **Res't Grill** City Sq 0113 2449625 www.therestaurantbarandgrill.co.uk   ㉖

Italian **Bibi's** Sovereign Street 0113 2430905 www.bibisrestaurant.com   ㉗

English **Brasserie 44** 44 The Calls 0113 2343232 www.brasserie44.com   ㉘

Pan asian **Chino Latino** Boar Lane 0113 3804080 www.chinolatino.eu   ㉙

Hotels (see map pages 151 and 152)

**

Travelodge Swingate 125 rooms 0871 9816155 www.travelodge.co.uk   ㉚

Travelodge Vicar Lane 132 rooms 0871 9846337 www.travelodge.co.uk   ㉛

IBIS Budget 2 Gateway North 218 rooms 0113 245 0725 www.ibis.com   ㉜

Premier Inn Wellington St 140 rooms 0871 52 8582 www.premierinn.com   ㉝

Ibis 23 Marlborough St 168 rooms   0113 2204100 www.ibishotel.com   ㉞

***

Jurys Inn Brewery Place 248 rooms 0113 2838800 www.JurysInns.com   ㉟

Merrion Wade Lane,109 rooms 0113 2439191 www.TheMerrionHotel.co.uk   ㊱

Comfort Inn BishopgateSt 90 rooms 01132422555 www.comfortinnleeds.co.uk ㊲

Novotel 4 Whitehall Quay 195 rooms 0113 2426446 www.novotel.com   ㊳

Cosmopolitan L'r Briggate 89 rooms 0113 2436454 www.cosmopolitanhotel.co.uk ㊴

Bewleys 7 City Walk 334 rooms 0113 23 2340 www.bewleyshotels.com   ㊵

Holiday Inn E'xs Kirkstall Rd 112 rooms 0113 242 6200 www.hiexpress.com   ㊶

Holiday Inn E'xs Armouries Dr 130 rooms 0113 3804400 www.hiexpress.com   ㊷

Premier Inn Claypit Lane 0871 52 8582 www.premierinn.com   ㊸

****

SAS Radisson The Light 147 rooms 0113 2366000 www.radissonblu.co.uk   ㊹

Crown Plaza Wellington St 135 rooms 0871 9429170 www.ichotelsgroup.com   ㊺

Metropole King Street 120 rooms 0113 245 0841 www.metropole-hotel.co.uk   ㊻

Malmaison 1 Swingate, 89 rooms 0113 3981000 www.malmaison-leeds.com   ㊼

42 The Calls 42 The Calls 41 rooms 0113 2440099 www.42thecalls.co.uk   ㊽

Marriott 4 Trevelyan Sq 236 rooms 0113 2366366 www.marriott.co.uk   ㊾

LEEDS

Doubletree Hotel Granary Wharf 333 rooms 50
0113 2411000 www.doubletreehilton.com/leeds
Hilton Neville St 208 rooms 0113 2442000 www.Hilton.co.uk/LeedsCity 51
Quebecs 9 Quebec St 45 rooms 0113 2448989 www.quebecshotel.co.uk 52
The Queens City Sq 215 rooms. 0113 2431323 www.qhotels.co.uk 53
Park Plaza Boar Lane City Sq 185 rooms 0113 3804000 www.parkplaza.com 54

Hotels outside the city centre
Leeds East
★★

Premier Inn Leeds East Selby Rd 87 rooms 0871 5278586 www.premierinn.com 55
Travelodge Styal Hill Way, Colton 87rooms 0871 9846235 www.travelodge.co.uk 56

★★★

Holiday Inn Ex's Oulton 77 rooms 0845 1126039 www.hiexpressleedseast.co.uk 57
Ramada Leeds North Ring Rd 102 rooms 0844 815 9108 www.ramadajarvis.co.uk 58

★★★★

Thorpe Park Century Way, 123 rooms 0113 264100 www.thorpeparkhotel.com 59
Oulton Hall Rothwell Lane Oulton 152 rooms 0113 2821000 www.devere.co.uk 60

South Leeds
★★

Premier Inn City West 1 125 rooms 0871 527858 www.premierinn.com 61

★★★★

The Village Tingley 115 rooms 0844 9800306 www.village-hotels.co.uk 62

North Leeds
★★

Travelodge Airport Whitehouse Lane 48 rooms 0871 9846275 www.travelodge.co.uk 63

★★★

Weetwood Hall Otley Road 106 rooms 0113 2306000 www.weetwood.co.uk 64
Britannia Hotel Bramhope 160 rooms   0871 2220027 www.britanniahotels.com 65

★★★★

The Village Otley Road 134 rooms 0844 9808031 www.village-hotels.co.uk 66
Mercure Parkway Otley Road 120 rooms 08448159020 www.mercure.com 67

LEEDS

Leeds Visitor Information Centre,
City Station 0113 2425242   www.visitleeds.co.uk

Car parks Ⓟ

① Merrion Centre	1,020 spaces	⑩ The Headrow Centre	313 spaces
② St Johns Centre	285 spaces	⑪ Basinghall Street	416 spaces
③ Templar Street	250 spaces	⑫ The Light	402 spaces
④ Lady Lane	270 spaces	⑬ City Station	749 spaces
⑤ Union street	300 spaces	⑭ Whitehall Road	380 spaces
⑥ Markets	646 spaces	⑮ West Gate	300 spaces
⑦ Quarry Hill	360 spaces	⑯ Wellington Place	507 spaces
⑧ Swinegate	630 spaces	⑰ West Street	238 spaces
⑨ Criterion Place	499 spaces	⑱ Woodhouse Lane	1287 spaces

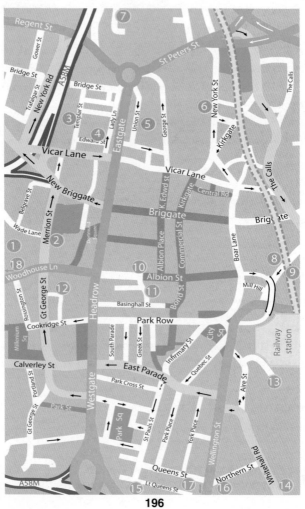

LEEDS

CASTLEFORD

the new castleford bridge

The largest of the so called five towns (the others being Norman-ton, Featherstone, Pontefract and Knottingley), positioned on the south side of the River Aire by its confluence with the River Calder and the Aire and Calder Navigation canal, Castleford is known primar-ily for its rugby league team and a large retail park with indoor ski slope.

History

There is evidence of Roman occupation in this area. The town is the site of an important Roman fort called *Legentium*, built to guard the crossing of the River Aire. The Roman road Ermine Street, from London to York via Lincoln, had to cross the Humber – a much more difficult crossing at two miles wide and one prone to attack from the Celtic Brigante tribes and the vagaries of win-ter weather. So the Romans devised an alternative route from Lincoln through what is now Bawtry, Doncaster, Castleford and Tadcaster, and *Legentium* was an important fort on this route. It was built in AD74 but the Romans had abandoned it by AD180, and Castleford reverted to being a small village for the next 1600 years, as it was not until the industrial revolution that any mate-rial change occured, when the development of coal mining saw rapid hous-ing expansion as demand mushroomed for labour to work in the mines. The demise of the coal industry in the 1980's left the town, like some other parts of the county, with deep seated economic and employment difficulties, but the emergence of a distribution industry, investment in nearby power stations, and a strong retail offering has offset the damage caused from coals decline.

Getting Here

Rail The train station lies south west of the town centre. There are regular services to Leeds (30 mins), and Sheffield (hourly). Connections to London and Manchester can be made at Leeds.

CASTLEFORD

Road the town is just north of the M62 (junction 32) and just west of the A1. Leeds is 30 mins; Manchester 1 hour, and Hull 45 mins. London is 3hrs 30 mins.

Bus all bus services arrive at and depart from the bus station on Albion Street. Regular services are to:

destination	service(s)	frequency
Leeds	163/166/167/168/189	15mins/30mins/15mins
Wakefield	125/134/135/136/187	hourly/15mins/20 mins
Pontefract	144/146/135/136	20 mins

Things to see and do

The small town centre, with a legacy of some late Victorian buildings, is centred around the Market and Carlton Street. The indoor market hall with over 80 stalls is open 6 days per week. The adjoining open air market is held Mon, Thurs, Fri, Sat. The Victorian free library in Carlton Street has a small museum with displays and artefacts from the roman fort. The museum is open Mon, Tue, Thurs,Fri, Sat.   Admission is free.   01924 305356   www.wakefield.gov.uk

Castleford Bridge is a new pedestrian bridge spanning the River Aire just to the north of the town centre. Its award winning graceful S shape alignment lends an attractive inviting air and gazing out over the river from its ship-like balustrades is a recommended experience.

Fairburn Ings Wildlife Sanctuary lies across the river 2 miles north east of the town centre. The Ings is a long established sanctuary for birds. Managed by the RSPB, visitors can use two trails hides and viewing platforms for views of species such as the reed warbler, and kingfisher. There is a small visitor centre on the sanctuary.   Access is along Newton Lane, off the A656 1 mile north of the town.   01977 628191   www.rspb.org.uk

Xscape sits alongside the M62 at one end of the large retail park. It contains one of the UK's largest indoor ski slopes as well as a skate park, a bowling alley, other leisure pursuits and a range of diners.   Open daily. There is an admission charge.   www.escape.co.uk/castleford

Diggerland on the A655 Willowbridge Lane west of the town, is a place where adults and children can drives diggers dumpers and tractors. It is open weekends April to October.   0871 2277007   www.diggerland.com/yorkshire

Sporting Life

Castleford Tigers   One of the national rugby league's more prominent and historically successful teams, "Cas Tigers" play at the Probiz Coliseum, Wheldon Road, ½ mile east of the town centre.   01977 552674   www.castigers.com

CASTLEFORD

Henry Moore -Sculptor 1898-1986

A sculptor and artist best known for his abstract monumental bronze sculptures which are globally renowned as pieces of public art. He was born in the town to a mining family, the seventh of eight children and spent his formative years here, gaining a scholarship to Leeds College of Art, and then to the Royal College of Art. Much of his prolific output of sculptures is on display at the Yorkshire Sculpture park.

Restaurants (see map page 200)

££

Chinese **Eastern Court** Colorado Way   01977 668668 www.easterncourt.com   **1**

Hotels (see map page 200)

★★★(GA)

The Bridge Inn Altofts Lane, Whitwood, 16 Bedrooms   **2**
01977 519696   www.thebridgeinncastleford.co.uk

★★★

Premier Inn Pioneer Way 119 Bedrooms 0871 5278218 www.premierinn.com   **3**

★★★★(GA)

Wentvale Court Great North Road 11 Bedrooms 01977 676714   **4**

not rated

The Village Motel Castleford Rd 40 Bedrooms 01977 897171   **5**

Parking

1 Bridge Street	285 spaces	**4** Welbeck Street	57 spaces
2 Castlefields	180 spaces	**5** Wesley Street	45 spaces
3 Railway station	66 spaces	**6** Aire Street	260 spaces

CASTLEFORD

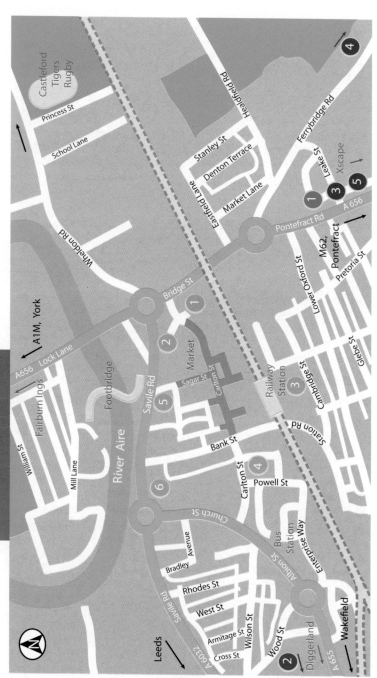

CASTLEFORD

PONTEFRACT

Sometimes referred to as Pomfret or Ponty Carlo by locals, Pontefract is a small town with a big history near the junction of the M62 and A1(M). It's main claim to fame is the liquorice industry. It is allegedly the only place in Britain where this unusual plant was grown. The name Pontefract derives from the Latin for broken bridge, as there was a small bridge over the River Washburn, thought to be a marshy area in medieval times which formed the original route of the great north road and served the town. In the 13thC, the bridge had to be abandoned because the extent of the marsh area made it impossible to maintain a road.

History

Although no mention is made of the town in the Domesday book, there is evidence of earlier settlement. Recent discoveries have included a neolithic henge just north of the town, some Anglo-Saxon remains of a small church close to the castle, and the Roman road known as the Roman Ridge, which acted as an alternative to Ermine Street between Lincoln and York, passed directly through the town. Not long after the Domesday Book however came a castle, built by the de Lacy family, whose ownership of much of Yorkshire had been granted by William the Conqueror, and although the castle was substantially demolished, by Oliver Cromwell after the English civil war, some remains are still evident. The castle had been a royalist stronghold for most of the civil war, and only surrendered after Charles I was beheaded. It is infamous for having been the place where Richard II met his death after being deposed by Henry IV in 1399; more romantic theories suggesting he had been murdered, less glamorous theories suggesting he died of starvation.

PONTEFRACT

pontefract castle

The town was also the site of a Cluniac Priory, founded by the de Lacy family following construction of the castle. Although no remains of the priory can be now be seen, a legacy of medieval papers from the priory survived (the so called cartularies of St John), and are in the Yorkshire Archeological Society's care. They give a rare insight into the life of a medieval priory. The market was established in medieval times, and still trades, centred around the town's Buttercross. There is an 18thC town hall, unlike the predominantly Victorian edifices which grace many former West Riding towns, and still used for a variety of public events. A liquorice industry developed in the Priory, from monks visiting from southern Europe -where liquorice grew in abundance- who introduced the plant, and found it thrived in the soft loamy soil. A local entrepreneur, George Dunhill, developed the product in the 18thC and the famed Pontefract cakes have been a feature ever since. By 1900, there were 17 liquorice factories in the town, and although the growing of liquorice locally had ceased by the late 1960's, today there are still two such factories in the town, and supplemented by a vibrant town centre, and other industries such as open cast coal mining and energy.

Getting Here

Rail the town is unusual in having three stations on two separate lines, but most services stop at Monkhill. There is a regular service to London via Doncaster, and to Bradford, Leeds and Halifax. Local services on the same line stop at Tanshelf station, and Baghill - one of the least busy stations in England - has direct, if infrequent, services between Sheffield and York.

Road the town lies near the M62/A1(M) junction, and main roads provide connections to Castleford, Wakefield, and Doncaster. London is 3 hrs Manchester 1 hr.

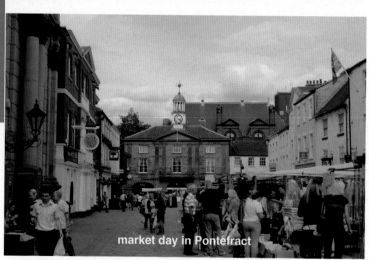
market day in Pontefract

PONTEFRACT

Bus all bus services arrive at and depart from the bus station in Horsefair/ Trinity Street just east of the town hall.

destination	service(s)	frequency
Wakefield	148/149/150/125	10mins/hourly
Leeds	410	30 mins
Barnsley	35/46	30 mins/hourly
Castleford	135/136144/145/146	20 min$_s$

Things to see and do

The historic core of the centre consists of cobbled streets, some pedestrianised, lined by many 18th and 19thC buildings. **The Town Hall** at the eastern end of the Market Place forms the effective centre of the town. Built in 1785, it replaced a former Moot Hall. The grand assembly room on the first floor now used for concerts and public events, was once the council chamber. On the ground floor, the building originally contained the town gaol.   A **market** is held in the Market Place on Wednesday and Saturday, with over 100 stalls open for business. The indoor market hall is open six days a week. At the other (western) end of the market place stands the **Buttercross**, built in 1734 to provide shelter for the farmers wives to stand and sell their market produce. It is on the site of a saxon cross. Opposite the buttercross is **St Giles Church**, where there has been a religious building since the 12thC. The present church, with its distinctive octagonal tower, was largely rebuilt in the 18thC, although parts are much earlier; the columns in the north arcade dating from the 14thC, and the font from the 16thC.   The **Cornmarket** and the **Courthouse** mark the western end of the core of the town centre, but BeastFair, Shoemarket and Ropergate are all worth a stroll.   Behind Beastfair, in Swales Yard, is the 14thC **Counting House**, possibly the towns oldest building. Of timber frame construction and now a pub, it was originally a merchants counting house.

The Buttercross and St Giles Church

PONTEFRACT

The towns **museum** is in Salter Row, which runs parallel to Market Place. Housed in an art nouveau style building, the museum has exhibitions and artefacts on the history of the town, including references to Richard II and the liquorice story. The museum is open Mon to Sat through the year. Admission is free. 01977 722740 www.wakefieldmuseums.org

To the east of the town centre, surrounding the castle, lies the oldest part of the town, although little remains. The **castle** was built by the de Lacy family, probably at the turn of the 12thC, and was once one of the most important defensive locations in northern England. Testifying to its strategic importance is the incarceration of Richard II, and later the weight attached by the Roundheads in the Civil War to capture what remained, throughout this war, a Royalist stronghold. The castle was largely demolished, at the request of the townspeople, shortly after, but its motte and bailey form, foundations, some cellars, and small sections of wall still remain set in a managed park. Admission is free.

To the south east of the castle, at the junction of Castle Garth and Baileygate, are recently uncovered foundations of a Saxon church which would have been at the heart of the old town centre - the triangle of grass behind suggesting this was the first spot for the market place. Across the road is **All Saints Church**, the parish church until 1789, when this designation passed to St Giles. A church has stood here since about 1220, with parts of the present building dating from 1300, and the scene of much fighting during the civil war siege of the castle; so much so that recent discoveries include a cannon ball plucked from one of the walls. The end of the war saw the church in ruins, and restoration did not begin until 1831 when part was restored to provide a chapel of ease for St Giles.

Pontefract races

One of Yorkshires 9 racecourses, Pontefract claims to have the longest continuous racing circuit in the country at 2 miles and one furlong. Race days occur regularly between April and October.

01977 702210 www.pontefract-races.co.uk

Festivals

July Liquorice Festival town centre www.experiencewakefield.co.uk

PONTEFRACT

Restaurants (see map page 206)

£

Indian Shahban Front Street 01977 70000 ①

££

Italian Mamma Mia 61 Northgate 01977 706825 ②

Italian Bellissimos 3-5 Front street 01977 690000 ③

gastropub Olde Church Tavern North Baileygate ④
01977 780619 www.theoldetavern.co.uk

Hotels (see map page 206)

★★★

Premier Inn Great North Road Darrington 28 bedrooms ⑤
0871 527888 www.premierinn.com

★★★★

Wentbridge House Wentbridge 41 bedrooms ⑥
01977 620444 www.wentbridgehouse.co.uk

★★★★★(GA)

Tower House 21 Bondgate 6 bedrooms ⑦
01977 699988 www.towerhouseguesthouse.co.uk

not rated

The Kings Croft Wakefield Road 22 bedrooms ⑧
01977 600550 www.kingscrofthotel.com

Parking

① Friarwood   94 spaces ② Newgate North   38 spaces
③ Newgate South   138 spaces

PONTEFRACT

205

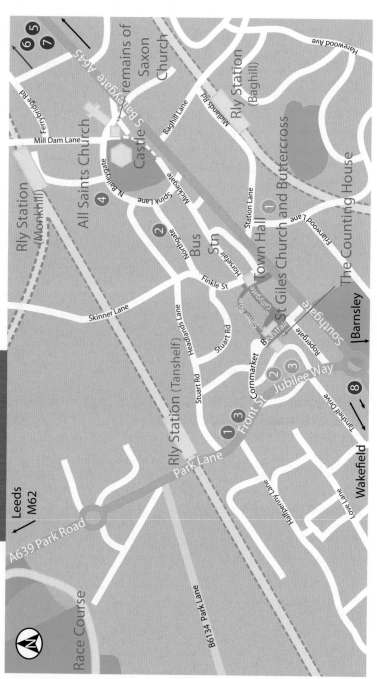

PONTEFRACT

HEBDEN BRIDGE

"Trouser Town" a name given to Hebden Bridge in the late 19thC as it became a centre for the production of ready to wear clothing.   It lies in the Calder Valley at the confluence of the River Calder and Hebden Water, its Yorkshire stone buildings clinging to the steep hillsides in a maze of straight Victorian terraces and narrow windy lanes. It is as close to Manchester as it is to Leeds and its resident workers equally likely to work "on the dirty side of the hill" as in the commercial centres of Yorkshire. In 2005 a well known in-flight magazine voted it "the funkiest place to live in Europe".

History

Hebden Bridge grew up around a river crossing on the packhorse trail between Halifax and Burnley. The original settlement was on a ridge above the valley, in what is now the much sought after village of Heptonstall.   The wool trade began early here with weavers cottages, some still evident today characterised by their large first floor windows to maximise light.   Hebden Bridge (named from the Saxon *Heb* and *Dene* which mean rose valley), became the dominant centre in the 17thC because of its bridge, which was the subject of a fierce battle in the English civil war. The Rochdale Broad canal (called broad because it would accommodate wider canal boats with greater carrying capacity) connected the town and its weaving industry in about 1800 to the Lancashire cotton mills and the port of Liverpool; an initiative which greatly enhanced its attractiveness and capacity for cloth production. 19thC industrialisation brought mills to the town and it became a centre for the production of corduroy, fustian and ready made clothing.   Steep valley sides and industrial growth of the mid to late 19thC created a challenge in building sufficient houses for the workers, and the solution was to build double decker (or top and bottom) properties; separate houses built on top of one another, with entries to the upper floors being from one side, and the lower floors from the other side. In the late 1960s and 70s the local economy declined with the collapse of textile manufacturing across the county but the town benefited from an influx of settlers who saw it's potential and the attractions of low house prices in a beautiful setting. These settlers brought new skills and helped the regeneration as a centre for tourism, small craft businesses and creative industries. More recently it has become a centre for alternative technology. Success has now created high house prices and made Hebden Bridge a popular tourism destination.

Bridgegate

Getting Here

Rail the station is south east of the centre with frequent services to Leeds (every 20 mins), Manchester (20 mins), Blackpool (hourly), and York (hourly).

Road the town lies on the A646 connecting Halifax with Burnley. Access to the national motorway network is via Halifax or Rochdale onto the M62. Manchester is 30 mins; Leeds 45 mins; London 4 hours; Glasgow 4 hours.

Bus there is no bus station. Most services call at New Road.

destination	service(s)	frequency
Keighley	500	hourly
Halifax	517/590/591/592/593	10 mins
Burnley	592	hourly
Rochdale	590	hourly

Hebden Bridge Visitor Information Centre
Butlers Wharf   01422 843831
www.hebdenbridge.co.uk

HEBDEN BRIDGE

Things to see and do

This is a small town, but its steep sides make it somewhat strenuous to wander around. It enjoys a reputation as a liberal, artistic and creative community, so a stroll through its streets is an interesting and rewarding experience. The core of the town is in the Bridgegate area, a pedestrianised main street with many independent shops, running parallel to Hebden water with St Georges Square at its higher end.

Rochdale Canal

To the south of the town centre in the Calder valley is the restored Rochdale Canal. This monument to Georgian endeavour and endurance is fully navigable and the towpath forms an attractive walk in both directions. It was built between 1797 and 1805 and links the Calder and Hebble Canal at Sowerby Bridge with the Bridgewater Canal at Manchester, running for some 32 miles over the Pennines. Travelling the whole length means navigating over 90 locks, so progress in a boat will be slow!! Unlike the Leeds Liverpool canal, there is only limited use of tunnels, so views from the higher sections of the route over the Pennine hills can be breathtaking. In the early 19thC, it rapidly became the main commercial artery between Lancashire and Yorkshire. Records show that, by 1890, the canal was carrying 50 barges a day despite strong competition from the railways. However, it declined in succeeding years, and by the second world war had fallen into disuse. Cut in two by the construction of the M62 in the late 1960's, but a later successful campaign to restore it to full use made the route navigable again by 2002. Canal boat hire and boat trips can be obtained from the Marina on New Road adjoining the canal.

Walkleys Clog Mill

Situated in the village of Mytholmroyd, 2 miles to the south east, Walkleys Clog Mill is Britains last remaining clog factory, manufacturing for both home and overseas markets. Clogs are an ancient form of shoe having been in regular use since Roman times, and although usually associated in folklore with Yorkshire and Lancashire, their usage has been widespread.The factory is open for visits to see clogs being made. 01422 885757 www.clogs.co.uk

the rochdale canal

HEBDEN BRIDGE

Little Theatre

Producing plays since 1924, the Little Theatre, in Holme Street, seats 120 and stages six different plays annually.   01422 843907   www.wix.com

Hardcastle Crags

A well frequented National Trust site north of the town, this is a beautiful wooded valley with deep ravines, tumbling streams and glorious waterfalls. There are over 25 miles of footpaths meandering through woodland rich in wildlife. In the midst is Gibson Mill, a former cotton mill, now a visitor centre which uses sustainable energy, and contains exhibits and information about the valley's 200 year history.   01422 844518 www.nationaltrust.org.uk

churches old and new at Heptonstall

Heptonstall

Overlooking the town is Heptonstall village, the original settlement in this area, characterised by a steep narrow cobbled main street and weavers cottages. In the churchyard, the abandoned tower and shell of the nave are all that remain of the original 13thC church destroyed in a thunderstorm in 1854. On the other side of the present church is the graveyard containing the grave of Sylvia Plath, the American poet and novelist married to the Poet Laureate Ted Hughes.   Heptonstall originally had a grammar school, dating from 1642. The building which housed the school dates from 1771 and is now used as a museum tracing the history of the village.   The museum is open weekends through the year. Admission is free.

01422 843738 www.calderdale.gov.uk

Festivals

Easter   Duck race   St Georges bridge   www.hebdenbridge.com
June/July Arts Festival   various venues   www.hebdenbridge.co.uk

HEBDEN BRIDGE

Restaurants

££

English **Moyles Hotel** New Road 01422 845272 www.moyles.com ①

Italian **Il Mulino** St Georges Square 01422 845986 www.ilmulino.co.uk ②

Thai **Rim Nim Thai** Butlers Wharf New Road 01422 846888 ③

£££

French **Kitties** 52, Market street 01422 842956 www.kittiesrestaurant.co.uk ④

Vegetarian **Greens** Albert St 01422 843587 www.greensvegetariancafe.co.uk ⑤

Hotels

★★★★(GA)

Bar Place 10 Crown St 8 bedrooms 01422 842814 www.barplace.co.uk ⑥

Moyles Hotel New Road 12 Bedrooms 01422 845272 www.moyles.com ⑦

not rated

White Lion Bridgegate 10 bedrooms 01422 842197 www.whitelionhotel.net ⑧

HEBDEN BRIDGE

HALIFAX

Halifax's iconic Piece Hall

The 17thC poet John Taylor, known as the water poet, pays a slightly sarcastic homage to the town in his well known poem the Beggars Litany:

"There is a Proverbe, and a prayer withall, That we may not to these strange places fall, From Hull, from Halifax, from Hell, 'tis thus, From all these three, Good Lord deliver us".

Halifax is a town of about 80,000 people, just north of the M62, set in the rolling hills of the east Pennines, with a chequered history and best known today for the Halifax Building Society, the Piece Hall, and the Eureka childrens museum.

History

Although there are a number of theories about the origin of the name, Halifax is believed to derive from the Saxon *Haly Flex Field,* which means a place where holy banners were made from flax. Indeed, the towns association with textiles has endured for over 1000 years. The first records, from the time of Henry I, describe the living from the church being granted by the Earl De Warrenne (William the Conquerors son in law) to the Priory of Lewes. The town grew significantly in the 15th and 16thC as the wool trade expanded, and in recognition of its growing stature, the Earldom of Halifax was created in 1677; an earldom whose bearers helped found Halifax in Nova Scotia and a current peerage. Expansion in the 15th and 16thC increased the incidence of theft. The penalties for stealing, called the Gibbet Law, were harsh. A gibbet was an early form of guillotine, and it is claimed the Halifax gibbet was a forerunner of that used in the French revolution. A replica is in Gibbet Street. The textile industry, in common with other towns in Yorkshire, expanded greatly in the late 18th to late 19thC. The large imposing Piece Hall which dates from 1779, suggests that by this time cloth manufacture was extensive throughout the town, and had become a key player in Yorkshire's booming textile industry. The mid to late19thC saw development of a planned town centre, together with a town hall, indoor market and theatre; most of this remaining today.

HALIFAX

The late 19th C also saw diversification with the emergence of a confectionery industry in the form of Macintoshes (famous for Rolos and Quality Street), and the development of a successful carpet weaving industry, mainly in the form of a company called Crossley who developed and operated from Dean Clough Mills. Today, Halifax has little or no textile manufacturing; it has however retained much of its Georgian and Victorian character and charm, with new uses being found for old buildings and an increasing array of attractions for visitors.

the vast courtyard space of the Piece Hall

Getting Here

Rail Halifax's busy station, south east of the town centre close to the Eureka museum, has regular services to service to London (3x per day), as well as to Leeds (20 min), Manchester (30 min), York (4x per day), and Blackpool (hourly).

Road the town lies at the intersection of the A58 Leeds to Oldham road and the A629 Sheffield to Keighley road. There is also a main road direct to Burnley, and a linkage south to the M62. Leeds is 40 min; Manchester 45 mins; London 4hrs; Glasgow 4 hrs.

Bus all bus services arrive at and depart from the bus station which lies at the northern edge of the shopping centre.

destination	service(s)	frequency
Leeds	255/508	hourly
Bradford	505/570/576	12 mins
Wakefield	278	hourly
Huddersfield	549	hourly
Rochdale	528/590	hourly
Burnley	592	hourly
London	465/564	2x per day

Halifax Visitor Information Centre
The Piece Hall 01422 368725
www.calderdale.gov.uk

HALIFAX

Things to see and do

Eureka

From an original idea promoted by Prince Charles and Vivien Duffield, a British philanthropist, Eureka is for children under 11. It encourages childlike inquisitiveness and features over 400 exhibits, many interactive, encouraging children to learn about themselves and the world around them. The museum is open Tues to Fri through the year, and on weekends during school term. There is an admission charge.   01422 330069 www.eureka.org.uk

Piece Hall

This vast structure was built in 1779 to provide a fitting place for the textile trade to buy and sell cloth. Piece halls, or cloth halls as they were sometimes known, were a common feature of British textile regions in the18thC although few survive. When built, the Piece Hall was a highly visible statement of the wealth, pride and ambition of cloth manufacturers. Not only has the building survived intact, but it is the largest such building in Britain. It is a quadrangular stone building enclosing a 10,000M2 courtyard with a rustic basement storey and two upper stories fronted with interior colonnades forming spacious walks leading to over 300 arched rooms where woollen (and later cotton) pieces of cloth in an unfinished state were deposited and exhibited for sale to the merchants.(A "piece of cloth " was a 30yard length of woollen cloth produced on a handloom). The courtyard is home to a variety of markets and exhibitions, and the building itself is filled with small shops selling sometimes quirky goods to visitors, and an art gallery.   www.thepiecehall.co.uk

Shopping Centre

The shopping core lies adjacent to the Piece Hall; generally in Market Street, Southgate, Cornmarket, and Commercial street, all built late 18th or 19thC. The busy indoor market between Cornmarket and Market Street is late Victorian with its lofty octagonal centre and decorative clock finished in gold leaf. It is a testimony to the wealth and elegance of the town as the 20thC approached. There are over 170 market stalls and 50 external shops, and is open daily.

HALIFAX

Town Hall

A little further north, at the top of Princess Street, the town hall is another building demonstrating the towns wealth and flamboyance in Victorian times. Its Italianate style was by Charles Barry, architect of the Palace of Westminster, and it was opened by the Prince of Wales in great pomp and ceremony in 1863. No expense had been spared to provide a sumptuous venue for transacting council business, hosting entertainment and public meetings (in the Victoria Hall with its richly decorated mosaic floor and decorative fibrous plasterwork), administer the law and house the local police force. The richly decorated tower, with spire is 180 ft high. There are four sculpted features, one on each facet of the clock tower to represent the four continents.

Halifax Gibbet

Sited, appropriately enough, on Gibbet Street just outside the town centre this replica tries to re-create the original 15thC structure. The origins of Gibbet Law are vague. There is a record of a beheading on the gibbet in the year 1286, and some historians claim it stems from the conditions attached to the award of powers by the king to the manorial court of the Earl of the Manor (John De Warrenne). The court had the right to execute anyone caught stealing woollen cloth, then known as the Staple because of its significant value to the realm. The last known beheading was in the 16thC. The gibbet was a form of guillotine which design was copied and developed by the French and used with such macabre effect throughout the French revolution.

Halifax Minster

To the east of the main shopping area on Lower Kirkgate is the Church of St John the Baptist. Documentary evidence suggests there was a church here by the early 12thC, and Anglo-Norman stone fragments of this are visible in some of the stonework on the north of the present building. There is a medieval grave cover in the south porch dated 1150, on which is carved croppers shears, providing evidence of the churches construction, and of the textile industry. The lofty interior contains Jacobean box pews - some with original nameplates- and an exquisite font cover said to be one of the best in English churches. Most of the stained glass is of Victorian provenance, although the western clerestory window contains glass of medieval origin. The church organ, part of which dates from the 18thC, is described as the Rolls Royce of church organs. William Herschel, a British astronomer, who is credited with the discovery of Uranus, was an organist in the Minster in the 18thC. The Minster is open daily and guided tours can be arranged with prior notice. 01422 355436   www.halifaxminster.org.uk

Square Chapel Arts Centre   10 Square Road

An arts venue, which puts on a regular programme of music, dance and workshops in a former chapel.   01422 349422   www.squarechapel.co.uk

Dean Clough

These towering edifices were built as carpet mills between 1840 and 1860 by Crossley and Sons, who went on to become the worlds largest manufacturer

HALIFAX

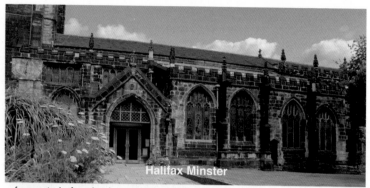
Halifax Minster

of carpets before business declined in the 1950s; the mills finally closed in 1980 and a successful regeneration scheme pioneered and led by a local entrepreneur and philanthropist, Sir Ernest Hall, was held up as a model for others. His vision has breathed new life into this rambling iconic complex, with both commercial and cultural activities. The site lies by the Victorian north bridge. In the building there are art galleries, artists studios and a small theatre, all open to the public. The artist studios cover several mediums, including painting, sculpture, ceramics and printmaking. 01422 250250   www.deanclough.com

the dark satanic Dean Clough mill

Shibden Hall and Folk Museum   Bradford Road

Built 5 years after the Battle of Agincourt in 1420, Shibden Hall is a Tudor manor house set in 90 acres of parkland above the town. The Hall is fully restored with each room authentically decorated and furnished. The hall also has some reconstructed workshops including a brewery, a tannery and stable, and these form a folk museum. The Hall has been the home to some influential Yorkshire families, starting with the Oates (who built it), and includes the Listers whose fame derives from the Bradford wool trade and Manningham mills. The extensive rolling parkland surrounding the house is also a popular attraction, with landscape and rock gardens, a boating lake and a miniature railway.

House and park are open every day. There is an admission charge. Shibden is accessed from Lister road. It is served by bus service 681, 682, 548, 549, 509, 534, 227, 508, 226 from Halifax, Bradford, Brighouse, Huddersfield and Leeds.
01422 352246   www.calderdale.gov.uk

Wainhouse Tower   Washer Lane

The tower is at Kings Cross, 1 mile west of the town. It sits on a ridge and those with sufficient energy to climb its 400 steps can enjoy unrivalled views over the Pennines and across to the Vale of York. At 275 feet it is aclaimed to be the tallest folly in the world, and erected between 1871-1875, originally to provide for a nearby dye works, which needed a chimney of considerable height to safely emit smoke. It did not have to be as high as it is built, but the dyeworks owner insisted it should be a structure of beauty. It was to be connected to the works with a pipeline, but following a dispute between the owner and his manager, the pipeline was never completed; the dyeworks were sold, and the tower became a folly. The tower is open to access the viewing platform on bank holidays only, although private viewings are possible by prior arrangement, for which there is a fee. 01422 323824

Bankfield Museum   Boothtown Road

The house, now a museum, was built by Edward Akroyd to replace a much smaller earlier(18thC) one. His father, Jonathan Akroyd, a wealthy worsted mill owner left him sufficient money to let his grandest desires come true, and Edward spared no expense in creating a grand Italianate style villa set in extensive parkland grounds, in which he could lavishly entertain guests. The villa was sold to the local Council shortly before his death in 1887 and the museum focuses on costumes, fabrics and textiles, as well as being the regimental museum for the Duke of Wellington's regiment. Open Tues to Sun. There is no admission charge.
01422 354823   www.calderdale.gov.uk

Victoria Theatre   Fountain Street

Built as a theatre over 100 years ago, this Edwardian building with its prominent twin cupolas marking the frontage, is still in everyday use as a theatre and concert venue, putting on a diverse programme in its 1500 seat auditorium.
01422 351158   www.calderdale.gov.uk

Halifax Playhouse   King Cross Street

A converted, ivy clad Methodist chapel, the 245 seat playhouse is the home to Halifax thespians and arranges a series of different events across the year.
01422 365998 www.ukattraction.com

HALIFAX

Edward Akroyd   Textile Magnate   1810–1887

Born into a textile dynasty, he grew the family firm into one of the country's largest worsted manufacturers.   He established mills at Haley Hill and subsequently another one at Copley about two miles away. He was a learned man, but ambitious, successful, and charming.   He was concerned about the fortunes of the town and the terrible social conditions then prevalent. He funded a local allotment society and many institutions for the working classes: a school for child labourers, a workers' pension scheme, several churches and a cemetery.   He also founded a Working Men's College, the first one outside London. In the mid 1850s, he helped found the Yorkshire Penny Bank and he worked closely with the Halifax Building Society to promote home ownership through his model village Akroydon. This was built after the initial housing development, which he had undertaken with his brother at Copley, to show people how housing conditions could be improved, and although only small (90 houses as opposed to Saltaires 800+ houses), it demonstrated a strong philanthropic character. He was instrumental in bringing the railway to the town, and he became a member of Parliament for Halifax.   Failing health led him to retire to the south coast where he died at St Leonards on Sea. His funeral however was attended by over 15,000 people, demonstrating his innate popularity.

Festivals

May	Beer festival	Square Chapel	www.hxcalderdalecamra.org.uk
July	Halifax Festival	various venues	www.halifaxfestival.co.uk

HALIFAX

Restaurants (see map page 220)

££

Italian **Red Pepper Bistro** Broad St 01422 355694 www.redpepperbistro.co.uk ①

Eclectic **Design House** Dean Clough Arts and Business Centre
01422 383242 www.designhouserestaurant.co.uk ②

Eclectic **Inn Cognito** Winding Road 01422 353434 www.inncognitohalifax.co.uk ③

gastropub **The Maypole Inn** 32-34 Warley Town 01422 835861 ④

gastropub **Brasserie at the Bull** 5 Bull Green
01422 330833 www.brasserieatthebull.co.uk ⑤

Thai **Tum Nuk Thai** 5 Clare Road 01422 352500 ⑥

£££

English **Shibden Mill Inn** Shibden Mill Fold 01422 365840 www.shibdenmillinn.com ⑦

Italian **Julios** Princess Street 01422 349449 www.julios.co.uk ⑧

English **Gimbals** Wharf Street Sowerby Bridge 01422 839329 www.gimbals.co.uk ⑨

££££

English **Holdsworth Ho.** Holdsworth 01422 240024 www.holdsworthhouse.co.uk ⑩

Hotels (see map page 220)

**

Travelodge Dean Clough 51 Bedrooms 0871 9846144   www.travelodge.co.uk ⑪

Milans 6-8 Carlton Place 22 Bedrooms   01422 330539 ⑫

The Tower House Master Lane 16 Bedrooms ⑬
01422 345000 www.towerhousehotel.co.uk

***

The Rock Broad Carr, Holywell Green 27 Bedrooms ⑭
01422 379721 www.rockhotel.co.uk

Premier Inn   Salterhebble Hill 31 Bedrooms ⑮
0871 5278486 www.premierinn.com

Imperial Crown 42-46 Horton street 56 Bedrooms ⑯
01422 342342 www.imperialcrownhotel.co.uk

Holdsworth House Holdsworth 38 bedrooms ⑰
01422 240024 www.holdsworthshouse.co.uk

not rated

Shibden Mill Inn Shibden Mill Fold 11 Bedrooms ⑱
01422 365840 www.shibdenmillinn.com

Parking Ⓟ

① Bull Green	39 spaces		⑦ Mulculture Hall Road	167 spaces	
② Cow Green	226 spaces		⑧ North Bridge	367 spaces	
③ The Woolshops	300 spaces		⑨ St Johns Lane	27 spaces	
④ Hanover Street	27 spaces		⑩ Union Street	35 spaces	
⑤ High Street	238 spaces		⑪ Victoria street	29 spaces	
⑥ King Street	48 spaces				

HALIFAX

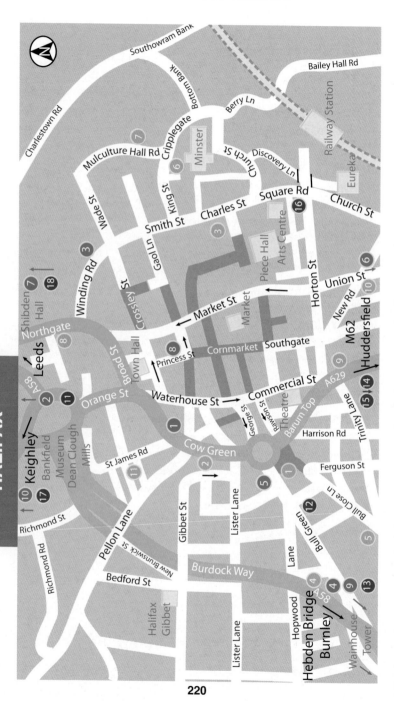

HUDDERSFIELD

"I rode over the mountains to Huddersfield. A wilder people I never saw in England...[they] seemed ready to devour us" (John Wesley, Methodist preacher 1757)

A town of some 120,000 people, Huddersfield stands on the edge of the high Pennines, its western suburbs sprawling across the ridges just below the Pennine hill tops. It is known as a woollen town, and more recently for its varied engineering and manufacturing and expanding university. Its19thC prosperity and wealth has endowed a legacy of fine Victorian architecture and of culture.

History

There is evidence of early occupation of this area. Castle Hill contains evidence of an iron age hill fort, whilst to the west of the town, at Outlane, Roman remains were uncovered in the 18thC, and Roman artefacts have been found elsewhere locally. The Domesday book records Huddersfield as *Oderesfelt*-the name deriving from *Oder* - a Celtic chieftain- and a Norman castle was built in Castle Hill. William the Conqueror gave lands in much of West Yorkshire, including Huddersfield, to the de Lacy family, and they remained lords of the Manor for more than two hundred years. Huddersfield developed on the back of the woollen trade, the abundant supplies of soft, subtly acidic water and the lack of any use for the hillsides other than the grazing of sheep, giving natural advantage. A market was established with a charter from King Edward I in the 13thC. An early industrial revolution brought prosperity and construction of the Huddersfield narrow canal linking with Manchester and ports on the west coast, although the impact of industrialisation briefly caused some civil unrest in 1817, stemming from the Luddite movement. Burgeoning development was given impetus with the arrival of the railway in 1846, the grand railway station being described by poet John Betjeman as "the finest facade in England"

HUDDERSFIELD

Unusually, the Ramsden family, long time lords of the Manor and therefore of much of the town centre, agreed to sell their town centre holdings to the council in the 1920s with the result that the Council became the dominant land-owner here. Decline of the woollen trade was countered in the 20thC with the emergence of other industries such as chemical and motor engineering and, more recently, with the rise to prominence of Huddersfield University as a national centre of excellence for computing and precision technology.

Getting Here

Rail the station is on the north side of the town centre on John William Street. There are regular services to Leeds (15 min), Sheffield (30 min), Manchester (15 min), Manchester airport (30 min), Liverpool (hourly), York (20 min), Hull (hourly) and other Yorkshire destinations. Journeys to London (Euston) take less than 3hrs via change at Manchester.

Road the town lies just to the south of the M62. Leeds is 30 mins; Manchester 30 mins; London 4 hours; Glasgow 4 hours.

Bus all bus services arrive at and depart from the bus station at Upperhead Row on the west side of the town centre, adjoining the Inner Ring Road.

destination	service(s)	frequency
town centre	FTB	10 mins
Manchester	184	hourly
Halifax	343/503/536/537/538	hourly/10 mins
Leeds	X6/202/203/220/229	20mins/hourly/30 mins
Wakefield	231/232	30 mins
Dewsbury	262	20 mins
Bradford	363	20 mins
Hebden Bridge	900/901	hourly
Sheffield	465	1x per day
London	465/M12	1x per day

Things to see and do

Shopping

Huddersfield centre has a strong and vibrant array of shops, restaurants and bars. The centre lies within the inner ring road; the railway station being the northerly point and contains most major brand names. Of particular note is **Byram Arcade** on the south side of Westgate. This delicately designed Victorian emporium with its ornate cartouche over the entrance (depicting the arms of the Ramsden family), has three floors of specialist shops and a café. The **Market Hall**, on the north side of the centre nearer the station, is a restored Victorian building which houses different markets across the week; a general market on Monday Thursday and Saturday, and second hand markets on Tuesday and Saturday. The more modern indoor market hall- the **Queensgate Market**- with over 100 stalls and shops is open six days a week, and contains a central demonstration area. The **Kingsgate Shopping centre** is a modern covered mall with over 50 brand name shops accessed from King Street. Other shopping centres include the Piazza Centre and the Packhorse centre.

Railway station

No visit to the town should miss the Railway station. A building designed by a well known local architect as part of the railway construction in 1850, it features an immensely long façade with an imposing portico, all in authentic classical style, and dominates the adjoining St Georges Square with its contemporary water features.

The Huddersfield Art Gallery
Princess Alexandra Walk

Housed on the 2nd floor of this distinctive art deco 1930's building, the gallery has an extensive collection of paintings and other including works by Lowry and Bacon. The gallery is open Mon to Sat. Admission is free.
01484 221964 www.kirklees.gov.uk

Other things to see in the town centre include the extensive facades of Victorian buildings that line many of the streets; indeed it is reputed that the town has more listed buildings than most others of its size in England - a testimony to its 19thC prosperity. The parish church and town hall are both of Victorian vintage. The former, the parish **church of St Peter**, dates from about 1830 (and designed by the architect responsible for the railway station) although it is substantially based on a 16thC building. The **town hall**, dating from 1881, like many in West Yorkshire of this period, exudes lavish elegance with it's ornate Italianate style and centrepiece magnificent concert hall seating 1200 where there are frequent orchestral and choral concerts as well as a programme of other entertainment events.

Castle Hill

At 800 ft high and standing conspicuously above the town to the south, archeologists attach considerable importance to Castle Hill as it was the site of a settlement for at least 4000 years. There was an iron age fort, constructed about 555BC, and subsequently a small castle, built by the de Lacy family in about 1140. Some earthworks are still visible from these constructions. The Victoria Tower sits atop the hill, built in 1897 to commemorate the Queen's diamond jubilee. This windswept summit, which has been the scene of political rallies and other gatherings over the centuries, gives panoramic views over the town and the Pennines. Access to the hill is via Almondbury. Buses run past the Hill from the bus station (services 336,337,341,354,368).

HUDDERSFIELD

Huddersfield Narrow Canal

The canal is Britain's highest navigable waterway, running for 20 miles between Huddersfield and Ashton-Under-Lyne. It includes 74 locks (nearly 4 locks per mile), and a three mile tunnel under the highest part of the Pennines. It was 17 years in the making, opening finally in 1811, and closed before the end of the second world war. Volunteers created a scheme to revive it, and it reopened for navigation in 2001. It is called narrow because, like many early canals, construction costs were very high, and so the canal and locks were built only as wide as the narrowest practical boat that could be constructed. There is a narrow towpath, suitable for walkers along the length of the canal as far as Standege tunnel. Boats can be hired from Sowerby Bridge for trips along the canal. 01422 832712 (Shire Cruisers) www.waterscape.com

Lawrence Batley Theatre   Queens Square

This theatre, created from a 19thC chapel, by a local philanthropist for whom it is named, is known for staging a variety of different entertainment and a community based performance venue.   01484 430528 www.lbt.org

Colne Valley Museum   Cliffe Ash Golcar

The museum is housed in former weavers cottages which have been restored to show how cloth was made by small independent weavers. Open weekends. There is an admission charge. The museum can be accessed by bus services 301A,302,303,304   01484 659762 www.colnevalleymuseum.org.uk

Tolson Museum   Ravensknowle Park

Originally a natural history museum, its wide range of exhibits allow the visitor to journey through the areas industrial and cultural history. The museum is open Mon to Fri and Sat and Sun afternoons. Admission is free. The museum can be accessed by buses 231/2.   01484 223830   www.kirklees.gov.uk

Holmfirth (Last of the Summer Wine)

A small town of stone built cottages, and an atmospheric centre, is 5 miles south of Huddersfield itself, nestling in the lee of the Holme Moss, it is best known as the location for a long running TV comedy Last of the Summer Wine.

Harold Wilson Politician 1916-1995

One of Britain's most prominent politicians in the period from 1950 to 1976, Harold Wilson was twice prime minister, and widely held to be the driving force behind many of the 1960's welfare reforms as well as the Open University, and was a formidable political operator. He was born in Huddersfield and attended Royds Hall Grammar school. Although he moved away, he continued association with the town and was a life long supporter of the football club. His statue is in St Georges Square.

HUDDERSFIELD

Festivals

The town and surrounding area plays host to a wide range of festivals and events throughout the years. Amongst the main annual events are *Organ and chamber concerts* performed by the Huddersfield Philarmonic Orchestra and the Huddersfield Choral Society, both with a proud Victorian heritage and renowned nationally for their accomplished performances not only in Huddersfield but also in venues such as London Barbican and Shakespeare's theatre in Stratford on Avon. www.huddersfieldchoral.com www.huddersfield-phil.org.uk

Town hall box office 01484 223200   www.tickets.kirklees.gov.uk

February *Mrs Sunderlands Music festival town hall and University*
www.mrs-sunderlandmusic.org.uk

March *St Patricks Day Parade town centre   www.theparadeonline.org*
Literature Festival various venues   www.litfest.org.uk

May *French Market New Street   www.kirklees.gov.uk*
Festival of Folk Music Holmfirth   www.holmfirthfestivaloffolk.co.uk
Film festival   Holmfirth   www.holmfirthfilmfestival.co.uk

June *Honley Show Farnley Tyas   www.honleyshow.co.uk*
July *carnival St Georges Sq   www.huddersfieldcarnival.com*
August *Food &Drink Festival St Georges Sq.*
www.foodanddrinkfestival.co.uk

October *Jazz Festival Marsden   www.marsdenjazzfestival.com*
November *Contemporary Music Festival variouvenues   www.hcmf.co.uk*
December *Light Fest town centre   01484 223200   www.kirklees.gov.uk*

HUDDERSFIELD

Sporting life

Huddersfield Town FC

Until the 1960's, probably the most prominent Yorkshire football club, Huddersfield Town FC have won cup and league honours throughout their history, becoming the first English league team to win league titles in three successive seasons in the 1920's. Home matches are played at the Galpharm Stadium, on the Leeds Road east of the town centre; a ground shared with rugby league side Huddersfield Giants.   01484 484123   www.htafc.com

Huddersfield Giants Rugby League Football Club

One of the worlds first rugby league clubs, formed in 1895 and after a turbulent post war history, has found new energy and style, consistently playing in premier competitions wearing distinctive claret and gold strip. Home games are played at the Galpharm.   01484 484123 www.giantsrl.com

Restaurants (see map page 228)

££

Indian **Nawaab** 35 Westgate 01484 422775 www.nawaabs.net ①

Mexican **Gringo's** Railway Arches 01484 422411 www.gringos-restaurant.co.uk ②

Thai **Thai Sakon** 5 St Johns Road 01484 450159 www.thaisakon.co.uk ③

Mongolian **Temujin** Manchester Road Milnsbridge
01484 461111 www.temujinrestaurant.co.uk ④

£££

English **Bradleys** 84 Fitzwilliam St 01484 56773 www.bradleyscatering.co.uk ⑤

Spanish **Les Caveaux** Victoria Square Holmfirth
01484 689003 www.lescaveauxholmfirth.co.uk ⑥

European **Live Lounge** 75 Lidget St 01484 646416 ⑦

European **Lounge 68** 68 John William St 01484 545454 ⑧

European **Scarlet** 3 Northumberland St 0845 8381833 ⑨

££££

European **Weavers Shed** 88 Knowl Road Golcar 01484 654284 ⑩

English **The Olive Branch** Marsden 01484 844487 www.olivebranch.uk.com ⑪

Hotels (see map page 228)

★★

Waterfront Lodge Brighouse 56 Bedrooms
01484 715566 www.waterfrontlodge.co.uk ⑫

Durker Roods Bishops Way Meltham 31 Bedrooms
01484 851413 www.durkerroodshotel.co.uk ⑬

★★★(GA)

Cambridge Hotel 4 Clare Hill 34 Bedrooms
01484 519892 www.newcambridgehotel.co.uk ⑭

★★★

Pennine Manor Nettleton Hill Road 30 Bedrooms
01484 642368 www.thedeckersgroup.com ⑮

Premier Inn New Hey Road 42 Bedrooms
0871 5278532 www.premierinn.com ⑯

Briar Court Halifax Road Birchencliffe 48 Bedrooms
01484 519902 www.briarcourt.co.uk ⑰

The Old Golf House New Hey Road 51 Bedrooms
01484 379311 www.corushotels.com/the-old-golf-hotel/ ⑱

HUDDERSFIELD

The George St Georges Square 60 Bedrooms ⑲
01484 515444 www.thegeorgehotel-huddersfield.co.uk

★★★★(GA)

The Central Lodge 11-15 Beast Market 22 Bedrooms ⑳
01484 515551 www.centrallodge.com

★★★★

Cedar Court Ainley Top 114 Bedrooms ㉑
01422 375431 www.cedarcourthotels.co.uk

Car parking

① Albion Street	41 spaces		⑦ Kingsgate	618 spaces
② Bath Street	54 spaces		⑧ Market Hall	550 spaces
③ Brunswick Street	26 spaces		⑨ Pine Street	588 spaces
④ Cambridge Road	250 spaces		⑩ Spring Grove	440 spaces
⑤ Alfred Street	113 spaces		⑪ Spring Wood	377 spaces
⑥ Bus station	450 spaces		⑫ St Andrew Road	350 spaces

**Huddersfield Visitor Information Centre
Princess Alexandra Walk
01484 223200 www.kirklees.gov.uk**

HUDDERSFIELD

panoramic views afforded from Castle Hill

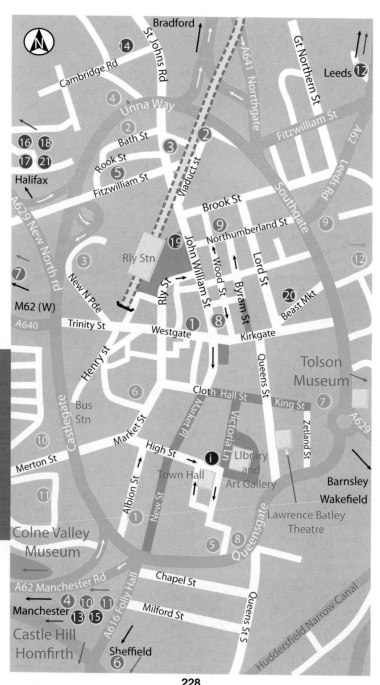

DEWSBURY

The largest town in what is known as the heavy woollen district, Dewsbury lies on the River Calder 8 miles south of Leeds.   The heavy woollen district comprises Dewsbury and the smaller towns of Batley, Heckmondwike and Ossett. The term stems from the nature of the cloth being manufactured for applications such as blankets, rope and twine. Some processes also involve the recycling of old cloth and combining with new. The old cloth is known as mungo or shoddy (the use of fibres from rags to produce new cloth).

History

The Domesday book records the town as *Deusberia*. The name is interpreted by some to mean fortified place by a stream. However, it is clear that the town was an important centre in Saxon times and Paulinus, the first Bishop of York preached in a church here in 627AD.   A market was in existence by the 14thC, and the town sustained religous significance until the18thC when the rise of non conformism began to take effect.   The first British Methodist society was formed in the town in 1746, with John Wesley a frequent visitor. The town was linked to the main canal system in the late 18thC and became a centre for heavy woollen manufacture in early Victorian times. The growth in industrial production, and the emergence of a powerful, but mainly disenfranchised, working class however was accompanied at times with agitation from reformers; Dewsbury was one of the places in Yorkshire that was a centre for both Luddite opposition in the period 1810 to 1820, and then a hotbed of Chartism 30 years later. History records that a speech given by the chartist leader Feargus O'Connor in the town resulted in a mob of 5-7,000 local people besieging the Poor Law guardians in the Royal Hotel; a feat repeated two years later when troops had to be called to quell the demonstration. Decline of the woollen industry in the town occurred later than in other parts of the county and there are still some operational mills producing heavy woollen products, but today the town relies more on commuters, a lively commercial centre and nearby outlet centres than its former heavy industrial heritage.

DEWSBURY

Getting Here

Rail the station is west of the town centre. There are services to Leeds (20 mins), Manchester (30 mins), Huddersfield (30 mins), Middlesbrough (hourly).

Road the town is close to the M1 (junction 40) and M62 (junction 28) with good links to Leeds and Wakefield. London is 3hrs 30 min, Manchester 1 hour.

Bus all services arrive at and depart from the bus station on Aldams Road on the south side of the town centre adjoining the inner ring road.

destination	service(s)	frequency
Wakefield	126/127/128/212/278	10mins/hourly
Leeds	202/253/254	15 mins/30 mins
Huddersfield	262	30 mins
Bradford	253/268/283	hourly/12 mins/30 mins
Halifax	278	hourly

Things to see and do

Dewsbury Market, on Cloth Hall Street, is amongst the larger in Yorkshire, with over 300 stalls. The outdoor market is held on Wed and Sat; the indoor market Mon to Sat.   In the core of the pedestrianised town centre is the Victorian **Town Hall**. Opened in 1889, this Italianate building has at its centre a 700 seat concert hall which hosts a regular programme of concerts and other entertainment   Also in the core of the town centre is **Batley Art Gallery**. Housed above the library in the Market Place, the gallery contains changing collections of art mainly of local artists. The gallery is open Mon to Sat.   **Dewsbury Minster** is close to the bus station. A Church was here in 966 AD with responsibility for an extensive parish area stretching nearly as far as Burnley. The earliest part of the present building dates from about 980 AD, and over the centuries changes and additions have produced a building of cathedral like proportions. Two fragments of a Saxon sandstone cross which commemorate Paulinus' visit to Dewsbury in 627 AD can be seen in the Minsters heritage centre. Much of the stained glass is 14thC, and includes depictions of the arms of well known Yorkshire families of the medieval period. The Minster is open daily to 3.00pm, and there is a refectory in the building.

01924 45705

www.dewsburyminster.org.uk

Dewsbury Museum   is in Crow Nest Park half a mile to the west of the town centre off of the Mirfield Road (A644). The park itself is attractively landscaped, and an ideal place for a summer picnic or short stroll through the fernery and the wildflower garden.   The summer season sees the park take on a role as a venue for pop concerts and other festivals.   The museum, housed in an early 19thC mansion, focuses upon history through the eyes of a local child, and has recently introduced new exhibitions which highlight well known figures who have a connection with the town.   The museum is open Mon to Fri, and Sat and Sun afternoons. Admission is free.   01924 325100   www.kirklees.gov.uk

DEWSBURY

Oakwell Hall and country park is nearby at Birstall, 4 miles to the north west on the A652. The house, built in 1583, is set out as it would have been towards the end of the 17thC. It is recast as "Fieldhead", home of the heroine in Charlotte Bronte's novel "Shirley". Outside, a formal 17thC garden has been recreated with octagonal knot gardens and box hedges. There is a visitor centre. The house is open Mon to Fri and Sat and Sun afternoons. There is an admission charge. The park is open daily. Bus service 283 passes close to the hall. www.kirklees.gov.uk

Red House museum   Dewsbury museum

Red House Museum at Gomersal off the Bradford Road 4 miles north west of the town, is a restored 17thC cloth merchants house with Bronte connections. The house has been recreated to appear as it would have done in the 1830s' as have the surrounding gardens. The house is open Mon to Fri and Sat and Sun afternoons. Admission is free. Bus services 220, 253,254,255 pass close to the site. 01274 335100 www.kirklees.gov.uk

Bagshaw Museum at Wilton Park, 2 miles north west of the town is dedicated to eclectic global collections, ranging from Egyptology to saucy seaside postcards. The house in Gothic style, formerly belonged to a wealthy Victorian mill owner. The surrounding park is part formal landscaped park with ornamental lakes and a butterfly house, and part informal woodland. Bus services 229,281,282,283 pass next to the park. 01924 326155 www.kirklees.gov.uk

Red Brick Mill is an innovative re-use of an old mill building. 1 mile north west of the town centre, it is now the home to cutting edge furniture and homeware retailers, including those associated with the London contemporary design scene. The building is open daily. 01924 460044 www.redbrickmill.co.uk

DEWSBURY

Festivals

May real ale festival   Town hall   www.dewsburybeerfestival.co.uk
July Festival in the Park   Crow's Nest Park
     Canal festival   Savils Wharf   www.waterscape.com

Restaurants (see map page 233)

££

Italian **Zucchinis** 260 Bradford Road 01924 473970 www.zucchinirestaurant.co.uk ①

eclectic **Oasis** 268 Bradford Road 01924 422202 www.oasisrestaurant.co.uk ②

Hotels (see map page 233)

★★★

The Village Capitol Boulevard Tingley 115 bedrooms ③
0844 9800306 www.village-hotels.co.uk

Heath Cottage Wakefield Road 28 bedrooms ④
01924 465399 www.heathcottage.co.uk

Healds Hall Leeds Road Liversedge 24 bedrooms ⑤
01924 409112 www.healdshall.co.uk

Gomersal Park Moor lane 100 bedrooms ⑥
01274 869386 www.gomersalparkhotel.com

not rated

Alderhouse Hotel Towngate Road 20 bedrooms 01924 444777 ⑦

Parking Ⓟ

① Wellington Rd	56 spaces	④ Railway Street	120 spaces
② Wellington Rd Station	292 spaces	⑤ Sports Centre	71 spaces
③ Cliffe Street	415 spaces	⑥ Whitehall Way	38 spaces

DEWSBURY

Dewsbury's busy town centre

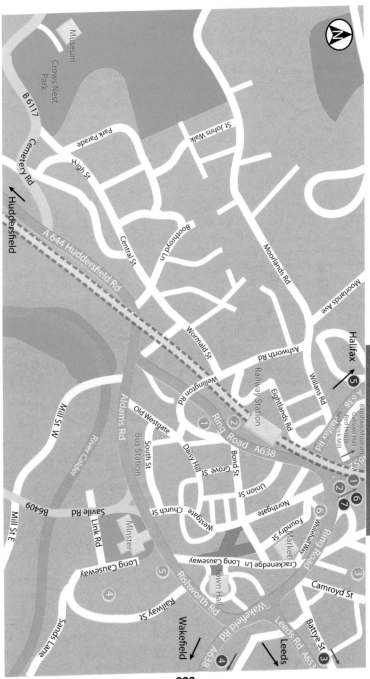

DEWSBURY

WAKEFIELD

Dubbed the "merrie city" in the middle ages, Wakefield is a large cosmopolitan town and administrative capital of the former West Riding. In the heart of the county, it sits in the lower Calder Valley close to the M1 and M62 junction.

History

There is evidence of a settlement in this area as far back as the iron and bronze ages, and there was a river crossing here for the roman road linking Pontefract with Manchester. During Anglo-Saxon times the town developed north of the river, near the present bridge. The streets of Northgate, Kirkgate and Westgate formed the core of the settlement, which was in a Manor owned by Edward the Confessor. The Domesday book lists the town as *Wachefield*, and William the Conqueror gifted the area to his long time confidant, William de Warrenne, whose descendants built Sandal Castle, which became the stronghold for the medieval settlement. The town was granted market charters in the early 12thC, and was the scene of a key battle in the Wars of the Roses in 1460 (the wars of the Roses was a long running clash between two rival households- the Lan-

castrians and the Yorkists, for the right to the English throne and was played out during most of the 15thC, although the main battles were all fought between 1455 and 1485). Two hundred years later, the town was again involved in the English civil war when, as a Royalist stronghold, it was laid siege to by the Parliamentarians under Sir Thomas Fairfax, and forced to surrender. Throughout, Wakefield prospered as a trading centre. Opening of the Aire and Calder Navigation canal in the 18thC and one of the largest cattle markets in northern England combined to solidify its status as a key commercial centre, and as a port trading in wool and corn. The 19thC saw the economy widen including a rapid increase in the number of coalfields around the town. It became the administrative centre for the West Riding County Council, a role it continued to perform, being accorded city status in 1888, until the abolition of that council in 1974, and then its successor in 1986. These extensive administrative functions endowed it with a legacy of fine civic buildings many of which survive.

Getting Here

Rail the city has two stations; **Westgate** with regular services to London, Manchester, Birmingham, Leeds, Doncaster and Newcastle, and **Kirkgate** with services to Nottingham, Sheffield, and Castleford.

Road the city lies immediately east of the M1 and just south of the M62. There are good communications to London, Manchester, Hull.

Bus All services arrive at and depart from the bus station in Union Street on the north side of the city centre, close to the markets.

destination	services	frequency
Leeds	110/117/189/444/X41	20 mins/30 mins/hourly
Bradford	253/425/427	hourly/30 mins
Barnsley	59/96	hourly
Pontefract	125/147/157/184/185	hourly/30 mins
Dewsbury	126/127/128/212/254	10 mins/hourly
Huddersfield	231/232	30 mins
Halifax	278	hourly
Wetherby	173/174	2 hourly
Castleford	187	30 mins
Doncaster	496	hourly
London	561/564/M12/M20	2x per day/1x per day
Heathrow/Gatwick	240	3x per day
Manchester	351	2x per day
Edinburgh	M20	2x per day

Things to See and Do

The administrative capital of the West Riding, the city has a busy atmospheric centre characterised by extensive civic and public buildings, many dating from the 19thC, and by the large shopping centres and commercial buildings. Markets are next to the bus station on Brook Street and are always lively and bustling. The main indoor market is open six days, the outdoor market five days (closed Sun and Wed). The shopping centre is focussed on the streets surrounding the cathedral with two large shopping malls. The newest, Trinity Walk, is on the north side of the centre adjoining the market. It contains over 50 large stores with most of the UK's top brands. The Ridings Centre on the south side of Westgate contains over 90 stores, again with many top brands represented. There are also a wide range of shops and stores fronting the Bullring, Westmoreland Street, Kirkgate, and Northgate.

Cathedral Church of All Saints

Bounded by Westgate to the south, and Westmoreland Street to the north, Wakefield's cathedral is an imposing stately building with the tallest spire in the county (247ft). There is evidence of a Saxon church on the site. The history of the present church, which gained cathedral status in 1888, spans over 800 years. The earliest surviving parts are the north arcade to the nave (1150) and the south arcade (1200). Like many churches, the building has developed

WAKEFIELD

and enlarged over the centuries, with a major rebuilding by Sir Gilbert Scott in the 19thC. The interior contains much of interest with carvings and sculptural features; notably the decorative choir stall misericords, dating from 1480, finely decorated ceilings, and lavishly carved capitals in the nave clerestory. The sundial in the south porch and the font both date from the early 17thC. The building forms an integral part of the city centre, its boundaries removed to open it up to the streets around. It is open daily, and a self guiding audio tour is available.
01924 373923   www.wakefield-cathedral.org.uk

Elizabethan Gallery   Brook Street

Originally the former Queen Elizabeth grammar School, this late 16thC hall is one of the city's oldest buildings, and tucked away in Brook Street is often missed, although close to the bus station and new Trinity Walk shopping centre. It houses varying exhibitions and hosts a number of community events.

Wakefield Museum   Wood Street

Near the town hall, in the civic quarter, the museum contains the Waterton Collection; artefacts collected by Charles Waterton, an archetypal eccentric aristocrat, but also a well known explorer and naturalist who, from his home near the city, travelled much of the world in pursuit of learning more about flora and fauna. The museum also hosts peripatetic exhibitions and provides a well documented and illustrated history of the city. The museum is open Tues to Sat. Admission is free.   01924 305357   www.wakefield.gov.uk

Hepworth Art Gallery   Bridge Street

This new gallery by the river Aire on the south side of the city centre, is one of the largest in the UK outside London and boasts ten gallery areas displaying historic and contemporary art. The Gallery is a tribute to the sculptor Barbara Hepworth (1903-75), a native of the city and whose Foundation has donated 40 pieces of her work to the gallery, which also contains works by contemporary and well known sculptors such as Graham Sutherland. The gallery is open Tues to Sat. Admission is free.   01924 247360   www.hepworthgallery.org

Barbara Hepworth   Sculptor   1903-1975

World renowned sculptor, Barbara Hepworth grew up in the city. She studied at Leeds College of Art and Royal College of Art in London. Her work is prodigious, and makes an immeasurable contribution to modern sculpture. It is in evidence all over the world, including the United Nations building in New York. Substantial collections are to be found in the Yorkshire Sculpture Park and in the newly opened Hepworth Gallery. She spent her later years in Cornwall, where she died in a fire in her studio.

WAKEFIELD

some of Barbara Hepworths work inside the hepworth gallery

Civic Area and St Johns

The city's historical role as an administrative centre is well evidenced in the area to the west and north of the city centre, with a range of buildings which illustrate this function. It is well worth a walk along Wood Street, where can be seen the old **Town Hall** (on Lee Street). In front, facing onto Wood Street, is the present town hall of 1877 in neo-gothic style. It was the ambition of inflential Wakefield men of the time to rival Leeds Town Hall. The building is stately and imposing, lavishly decorated with a strong flavour of Jacobean influence in the detail. It reflects the wealth and prosperity of the city in the mid Victorian era. The richly embellished interior is now the venue for weddings and other functions. Further along Wood Street is the former court house. Built in neo-Greek style in 1810, it is now used for a variety of commercial purposes. The former **West Riding County Hall**, now used as the local council's offices, is the next building on the street. This finely detailed and extensive structure was built in 1898 following a well subscribed architectural competition. As with the town hall, the style of this imposing building is ornate and lavish with an extenive array of different stone carvings on the façade. The richly decorated interior includes inlaid marble floors and mahogany panelling and has been described as a library of symbolism. Representations such as the owl and the scales on the main staircase reflect wisdom and justice; and there are many representations of the white rose of Yorkshire. Continuing along Wood Street and into Wentworth Street leads to **St Johns Square** and the surrounding area. Apart from the church, the area is characterised by neat rows of Georgian terraces fronting wide boulevards as well as the formally laid out St Johns Square. These were all built by wealthy merchants in the late 18thC when the city was a prime location for corn trading.

WAKEFIELD

Charles Waterton   Explorer   1782-1865

Charles Waterton was a renowned English naturalist and explorer. He was born into minor aristocracy at Walton Hall, an 18thC Palladian mansion (now a hotel), and the place where the Waterton family had been lords of the Manor since the mid 15thC. He travelled widely, including a spell in British Guyana managing family estates, and ventured into Brazil and other South American countries in search of flora and fauna , and rare undiscovered animals. A skilled taxidermist, he accumulated over his lifetime an extensive collection of stuffed birds and animals which is now in the Wakefield museum. He created a nature and wildfowl reserve in the grounds of Walton Hall and is credited with inventing the bird nesting box.

Yorkshire Sculpture Park   Bretton Hall

Set in the landscaped grounds of a 1720 Georgian country mansion, this is a so called "gallery without walls". The 500 acres park is home to a wide range of sculptures by artists such as Henry Moore and Barbara Hepworth. There are also indoor galleries. The park is close to junction 38 of the M1, 4 miles south west of the city and is open daily. Admission is free. The park is served by bus 96 (Wakefield to Barnsley), and 435/436 (Wakefield to Holmfirth).

01924 832631   www.ysp.co.uk

National Coal Mining Museum

This museum is in Caphouse Colliery, one of the earlier commercial colleries in Yorkshire, on the A642 5 miles west of the city.   Officially recognised as the national museum, it illustrates the rise and fall of Britain's coal mining industry. There are guided underground tours that demonstrate conditions many miners had to experience on a daily basis, and the tools and machines they used.   On the surface, a visitor centre traces the development of the British coal industry, and visitors can see the former pithead baths, the winding gear and other features of a large working coal mine.   The museum is open daily. Admission is free. Bus 128 (Wakefield to Dewsbury) and 231/232 (Wakefield to Huddersfield) pass the site.   01924 848806 www.ncm.org.uk

Sandal Castle   Manygates Lane

This is a ruined medieval castle in the suburb of Sandal two miles south of the city centre. Built by William de Warenne with earthwork motte and bailey and wooden towers in the 12thC, and rebuilt in stone in the 13thC, it was the scene of the Battle of Wakefield during the Wars of the Roses in 1460. It fell into neglect after the death of Richard III in 1485, and was a ruin by the time of the English civil war. The castle grounds are open all year. The visitor centre is open Wed to Sun Admission is free. There are guided tours available for a fee. Bus services 59, 96, 110 pass near to the castle.   01924 249779 www.wakefield.gov.uk

WAKEFIELD

Chantry Chapel

The oldest of the four surviving chantry chapels in England, the 14thC St Mary the Virgin was restored in the 19thC following closure in the Reformation. It survived though only because it is an integral part of the bridge! The interior possesses ornate stained glass dating from a 19thC restoration. It was built to enable priests to say mass for the souls of the dead, and today used for a monthly church service. There are limited opening hours for viewing.

www.wakefieldfhs.org.uk

Nostell Priory

A Palladian style mansion built in 1733 for the Winn family, wealthy London textile merchants, in the grounds of a former 12thC Augustinian priory dedicated to St Oswald. The house is surrounded by 300 acres of landscaped parkland including lakeside walks and extensive collections of rhododendron and azaleas. Parts, including the stableblock, were designed by the then in demand Robert Adam, although much of his designs and plans for the house were never realised. The sumptuous interior of the house contains an extensive collection of Thomas Chippendale furniture as well as paintings by such notable artists as Breughel and Hogarth. House and gardens are open Wed to Sun afternoons. There is an admission charge. The parkland is open throughout the year. Bus services 485/496 from Wakefield stop in Nostell village.

01924 863892 www.nationaltrust.org.uk

"The Rhubarb Triangle"

The rhubarb plant is a native of Siberia, and said to have manifold medicinal properties, as well as being a favourite dessert. The plant thrives in the climatic and soil conditions found in this part of the county. A small area to the north of the city is known as the rhubarb triangle, where the crop is grown in dark and warm conditions in what are called forcing sheds, by small holders and market gardeners. There is a rhubarb festival every February and Yorkshire rhubarb now, like champagne and parma ham, enjoys a protected name status.

WAKEFIELD

Festivals

February Rhubarb festival   city centre   www.wakefield.gov.uk
April   World Coal Carrying Championship Gawthorpe
                                         www.experiencewakefield.co.uk

Restaurants (see map pages 241 242)

££

Italian **Bellaroma** 63 Northgate 01924 371059 www.bellaromawakefield.co.uk ①

Italian **Rustico** 29 Northgate 01924 291297 www.dinerustico.co.uk ②

Italian **Prego Pizzeria** 107 Westgate 01924 377977 www.pregowakefield.co.uk ③

Oriental **Bollywood Lounge** 34 Smyth Street
01924 362111 www.bollywood-lounge.co.uk ④

Chinese **China Wok** 24 Teall street   01924 370011 ⑤

Kashmiri **Lala's** 17 George Street 01924 377550   www.lalasrestaurant.co.uk ⑥

Kashmiri **Aagrah**   108, Barnsley Road 01924 258725   www.aagrah.com ⑦

£££

English **The Cow Shed** 53 Northgate 01924 291044 www.cowshed.uk.com ⑧

Italian **Boccaccio** Smyth Street   01924 360018 www.boccaccio.co.uk ⑨

Italian **Sloanes** 10-12 Drury Lane 01924 372069 www.billybuddleisure.co.uk ⑩

Cuban **Qubana** 25-27 Northgate 01924 299000 www.qubana.co.uk ⑪

Thai **Thai on the Square** 3-9 Cross Square
01924 298555 www.thaionthesquare.co.uk ⑫

Hotels (see maps page 241 242)

★★★

Premier Inn Central Thornes Park Denby Dale Road.42 bedrooms
0871 5279114 www.premierinn.com ⑬

Chasley Queens Street 62 bedrooms 01924 372111 www.chasleyhotel.com ⑭

St Pierre Barnsley Road Newmillerdam   54 bedrooms
01924 255596   www.hotelstpierre.co.uk ⑮

York House 10-12 Drury Lane 20 bedrooms
01924 372069   www.billybuddleisure.co.uk ⑯

Days Inn Fryers Way 100 bedrooms 01924 274200 www.daysinn.com ⑰

Holiday Inn Queens Drive 104 bedrooms 0871 4234896 www.holidayinn.com ⑱

★★★★

Cedar Court Denby Dale Road 149 bedrooms
01924 76310   www.cedarcourthotels.co.uk ⑲

Waterton Park Walton Hall 65 bedrooms
01924 257911 www.watertonparkhotel.co.uk ⑳

WAKEFIELD

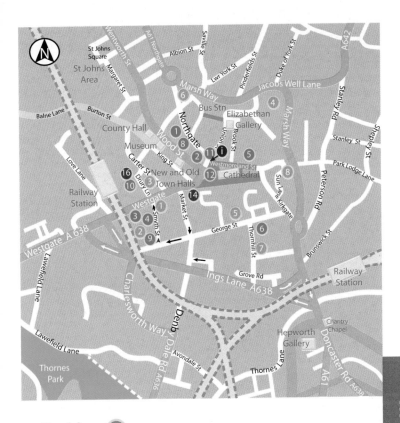

Parking

1	Smyth Street	74 spaces	5	The Ridings	1000 spaces
2	Garden Street	62 spaces	6	Rishworth Street	388 spaces
3	Carter Street	85 spaces	7	Thornhill Street	47 spaces
4	Trinity Walk	1000 spaces	8	Lower Warrengate	150 spaces

Wakefield Visitor Information Centre
The BullRing
0845 60128353
www.experiencewakefield.co.uk

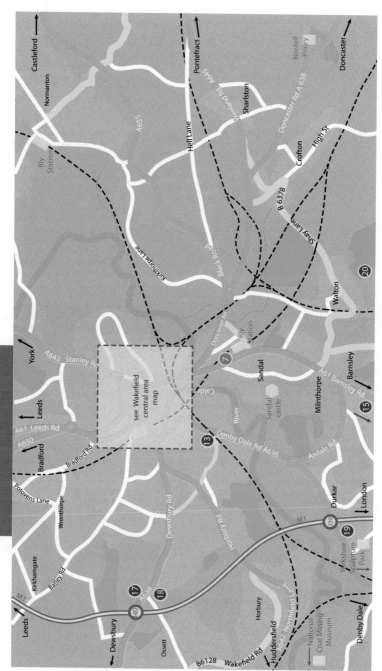

WAKEFIELD

Castleford
Normanton
A655
Rly Station
York
A642 Stanley Rd
Leeds
A61 Leeds Rd
A650
Bradford
Bradford Rd
Potovens Lane
Wrenthorpe
Kirkhamgate
Batley Rd
M1
Leeds
Dewsbury
Ossett
A638
17
18
40

Hell Lane
Kirkthorpe Lane
Black Road
Doncaster Rd
Pontefract A645
Sharlston
Wakefield Rd A645
Doncaster Rd A 638
Crofton
High St
Nostell Priory
Doncaster
B 6378
Shay Lane
Walton
20

see Wakefield central area map

Doncaster Rd
Rly Station
7
Calder
River
Sandal
Sandal castle
13
Denby Dale Rd A636
Milnthorpe
Asdale Rd
A61 Barnsley Rd
Barnsley
15

Dewsbury Rd
Horbury Rd
Durkar
London
M1
39
19
Yorkshire Sculpture Park

Horbury
Huddersfield
A642 Northfield Lane
B6128 Wakefield Rd
Denby Dale
National Coal Mining Museum

BARNSLEY

The town of Barnsley lies on the River Dearne midway between Sheffield and Wakefield, in the heart of the former West Riding industrial area. It is known for its long association with the coal industry, with glassmaking and with brass bands. The classic film *Kes* was filmed in and around the town, and the local community is renowned for its friendliness, its cohesion and mutual support.

History

The Domesday book describes what was then a small settlement of no more than 200 people as *"Berneslai"*, but which was in Silkstone parish. The current town was started in the 12thC by the monks of St Johns Priory in Pontefract, to whom the land had been given, and it grew up around the junction of the three roads linking Wakefield with Sheffield, Rotherham with Huddersfield, and Doncaster with Manchester.   A market charter was granted in the mid 13thC, and from the 17thC it became both a stopping off point for travellers between Sheffield Leeds and London, as well as a centre for linen weaving.   In the early 19thC, the town became the focal point for many of Yorkshire's coal mines.   The 20thC witnessed the rise of civic pride and investment, with an iconic town hall and redevelopment of the town centre and, by contrast, the demise of the coal industry and its associated commerce; an experience which the town has found difficult to recover from, although alternative commercial activity is now evident.

Getting Here

Rail the railway station adjoins the bus station on Eldon Street with regular services to Leeds, Sheffield, Huddersfield, and Nottingham.   Links to London services can be made at Sheffield, and links to Manchester at Huddersfield.

Road the town lies adjacent to the M1 motorway. London is 3 ½ hours, Leeds c. 30 mins.

Bus all services arrive at depart from the interchange on Eldon Street, adjoining the railway station.   There are regular services to:

BARNSLEY

destination	service(s)	frequency
Wakefield	57/59/96/97	15 mins/hourly
Sheffield	265	30 mins
Rotherham	229	30 mins
Pontefract	35/46	30 mins/ hourly
Doncaster	219/222	30 mins
London	560	3x per day
Blackpool	351	2x per day
Robin Hood Airport	X19	hourly

Things to see and do

Much of the **town centre** is pedestrianised, with most shopping activity in Queen Street, Cheapside and Peel Square.   The enclosed mall known as the Alhambra centre on New Street forms the southern edge of the shopping area, and adjoins the lively **Market Hall** which has a market, indoor and outdoor, most days of the week with over 300 stalls giving a wide range of choice for the visitor. To the north of the shopping area lies the **town hall**. Built in the early 1930's at the height of inter war depression, it is a monument to civic splendour and largesse. The author, George Orwell, who lived in the town at the time, was vociferous in condemning the project saying the funds should have been directed towards the homeless and the unemployed.

Wentworth Castle Gardens

Not to be confused with Wentworth Woodhouse (see page 267), the extensive gardens forming the grounds of Wentworth Castle are open to the public and offer a family day out. There are over 500 acres of maintained parkland, containing the castle itself - an 18thC Palladian mansion which is not open to the public - an 18thC folly known as Stainborough Castle, a number of other follies, a heronry and nationally recognised collections of magnolia, rhododendrons and Camilla plants.   The gardens are open year round. There is an admission charge. A regular bus service (23,24) from Barnsley interchange passes the entrance. 01226 776040 www.wentworthcastle.org

Cannon Hall Country Park and Museum

Cannon Hall is an 18thC mansion in extensive grounds now a museum and country park. The museum houses art collections   including ceramics and paintings as well as being home to the regimental museum of the Royal Hussars. The parkland, open all year round, includes a walled garden amidst its 70 acres. There is a working farm adjoining the park.   The museum and park lie close to the A635 about 4 miles west of the town centre. Bus service 92 goes to Cawthorne village which adjoins the park. The Museum is open Sat to Wed from Easter to October. Admission is free. The adjoining farm has an admission charge.   01226 790270 www.barnsley.gov.uk

Pot House Hamlet   Silkstone

A small complex of former mill buildings, in a village 3 miles west of the town, Pot House began as a 17thC glassworks, and expanded to include a pottery

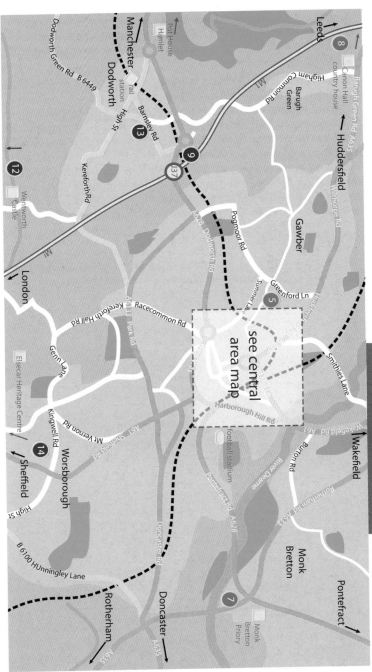

BARNSLEY

and grain mill. The renovated buildings now provide a series of independent shops, café, ice cream parlour and a walk along an ancient wagon way beside the beck. The complex is open daily.   www.pothousehamlet.co.uk

Monk Bretton Priory ⊞ Lundwood

The site at Abbey Lane Lundwood, two miles east of the town centre, contains substantial ruins of a 12th Cluniac monastery.   The site is entered through the remains of the late 14thC gatehouse, though only limited parts of the main monastic buildings survive - a few low sandstone walls, indicating the transepts and chancel of Monk Bretton Priory church; the south wall of the refectory remains standing to a good height, and even two of the original windows exist. Parts of the west range also remain remarkably intact. A surprisingly sophisticated drainage system existed during monastic times, and much of this remains. Bus service 46 passes near the site on Pontefract Road.   The priory is open daily between April and October.   Admission is free. www.englishheritage.org.uk

Elsecar Heritage Centre

5 miles south of the town, the Elsecar Heritage centre is a small complex of former iron works and colliery buildings attractively converted into a craft and antique centre and includes a short stretch of restored railway line.   The centre is open daily.   Bus service 66 passes the complex.
01226 740203   www.elsecar-heritage-centre.co.uk

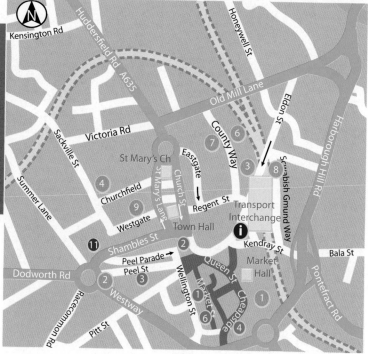

Sporting life

Barnsley AFC

A middle ranking English League club, Barnsley AFC play home games at Oakwell, a long established ground east of the town centre. Home games regularly attract a noisy crowd of around 12,000. 0871 2266777 www.barnsleyfc.co.uk

Monk Bretton Priory

Restaurants (see map pages 245 246)

££

Indian Chilli 66-68 Market Street 01226 290333 www.chillirestaurant.co.uk

English Blah Bar &Grill 1 Market Hill 01226 734195 www.blahbarandgrill.co.uk

Chinese China Moon 37, Peel Street 01226 283331

Italian Pinocchios 15 New St 01226 770121 www.pinocchios-restaurant.co.uk

Indian Gate of India 44 Gawber Road 01226 242242

£££

English Grille Market Street 01226 294333 www.grillesteakhouse.co.uk

Italian Vecchio Mulino 81, Grange Lane 01226 24224

££££

English Beatson House Darton Road Cawthorne
01226 791245 www.beatsonhouse.co.uk

Hotels (see map pages 245 246)

★★★

Ramada Encore Whinby Road Dodworth 113 Bedrooms
01226 729930 www.encorebarnsley.co.uk

Ardsley House Doncaster Road 75 Bedrooms
01226 309955 www.ardsleyhousehotel.co.uk

Premier Inn Central Sackville Street 110 bedrooms
0871 5279114 www.premierinn.com

BARNSLEY

★★★★(GA)

Wortley Hall   Wortley 49 Bedrooms   0114 2882100   www.wortleyhall.org.uk

★★★★

Holiday Inn   Barnsley Road Dodworth 77 Bedrooms
01226 299571   www.hibarnsley.com   ⑬

Tankersley Manor   Church Lane   Worsbrough 99 Bedrooms
01226 744700   www.qhotels.co.uk   ⑭

Elsecar Heritage Centre

Parking Ⓟ

① Alhambra Centre	496 spaces		⑥ County Way (east)	200 spaces	
② Peel Street	359 spaces		⑦ County Way (west)	200 spaces	
③ Interchange	82 spaces		⑧ Eldon Street	300 spaces	
④ Sackville street	112 spaces		⑨ Lancaster Gate	40 spaces	
⑤ Mark Street	55 spaces				

ⓘ **Barnsley Visitor Information Centre**
Eldon Street
01226 206757   www.barnsley.gov.uk

Cannon Hall, set in extensive country grounds and which houses Barnsley's collection of art and ceramics as well as the regimental museum of the Royal Hussars

BARNSLEY

SHEFFIELD

"Ay by his belt he baar a long panade,
And of a swerd ful trenchant was the blade.
A joly poppere baar he in his pouche;
Ther was no man, for peril, dorste hym touche.
A Sheffeld thwitel baar he in his hose.
Round was his face, and camus was his nose"

Thus runs the Reeves Tale, from Geoffreys Chaucers Canterbury Tales, refer-
ring to Sheffield as an acknowledged centre for the manufacture of knives as
far back as the 14thC. Yorkshire's second city is bustling and cosmopolitan as
it renews itself from the trials and tribulations of the 1980's and 1990's where
demise of its long established prosperous economic base shattered illusions of
immortality and instilled a determination to renew, to innovate and to become a
stylish international destination for commerce, sport, and culture.   Its reputation is as a "steel city"; the ubiquitous metal in its earlier and later forms having
been made here for over 600 years.   It lies at the foot of the county, on the
Pennine foothills, at the confluence of the River Sheaf and River Don and close
to the Peak District National Park. It is served by the M1 motorway, a regular
rail service to London St Pancras, and a regional airport.   It is also known as a
city with strong and vociferous political traits, and as well as where the concept
of the TUC (Trades Union Congress) was first developed. The city has reared a
number of famous politicians, Chartists and union activists – past and present -
such as the Chartist, Samuel Holberry (1816 -1842), William Broadhead (1815-
1879), and William Dronfield (1826-1894) union activists; Nicholas Liverpool,
president of Dominica and Roy Hattersley and David Blunkett, Labour politicians.

SHEFFIELD

water features in Sheaf Square

Time spent in Sheffield is time well rewarded, with the cities many attractions from the retail offering at one of the UK's largest enclosed shopping centres, Meadowhall; the top class entertainment and sporting events hosted at the Sheffield Arena, to the panoply of museums, galleries and restaurants in the city centre.

History

Sheffield's roots - the name derives from the river Sheaf, and field - a clearing in old English - can be traced back to the founding of a settlement beside the river in the second half of the 1st millennium AD. The area had seen human occupation, probably following the last ice age, but like many modern cities in the north of England, significant growth only occurred as recently as the 19thC with the arrival of the industrial revolution. There is evidence of a Mesolithic "house" – a circle of stones in the form of a hut base – at Deepcar to the north west of the city, and stone circles and urns from the bronze age can be found to the west by the gritstone escarpments. The Iron Age saw the rise of the Brigantes, a powerful Celtic tribe who dominated much of the county, with Sheffield being their southern most area of occupation. The remains of a hill fort built by the tribe exists at Wincobank in the north eastern suburbs of the city, close to Meadowhall. There is only limited evidence of Roman occupation in the area, and it was unlikely to have been a settlement of any significance, the closest remains of a settlement of any size being at Templeborough in Rotherham, but following the Roman withdrawal from Yorkshire in the early part of the 5thC, the area now occupied by the city became part of the Celtic kingdom of Elmet, close to its boundary with Mercia. Anglo Saxons gradually pushed west from Deira (the eastern side of the county) to inhabit the Sheffield area in the 7thC and beyond, and the site of the present city is thought to have started between the 6th and 9thC. Norse settlers arrived in the 9thC and there were pitched battles fought between the Anglo Saxons and the Norse tribes for possession of the North of England, one of which, c.937 AD, was thought to have been at or near Tinsley to the east of the city. The arrival of the Normans following the1066 invasion sees the city described as *Scafeld* in the Domesday Book with the land being owned by Roger de Busli, who built Sheffield castle close to the confluence of the Rivers Sheaf and Don - in the Castlegate area of the city centre. Although developed and updated over the centuries (Mary Queen of Scots was a prisoner in Sheffield castle between 1570 and 1584), the castle was razed to the ground following the English civil war and there is now no visible trace. Medieval Sheffield grew up around the castle. It was granted a market charter in 1296, and became a borough the following year. The oldest buildings surviving in the city centre date from the15thC - notably the Old Queens Head pub in Pond Hill and parts of the Cathedral. The Bishops House and Broom Hall (now a private nursery on leafy Broomhall road south west of the city centre) also date from the same era. By the middle of the 14thC, the town had become noted for its manufacture of knives, and by 1600 had become the main centre in England for the manufacture of cutlery.

The history of cutlery production is traced at the Abbeydale Industrial Hamlet (see page 259), and Daniel Defoe's book of 1727, "A Tour through the Whole Island of Great Britain" refers to Sheffield as *".......the streets narrow, and the houses dark and black, occasioned by the continued smoke of the forges, which are always at work: Here they make all sorts of cutlery-ware, but especially that of edged-tools, knives, razors, axes, &c. and nails; and here the only mill of the sort, which was in use in England for some time was set up, for turning their grindstones, though now tis grown more common......"*

The steel making process implicit in production of cutlery widened and grew. 18thC Sheffield saw the invention of new forms of metal manufacture, including a process to fuse silver onto copper to give silverplate, a technique since widely used across the world, and the early 19thC witnessed the introduction of the Bessemer Converter, a process for converting pig iron into steel cheaply and efficiently, and used worldwide until the 1960's.

These developments, and the manufacturing production which accompanied them, made the city a world class centre for the production of steel.

One of the original converters used by its inventor, Henry Bessemer, can be seen at the Kelham Island Museum (see page 257). The importance of steel and metal production was reflected in the granting, by Act of Parliament, of the right to have an Assay Office, which opened in 1773. Only Birmingham and Edinburgh outside London possess such offices, and the Sheffield one is still trading. Like many of the West Riding towns, the 19thC saw massive growth; steel and metal products, particularly cutlery production multiplied, and prosperity based on this did not falter until the 1970's. City status was conferred in 1893, and the creation of the Sheffield Diocese in 1914 made the city's parish church a cathedral. Rapid decline of the steel and metal industries in the late 20thC led to renewed vigour in creating new economic activity, reflected in the Meadowhall shopping complex, the introduction of a new tram network as well as museums, galleries, entertainment and sports venues. The city's Don Valley stadium hosted the World Student Games in 1991.

SHEFFIELD

SHEFFIELD

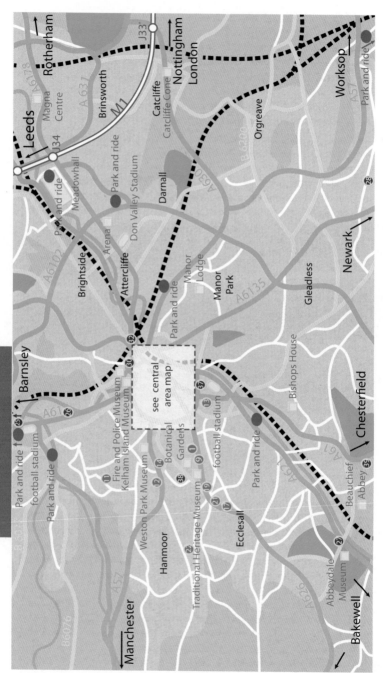

Getting Here

Rail The main station is on the south east side of the centre with regular services to most UK destinations. London (St Pancras) takes 2hrs and there are frequent services to Leeds, Birmingham, Newcastle and Manchester.

Road The city lies immediately west of the M1, close to its link with the M18. Journeys to London take c.3 hrs; Manchester c.1hr; Leeds c.45 mins.

Bus Most bus services arrive at and depart from the Interchange, located near the station between Pond Street and Sheaf Street.

destination	service(s)	frequency
Barnsley	265/465/560	30 mins/1x per day
Birmingham	310/320/321/324	4x per day
Bradford	321/324/465	3x per day
Chesterfield	43/44/X17/321/465/560	hourly/5x per day
Doncaster	X78	10 mins
Glasgow	537	1x per day
Halifax	465	1x per day
Huddersfield	465	1x per day
Leeds	321/324/326	3x per day
Liverpool	350	1x per day
London	560	3x per day
Heathrow/Gatwick	240	3x per day
Manchester	350	1x per day
Newcastle	326	1x per day
Rotherham	69/X78	10 mins
Wakefield	465	1x per day
York	326	1x per day

Park and Ride the city has excellent park and ride services, with frequent links into the city centre. Park and ride sites (see map page 252) are at:

Middlewood Rd	340	tram and bus
Nunnery Sq	390	tram
Halfway	200	tram
Malin Bridge	104	tram and bus
Meadowhall	328	tram bus and train
Valley C'ment	200	tram
Abbeydale	200	bus

Things to see and do

Journeys in and around the city are made easier for the visitor by a free-bus, which runs in a circular route around the city centre, and by a comprehensive citywide tram network. The heart of the city centre lies around the **Town Hall** and the **Peace Gardens** with the major shopping streets being High Street, Fargate, Orchard Square, Pinstone Street, and The Moor. Retail therapy can be had here with most major brands represented.

SHEFFIELD

SHEFFIELD

The city has a number of markets. There are outdoor markets operating six days a week; one with about 45 stalls on the north east side of the centre at King Street/Exchange street, and the Moor market with about 30 stalls on the south side of the centre.   Castle Market is a large indoor market with over 200 stalls fronting onto Castlegate on the northern edge of the centre and built over the site of Sheffield Castle. Open six days a week, it sells meat and fish as well as other goods.   A walk through the city centre's main sights, starting from the station to the City Hall, leads first of all to Sheaf Square which presents an unusual and dramatic sight on leaving the railway station, with an unusual steel and water sculpture dominating the space. Designed by Japanese glass artist Keiko Muikade and using locally produced steel, it is a testimony to the city's long history in steel manufacture. From here, walk up the tree lined pedestrianised Howard Street and cross Arundel Gate into the Millennium Galleries. This light and airy building houses four individual galleries. The *Craft and Design Gallery* has both historic and contemporary collections, and showcases recent work by modern designers and craftspeople.   The *Metalwork Gallery* celebrates the city's role as a steel and metal manufacturing centre and contains both historic and contemporary pieces of metalwork.   The *Ruskin Gallery* shows the comprehensive collection of the well known Victorian artist and scholar.   There is a *special exhibition gallery* which puts on four different themed displays of art a year; many works of national importance loaned from London or overseas. The galleries are open daily. Admission is free. 0114 2782600 www.sheffield-museums.org.uk

The Winter Gardens are on the north side of the gallery. There is direct access into the unashamedly modern, spectacular wood and glass arcade. Large enough to contain over 5000 domestic greenhouses it has over 2,500 plants from all around the world. The gardens are open every day. Admission is free.   Exiting the northern side of the gardens is Tudor Square, a formal civic space, containing the Graves Art Gallery, The Crucible Theatre and the Lyceum theatre.

Sheffields galleries and winter gardens

The **Crucible Theatre** is an icon venue, and unusually a modern listed building. It has long associated the city with the world snooker championship, but is also one of the city's main entertainment venues with a year round programme of concerts, plays, and an annual pantomime. The **Lyceum Theatre** by contrast is a late Victorian building with lavish internal design and decoration and puts on programmes of opera, ballet, contemporary dance and West End hits.   0114 2496000   www.sheffieldtheatres.co.uk

On the southern side of the gardens is **Millennium Square.** This triangular shaped space features a number of water features in the form of steel spheres, and leads into the **Peace Gardens** which, with a backdrop of the town hall, is the civic core of the city. Built on a former churchyard to celebrate the 1938 Munich Agreement, the gardens were rebuilt for the second Millennium. They contain all the aspects of a contemporary English garden, together with locally designed water features. The **Town Hall** was opened in 1897. It was designed in renaissance revival style by the London architect of The Old Bailey. The clock tower, some 200ft high, is topped by a statue of Vulcan, the Norse god of fire, and the frieze along the facade depicts Sheffield industries. The interior is embellished with a grand marble staircase; and lavishly decorated walls and ceilings. The town hall is open to group tours by prior arrangement.
0114 2734567 www.sheffield.gov.uk

City Hall at night

To the west of the town hall through town hall square, is **Barkers Pool**, a shopping street which leads to Barker Pool Square, containing the city's war memorial and the **City Hall**. This is a restored art deco concert hall, designed in neo classical style with an imposing front portico and opened in 1932. It hosts a comprehensive programme of concerts throughout the year in its main 2,200 seat auditorium.
0114 2233740 www.sheffieldcityhall.co.uk

SHEFFIELD

The Cathedral Quarter forms the northern part of the city centre, and is the oldest part of the city. **St Peter and St Paul's Cathedral**, on Church Street, is on a site occupied by a church since Saxon times. The only relic from this era is a stone cross which is now in the British Museum. The Norman church built here by William de Lovetot was replaced in the late 13thC. The sole surviving remnant of this are the dogtooth pattern stones set in the east wall, and the cathedrals main tower is the only survivor of the medieval building. Most of the church was rebuilt in the present cruciform pattern in the 15thC, and had been completely rebuilt bar the tower and the chancel by the end of the 19thC. It was consecrated as a cathedral in 1914. The most recent additions were in the 1960s with the modern Lantern Tower built in 1966. The interior of the Shrewsbury Chapel contains an alabaster monument to the 6th Earl of Shrewsbury, Lords of the Manor of Sheffield, one of the most senior British peerage titles, who was responsible for the incarceration and safe keeping of Mary Queen of Scots during her time in Sheffield Castle in the late 16thC. Many family members are buried in the vault underneath the chapel. The lantern tower has a contemporary glass roof put in place in 1998 and designed by the well known stained glass artist, Amber Hiscott. The richly carved hammer beam roof of the chancel is decorated with eight gilded angels. The St George chapel is now dedicated as the Regimental Chapel of the York and Lancaster regiment. The cathedral is open most days. Guided tours are available by prior arrangement.

Cathedral

0114 2753434 www.sheffieldcathedral.org

The area around the cathedral is mainly occupied by commercial offices with many 18th and 19thC buildings. Streets such as Meetinghouse Lane, Paradise Street and Paradise Square gives a strong flavour of what the city might have been like in times gone by. Cutlers Hall is a further example of the city's 19thC heritage and prosperity. Opposite the Cathedral, the Hall was built in 1832 with a handsome neo-Grecian facade and opulent interior. It is primarily a banqueting hall, originally for the Guild of Master Cutlers, the city's premier craft guild established as the Hallamshire Company of Cutlers, by Act of Parliament in 1624. Despite the decline of the cutlery and steel industry, the guild is still active. An extensive membership elects each year a Master Cutler to head the guild. To the east of the cathedral lies the Old Town Hall, in Waingate, currently disused but a court for many years after the present town hall was opened in 1897. One of the oldest buildings in the city, the Old Queens Head Pub in Pond Hill is behind the bus station. Originally a house, this timber framed building dates from c.1475, and was used as a banqueting hall for the parties hunting wildfowl on the Earls of Shrewsbury estates during the 16thC.

SHEFFIELD

Sheffield's **Botanical Gardens** on Clarkehouse Road, 1 mile west of the station, offer 19 acres covered with plant collections from across the world. There are national collections in the gardens, including *weigela* and *diervilla* (bush honey-suckles). Some are housed inside recently restored glass pavilions which date from 1832, the work of Victorian garden expert Robert Marnock, best known for his work on Regents Park in London. The gardens are open daily. Admission is free. Bus services 10, 30 and 505 from the bus station pass the main entrance.

0114 2686001   www.sbg.org.uk

Manor Lodge is the remains of a 16thC grand manor house which would originally have stood in the middle of a vast deer park then owned by the Earls of Shrewsbury,   The lodge fell into disrepair during the 17th /18thC and coal mining later took place in the grounds   The Turret House built in 1574, probably as a gatekeepers house and a hunting tower, remains the only roofed building on the site today. Activities here including a farm shop, and a heritage skills training centre.   The site, to the east of the city centre on Manor Lane, is served by bus 10 (from Arundel gate) which passes directly in front of the site, and by bus 56 (from the interchange) which goes along City road. A short walk up Moor lane will reach the site.   0114 2762828 www. manorlodge.org.uk

The Bishops House is on Norton Lees road, 2 miles south of the city centre, tucked into the corner of Meersbrook Park. This is one of the city's oldest build-ings, dating from 1500 and typifies the domestic house of the 16thC. The house is open Sat and Sun. Admission is free. Bus services 20 and 33 from the Inter-change pass the site.   0114 2782600 www.museums-sheffield.org.uk

Weston Park Museum is in Weston Park, on the A57 west of the city centre. It has collections devoted to archeology, natural history and decorative art. The Museum is open daily. Admission is free. Bus services 51/52, from Arundel Gate pass the site.   0114 2782600 www.museums-sheffield.org.uk

Kelham Island Museum contains machinery, artefacts and archives re-counting the city's illustrious history with heavy industry. It is sited north of the city centre where, historically, the mainstay of Sheffields industry

SHEFFIELD

Sir Frederick Mappin Master Cutler 1821- 1910

His father started a cutlery company which Frederick assumed control of when he was 20. He built the company up becoming the youngest ever Sheffield Master Cutler. The company became the world renowned Mappin and Webb famed for its high quality cutlery, jewellery and glass. Elected to the city council twice; the second term serving a year as Mayor, he was elected to Parliament as an MP for nearby Retford, but he maintained an active involvement in the Sheffield community and funded the creation of an art gallery (now part of Weston Park Museum) as well as being instrumental in the formation of Sheffield university; becoming its first pro chancellor.

has long been. There are galleries devoted to the history of steel including an original Bessemer converter, equipment which transformed modern steel making (and one of only three left in the world); to power; and to working conditions in the Victorian age. The museum is open Sun to Thu. There is an admission charge.   0114 2722106 www.simt.co.uk

The Fire and Police Museum is to be found at the junction of West Bar and Corporation street in the north west of the city centre. It contains collections of fire and police service memorabilia.   The museum is open on Sun. There is an admission charge.   0114 2491999   www.firepolicemuseum.org.uk

Turner Museum of Glass houses a vast collection of glass from all over the world ranging from the18thC to the modern day. It is located in the University of Sheffield (Sir Robert Hadfield Building) on Newcastle Street, in the westen part of the city centre   The museum is open Mon to Fri. Admission is free.
www.turnermuseum.group.shef.ac.uk

The Traditional Heritage Museum on Eccleshall Road forms part of the National Centre for English Cultural Tradition, based in the University. The Museum houses a material culture collection, which provides a unique insight into the life and work of the city and vividly illustrates how people lived and plied their trades in years gone by. Open on last Sat of each month. Admission is free.   Frequent bus services pass the site 10, 65, 81, 82, 214, 272
0114 2681270   www.thegroup.shef.ac.uk

The Site Gallery near Sheaf Square is a venue for the display and development of contemporary art, particularly focussing new artists and on digital media and visual arts. It hosts national and international exhibitions of emerging artists and is a key national player in the UK visual arts sector. Open Tues to Sat. Admission is free.   0114 2812077 www.sitegallery.org

Graves Gallery situated above the central Lending library in Surrey Street houses the city's primary traditional fine art collection focussing on classical and contemporary paintings. The museum is open Monday to Saturday. Admission is free.   0114 2782600 www.museums-sheffield.org.uk

SHEFFIELD

Henry Bessemer Steel Inventor 1813-1898

Although not a native of the city, Bessemer created the Bessemer Convertor, which revolutionised the scale quality and efficiency of steelmaking and did so by setting up a brand new steelworks in the city which used his invention. It was a runaway success and the emergence of the Bessemer Convertor helped strengthen Sheffields dominant role in British steel manufacture and greatly enhanced its wealth and prosperity.

Yorkshire Artspace is small artist studios which welcomes visitors. Most studios are in the Cultural Workshop quarter, centred around Brown Street. The main buildings are Persistence Works and Porterbrook Studios, between them providing nearly 70 studios. 0114 2761769 www.artspace.org.uk

To the south of the city is **Beauchief Abbey**, a 12thC Premonstratensian order abbey built by Robert Fitzranulf, purportedly as a penance for the murder of St Thomas a Becket. The Abbey is on Beauchief Abbey Lane, not far from the junction with the A621 Abbeydale Road. The Abbey would originally have had a church, cloisters, chapter house, and dormitory. Like most such institutions, Henry VIII's dissolution of the Monasteries spelt the end of the Abbey; the lands were sold and and it fell into disrepair. Today, only the western tower of the church remains, although some of the foundations of other buildings are visible, as are the medieval fishponds. The Abbey is open after each Sunday service. Bus services from the interchange, 97,98,218,293 pass along Abbeydale road. 0114 235326 www.beauchiefabbey.org.uk

Nearby **Abbeydale Industrial Hamlet** off Abbeydale Road (A621), is a collection of buildings, associated machinery and objects relating to the manufacture of edge tools, particularly scythes. The exhibits include water powered tilt hammers and blacking shop as well as a worker's cottages. It provides glimpses of industrial processes which existed prior to the industrial revolution and which made Sheffield the powerhouse of the metal industry. There is a works gallery with displays and activities, and the crucible furnace is the only one of its kind in the world left intact. It is open Sun to Thu between April and October. Admission is free. Bus services 97 and 98 from the Interchange pass by the site. 0114 2722106 www.simt.co.uk

To the east of the city, adjoining the M1, lie two major attractions whose success keeps the city on the national and international map. **Meadowhall** is one of the UK's largest shopping malls with nearly 300 stores, most major brands represented, together with 12,000 car parking spaces, a rail station and tram stop. The complex attracts over 25m visitors annually and is a popular family day out with attractions for children, including cinemas and play areas. (0845 6006800 www.meadowhall.co.uk) Close by, in Broughton Lane, is **Sheffield Arena**. This is one of the North of England's biggest entertainment and concert venues. With a capacity

SHEFFIELD

of some 13,000 visitors, the Arena puts on a diverse programme of events from ice hockey matches to indoor motocross, and frequently large pop concerts. Buses 17 and 69 and the tram run on Attercliffe road to the city centre. 0114 2565656   www.motorpointarena.co.uk

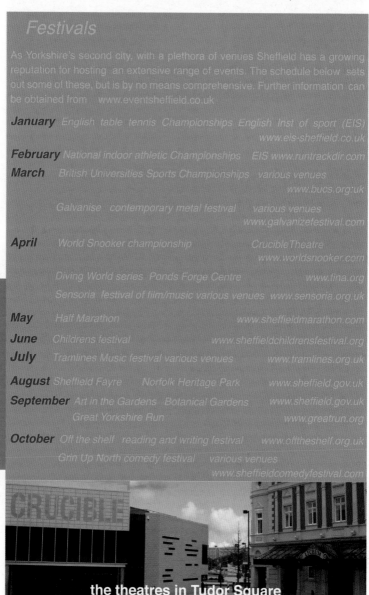

Festivals

As Yorkshire's second city, with a plethora of venues Sheffield has a growing reputation for hosting an extensive range of events. The schedule below sets out some of these, but is by no means comprehensive. Further information can be obtained from   www.eventsheffield.co.uk

January English table tennis Championships English Inst of sport (EIS)
www.eis-sheffield.co.uk

February National indoor athletic Championships   EIS www.runtrackdir.com

March British Universities Sports Championships   various venues
www.bucs.org.uk

Galvanise   contemporary metal festival   various venues
www.galvanizefestival.com

April World Snooker championship   Crucible Theatre
www.worldsnooker.com

Diving World series Ponds Forge Centre   www.tina.org

Sensoria festival of film/music various venues www.sensoria.org.uk

May Half Marathon   www.sheffieldmarathon.com

June Childrens festival   www.sheffieldchildrensfestival.org

July Tramlines Music festival various venues   www.tramlines.org.uk

August Sheffield Fayre   Norfolk Heritage Park   www.sheffield.gov.uk

September Art in the Gardens Botanical Gardens   www.sheffield.gov.uk
Great Yorkshire Run   www.greatrun.org

October Off the shelf   reading and writing festival   www.offtheshelf.org.uk

Grin Up North comedy festival   various venues
www.sheffieldcomedyfestival.com

the theatres in Tudor Square

SHEFFIELD

Sporting life

Ponds Forge, in the city centre, is a large leisure complex with Olympic and World class swimming and diving facilities. Named for the former steel works it frequently hosts major championships. 0114 2233400 www.ponds-forge.co.uk

Don Valley stadium, built for the World Student Games in 1991, is the largest athletics stadium in the country with a spectator capacity of over 25,000. It regularly hosts major athletics championships besides being home to the Sheffield Eagles Rugby League football club and occasionally the venue for large pop concerts. 0114 2233600 www.donvalleystadium.co.uk

Sheffield Wednesday is one of two league football clubs carrying the name of the city in football circles; the "Owls" are one of the oldest clubs in the world being a founding member of the Football League in 1889. The name derives from starting as a cricket club and habitually playing on a Wednesday. Home games are at Hillsborough in the north of the city, with crowds over 17,000. Bus services 66,77,78 run past the ground. 0871 9001867 www.swfc.co.uk

Sheffield United's ground lies on the south side of the city, within walking distance of the centre, on Bramall Lane. The club, like its counterpart, is long established and it too has enjoyed an illustrious history since its formation in 1889. Known as the "Blades" after the city's cutlery industry, the club were the dominant English league team for 30 years between 1895 and 1925, winning the FA cup on a number of occasions, and although fortunes have ebbed and flowed in more recent years, the Blades still attract over 20,000 fans for home games. 0871 9951889 www.sufc.co.uk

Restaurants (see map pages 252 264)

£

Tex Mex **Uncle Sams** 298 Eccleshall Road 0114 2668588　①

Vegetarian **Blue Moon Café** 2 St James Street 0114 2763443　②

££

Italian **BB's** 119 Devonshire Street 0114 2799394　③

Indian **Aagrah** 2 Leopold Square 0114 2795577 www.aagrah.com　④

Italian **Mama & Leonies** 111 Norfolk St 0114 2720490 www.mamas.co.uk　⑤

Italian **Piccolos** 3 Convent Walk 0114 2495040 www.piccolositalian.co.uk　⑥

Italian **La Gondola** 33 Carver Street 0114 2755264　⑦

Italian **Antibo** The Plaza Fitzwilliam Street 0114 2727222 www.antibo.co.uk　⑧

Indian **Ashoka** 307 Eccleshall Road 0114 2683029 www.ashoka1967.com　⑨

Spanish **La Mancha** 152-154 West Street 0114 2738885　⑩

Italian **Casanova** 200 Crookes 0114 2666684 www.casanova-sheffield.co.uk　⑪

Spanish **El Toro** 129 Newbould Lane 0114 2666956 www.el-toro-sheffield.co.uk　⑫

Chinese **Hong Kong Wok** 200 London Rd 0114 2588694 www.hkwok.co.uk　⑬

African **Zanzibar** 257 Fulwood Rd 0114 2687807 www.zanzibarsheffield.co.uk　⑭

SHEFFIELD

£££

European **23 Bar Restaurant** 3 West One Fitzwilliam Street
0114 2722323 www.23barandrestaurant.co.uk **(15)**

British **Silversmiths** 111 Arundel Street
0114 2706160 www.silversmiths-restaurant.com **(16)**

Italian **La Luna** 968 Eccleshall Road 0114 2676161 www.laluna-restaurant.co.uk **(17)**

British **London Club** 33 Surrey St 0114 2700655 www.londonclubsheffield.co.uk **(18)**

Thai **Patoo** 607-609 Eccleshall Road 0114 2668916 www.patoothai.com **(19)**

South American **Las Iguanas** 8-9 West One Fitzwilliam Street
0114 2521010 www.iguanas.co.uk **(20)**

French **Le Bistrot Pierre** 837 Eccleshall Rd
0114 2678687 www.lebistrotpierre.co.uk **(21)**

££££

English **Rafters** 220 Oakbrook Road 0114 2304819 www.raftersrestaurant.co.uk **(22)**

Hotels (see map pages 252 264)

**

Ibis Shude Hill 95 bedrooms 0114 2419600 www.ibishotel.com **(23)**

Travelodge 1 Broad St West 80 bedrooms 0871 9846305 www.travelodge.co.uk **(24)**

***

Whitley Hall Elliot Ln Grenoside 31 bedrooms 0114 2454444 www.whitleyhall.com **(25)**

Garrison 635 Penistone Rd 42 bedrooms 0114 2499555 www.garrisonhotel.co.uk **(26)**

Beauchief 161 Abbeydale Road South 50 bedrooms 0114 2624444 **(27)**

Mosborough Hall High Street Mosborough 43 bedrooms
0114 2484353 www.mosboroughhall.co.uk **(28)**

Jury's 19 Eyre Street 259 bedrooms 0114 291222 www.jurysinns.com **(29)**

Park Inn Blonk Street 111 bedrooms 0114 2204000 www.parkinn.co.uk **(30)**

Cutlers George Street 45 bedrooms 0114 2739939 www.cutlershotel.co.uk **(31)**

****

Holiday Inn Victoria Station Road 107 bedrooms
0114 2768822 www.holidayinnssheffieldco.uk **(32)**

Mercure St Pauls Norfolk Street 161 bedrooms 0114 2782000 www.mercure.com **(33)**

The Leopold Leopold Street 90 bedrooms 08450 780067 www.leopoldhotel.co.uk **(34)**

Novotel Arundel Gate 144 bedrooms 01142 781781   www.novotel.com **(35)**

Hilton Victoria Quays, Furnival Rd 128 bedrooms 0114 2525500 www.hilton.co.uk **(36)**

SHEFFIELD

Copthorne Bramall Ln 158 bedrooms 0114 2525480 www.milleniumhotels.co.uk

Rutland Glossop Rd 63 bedrooms 0114 2664411 www.rutlandhotel-sheffield.com

Sheffield Park Chesterfield Rd South 95 bedrooms
0114 2829988 www.doubletree3.hilton.com

Parking

① Arundel Gate	558 spaces	② Castlegate	403 spaces
③ Hartshead Square	505 spaces	④ Ponds Forge	200 spaces
⑤ Bailey Lane	26 spaces	⑥ Campo Lane	150 spaces
⑦ Velocity Tenter St	552 spaces	⑧ Charles St	552 spaces
⑨ Cross Burgess St	415 spaces	⑩ Turner St	678 spaces
⑪ Wellington Street	438 spaces	⑫ Furnival Gate	327 spaces
⑬ Rockingham Way	249 spaces	⑭ Charter Row	433 spaces
⑮ Arundel Street	76 spaces	⑯ Carver Lane	71 spaces
⑰ Carver Street	58 spaces	⑱ Rockingham Street	81 spaces
⑲ Sidney Street	210 spaces	⑳ Fitzwilliam Street	210 spaces

**Sheffield Visitor Information Centre
The Winter Garden Surrey Street
0114 2211900
www.welcometosheffield.co.uk**

SHEFFIELD

the steel and water feature in Sheaf Square

263

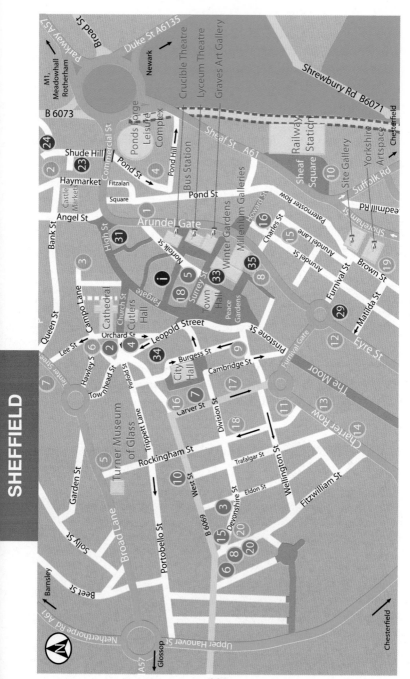

SHEFFIELD

ROTHERHAM

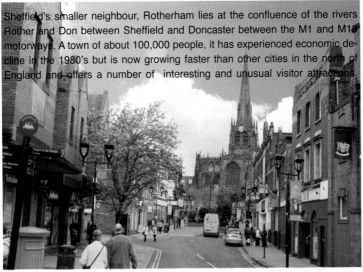

Sheffield's smaller neighbour, Rotherham lies at the confluence of the rivers Rother and Don between Sheffield and Doncaster between the M1 and M18 motorways. A town of about 100,000 people, it has experienced economic decline in the 1980's but is now growing faster than other cities in the north of England and offers a number of interesting and unusual visitor attractions.

History

The Domesday book lists the town as *Roderham*, meaning the settlement on an important river. It began its existence during the early Saxon period, by a crossing point of the River Don on a former roman road, quickly becoming a small market town. Norman conquests saw its lands given to largely absentee landlords, whose descendants eventually bequeathed the town and the surrounding area to the Cistercian monks of Rufford Abbey (in north Nottinghamshire); a position which prevailed until the 16thC. During the 15thC, the then Archbishop of York, Thomas Rotherham (who had been born in the town) founded a College of Jesus, intended to rival Oxford and Cambridge Universities (he had earlier helped to found Lincoln College Oxford). The success of the college, plus the role of the local parish church produced an enviable modern town but one which fell into decline following Henry VIII's dissolution of the monasteries. It was not until the late18thC that the towns iron industry expanded with the exploitation of underlying coal seams which created a large number of ironworks, and subsequently steelworks; industries which survived until the early 1990's.

Getting Here

Rail the station - Rotherham Central- on the western side of the town centre provides regular services to and from Leeds, Sheffield, Lincoln, and York.

Road the town enjoys direct access to the M1 and M18 motorways, London is 2½ hrs; Leeds 45 mins; Newcastle 2½ hrs, and Manchester 90 mins.

ROTHERHAM

Bus Most bus services   arrive at and depart from Rotherham Interchange on College Walk, just north of the town centre and east of the railway station. There are regular services to:

destination	service(s)	frequency
Sheffield	69/X78	20 mins/10 mins
Barnsley	X12/229	hourly/10 mins
Doncaster	X78	10 mins
Meadowhall	X78	10 mins

Things to see and do

Rotherham's town centre is dominated by the Minster. Described by the architectural historian, Niklaus Pevsner, as "the best perpendicular church in the country", All Saints Minster, towering above All Saints Square, is largely 15thC construction, built on the site of former churches originating in the early Saxon period. The building's detailing and decoration is testimony to the wealthy heritage of the town in the 15th and 16thC.   The interior contains a Saxon coffin, inscribed with the outline of a sword, and 15thC chancel stalls with carved misericords. The Minster is where the family of Jonathan Swift, author of Gullivers Travels, are buried, and where Anthony Trollope the Victorian novelist was married in 1844. The main shopping streets of Effingham Street, Frederick Street and College Street contain high street brands as well as independent shops. The market in the town is held on six days a week (not Sun) both indoors and outdoors with a weekly street market in Effingham Street. The Chantry Chapel, on the Frederick Street bridge is one of only four examples in the UK of a surviving bridge chantry. Built in 1483, the chapel was primarlly for the use of travellers to give thanks for a safe arrival in the town after a long and arduous journey. It did not survive the dissolution of the Monasteries and became almshouses and then a jail for a while before being restored in the early 20thC. It is still used for church services. The Civic Theatre in Catherine Street, a conversion of a redundant church, seating 350, provides an eclectic programme of drama, children's theatre, musicals, and comedy.   01709 823640 www.rotherham.gov.uk/theatre
On Clifton Lane, a short distance to the south east of the town centre, Clifton Park Museum is housed in Clifton House, a John Carr designed building of 1783 and originally the home of the Walker family who made their fortune in the early industrialisation of the steel industry in Rotherham.   The museum contains collections illustrating local history, archaeology and fine arts as well as a collection of locally made Rockingham pottery. The museum is open every day, except Fri. Admission is free.   01709 336633 www.rotherham.gov.uk

Rotherham's Central Library in Walker Place is also home to the Art Gallery, and the Yorkshire and Lancashire Regimental Museum, and is open six days (closed Sun). Admission is free.   01709 336633 www.rotherham.gov.uk

Lying 2 miles north of the town centre, Wentworth Woodhouse is sometimes called "one of the great Whig political palaces" and, at 600ft in length, has the longest country house façade in Europe –twice as wide as Buckingham Palace.   The house itself is vast, its 365 rooms covering an area of 2.5 acres, and set imposingly in 150 acres of parkland with uninterrupted views from the facade.   It was built c.1730 by Thomas Wentworth-Woodhouse, the 1st Marquis of Rockingham and subsequently modified until by 1790, it had broadly assumed the form visible today. The well known landscape gardener Humphrey Repton is responsible for the creation of the extensive surrounding parkland in the late 1700's; a transformation which included the erection of a number of follies, some poking fun at then unfashionable Whig politicians. The gardens and parkland are open although the house is not. Bus service 227 from Rotherham interchange goes to the adjoining estate village of Wentworth. The unusual sight of the Catcliffe Cone (for location see Sheffield district map) lies on the main street of Catcliffe, 2 miles south of the town just beyond the M1

motorway, This is the oldest surviving structure of its type in Europe. It was built in 1740 as part of a glassworks factory, which made glass bottles and window glass until the late 19thC.   The Magna Centre, at Templebrough, on the west side of the town, (for location see Sheffield district map) is a former steelworks, which is itself sited over a roman fort. It is a major UK attraction for families. An educational experience,it explains the powers and effects of earth air, fire and water. The exhibits include a regular feature called "The Big Melt" which shows how steel was made in an electric arc furnace. The attraction is open daily. There is an admission charge.   The site is served by bus 69 between Sheffield and Rotherham.   01709 720002 www.visitmagna.co.uk

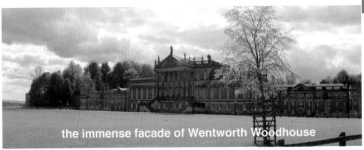

the immense facade of Wentworth Woodhouse

ROTHERHAM

7 miles to the south east on the A634 Retford Road is **Roche Abbey** . Set in a secluded lush valley, this is a Cistercian Abbey founded around 1170 by the Norman baron Richard de Busli and, like many abbeys, destroyed by Henry VIII, only a few parts of the buildings surviving. Ownership of the site passed through a number of hands until, in the 18thC, the Earl of Scarborough, who occupied the nearby Sandbeck Hall, enlisted the assistance of Capability Brown, the renowned landscape gardner, to enhance the valley setting for the abbey, although some of his work covered over the ruins, which were only restored in the early 20thC.   The abbey is open Thu to Sun from April to October. There is an admission charge.   The nearest bus services are the No 2 and No 10 services from Rotherham to Maltby, 1.5 miles away.   01709 812739 www.english-heritage.org.uk

secluded Roche Abbey

Sporting Life

Rotherham United known as The Millers are consistently in football's league one or two, play in a new venue, the New York Stadium off Centenary way to the south of the centre. The ambience and 12,000 capacity is expected to increase attendance.   08444 140737 www.themillers.co.uk

ROTHERHAM

Thomas Rotherham Religious Leader *1423-1500*
Born in the town, he was educated at Eton, and Cambridge university, sub-sequently entering the church, where he rose to become Archbishop of York in 1480. He was ambassador to France and served as Edward IV's Lord Chancellor. He endowed Lincoln College at Oxford University, and created a religious college in his home town - the College of Jesus - which was intended to create a northern rival to Oxford and Cambridge but failed to survive Henry VIII's dissolution of the Monasteries. He is buried in a tomb in York Minster, and the present secondary school in the town is named for him.

Festivals

May *World Folk and Music Festival Wath*
July *Brass Band Festival   Kiveton Park*
September *Rotherham Show community festival www.rotherham.gov.uk*
October *Open Arts Festival various venues www.rotherhamfestival.com*

Restaurants (see map page 270)

££

Indian Amaans 192 Bawtry Road   01709 701700

Indian **Apna** 113 Psalters Lane 01709 550077 ②

English **Mayors' Parlour** 16 Effingham Street 01709 820225 ③

Mediterranean **Blue Mountain** 127E Bawtry Road 01709 541133 ④

Italian **Alfonso's** 9A High Street 01709 820150 ⑤

Italian **El Lupo** 147-149 Effingham Street 01709 362279 ⑥

Asian **Orient Express**   Princes Street 01709 555527 ⑦

£££

English **Le Bistro** Main Street Wentworth ⑧
01226 746162 www.lebistrowentworth.co.uk

English **Vasco's** 169 Bawtry Rd 01709 531999 www.vascobarandrestaurrant.com ⑨

Hotels (see map page 270)

★★

Ibis Moorhead Way Bramley 86 Bedrooms 01709 730333 www.ibis.hotel.com ⑩

Restover Lodge Denby Way 51 Bedrooms ⑪
01709 700255 www.restoverlodge.co.uk

★★★

Brentwood 114 Moorgate Road 28 Bedrooms ⑫
01709 382772 www.goodnightinns.co.uk

Brecon 49-51 Moorgate Rd 20 Bedrooms 01709 828811 www.breconhotel.co.uk ⑬

The Elton Main St Bramley 27 Bedrooms 01709 545681 www.bw-eltonhotel.co.uk ⑭

Carlton Park 102-104 Moorgate Road 80 Bedrooms ⑮
01709 849955 www.carltonparkhotel.com

The Consort 8 Brampton Road Thurcroft 27 Bedrooms ⑯
01709 530022 www.bw-consorthotel.co.uk

★★★★

Hellaby Hall Hellaby Lane 90 Bedrooms 01709 702701 www.primahotels.co.uk ⑰

Holiday Inn Bawtry Road   104 Bedrooms 01709 830630 www.holidayinn.com ⑱

ROTHERHAM

Parking Ⓟ

① Wellgate	291 spaces	② Rotherham interchange	730 spaces
③ Sheffield Road	80 spaces	④ Drummond Street	240 spaces
⑤ Bailey House	30 spaces	⑥ St Annes	30 spaces
⑦ York Road	105 spaces	⑧ Fitzwilliam Road	206 spaces

Rotherham Visitor Information Centre
40, Bridgegate
01709 835904 www.visitrotherham.org

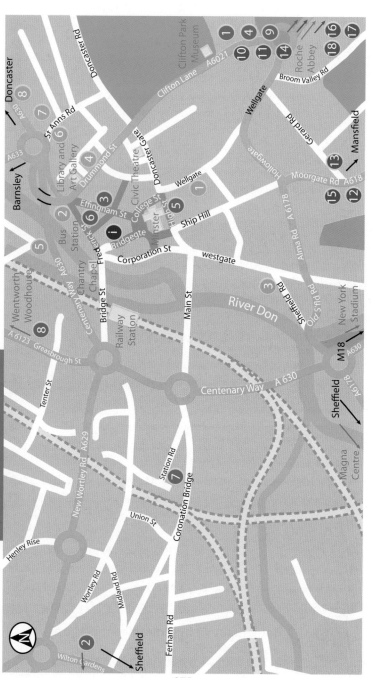

ROTHERHAM

PART FOUR
NORTH EAST YORKSHIRE

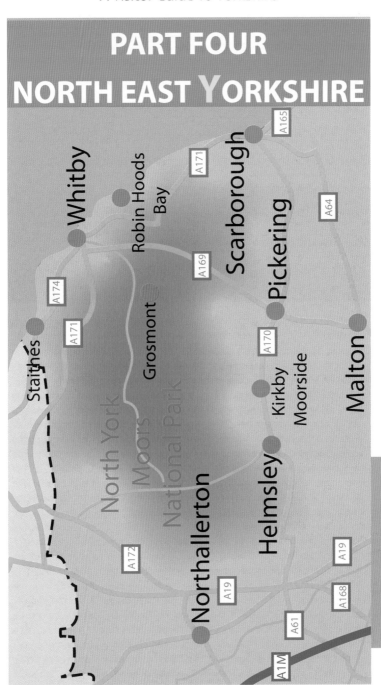

THE MOORS

The North Yorkshire Moors is a beautiful, and in places wild, open upland area covering most of the north east part of the county, much of it being a National Park. There is over 600 sq miles, mainly flat top moorland covered with heather and peat bogs, the bright purple flowers of the heather providing splashes of colour and warmth on the moortops in late summer and early autumn. The Moorlands are broken up with deep narrow river valleys running north south, although the biggest- the Esk- carves an eastward path to the sea at Whitby. The valleys are small, steep sided and covered in bright green pastureland, occasionally interrupted with small villages. The area is bounded by the Hambleton Hills on the west, the Vale of Pickering on the south, and the sometimes high sea cliffs of the North Sea on the east and north. The Moors can be viewed on a clear day from as far away as north Leeds, with the White Horse of Kilburn always a prominent landmark, and in the north the round topped hill of **Roseberry Topping** looms high on the skyline on a clear day. There are only a few small villages in the Moors, most settlements being dotted around the edges (see Whitby, Scarborough, Pickering, Helmsley, Thirsk and Northallerton chapters). Sparseness however is what endows the Moors with such atmosphere and feeling. On the northern edge is the North Sea coast. Probably at its wildest here, the soaring sea cliffs continue some 30 or more miles to Scarborough. **Boulby cliffs,** near the county border with Cleveland, and at 690ft the highest on Englands east coast, can be viewed from the long distance footpath – the Cleveland Way. A short distance to the east is **Staithes**. A haunt of artists and photographers, and often described as quaint, the village and its harbour nestle dramatically in a narrow gap in the rugged coastline. Despite its artistic qualities, the village is a small

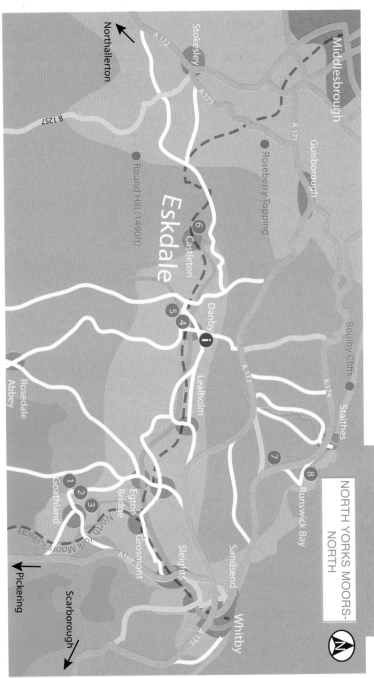

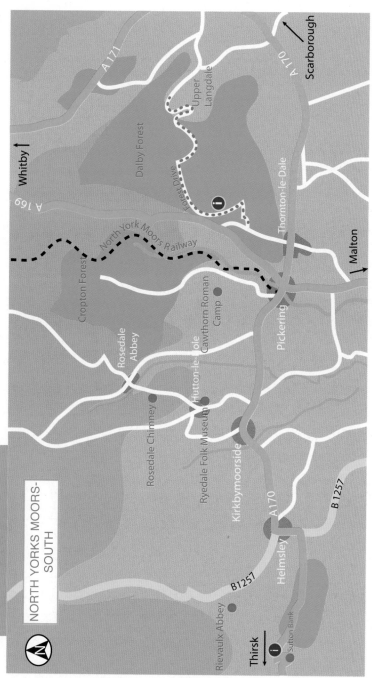

THE MOORS

NORTH YORKS MOORS-SOUTH

Scarborough

Whitby

A171

A169

Dalby Forest

Upper Langdale

A170

Forest Drive

Thornton-le-Dale

North York Moors Railway

Malton

Cropton Forest

Rosedale Abbey

Cawthorn Roman Camp

Hutton-le-Hole

Pickering

Rosedale Chimney

Ryedale Folk Museum

Kirkbymoorside

A170

B 1257

Helmsley

B1257

Rievaulx Abbey

Sutton Bank

Thirsk

fishing community, although the extensive fleet of a hundred years ago is nowadays reduced to just a few. The harbour area is busy in the high season with a number of cafes and restaurants. Bus service 5 between Whitby and Middlesbrough passes along the main road above the village. **Runswick Bay** is a tiny picturesque holiday village on the west, and more sheltered, side of the Bay of the same name. The sandy beaches here make the village a popular family holiday spot, and the Bay has long provided a safe anchorage for fishing vessels and leisure craft. Stunning panoramic views over the red pantiles roofs of the village out into the bay can be had from Runswick Bank top. **Sandsend**, under the lee of Lythe Bank, marks the abrupt western end of the long sandy beach linking the village with Whitby. A popular pastime in the summer is to walk the length of the beach between here and Whitby. Beyond Whitby, the coast turns in a more southerly direction, although the dramatic coastline remains. **Robin Hoods Bay**, 5 miles south of Whitby is a well known iconic Yorkshire village. Built in a fissure between two cliffs, its sandstone and pantile roofed buildings tumble steeply down to the sea. The origin of the name is unclear, but is

highly unlikely that this 13thC folk hero was ever here, although the settlement was more important than Whitby until the mid 17thC. With its maze of steep windy narrow cobbled streets and alleys, it was a smugglers favourite port, as during much of the 18thC smuggling was rife on the Yorkshire coast. Tea, gin, rum, brandy and tobacco, were amongst the staple goods smuggled ashore here to evade duty. In 1779, a pitched battle was fought in the bay over consignments of brandy and tea. To the south is **Boggle Hole**, a popular spot for beachcombing for fossils or marine life in rock pools. The name boggle is said to derive from goblins who, in legend, haunted the cliffs here. The village is served by buses 93 (Scarborough to Middlesbrough), and 94, to Whitby. **Ravenscar** midway between Whitby and Scarborough, is a small village with a wild rugged headland. It lies over the site of a small Roman signal station and grew up in response to the mining of alum, once vital in the dyeing industry. The former alum works are now a visitor centre, in the care of the National Trust, with a visitor centre retracing the industrial heritage of this area. The centre is open daily between April and September. 01723 870423 www.nationaltrust.org.uk

The Esk Valley winds its way eastwards from headwaters at Westerdale north east of Northallerton, through steep valley sides and out to the sea at Whitby. Its clear sparkling waters are home to a wide variety of wildlife, notably salmon. The small attractive villages lying astride the river were once hives of activity in coal and iron ore mining, and although both industries

THE MOORS

died out a long time ago, remains of deserted mine shafts are evident. The railway line from Middlesbrough to Whitby wends its way through the valley bottom. With a junction at Grosmont with the heritage North York Moors Railway, seeing the valley by train is one way to fully appreciate its natural splendour. The villages of Castleton, Danby and Lealholm lie towards the head of the valley. There is the remains of a Norman motte castle at Castleton dating from the mid 12thC and, at Danby, is the very informative and comprehensive National Park visitor centre, which is open all year. (01439 772737 www. northyorkmoors.org.uk) Between Danby and Lealholm, the river drops steeply through a wooded ravine known as Crunkly Gill. Between Glaisdale and Egton Bridge, the river drops steeply again through Limber Hill Wood. Below the village is the early 17thC Beggars Bridge which, according to legend, was built by a local man to enable him to never to have to be separated from his fiancee who lived on the other side of the river. Egton Bridge's catholic

church - St Hilda's - contains the relics of Nicholas Postgate, a 17thC martyr, executed because he steadfastly continued to practice Catholicism; as with many in this area at the time commitment to Catholicism remained strong. Grosmont, so named because a 13thC priory was established here until the dissolution, is where the North Yorks Moors Railway (NYMR - see page 296) maintain an engine shed which doubles up as a workshop for the restoration of steam and diesel locomotives. Above the village are remains of a Roman fort on Lease Rigg. As the river nears the sea, the valley widens as it passes through the villages of Sleights and Ruswarp before entering the harbour at Whitby.

The Moor Tops

South of the Esk, the landscape is that of the high moorland, with a plateau at 1200ft, the flat topped moors stretch from Bilsdale to the sea. The highest point, 1490ft, is Round Hill, on the northern edge of the Moors. Ancient crosses, some dating from the 10thC, mark the high points of some of the moors; there are more than 30 dotted across the area. This is wild, open and inherently peaceful countryside affording long distance views, particularly from the minor roads which cross the Moors; again mainly in a north to south axis. The extensive coverage of heather, brilliantly purple in the late summer, is home to many bird species such as marlin, grouse and ring ousel. Goathland, a few miles south of the Esk Valley, is the location of the fictional village of Aidensfield in the long running TV drama series, "Heartbeat", with much of the village now a popular haunt for visitors seeking to experience the 1960's atmosphere in which the series is set.

THE MOORS

The attraction of the TV connections combined with its position on the NYMR makes for a packed day out for visitors, whether starting from Pickering or from Whitby. The village itself is of Viking origin, and in the 19thC became a small spa destination with a number of hotels established here, the most well known being the Mallyan Spout Hotel, named for the nearby waterfall. A long distance walk across the moors, from Scarth Wood Moor near Osmotherley in the west, to Ravenscar in the east, is the Lyke Wake Walk. Some 40 miles long, the intention is that walkers complete within 24 hours. It crosses the high points of the moors following paths set in the heather. Towards the southern side of the moors, extensive afforestation in the inter war years with the creation of the Forestry Commission has led to about 20% of the moors area now being under active woodland management. Much of this area is open to visitors.

The forests of Cropton, Dalby, Staindale and Langdale contain a well developed network of tracks and footpaths, picnic areas, and in Dalby forest there is a modern self sustaining visitor centre at the start of Forest Drive, a 9 mile tour snaking through the varied woodlands ending in Upper Langdale. The forests host a variety of regular outdoor activities. The visitor centre organises ranger led walks and talks; there is a well developed network of mountain bike trails, frequently used for major bike races, the world mountain biking championship having been held here; a number of car rallies and motorbike trials are held in the forests during the year. The forests are also home to a variety of wildlife including roe deer and badgers, nightjars and crossbills. Access to Dalby forest is north of Thornton–le-Dale on the A170, through Low Dalby village, or from the Scarborough direction, off the A171 to Hackness and Langdale End. For motorists there is an admission charge. Wending its way through the eastern side of Cropton forest is the North Yorks Moor Railway. From the terminus at Pickering, nostalgic steam trains haul passengers through the narrow defile of Newtondale for several miles, before reaching a halt where walkers can alight straight onto the well trodden network of paths and trails in Cropton forest. The line continues north to Goathland and then to the junction with the public line at Grosmont. Cawthorn Camp, the site of Roman occupation lies 3 miles north of Pickering. Here was a major Roman military installation, in three separate camps, and the defensive banks and ditches which formed the camp are still evident. The camp can be reached from Swainsea Lane off Middleton Road in Pickering. To the west of Cropton lie the narrow, deep valleys of Rosedale and Farndale. Rosedale Abbey is the main village here, named for the Cistercian abbey which once stood in the valley bottom, the village is set around a small green but all that remains of the abbey is a sundial and a stone pillar. In the 19thC the village provided homes for

THE MOORS

those working in the iron ore mines, an industry that died out here in the 1920s. Evidence of the mines can be seen on the top of Rosedale Chimney, a fearsomely steep climb up to Spaunton Moor on the south side of the village. This road zig-zags steeply down to Hutton le-Hole on the eastern shoulder of Farndale, a small village where sheep graze contentedly on the extensive village green. The Ryedale Folk museum is here. Dedicated to recounting the history of the people of Ryedale, it features displays from an iron age settlement to a second world war air raid shelter. The museum is open daily. There is an admission charge.   01751 417367 www.ryedalefolkmuseum.co.uk

At the foot of Farndale where the river emerges into the Vale of Pickering, lies Kirbymoorside, a small market town which describes itself as the gateway to the moors. Listed as *Chirchebi* in the Domesday book, it was granted a market charter in 1254 and still holds a weekly Wednesday market. The church of All Saints, although substantially rebuilt in the 19thC, by Sir George Gilbert Scott, retains a 13thC interior.   Behind the church lies the site of a moated wooden castle built in the early 13thC by the de Stuteville family, in a defensive position on Vivers Hill overlooking the town. There are only limited remains of the moat still visible.   In the town centre is the Tollbooth and Memorial hall which date from the mid 18thC.   Further to the west, on the A170 and marking the south west corner of the Moors is Sutton Bank.   Renowned as a steep climb from the Vale of York to the plateau above, it is said to offer one of the most panoramic and spectacular views in the county. Sutton Bank was the site of an important iron age hill fort, with an enclosed area of over 60 acres and a perimeter 1.3 miles circumference, although now it is better known as the site of a gliding club, where the combination of the escarpment and the prevailing winds produce ideal gliding conditions and gliders can often be seen riding the thermals above the hill.   At the summit of the hill is a visitor centre that provides information about the National Park, as well as being furnished with some modern sculptures representing local features. The centre is open daily most of the year.   01845 597426 www.northyorkmoors.org.uk

THE MOORS

The Moors Restaurants and Hotels
(see maps page 273 274)

Goathland **Mallyan Spout** country hotel 20 bedrooms ①
01947 896486 www.mallyanspout.co.uk

Goathland **The Goathland** country hotel pub food 8 bedrooms ②
01947 896203 www.thegoathlandhotel.co.uk

Goathland **The Beacon** guest house 6 bedrooms ③
01947 896409 www.thebeaconguesthouse.co.uk

Danby The Duke of Wellington country hotel pub food 9 bedrooms ④
01287 660351 www.dukeofwellingtondanby.co.uk

Ainthorpe **The Fox andHounds** coaching inn pub food 7 bedrooms ⑤
01287 660218 www.foxandhounds-ainthorpe.com

Castleton **The Downe Arms** country hotel pub food 5 bedrooms ⑥
01287 660223 www.thedownearms.com

Ellerby **The Ellerby Hotel** country hotel 01947 840342 www.ellerbyhotel.co.uk ⑦

Runswick Bay **Cliffemount** country hotel English food 20 bedrooms ⑧
01947 840103 www.cliffemounthotel.co.uk

Robin Hoods Bay **The Victoria** 12 bedrooms 01947 880205 www.victoriarhb.com ⑨

Robin Hoods Bay **The Grosvenor** English food 10 bedrooms ⑩
01947 880320 www.thegrosvenor.info

Fylingthorpe **Thorpe Hall** country hotel 7 bedrooms ⑪
01947 880667 www.thorpe-hall.co.uk

Ravenscar **Raven Hall** country hotel 52 bedrooms ⑫
01723 870353 www.ravenhall.co.uk

Ravenscar **Wayfarer** guest house/restaurant English food 5 bedrooms ⑬
01947 880240 www.wayfarerbistro.co.uk

Lastingham Lastingham Grange country hotel gourmet food 11 bedrooms ⑭
01751 417345 www.lastinghamgrange.com

Kirbymoorside **The Cornmill** guest house 5 bedrooms 01751 432000 ⑮

Kirbymoorside **George and Dragon** coaching Inn pub food 20 bedrooms ⑯
01751 433334 www.georgeanddragon.net

The Moors National Park Centres
- **Danby 01439 772737**
- **Sutton Bank 01845 597426**
www.northyorkmoors.org.uk

Dalby Forest Visitor Centre Low Dalby
01751 460295 www.forestry.gov.uk

THE MOORS

NORTHALLERTON

Northallerton is the county town for the present administrative area of North Yorkshire and prior to that for the North Riding. Lying in the Vale of York it is an administrative and transport centre.

History

There is some evidence of Roman occupation in this area although mainly to the east where the Roman road connecting Aldborough and York with Durham and Hadrian's wall was established. There was likely a signal station here. The Domesday Book however simply refers to the area as a waste. Following the Norman invasion, the area was given to the See of Durham, and in the early 12thC, the bishops built a motte and bailey castle on land where the cemetery now is, west of the town centre. The Battle of the Standard in 1138, where an English army defeated the Scottish one under the command of King David of Scotland, took place about two miles due north of the town. A monument to the battle – whose English victory safeguarded the sovereignty of northern England- can be seen on the roadside of the A167. The castle was replaced at the start of the 13thC by a larger fortified palace, and the town's role as an administrative centre took shape. Because the palace lay on the main road between York and Durham, it became a key rest halt for VIP travellers – a function continued well into the 20thC. A Carmelite priory was founded here c.1350, but destroyed with the dissolution of the monasteries. The site is where the Friarage hospital now stands, and digging the foundations for a recent redevelopment uncovered skeletons of several monks from this era.The town developed its role as a commercial centre with a cattle market and other key agricultural functions, and as a resting place for travellers. At one time there were four coaching inns on the High Street. The arrival of the great north eastern railway - and other links directly into the West Riding and into the Teesside ports - helped strengthen the towns administrative and transport functions in the 19thC. Today the town remains an important agricultural service and administrative centre for North Yorkshire.

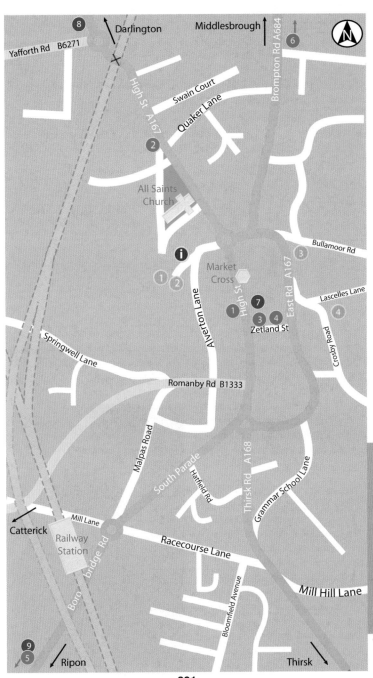

Getting Here

Rail the town is on the east coast main line with regular services to and from London (2hr 30 min) York (25 min), and Newcastle (45min).   Both intercity and local services stop here. Additionally, there is a direct service into Middlesbrough (30 mins). The station is on the south side of the town, close to the offices of North Yorkshire County Council.

Road   although the town no longer lies on a major road, it is close to two national routes; the A1 6 miles to the west; the A19 4 miles to the east.

Bus Most bus services arrive at and depart from the Buck Inn, at the southern end of the High Street.

destination	service	frequency
York	58	1x per day
Darlington	72	2 hourly
Richmond	55	hourly
Whitby	27	1x per day
Ripon	70	2 hourly
Thirsk	153	3x per day
Helmsley	M11	1x per day

Things to see and do

The heart of the town lies in the High street; a wide, long street lined with shops, both national brands and more distinctive local independent ones. At the centre is the town Hall, a Victorian building still in use as such, and nearby is the market cross, restored in 1914 but thought to date from the 15thC.   A lively twice weekly market is held on the High Street - on Wed and Sat - with a small country market being held in the town hall on Fridays and a farmers market on the fourth Wed of each month.

All Saints Church

This large and imposing edifice marks the northern end of the High Street. Parts date from the early 12thC, although there was undoubtedly a previous church on the site, as remnants of a Saxon previous building have been unearthed and are displayed inside the present church. The building itself was altered and extended over a period and the overall appearance is that of a late 14th/early15thC ecclesiastical building in the perpendicular style.

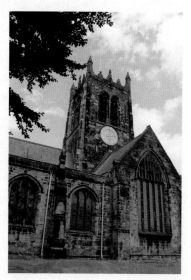

NORTHALLERTON

Restaurants (see map page 281)

££

English **Betty's Tea rooms** High Street 01609 775154 www.bettys.co.uk ①

Indian **Red Chilli** 297 High St 01609 775552 www.redchillinorthallerton.co.uk ②

English **The Golden Lion** High St 01609 777411 www.golden-lion-hotel.co.uk ③

Indian **Aroma** Zetland street 01609 774239 www.aroma-restaurant.co.uk ④

££££

English **Solberge Hall** Newby Wiske 01609 779191 www.solbergehall.co.uk ⑤

£££££

English **Cleveland Tontine** Staddlebridge ⑥
01609 882671 www.theclevelandtontine.co.uk

Hotels

★★

The Golden Lion High St 14 Bedrooms ⑦
01609 777411 www.golden-lion-hotel.co.uk

★★★

Allerton Court Darlington Rd 28 Bedrooms ⑧
01609 780525 www.allertoncourthotel.co.uk

Solberge Hall Newby Wiske 24 bedrooms ⑨
01609 779191 www.solbergehall.co.uk

Parking

① **Applegarth (shortstay)** 148 spaces   ③ **Hambleton Forum**   137 spaces
② **Applegarth**   269 spaces   ④ **Crosby Road**   228 spaces

 Northallerton Visitor Information Centre
Applegarth Car Park
01609 776864
www.hambleton.gov.uk

NORTHALLERTON

HELMSLEY

Helmsley is a small market town at the foot the North Yorkshire Moors, dominated by it's castle and church tower. For such a small town it has much to offer the visitor, whether staying or simply coming to the town for the day.

History

The town is referred to in the Domesday book as "*Elmeslac*"- which means narrow vale- and was owned by William the Conquerors half brother, Robert de Mortain, although he forfeited the lands in favour of another Norman earl, Walter L'Espec. It was he who built the castle in the 12thC. The lands then passed to the Roos family who developed the town as a commercial centre with corn mills and weaving businesses.   The castle was largely destroyed in the English civil war, although parts were rebuilt, and acquired in 1687 by Sir Charles Duncombe, a wealthy London goldsmith, but his family subsequently abandoned it and built a new residence, designed by Vanbrugh, called Duncombe Park. The Duncombes remained as Lords of the Manor and were ennobled in the early 19thC, becoming the Earls of Feversham; the family still reside in the house, set in the extensive 13,000 acres of parkland.   Today, the town is a visitor magnet, its attractive centre peppered with galleries and other visitor related shops, whilst it has accommodation that make it an excellent touring base for much of North Yorkshire, and it sits handily on the edge of the North York Moors National Park.

Getting Here

Rail The nearest rail stations are at Thirsk (11 miles), Malton (15 miles), and York (20 miles). Both Thirsk and York are on the east coast main line with regular services to all parts of the country.

Road the town sits astride the A170 Thirsk to Scarborough road, Thirsk is 20 min; Scarborough 45 min. Minor roads to the north go to Stokesley and Middlesbrough, a 45 min scenic drive over the North York Moors, and to the south to York (40 min), and Malton (20 min) to the south east.

Bus buses arrive at and depart from the market place.

destination	service	frequency
York	31X	2 hourly
Scarborough	128	hourly
Pickering	128	hourly

Things to see and do

Helmsley is a small place, and most points of interest can be reached easily from the spacious Market Place with its weekly Friday market.

In the Market Place is a statue to the 2nd Earl Feversham (1798-1767), and the buildings lining its sides are mainly 18th and 19thC, although a timber framed property dating from the late 15thC is evident on the west side. The Market place and surrounding streets have plenty of galleries, souvenir shops, restaurants and cafes, so as well as visiting the attractions, browsing around the centre is interesting and rewarding in itself.

Helmsley Castle

Sat atop a grassy knoll to the west of the Market Place, Helmsley castle is of Norman origin. Built by Walter L'Espec in the early 12thC, it was rebuilt by his nephew, Robert de Roos at the turn of the 13thC. During the English Civil War it was the scene of battles and substantially demolished by Thomas Fairfax in 1644, only to be partially rebuilt and occupied by the then owner, the second Duke of Buckingham. The Duncombe family acquired the Castle and its lands in 1687. Sir Charles Duncombe was a successful London goldsmith and used his fortune to move the family seat to Helmsley. His successors however did not favour the castle, and instead built Duncombe Park in the surrounding lands. The castle fell into a state of ruin. However, there is still much visible on a visit today; the south barbican entrance; some of the living quarters built in Tudor times above the west walls, and substantial defensive ditches. Open daily from March to October. There is an admission charge.

01439 770442   www.english-heritage.org.uk

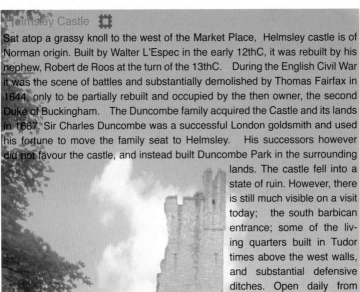

HELMSLEY

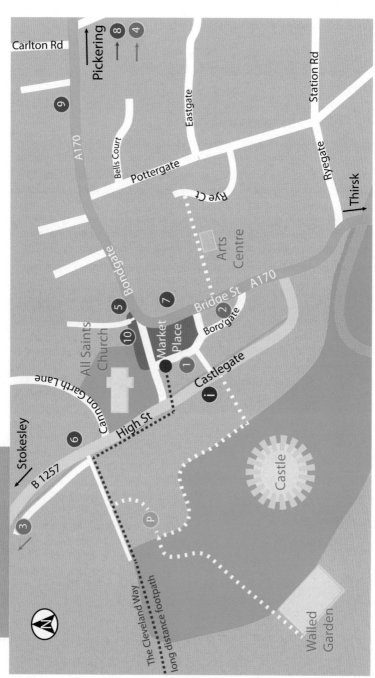

All Saints Church

The large church of All Saints above the Market Square is Victorian and built over the previous Norman building, parts of which are still evident such as the south entrance porch, some interior pillars and arches. The murals in the north aisle, although of medieval style, are relatively recent and designed by a former incumbent in 1909. The stained glass windows tell the story of Walter L'Espec. The church is open daily.

Helmsley Arts Centre

Occupying the former Friends Meeting house of 1812, and substantially extended with a modern structure, the Arts Centre is the focus of the town's entertainment and culture. It is in a small courtyard at the eastern side of Bridge Street and accessed through a narrow arched opening in the street frontage. It has an eclectic but rich programme of films concerts plays and other arts events put on constantly through the year. 01439 771700 www.helmsleyarts.co.uk

Walled Garden

Against the backdrop of the Castle and Duncombe Park, this 5 acre walled garden of 1756 has been restored to its original form. It contains a19thC glass house, fruit trees, vines, a peony garden, dipping pond and over 250 varieties of clematis.It is open from April to October. There is an admission charge.
01439 771427 www.helmsleywalledgarden.org.uk

Helmsley is also close to the major attractions of Rievaulx Abbey, Bylands Abbey and Nunnington Hall (see pages 391,392,395) as well as the North Yorks Moors.

Cleveland Way

The 110 mile long distance footpath which traces an upland route around the edges of the North York Moors before finishing in Filey, starts from Helmsley. A popular route for walkers, it covers varied and spectacular scenery and much of historical interest before arriving in Filey.

Walter L'Espec *Norman nobleman* d.1153

Walter L'Espec was a favoured knight of Henry I (1100-1135). He controlled, with Eustace Fitz John, much of the north of England on behalf of the king. He built Helmsley castle, but much more besides He was an enthusiastic supporter of religious reform, founding an Augustinian priory at Kirkham in 1122, before founding the first Cistercian abbey in Yorkshire, at Rievaulx. He also founded Rievaulx's daughter-house at Warden in Bedfordshire Walter led the Yorkshire barons against King David of Scotland in 1138 at the Battle of the Standard, fought at Northallerton, following the Scots' incursion into the North of England. He was by nature a philanthropist and had the well being of the community, dominated by religious orders, at heart, and was evidently highly regarded by the monks of Rievaulx. He entered the Cistercian community shortly before his death. He died leaving no male heirs. His inheritance was divided and patronage of Rievaulx passed to the Roos family.

HELMSLEY

Other points of interest near the town include Ampleforth college, the well known boys catholic public school, and Gilling Castle, also owned by the school.

Restaurants (see map page 286)

££

pub food Royal Oak Market Place 01439 770450 www.theoak-helmsley.co.uk ①

Italian Gepetto's 8 Bridge Street 01439 770479 www.gepettos-helmsley.co.uk ②

£££

English The Inn at Hawnby Hawnby 01439 798202 www.innathawnby.co.uk ③

££££

English The Star Harome 01439 770397 www.thestaratharome.co.uk ④

Hotels (see map page 286)

**

The Crown Inn Market Place 12 Bedrooms 01439 770297 ⑤

***

Feversham Arms 34 bedrooms 01439 770766 www.fevershamarmshotel.com ⑥

The Feathers Market Place 23 bedrooms
01439 770275 www.feathershotelhelmsley.co.uk ⑦

The Pheasant Hotel Mill Street Harome 14 Bedrooms
01439 771241 www.thepheasanthotel.com ⑧

****(GA)

Carlton Lodge Bondgate 8 Bedrooms 01439 770557 www.carlton-lodge.com ⑨

****

The Black Swan Market Place 45 Bedrooms ⑩
01439 770466 www.blackswan-helmsley.co.uk

**Helmsley Visitor Information Centre
Castlegate
01439 770173
www.ryedale.gov.uk**

HELMSLEY

MALTON

Malton lies astride the River Derwent in the Vale of Pickering, 20 miles from York and about the same distance to Scarborough. Founded in Roman times, it has historically been a small commercial centre for the fertile agricultural land in the Vale of Pickering; a role it continues today.

History

The town is the site of a Roman settlement called *Derventio*. It was a strategically important cavalry fort, at the hub of a Roman road network across North and East of Yorkshire. The fort was on what is now Orchard Fields, to the south of Old Maltongate. The Roman occupation ended around 400AD and the fort and associated settlement largely destroyed. A castle was built in the 11thC but had been demolished by 1569 when a new grand house, allegedly rivalling such notable houses as Audley End in Essex, was built by Ralph 3rd Lord Eure. The only remains of this – and which is thought to be but a fragment - is now incorporated into the Old Lodge Hotel on Old Maltongate; this gives an idea of the size of the original Jacobean house. Malton has continued as a small market town and agricultural centre, fortified by the coming of the railways in the mid19thC, and it has expanded its economic role with a number of horse racing stables nearby.

Getting Here

Rail the Scarborough -York line provides fast hourly services with connections to the national rail network in York 25 mins away; Leeds is 50 mins and Manchester Airport 2 hrs 30 mins.

Road the town lies just off the A64 York to Scarborough road. York is 30 mins drive; Leeds 1 hour; Scarborough 40 mins

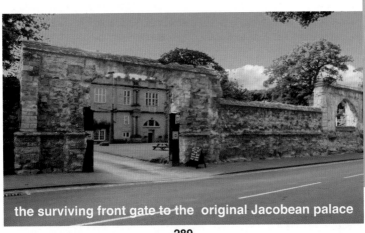

the surviving front gate to the original Jacobean palace

MALTON

Bus arrive and depart from the bus station adjoining the railway station.

destination	service(s)	frequency
York	840/843	30 mins
Leeds	840/843	30 mins
Scarborough	840	hourly
Pickering	843	hourly
Whitby	843	3 hourly

Things to see and do

The **Market Place** has long been the heart of the town. An interesting walk from the Market Place leads from the16thC old town hall, past **St Michaels church**, of Norman origins, along Finkle Street and then right into Wheelgate.   The Cross Keys pub is built over the crypt of a hospice for pilgrims.   Turn left onto Old Maltongate, up the hill. The **Old Lodge hotel** is on the right; the remaining fragment of the once great Jacobean palace which stood here.   The footpath to the right a little way beyond leads to Orchard fields, the site of the original Roman fort on the left; and on the right the field behind the hotel is the site of the castle.   Continuing on the footpath leads to Sheepfoot Hill where turning back towards the town centre, and then left reaches the County bridge over the river Derwent; once marking the boundary between East and North Ridings. Retracing steps and proceeding up **Castlegate** and then left along Yorkersgate to the Talbot hotel. This was a 16thC hunting lodge owned by a well known local family.   Turn right into Market Street and back to the Market place where there is a weekly Saturday market.   In **Old Malton** 1 mile from the town centre, is St Mary's church, known as Malton Priory, part of a Gilbertine Priory founded 1150 but destroyed with the dissolution of the monasteries. There is hardly a trace of the monastic priory, but there is a surviving undercroft under Abbey House.

Eden Camp   Pickering Road

This is a museum in a former second world war prisoner of war camp, devoted to military and social history of the two world wars. Its range of original and sometime interactive exhibits and atmosphere make it a good day out for families.   It is open all year round from Mon to Sat. There is an admission charge.
01653 697777   www.edencamp.co.uk

Flamingoland   Kirby Misperton

A large theme park, on US lines, incorporating a range of facilities from gentle children's rides to white knuckle ones, together with over 1000 animals birds and exotic fish.   The park covers nearly 400 acres and boasts it has more roller coaster rides than any other UK theme park.   The park is open daily from April to October. There is an admission charge.
0871 9118000 www.flamingoland.co.uk

MALTON

Kirkham Priory ♯ Whitwell on the Hill

This is a little known Augustinian priory of the 12thC, founded by the Norman baronWalter L'Espec, although there are only limited remains standing. The remains sit peacefully in the Derwent valley 4 miles south west of the town, with access from the A64. The site is open daily from April to October. There is an admission charge. 01653 618768 www.english-heritage.org.uk

Castle Howard

This well known stately home is 4 miles west of the town. Visiting will occupy a full day. Castle Howard is covered in more detail on pages 396-397.

Wharram Percy ♯

This is an abandoned medieval village, the best researched and analysed of some 3000 such sites across the UK, some 6 miles south of the town off the B1248. First settled in prehistoric times, Wharram flourished as a village between the 12th and 14thC before final abandonment in about 1500. The site, accessed from a footpath only, contains a church and clear traces of a range of abandoned buildings. Interpretative panels help visitors understand the village's story.

www.english-heritage.org.uk

Restaurants (see map page 292)

££

Eclectic **Market Place Bistro** Market Place
01653 697100 www.the-market-place.co.uk ❶

Thai **Tui's** 29 Yorkersgate 01653 692865 www.tuisofmalton.co.uk ❷

Tex-Mex **El Gringo's** 5 Saville Street 01653 691507 ❸

pub food **The Stone Trough** Whitwell on the Hill
01653 618713 www.stonetroughinn.co.uk ❹

£££

English **The Worsley Arms** Hovingham 01653 628234 www.worsleyarms.co.uk ❺

English **Priory Restaurant** Burythorpe
01653 658200 www.burythorpehouse.co.uk ❻

English **Bay Horse Inn** Burythorpe
01653 658302 www.bayhorseburythorpe.co.uk ❼

MALTON

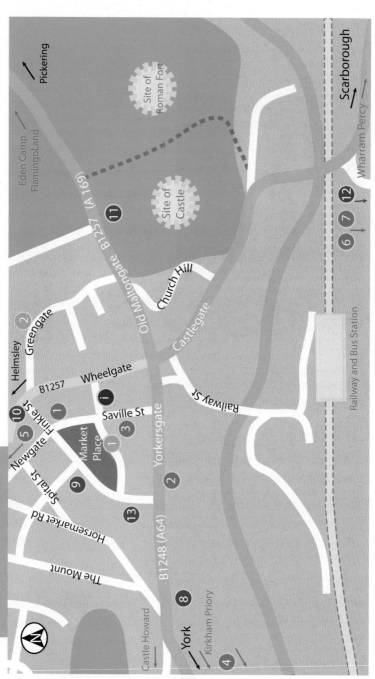

MALTON

Pickering

Site of Roman Fort

Scarborough

Wharram Percy

Eden Camp
FlamingoLand

Site of Castle

⑪

⑫
⑦
⑥

Old Maltongate B1257 (A169)

Church Hill

Castlegate

Railway and Bus Station

②
Greengate

Helmsley

Wheelgate

B1257

Finkle St

⑩
⑤
①

Saville St

ⓘ

③

Railway St

Newgate

Market Place

①

Spital St

Yorkersgate

②

⑨

⑬

Horsemarket Rd

The Mount

B1248 (A64)

⑧

Castle Howard

York

Kirkham Priory

④

Hotels (see map page 292)

**

The Talbot Yorkersgate 31 bedroom 01653 694031 www.talbotmalton.co.uk ⑧

***(GA)

The Kings Head Market Place 6 bedrooms 01653 692289 ⑨

***

Worsley Arms Hovingham 20 bedrooms 01653 628234 www.worsleyarms.co.uk ⑩

****

The Old Lodge Old Maltongate 20 bedrooms ⑪
01653 690570 www.theoldlodgemalton.co.uk

Burythorpe House Burythorpe 12 bedrooms ⑫
01653 658200 www.burythorpehouse.co.uk

not rated

The Green Man Market Street 01653 693567 ⑬

Parking Ⓟ

① Market place   95 spaces   ② Wentworth street   130 spaces

Malton Visitor Information Centre
St Michael Street
01653 600048
www.ryedale.gov.uk

MALTON

PICKERING

This small market town sits quietly at the foot of the North York Moors, astride the crossing of the Thirsk to Scarborough and York to Whitby roads,and is now best known as the home of the North York Moors steam railway. It is an ideal touring base for this part of the county with easy access to countryside and coast, and a small but friendly town centre.

History

Pickering's location on the edge of moorlands to the north, wetlands to the south and forests all around made it suitable for a settlement. It's history is said to stretch back to about 270 BC, and there is evidence, close to the town, of Celtic and Roman era settlement. The Anglo Saxons called it *Piceringas,* a spelling used in the Domesday book. The castle and church originated in the early Norman period and the castle and surrounds are still in the ownership of the monarchy (through the Duchy of

15thC mural in the church

Lancaster). The town developed and prospered over the centuries as a market town and agricultural centre, and more recently as a touring base. It has a long liberal tradition, and non conformist religions have prospered here over the last two centuries with a strong Methodist and congregational presence.

Getting Here

Rail the nearest station is Malton (9 miles south) with regular services to Scarborough and York.

Road The town lies on the cross roads of the A169 and A170. Travelling from the south is via the A64, and A169; alternatively via the A19 and Thirsk Helmsley. Whitby is 40 min and Scarborough 30 min.

Bus buses arrive at and depart from Eastgate and the Ropery.

destination	service	frequency
York	840(Eastgate)	hourly
Leeds	840	hourly
Whitby	840	3 hourly
Scarborough	128(The Ropery)	hourly
Helmsley	128(The Ropery)	hourly

Things to see and do

Pickering is small and compact and easily walkable. The centre of the town is the Market Place, more a street than a square, with a small open market on Mondays. A wander along Smiddy Hill and the Market Place, Bridge Street and Potter Hill captures the essence of the town.

PICKERING

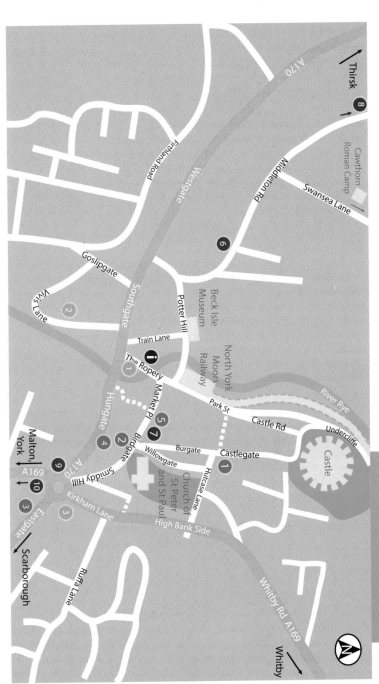

Castle ⊞

Built shortly after the Norman conquest, with an earthwork motte and bailey and a simple timber constructed keep. There may have been an earlier fortification here. Henry II built the s keep in 1180, and Edward II the outer walls, much of which remain intact. Within the walls are a restored chantry chapel of 1227, and the Coleman tower which would have originally housed the soldiers who guarded the entrance to the castle. The castle's useful life ended by the mid 17thC, although it has remained in the possession of the monarchy. It is open daily April to September. There is an admission charge.

01751 474989 www.english-heritage.org.uk

Church of St Peter and St Paul

The church of St Peter and St Paul stands on high ground at the eastern end of the Market Place above Biddygate, with access by footpath and steps between the frontage buildings. Built in the 12thC probably on the site of an earlier Saxon church – the bowl of the font is thought to be Saxon- and like many parish churches it was added to and altered over the following two hundred years. The interior is notable for its original 15thC murals which are clear and unambiguous in telling religious stories, such as St George and the Dragon, Herods feast etc. They also give a vivid representation of what ecclesiastical interiors may have been like in medieval times. The church is open most days.

North Yorkshire Moors Railway

Said to be the most popular heritage railway in the country, it carries over 350,000 passengers a year, and ranks amongst the busiest such railway anywhere in the world. Passengers travel from Pickering through stunning colourful scenery of the North Yorkshire Moors to Grosmont and on the Eskdale national rail line to Whitby. First built in the 1830's, it was part of the railway line from York to Whitby, pioneered by George Stephenson, to haul goods inland from Whitby port. It closed in 1965, re-opening in 1973 as a charitable trust run line operating in peak season, originally to Goathland, and in the 1990's extended through to Whitby. In Pickering, the original station has been faithfully restored to its 1937 condition. The railway has over 20 steam locomotives providing regular services during the summer months and a more limited service during the winter.   01751 472508   www.nymr.co.uk

Cawthorn Roman Camp

Some 3 miles north of the town, on the edge of the North York Moors, Cawthorn Camp was an important Roman military installation, with the remains of the defensive ditches still evident. There is an interpretive trail around these and the leaflet for this can be obtained from Pickering Visitor Information Centre.

PICKERING

Beck Isle Museum

An elegant Regency period house on Bridge Street is home to this celebration of rural crafts and way of life in this part of Yorkshire. It was here that William Marshall tried to establish England's first agricultural institute in the early 19thC. The collections include local photographs of Sydney Smith, a renowned photographer of local life in the first part of the 20thC. Open daily mid February to end October. There is an admission charge.   01751 473653   www.beckislemuseum.org

Restaurants (see map page 295)

££

Spanish **Castlegate Taberna** Castlegate ①
01751 476481 www.castlegatetaberna.co.uk

Italian **Figaro's** Birdgate 01751 477733 ②

Indian **Noyon** Eastgate   01751 476969 ③

Indian **Spice4U** 41 Hungate 01751 473334 www.spice4u.co.uk ④

£££

English **White Swan Inn** Market Place 01751 472288 www.white-swan.co.uk ⑤

Hotels

**

Old Manse Hotel 19 Middleton road 10 bedrooms ⑥
01751 476484 www.oldmansepickering.co.uk

***

White Swan Inn Market Place 21 bedrooms 01751 472288 www.white-swan.co.uk ⑦

Tantara Country Hotel Nova Lane Middleton 11 bedrooms 01751 472129 ⑧

Forest and Vale Hotel Hungate 22 bedrooms ⑨
01751 472722 www.bw-forestandvalehotel.co.uk

****(GA)

Beansheaf Hotel Kirby Misperton 18 Bedrooms ⑩
01653 668614 www.beansheafhotel.com

Parking Ⓟ

① The Ropery (short stay)   90 spaces   ② Vivis Lane   100 spaces
③ Eastgate   120 spaces

Pickering Visitor Information Centre
The Ropery
01751 473791
www.ryedale.gov.uk

PICKERING

297

WHITBY

"*This is a lovely place. The little River Esk runs through a deep valley which broadens out as it comes near the harbour... The houses of the old town are all red-roofed and seem piled up one after the other anyhow... Right over the town is the ruin of the Abbey, a noble ruin of immense size. Between it and the town is another church, the Parish one, round which is a big graveyard, all full of tombstones. It descends so steeply over the harbour that part of the bank has fallen away, and some of the graves have been destroyed.*" (Bram Stoker, author of the famous novel Dracula)

Whitby is an iconic name in British history; the stomping ground of early Benedictine monks, and sometime home to explorer James Cook. The town is built on the steep sides of the River Esk - the only salmon river in the county - as it flows into the sea, creating a natural harbour and port. Overlooked on the east cliffs by the church and abbey ruins, Whitby has earned its living from more than just the sea and today is not only a popular tourist town, but a fishing port and a vibrant commercial centre.

History

The first mention of Whitby is in 656 AD when it was called *Streonsahl* by Oswy, the Christian King of Northumbria who founded Whitby Abbey. He appointed Lady Hilda, Abbess of Hartlepool as Abbess, and the Abbey witnessed a pivotal moment in monastic history at the 664 Synod of Whitby when the King ruled that the church in his kingdom (most of northern England) would follow Christian traditions which conformed to Roman interpretations rather than those which followed the Ionian (or Irish) version of the religion. This ruling effectively allied the Christian church in northern England to Rome, whence it stayed until the dissolution of the monasteries by Henry VIII in the 16thC.

298

The Abbey fell into disrepair and was substantially destroyed by Viking raiders in the 9thC. It was not until some years after the Norman conquest that it was re-founded – by William de Percy, one of William the Conquerors senior generals - as a reward for his part in the Norman conquest - and the town renamed *Witebi* (meaning white settlement in old norse) and over the years this has changed to the present name. The Abbey was probably larger than the town until the dissolution of the monasteries, being just a small fishing port with most buildings on the east side of the river. Growth of the alum industry, soon after the dissolution, transformed the size of the town and its role. Alum was an important chemical compound in all sorts of manufacturing processes during this period - it was used to cure leather for fixing dry cloth, and had wide application for medicinal purposes. Rock from which alum was made was found nearby, and skills to make it were secretly imported from Italy. Whitby became a port that exported the alum product and imported coal to be used in its production process. This in turn led to prosperous shipping and related industries and expansion of the port with piers being extended out into the North Sea. Together with the rise of the whaling industry, the late 18thC saw

the town as one of the more prominent coastal centres in Northern England. Testimony to its prosperity about this time is the fine Georgian property on the west cliff. Arrival of the railway in the 1840's strengthened the town's economy, bringing in large numbers of visitors from Teesside and the West Riding - a pattern still evident today. The novelist Bram Stoker, author of the acclaimed novel Dracula spent much time in Whitby and parts of the book are set in the town. The cult around Dracula makes the town a popular destination for "Goths". Today, the town earns its living from the visitor; from the fishing industry, although sadly not the force it once was, from the nearby potash mine at Boulby – the UK's only such mine - and from its freight capacity as a small commercial port. The fishing industry gives rise to an ad hoc fish market on the quay as and when catches are landed and that in turn has endowed the town with a plethora of fish and chip shops and restaurants; some of national renown.

WHITBY

Getting Here

Rail There are regular services via the Esk Valley line to Middlesborough (90 min). The station is also the northern terminus of the North York Moors Railway which runs from Pickering.

Road The town lies at the end of the A169, which leads from Malton; the A174 which leads east from Middlesbrough, and the coastal road, the A171 which leads from the southeast and Scarborough.

Bus The town is served by a number of long distance routes all of which terminate at the bus station in Station Square.

destination	service	frequency
Leeds	840	3x per day
York	840	3x per day
Malton	840	3x per day
Middlesbrough	X5/93	30 mins/hourly
Scarborough	X60/93	1x per day/hourly

Things to see and do

Although Whitby is a small place, with its buildings clinging to the steep hillsides either side of the harbour, its character and ambience demand time for exploration. On the eastern side of the harbour, the buildings are older and appear more organic. The narrow cobbled streets of Sandgate, Market Place and Church Street invite exploration to sample the atmosphere of Whitby 200 years ago and enjoy browsing in the shops, many of which sell the well known Whitby precious stone, the whitby jet. At the far end of Grape Lane, on the south side of the bridge, is the house where Captain James Cook lived, and is now a museum. Walking up to the Church and the Abbey is via the north end of Church Street and the steep climb up the 199 steps of Church Lane. Crossing the bridge (a bridge was first built here as far back at the 14thC) the quaysides on both sides of the harbour can clearly be seen with the backdrop of long irregular rows of buildings; much in contrast to the Abbey's splendour. On the west side, St Anns Staith and Pier Road follow the edge of the quay,

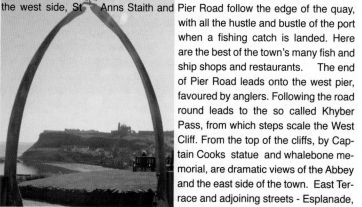

with all the hustle and bustle of the port when a fishing catch is landed. Here are the best of the town's many fish and ship shops and restaurants. The end of Pier Road leads onto the west pier, favoured by anglers. Following the road round leads to the so called Khyber Pass, from which steps scale the West Cliff. From the top of the cliffs, by Captain Cooks statue and whalebone memorial, are dramatic views of the Abbey and the east side of the town. East Terrace and adjoining streets - Esplanade, North terrace and Royal Crescent were built as part of a grand master plan devised by George Hudson (the railway king) although his vision was never completed because of Hudsons financial and personal difficulties - the Royal Crescent for example is only half a crescent; the western section was never built.

WHITBY

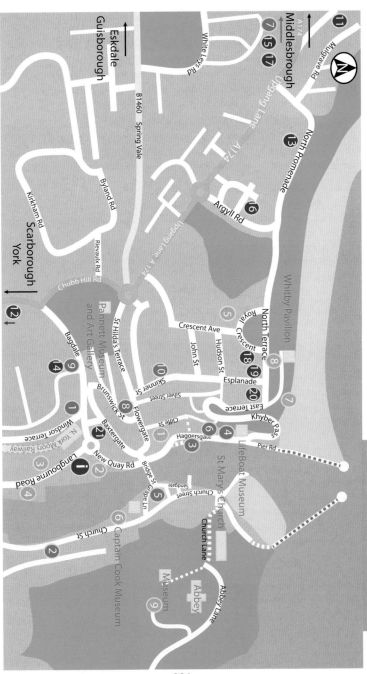

The streets behind- Silver Street, Skinner Street, Flowergate, Baxtergate reflect the towns prosperity in the late 18thC, although many buildings are of an earlier time. These streets were often used for filming the well known TV series "Heartbeat". A regular feature of Whitby are the opentop bus tours of the town, taking about 1hr, visitors can explore the town in a quirky steam bus or vintage charabanc are. The tours depart from the railway station between April and September.

The Beach

Whitby has a sandy beach on the west side of the harbour. It is safe, clean, gently sloping and stretches all the way to the village of Sandsend 2.5 miles away and walking to Sandsend on the beach is a popular activity Here are donkey rides, ice cream sellers, and the hotly sought after beach huts.

Abbey and Museum ⊞

Whitby Abbey sits proudly on the east headland, overlooking the town and sea; a dramatic, romantic setting, unequalled by any other English abbey. It can be reached by climbing the 199 steps from Church Street in the town below, a strenuous but rewarding route. By road, access is from the A171 just to the east of the road bridge over the Esk, and then along Spittal Bridge, and Green Lane. There is a large car park adjoining the site, although this can get full quickly in high season. The first monastery here was founded in 657 by King Oswy of Northumbria. This was an Anglo-Saxon style 'double monastery' for men and women, and the King installed Hilda as its first ruler; she remained here until her death in 680, and was present at one of the epic moments in English history, where the future of the English church was decided by the Synod of Whitby in 664. It was in the abbey that the relics of Northumbrian kings and saints were enshrined and the Anglo-Saxon poet Caedmon was educated. Nothing remains of the original monastery - the Danes saw to that in 867. The imposing ruins are those of the Benedictine abbey re-founded on the same site by the William de Percy about 1220. Adjoining the Abbey is Cholmley House, built in the aftermath of the Dissolution of the Monasteries in the 16thC; Sir Hugh Cholmley, having done Henry VIII service in this regard, was given the abbey and grounds. The courtyard here has been restored and has, at its centrepiece, a specially commissioned bronze copy of the famous 'Borghese Gladiator' statue. (The original of 1stC BC is in the Louvre Paris). The house is now a large visitor centre, which enables visitor to learn about much of Whitby's history as well as the Abbey and Cholmley House. There is an admission charge. 01947 643568 www.english-heritage.org.uk

WHITBY

St Mary's Parish Church

Best visited on the way up to the Abbey, much of this church dates from Norman times. Its low flat tower and battlements give it a fortress like appearance, some say in keeping with its need to fight off the fierce winter storms which blows in from the sea over the headland. The interior is crammed full of pews and galleries, and a notable triple-decker pulpit of 1778.   The surrounding bleak exposed graveyard is full of tombstones and graves of sailors, fishermen, navy seamen and lifeboatmen.   The church is open daily.

Captain Cook Museum

This celebration of the life and achievements of perhaps the towns most famous son is a small museum in Grape Lane. It is in the 17thC house where the young James Cook lived whilst he served his apprenticeship as a seaman. The Museum is on four floors. It is open daily between April and October. There is an admission charge.   01947 601900 www.cookmuseumwhitby.co.uk

Captain James Cook - Seafarer 1728-1779

Born near Middlesborough, James Cook is a renowned English seafarer, cartographer and explorer. He came to Whitby about 1745 and was apprenticed in a local merchant shipping company where he served his apprenticeship on coal vessels which plied this part of the coast, rising to working on larger ships in the Baltic sea.

He joined the Royal Navy in 1755 and rose quickly to the rank of captain. He saw service in the seven years war and developed a talent for exploring and mapping – he was responsible for the first mapping of Newfoundland in the early 1760's.   In the latter years of his naval service he became well known as an explorer, making three exploratory voyages to the far east and Australasia- he mapped the New Zealand coast, discovered and named Botany Bay; he discovered Antarctica, and on his third, and last voyage, and having mapped the coastline of Alaska, he sailed south to the Hawaiian Islands where he met his death in February 1779.

The ship he used for his first voyage was the Endeavour which had been built in Whitby. It saw service on a number of voyages after Cooks first voyage, and was eventually scuttled off Rhode Island in 1778 during the American War of Independence. The Endeavour's name has been used for many other exploration craft, including the NASA space shuttles. A replica ship was built in 1994 and is berthed in Sydney Harbour.   The harbourside at Whitby is named after the ship.

WHITBY

Lifeboat house and Museum

Whitby operated a lifeboat service long before the formation of the RNLI; the original lifeboat station was built in 1802. The present Lifeboat station is on Fish Pier and the previous station, on Pier Road is now the Museum. Here are exhibits and stories of the significance of the lifeboat to seafarers and the courage and derring-do of the volunteer lifeboatmen who have consistently graced the towns marine heritage. Open daily from Easter to November, and weekends in the winter. Admission is free.   01947 602001 www.rnli.co.uk

Fishing

The town is a popular spot for anglers. There are opportunities for sea angling, from boat trips out of the harbour, shore angling from the beach and on the pier, and river angling on the River Esk. Sea anglers can use charter boats from the harbour for expeditions to the best grounds offshore, sometimes close to the shipwrecks common to this part of the coast, and are usually rewarded with catches of a range of fish ranging from mackerel through to seabass. Shore anglers have opportunities to land catch from both piers and the beach, whilst freshwater anglers can expect to catch salmon and trout in the clear waters of the Esk; although most of the fishing rights are private there are a limited number of free fishing areas upstream out of the town at Ruswarp and Sleights.

North York Moors Railway

The station marks the northern end of the North York Moors railway, reputedly the UK's most popular vintage railway line which runs regular daily services from Pickering across the Moors to Whitby during the April to October period, and a more limited service in the winter months (see page 296).

Jet heritage

Whitby Jet is a black gemstone dating back to the Iron Age, created from jet bearing shale rocks, containing fossilised remains of *araucaria*, or monkey puzzle trees. These shales are only found on a nearby stretch of coastline, and the town has long been a centre for jet jewellery. In Sandgate and Church Street are shops specialising in jet stone products. The Whitby Jet Heritage Centre in Church Street, besides retailing artefacts, contains a wealth of information about its history and its applications.   01947 821530 www.whitbyjet.co.uk

Whitby Museum and Pannett Art Gallery

These two venues are in Pannett Park, named for a local solicitor who provided the land for the park and built the art gallery.   The park can be reached from St Hildas Terrace.   The Museum has a distinct Edwardian ambiance. It has an eclectic collection of fossils, jet artefacts, an ethnographic collection as well as material relating to Captain Cook and other Whitby personalities. It is open Tues through Sun through the year. There is an admission charge. The Art Gallery is relatively small containing Robert Pannetts art collection and periapatetic exhibitions. The opening times are the same as the museum, but admission is free.   01947 601908   www.whitbymuseum.org.uk

WHITBY

Festivals

April	Goth Weekend Pavilion	www.topmum.co.uk
May	Moors and Coast Festival	
June	60's music festival Pavilion	www.whitbylive.co.uk
July	Northern Soul weekend Pavilion	
August	Regatta	www.whitbyregatta.co.uk
	Whitby Folk week	www.whitbyfolk.co.uk

St Hilda Religious Leader 614-680

A prominent figure in the Anglo Saxon period in providing direction to the English church as it veered from Ionian Christianity to that of the Church of Rome. She was an abbess at several monasteries and renowned for her ability to draw Kings to her for advice. She was of Royal blood, and after the murder of her parents was raised at Kings Edwin's court in Northumbria.   She entered a convent on the banks of the River Wear and quickly succeeded to become Abbess at Hartlepool.   It was King Oswui who persuaded her to become founding Abbess at Whitby, a post she retained until her death.   She discovered Caedmon, the first known English poet, who was a cowherder at the Abbey, and was instrumental in developing the talents of two fellow monks who went on to become bishops and then were beatified; St John of Beverley and St Wilfrid of Ripon. Her legacy includes the naming of a number of womens colleges at blue chip universities across the world as well as many churches.

Restaurants (see map page 301)

££

Indian **Passage to India** Windsor Terrace
01947 606500 www.passagetoindia.eu ❶

Pub food **White Horse and Griffin** Church Street
01947 604857 www.whitehorseandgriffin.co.uk ❷

Fish **The Marine Hotel** Marine Parade 01947 605022 www.the-marine-hotel.co.uk ❸

Fish **The Quayside** 7 Pier Road 01947 825346 www.fuscowhitby.com ❹

£££

Fish **Green's Restaurant** Bridge St 01947 600284 www.greensofwhitby.co.uk ❺

Fish **The Magpie Café** 14 Pier Road 01947 602058 www.magpiecafe.co.uk ❻

English **Crossbutts Stable** Guisborough Road 01947 820986 ❼

English **Red Chard Grill Room** 22-23 Flowergate 01947 606660 ❽

English **Bagdale Hall** 1, Bagdale 01947 602958 www.bagdale.co.uk ❾

English **Ditto Restaurant** Skinner St 01947 601404 www.ditto-restaurant.co.uk ❿

WHITBY

Hotels (see map page 301)

★★

The White House Hotel Upgang Lane 15 Bedrooms ⑪
01947 600469 www.whitehouse-whitby.co.uk

★★★(GA)

Ruswarp Hall Ruswarp 13 Bedrooms 01947 602801 www.ruswarphallhotel.co.uk ⑫
The Seacliffe 12 North Promenade 20 Bedrooms ⑬
01947 603139 www.seacliffehotel.com

★★★

Bagdale Hall 1, Bagdale 26 Bedrooms 01947602958 www.bagdale.co.uk ⑭

Dunsley Hall Country House Dunsley Lane 26 Bedrooms ⑮
01947 893437 www.dunsleyhall.com

Saxonville Hotel Ladysmith Avenue 23 Bedrooms ⑯
01947 602631 www.saxonville.co.uk

★★★★

Raithwaite Hall Sandend Road 01947 661661 www.raithwaitehallwhitby.co.uk ⑰

★★★★★(GA)

The Langley Royal Crescent 6 Bedrooms 01904 604250 www.langleyhotel.com ⑱

not rated

Sandbeck Hotel 1-2 Crescent Terrace 23 Bedrooms 01947 604012 ⑲
Royal Hotel West Cliff 115 Bedrooms 01947 602234 www.shearings.com ⑳
George Hotel Baxtergate 19 Bedrooms ㉑
01947 602565 www.georgehotelwhitby.co.uk

Parking Ⓟ

① Cliff Street	37 spaces	⑥ Church Street	92 spaces
② Endeavour Wharf	250 spaces	⑦ Pavilion Drive	63 spaces
③ Marina Back	232 spaces	⑧ Pavilion Top	68 spaces
④ Marina Front	96 spaces	⑨ Abbey Headland	415 spaces
⑤ Royal Crescent	424 spaces		

WHITBY

Whitby Visitor Information Centre
Langbourne Road
01723 383636
www.discoveryorkshirecoast.com

SCARBOROUGH

Often acclaimed as the UK's first seaside resort, Scarborough has long catered for visitors in large numbers and remains a popular family destination on Yorkshire's east coast, having a wide range of attractions and activities for all ages and tastes. Despite rival attractions of foreign beaches and warmer climes, the town has retained its lure for visitors and ranks amongst Britain's most popular seaside resorts; the Victorian travel writer Bradshaw describing the town as England's most interesting marine spa.   Set around a headland on which is perched dramatic ruins of a Norman castle, it has two large bays; wide, safe, gently shelving sandy beaches; a working harbour; many attractions and a seemingly endless supply of guest houses and self catering accommodation as well as a number of classy hotels. There is a busy town centre, and a wide range of entertainment and nightlife.

south bay beach

History

Archaeological evidence shows an Iron Age settlement as well as a Roman signal station on the castles rocky headland, but much of the towns early development can be ascribed to the Vikings.   The name Scarborough derives partially from the nickname *"Skarthi"* given to one of Viking invaders- Thorgils – on account of his hare lip, and partially from the Viking word *Borg* which means stronghold; the combination giving the name *Skarthiborg*. The Vikings established themselves here in c.966. The town was then invaded and burned by the Norwegian King Harold Hadrada in 1066, but despite the Norman conquests, there is no mention of it in the Domesday Book.   The castle was built in 1136 by King Henry II, and the town granted a royal charter shortly afterwards. Scarborough Fair (for which the well known song was written) was established in the 13thC as a six week long festival attracting merchants across Europe and continued for nearly 500 years.   The English civil war saw the town change hands a number of times between Parliamentarians and Royalists, including two long and bloody sieges.   At the end of the war, much of the town lay in ruins. The birth of the resort happened in the early

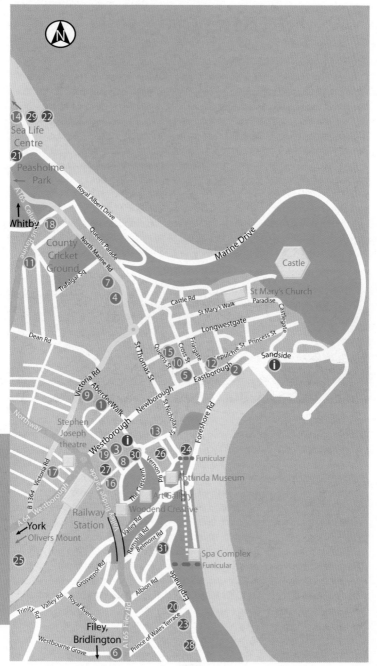

SCARBOROUGH

The Grand Hotel dominates the south bay beach

17thC with the discovery of the spa waters, and the development of the spa; this was not long after Harrogate had developed a similar trade. A book promoting the health benefits of the towns spa waters in 1660 brought a tide of visitors seeking cures for ailments, and it has been a resort ever since. The first bathing machines in Britain were introduced on Scarborough's beaches in the mid 18th century. The arrival of the railway in 1845 gave a fillip to the attractions of the resort to those in the industrial West Riding, as the town became less than a days travel away. The number of large hotels, guest houses, and resort attractions then mushroomed and endowed the town with much of its present character.

Getting Here

Rail the station is at the western edge of the town centre, but within easy walking distance of the seafront. There are regular services to Hull (90min), York (50 min), Leeds (80 min), and Manchester(140 min).

Road the A64 links the town with the national road network. Journey times by car from Leeds are c.90 min; 150 mins from Manchester, although the main road can become congested in peak season and longer journey times should be allowed for. A park and ride scheme is operation. See page 320.

Bus most longer distance routes start from or finish at the railway station. There are routes from a wide range of destinations.

destination	service(s)	frequency
Leeds	843	hourly
York	843	hourly
Whitby	93/X60	30 mins/1x per day
Hull	121	hourly
Bridlington	121	hourly
Filey	121	hourly
Middlesbrough	93/X60	hourly/1x per day
London	563	1x per day

SCARBOROUGH

Walks around the town Scarborough is a big resort. There is much to see and do. It is impractical to try and capture it's atmosphere in one go; several visits are probably necessary to gain a real feel for this quintessentially traditional seaside town. Two walks are suggested to gain a taste of what is on offer.

● ● ● ● ● ● Walk 1 The Resort Walk

Start at the railway station, an iconic building of 1845 with the tall imposing Baroque middle tower added in 1882. Across the road is the Stephen Joseph Theatre ①. The theatre company started by Stephen Joseph in 1955 introduced the theatre in the round concept to the UK, but not until 1988 did it come occupy the present building, a former Odeon cinema. The Theatre, renowned for innovative, thought provoking plays and dramas, many of which go on to be West End and Broadway hits, has been continually championed by playwright Alan Ayckbourn. It has two theatres, one in the round which seats about 400, and one traditional stage end seating 160. There is a full programme of plays throughout the year. (01723 4370540 www.sjt.uk.com) Turn into Newborough, the heart of the shopping centre and Brunswick Mall ②. This modern complex provides an array of big high street brand names together with one of the towns two visitor information centres. Returning to Newborough, keep going downhill and into Eastborough, the older end of the shopping centre. On the beach side of the street is Merchants Row ③, once the main street of the historic town and where Scarborough Fair took place. A little further down is the small but fascinating Museum of Scarborough's Maritime heritage ④. This centre has a collection of material of maritime life on the Scarborough and Yorkshire coast. It has exhibits and archives on shipwrecks, the lives of fishermen and their families and the fishing industry. The Centre is open Wed through Sun. Admission is free. (01723 369361 www scarboroughsmaritimeheritage. org.uk). At the bottom of Eastborough is the waterfront. Here, to the left is Sandside and the Harbour, and to the right Foreshore Road, amusement arcades and other typical seafront shops.At the far end of Sandside, below the castle grounds, is a gatehouse with a round tower and although it looks old, in fact dates from 1906. The Newcastle Packet pub lies on the corner of Sandside with East Sandgate and reputedly the oldest pub in the town; the origins of the building, although appearing Elizabethan, are thought to to date from the 13thC. The Harbour ⑤ is worth exploration. A working port ever since the early 14thC, with the west pier dating from this period. There is an inner and an outer harbour; the inner houses the fishing fleet and the outer, leisure craft. The harbour is used by a range of fishing boats - from large whitefish trawlers to smaller day fishing shellfish vessels. The landed catches are auctioned in the fish market on the adjoining quay, with the largest market generally on a Saturday. During the summer season, visitors can enjoy short sea trips and cruises in pleasure boats such as the Hispaniola.

SCARBOROUGH

310

—A Visitor Guide To Yorkshire—

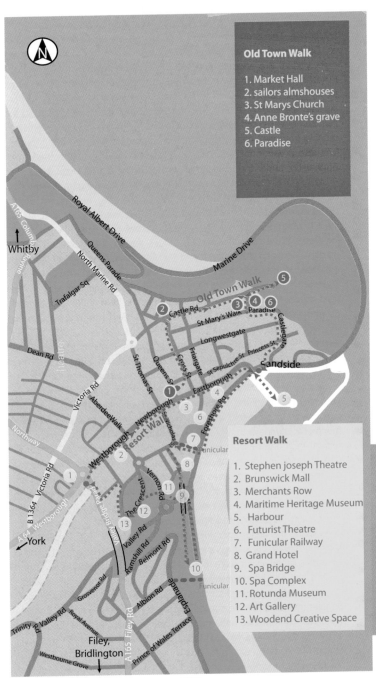

Old Town Walk

1. Market Hall
2. sailors almshouses
3. St Marys Church
4. Anne Bronte's grave
5. Castle
6. Paradise

Resort Walk

1. Stephen joseph Theatre
2. Brunswick Mall
3. Merchants Row
4. Maritime Heritage Museum
5. Harbour
6. Futurist Theatre
7. Funicular Railway
8. Grand Hotel
9. Spa Bridge
10. Spa Complex
11. Rotunda Museum
12. Art Gallery
13. Woodend Creative Space

SCARBOROUGH

WALK 1 ▼

SCARBOROUGH

The central pier, dividing the harbour, was built 1752 complete with lighthouse. This is manned in the summer months, and open to the public. During peak season opening hours extend into the evening, and at night visitors are afforded splendid views of the town.   Returning to Foreshore Road, the panoramic view is of the South Bay, with its wide sandy beach and backdrop of the Spa complex and South Cliffs.   Facing the sea is the Futurist Theatre 6 , well known in Yorkshire as a centre of nightlife and entertainment, it offers a full programme for families ranging from well known comedians to dance troupes and pop groups. It is also a venue for film.   (01723 374500 www.futuristtheatre.co.uk) Further on, under the towering elevations of the Grand Hotel is the funicular lift 7 that offers an exertion free way of climbing up to the town centre. It was one of five such funiculars in the town, only two of which remain in operation, the other adjoining the Spa (and the first funicular in the UK when opened in 1878).   The alternative to using the funicular, for those with energy to spare, is to use the winding pathways in the gardens between the Futurist and the funicular station which leads to the Town Hall and St Nicholas Street. At the top of the funicular, the Tramway station opens onto St Nicholas Street. The Town Hall is on the right, a neo - Jacobean red brick building dating from 1870. Turn left and go round into St Nicholas Cliff.   On the left hand side is the imposing Victorian edifice of possibly Scarborough's finest hotel building 8 and historically one of its most important. In many published pictures of the town, the dramatic setting of the domineering Grand Hotel overlooking the harbour and the South Bay is prominent. Opened in 1867 and designed by Hull architect Cuthbert Brodrick, it was one of Europes first purpose built hotels. Its design is based on the concept of time; there are four towers to represent each season; twelve floors to represent each month; 52 chimneys to represent each week, and 365 bedrooms to represent each day of the year. It is V shaped in plan form in honour of Queen Victoria. Beyond the Grand Hotel a footpath leads onto the Cliff or Spa Bridge. This crosses the Valley close to the sea and was built in 1827.It leads directly to the Spa Complex 10 , one of the town's long established attractions, well worth a visit, even if not to see a concert or other event. This 1877 complex sits grandly at the foot of the south cliffs overlooking the beach and adjoining the funicular lift. This is where the spa waters were discovered a hundred years before. The present building was adapted following a fire, but still follows the broad design of Joseph Paxton, the architect better known for his stunning design of London's Crystal Palace.   During its heyday the Spa was renowned as the most popular music hall venue outside of London. It provides a multi-purpose venue for conferences and entertainment and there is a full programme of events through the year.(01723 376774 www.scarboroughspa.co.uk) Return via the beachside path, and under the Cliff Bridge is the Rotunda Museum 11 recently re-opened and run by Scarborough Museums Trust.

rotunda museum

The Museum tells the story of the town as well as possessing a comprehensive geological archive derived from William Smith, the father of British geology, and who inspired the design and construction of this rather unique building which opened as a museum of geology as long ago as 1829. (01723 353665 www.rotundamusem.co.uk) From the Museum, turn up Vernon Road, and then up a short ramp to St Nicholas Cliff, over the bridge above Vernon Road which leads to a winding footpath through a small park into The Crescent. On the south side, facing over The Valley, are two more small museums; The **Art Gallery** 12 , a large Italianate villa, contains Scarborough's eclectic art collection, dating from the late Georgian times, and built over the years from bequests and donations. There is an admission charge. (01723 374753 www.scarboroughartgallery.co.uk) Beyond the art gallery, the building occupied by **Woodend Creative Workspace** 13 was once the home of the literary family, the Sitwells, and is now a facility for new and growing businesses with a creative bent. Housed in the foyer and main gallery space is an Art and Craft Gallery offering a range of original art works as well as a unique assortment of hand made products including fine art, jew-

The old town sits snugly under the lee of the castle

ellery, ceramics and textiles. (01723384500 www. woodendcreative.co.uk). This area is where the town most resembles the grandeur to be seen in the cities of Bath or Edinburgh with an imposing terrace of late Georgian houses that follow the curve of road, overlooking the small park. From the Crescent, return along Somerset Terrace and back to the Station.

Walk 2

Old town walk

A shorter, but more strenuous, walking tour which climbs up to the Castle and back to the beaches.

Starting in Newborough, head towards the Market Hall and Vaults. This neo classical building of 1853 still provides a lively daily indoor market. In the vaults is a set of shops and stalls selling all sorts of bric-a-brac and antiques. Continue up Cross Street and Auborough Street. At the top, turn onto Castle Road. On the left are almshouses for retired seamen ②. Turn into Blenheim Street which, at the top, gives a spectacular view out over North Bay. The Castle can be seen to the right and there is a footpath to follow across the front of the Bay Hotel to Mulgrave Place, with similarly spectacular views of South Bay. St Marys Church ③ is on

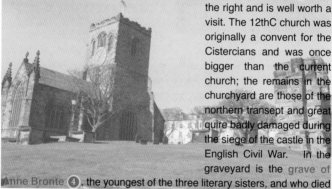

the right and is well worth a visit. The 12thC church was originally a convent for the Cistercians and was once bigger than the current church; the remains in the churchyard are those of the northern transept and great quire badly damaged during the siege of the castle in the English Civil War. In the graveyard is the grave of Anne Bronte ④, the youngest of the three literary sisters, and who died in the town in 1849. The entrance to the Castle ⑤ lies ahead, and a visit well rewarded. The prominent setting on a rocky headland has always formed a defensive structure protecting the town from sea borne invasion. Archaeological digs have recovered artefacts showing evidence of an Iron Age fort on the headland, as well as some evidence of an earlier Bronze Age settlement. The Romans occupied the headland with a Signal Station in c.370AD, and the Anglo-Saxons built a small chapel on the site. The present stone structure was built by Henry II to replace an earlier wooden one. Only the keep survives as a part shell, together with the later outer walls and barbican. The castle was heavily damaged during the English civil war and never recovered. It was used as a prison in the 17th and 18thC and briefly re-fortified during the 1745 Jacobite Rebellion.There is a museum and and visitor centre in the grounds. The site is open through the year; times may vary. There is an admission charge. (01723 372451 www.english-heritage.org.uk). Leaving the Castle, pass by the churchyard and descend via the quaintly named street of Paradise ⑥. A house here commemorates the sometime home of George Cayley, briefly Scarborough MP from 1832 to 1835 but whose lifetime work was exploration and study of aeronautics. Continue down Castlegate, fronted with elegant Georgian houses and turn through Princess Street and St Sepulchre Street. Halfway along, there is a small ginnel called Palace Hill that leads down onto the north side of Eastborough, and thence to the harbour and the beaches where the walk finishes.

SCARBOROUGH

Sir George Cayley   Aeronautical Pioneer 1773-1857

Sometimes called the father of aeronautics, George Cayley was responsible for the creation of the concept of an airplane as a fixed wing flying machine, although his concept would not achieve practicality for another 50 years after his death. his ideas and theories laid the foundation which enabled the creation of manned flight.   His engineering achievements went well beyond flight. He invented the self- righting lifeboat, caterpillar tractors, and many other engineering applications we take for granted today.   He was born in Brompton near Scarborough and was MP for the town between 1832 and 1835, and although in great demand in London chose to spend much of his time at Brompton Hall where he had been born. He did live, as a child at a house in Paradise; a plaque on the wall marks the position.

The Sitwells   Literary Figures

The Sitwells were a well-to-do family, whose wealth had come from iron. They came to Scarborough, at first just to take the waters of the then spa resort, and when misfortune forced sale of their Derbyshire home in 1865, they came to live in the town. They soon moved into the Italianate villa, Woodend, which they owned until 1934, and which is now a creative arts workspace.   The family is however best known for the literary trio of children born to Sir George Sitwell in the late 19thC, and who was briefly the towns MP. The children were brought up in the town and their literary works often refer to it.   The oldest child was Edith (1887-1964) who gained fame as a poet and author, publishing literary books and verse over a long period both in the UK and latterly in the USA.   The middle child Osbert (1892-1969) was a consummate socialite, but devoted his life to poetry, art criticism and controversial journalism, as well as publishing a large number of works of fiction and non fiction.   The youngest was Sacheverell (1897-1988), and the only one who produced heirs to the baronetcy; neither Edith nor Osbert had any children. He too was a prolific writer of verse and expanded his writings with a considerable amount of non fictional books on art and nature.

SCARBOROUGH

Paradise overlooking the south bay

The Beaches

North Bay Beach extends from the headland north to Scalby Mills and the Sea Life Centre. It is the lesser developed of Scarborough's two beaches, and enjoys blue flag status as a clean safe beach. Prince Albert Drive runs along the back of the beach and provides parking all the way along. The beach and waters of the bay are a favoured spot for surfers at all times of the year. At the northern end, just before the Sea Life Centre, the pedestrian promenade is lined with colourful beach huts, where families base themselves all day during their holidays in the resort. The supply is limited and there is great demand for this kind of facility - purchase prices being in many thousands of pounds - so to visitors seeking a base for a day on the North Bay beach, a beach hut may remain but a distant dream.   **South Bay Beach** extends from the harbour to just beyond the South Cliff funicular railway. It boasts wide smooth sand and with the traditional amusement arcades and other traditional resort shops on the seafront, is often very crowded during peak seasons. Here are the donkey rides and the sandcastle competitions, the deckchairs and ice cream sellers, all making up a typically British seaside scene.

Peasholm Park

Open through the year, the Park lies on the north side of town, behind North Bay beach. It is a pleasant place to walk, and enjoy a range of activities, many based around the lake. There are rowing boats and pedalos for hire, and three times a week during August, a mock naval battle is fought using scale warships.

SCARBOROUGH

There are also band concerts and firework displays during the summer season. The park is over 100 years old, laid out in Japanese style with a pagoda; oriental statues, shrubs and plants. A tree trail reveals a range of rare and unusual trees. The park is walkable from the town centre (½ mile), but for those less fleet of foot, the bus (3,12,21) departs regularly from York Place.

Open Air Theatre

The theatre is near Peasholm Park and is Europe's largest open-air theatre, seating over 6000. It was first opened in 1930 and has recently been refurbished for summer performances with top line celebrity singers on the bill. The bus services to Peasholm Park (3,12,21) also serve this venue.
0844 8889991 www.scarboroughopenairtheatre.com

North Bay Railway

This miniature gauge railway has been operating for over 80 years. Trains run from Peasholm Park to Scalby Mills and the Sealife Centre at weekends in the winter and daily during the summer months. 01723 368791 www.nbr.org.uk

Sea Life Centre

The centre is at Scalby Mills, on the northern end of North Bay. An aquarium and marine sanctuary, it offers a range of ever changing exhibits and experiences of the marine world. The pyramids in which the attraction is set have sanctuaries for seals, penguins and otters, as well as more exotic marine life such as leopard sharks, turtles and giant crabs. The North Bay Railway serves the centre, as well as bus services 3,12,21. The attraction is open all year round. There is an admission charge. 01723 376125 www.visitsealife.com/Scarborough

Olivers Mount

Dominating the landscape to the south of the town, Olivers Mount is a flat topped hill with heavily wooded steep sides which, besides providing panoramic views over the town, also contains Scarborough's war memorial and a motor cycling road race circuit; probably the only one left in mainland Britain. There is a full programme of motor bike racing across the year. Access to the site is off the A64 on Queen Margarets Road, and Mere Lane. From Filey Road, the site is accessible from College Lane. 01723 373000 www.auto66.com

Opera House Casino

The only licensed casino on the east coast of Yorkshire, this late night entertainment venue is in St Thomas St. 01723 357940 www.operahousecasino.co.uk

Cricket

County cricket is played in the town at the Scarborough Cricket Club in North Marine Road just north of the town centre. It is now the only venue apart from Headingley (Leeds) to host county matches. The ground also hosts other cricket events through the year including the popular Scarborough Festival held annually towards the end of August. 01723 365625
www.scarboroughcricketclub.co.uk

SCARBOROUGH

Restaurants (see map page 308)

£

Italian **Florios** Aberdeen Walk   01723 351124   wwwflorios-restaurant.co.uk   ①

Fish **The Famous Fishpan** Foreshore Road   01723 371299   ②

££

Tex Mex **Chillis** 17 York Place   01723 503900   ③

Italian **CoGonis** 36 North Marine Road   01723 506979   ④

French **Le Chat Noir** 10 Eastborough   01723 350653   ⑤

Italian **Tuscany Too** 6 Filey Road   01723 35590   ⑥

Thai **Manor Thai** 50 North Marine Road   01723 507744   ⑦

Greek **George Michaels** 5 York Place   01723 372646   ⑧

Italian **Gianni's** 13 Victoria Road   01723 507388   ⑨

Indian **Eastern Paradise** 5 St Helens Square   01723 375227   ⑩

Turkish **Haz** Columbus Ravine   01723 366180   ⑪

Italian **Tricolos** 36-39 Newborough   01723 367842   www.tricolos.co.uk   ⑫

£££

Italian **Da-Claudio** 4 Harcourt Place   01723 354648   www.da-claudio.co.uk   ⑬

English **Four Seasons** Wrea Head Hotel   Barmoor Lane
01723 371190   www.wreaheadhall.co.uk   ⑭

Italian **Lanterna** 33 Queen St   01723 363616   www.lanterna-ristorante.co.uk   ⑮

English **Marmalades** The Crescent   01723 350349   www.beiderbeckes.com   ⑯

English **The Green Room** 138 Victoria Road
01723 501801   www.thegreenroomrestaurant.com   ⑰

English **Jeremy's** 33 Victoria Park Avenue
01723 363871   www.jeremysrestaurant.co.uk   ⑱

Fish **Cafe Fish** 19 York Place   01723 500301   ⑲

SCARBOROUGH

Hotels (see map page 308)

**

Red Lea Prince of Wales Terrace 68 Bedrooms 01723 362431 redleahotel.co.uk   ⑳

Park Manor Northstead Manor Drive 42 Bedrooms   ㉑
01723 372090   www.parkmanor.co.uk

***

Oxpasture Hall Lady Ediths Drive, 23 bedrooms   ㉒
01723 365295   www.oxpasturehall.co.uk

Brooklands Esplanade Gardens 63 Bedrooms   ㉓
01723 376576   www.brooklands-scarborough.co.uk

Grand St Nicholas Cliff 365 Bedrooms   ㉔
0871 2220047   www.scarboroughgrandhotel.co.uk

Clifton Queen Margarets Road 70 Bedrooms   ㉕
01723 356772   www.britanniahotels.com

Palmcourt St Nicholas Cliff 44 Bedrooms   ㉖
01723 368161   www.palmcourtscarborough.co.uk

Beiderbeckes 1-3 The Crescent 27 Bedrooms   ㉗
01723 365766   www.beiderbeckes.com

Ambassador 36 The Esplanade 59 Bedrooms   ㉘
01723 362841 www.ambassadorspahotel.co.uk

Wrea Head Barmoor Lane Scalby 20 Bedrooms   ㉙
01723 375844 www.wreaheadhall.co.uk

The Crescent 1 Belvoir Terrace 20 Bedrooms   ㉚
01723 360929 www.thecrescenthotel.com

****

Crown Spa The Esplanade 91 Bedrooms   ㉛
01723 357400 www.crownspahotel.com

SCARBOROUGH

Parking P

As with many resorts, high season means parking can become extremely difficult, whereas ample space is available at other times. A park and ride system operates through the year, and visitors travelling in peak season for a day trip will be well advised to take advantage of this service.   The sites are on the A64 (approach from York) and A165 (approach from Filey). Each site has 600 spaces. Bus services operate each way from each car park at 12 min intervals from 7.00 am to 7.00pm throughout the year. Parking is free; there is a small fare for the bus.

Other car parks   (* short stay only)

1	Albion Road	66 spaces	11 Quay St	38 spaces
2	Burniston Road	770 spaces	12 Scalby Mills	180 spaces
3	Brunswick Centre	350 spaces	13 South Bay	168 spaces
4	Castle road	60 spaces	14 Spa Drive	38 spaces
5	Eastborough	43 spaces	15 Spa Forecourt	64 spaces
6	King St *	75 spaces	16 St Thomas St *	125 spaces
7	Marine Drive	349 spaces	17 Weaponess Valley Rd	334 spaces
8	N'hstead Manor Drive	654 spaces	18 West Pier	74 spaces
9	Balmoral Centre	445 spaces	19 Westwood	106 spaces
10	North St *	165 spaces	20 William St	248 spaces

Scarborough Visitor Information Centres
- **Brunswick Mall**
- **Sandside**
01723 383636
www.discoveryorkshirecoast.com

SCARBOROUGH

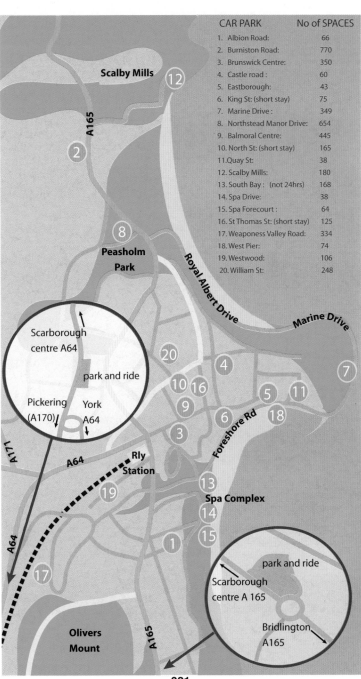

CAR PARK	No of SPACES
1. Albion Road:	66
2. Burniston Road:	770
3. Brunswick Centre:	350
4. Castle road :	60
5. Eastborough:	43
6. King St: (short stay)	75
7. Marine Drive:	349
8. Northstead Manor Drive:	654
9. Balmoral Centre:	445
10. North St: (short stay)	165
11.Quay St:	38
12. Scalby Mills:	180
13. South Bay : (not 24hrs)	168
14. Spa Drive:	38
15. Spa Forecourt :	64
16. St Thomas St: (short stay)	125
17. Weaponess Valley Road:	334
18. West Pier:	74
19. Westwood:	106
20. William St:	248

Scalby Mills

A165

Peasholm Park

Royal Albert Drive

Marine Drive

Scarborough centre A64

park and ride

Pickering (A170)

York A64

A171

A64

Rly Station

A64

Foreshore Rd

Spa Complex

Olivers Mount

A165

park and ride

Scarborough centre A 165

Bridlington A165

SCARBOROUGH

321

PART FIVE

EAST AND SOUTH EAST YORKSHIRE

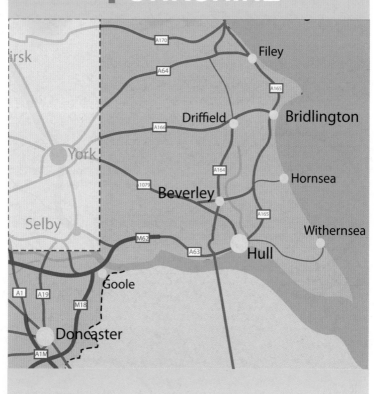

FILEY

Once a tiny fishing village in a peaceful sheltered bay, Filey lies midway between Scarborough and Bridlington, and is everything they are not. A small, discrete and gentle resort, for those who prefer a quieter visit to the seaside.

History

There is a record of the Romans having inhabited this area- there are the remains of a Roman signal station on Carr Naze (the headland leading out to Filey Brigg) and possibly the remains of a harbour wall on the Brigg itself. But Filey was, until the 19thC, little more than a fishing village with a small weekly market and an annual fair. Scarborough and Bridlington's rapid growth led some visitors to seek a liitle more peace and quiet, and Filey provided a perfect answer. There was a spa function in the early 19thC, but the spa well, close to Carr Naze, was eventually washed away by the sea. A well to do regular visitor conceived a grand plan in 1835 to develop the town as a fashionable resort, and boosted by the coming of the railway in 1846, this plan resulted in what is now The Crescent and adjoining streets. Filey's growth continued through the19thC, but always as a resort different to its neighbours; and the Edwardian period probably reflected its apotheosis as a desirable but genteel destination. That characteristic is still evident today as the town continues to serve the needs of visitors wanting gentility, peace and quiet and a safe haven to venture into the water.

Getting Here

Rail Filey station is on the Hull to Scarborough line, with regular services to both. Leeds and Manchester can be reached via both.

Road The A165 coast road linking the east coast resorts. From Leeds via the A64 to Staxton and then the A1035 is a journey time of c.90 mins.

FILEY

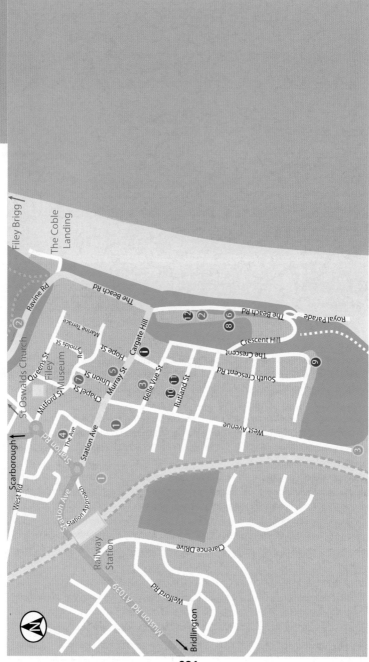

Filey Brigg

The Coble Landing

Ravine Rd

The Beach Rd

Marine Terrace

Cargate Hill

Royal Parade

The Beach Rd

Crescent Hill

The Crescent

South Crescent Rd

St Oswalds Church

Queens St

Filey

Mitford St

Museum

Reynolds St

Hope St

Muray St

Union St

Chapel St

Belle Vue St

Rutland St

West Avenue

The Ave

Station Ave

Station Rd

West Rd

Scarborough

Station Approach

Station Ave

Railway Station

Clarence Drive

Welford Rd

Muston Rd A1039

Bridlington

Bus The bus station is near to the railway station. The regular services are:

destination	service(s)	frequency
Scarborough	118/121	2 hourly/hourly
Bridlington	121	hourly
Hull	121	hourly
York	845	4x per day
Leeds	845	4x per day

Things to see and do

Getting around is easy although the short climb from the beach to the centre can be strenuous. A suggested walk is to start at St Oswalds Church and walk down the Ravine. At the bottom, is the coble landing from which you can walk onto the Brigg. Alternatively, turn right onto the promenade, and follow the seafront as far as Crescent Hill, and climb up to the Crescent. The Crescent, the Victorian development which remains largely intact, fronts a small park along its length with good views over Filey Bay, and space to sit and admire the view. At the northern end of the Crescent turn into the town and, using the back streets, lined with pleasant Victorian terraces, return to Queen Street, near the Church and finish up at the Filey Museum.

St Oswalds Church

Niklaus Pevsner, the celebrated architectural historian describes the church as "easily the finest in the NE corner of the East Riding". It is of early Norman origin and rebuilt at the end of the 12thC.

Filey Museum

The museum dedicated to the towns history is in Queen Street occupying two of Fileys oldest buildings (late 17thC) which are easily recognisable with their bright whitewashed facades, and an original plaque on the wall dated 1696, stating simply *"The fear of God be in you"* The museum is open Easter to October. Opening times may vary. There is an admission charge.

01723 515013   www.fileymuseum.co.uk

The Beach

One of the towns major assets, the beach is long, gently shelving and stretches across Filey Bay, only finishing east of Speeton as the Flamborough cliffs rise from the landscape. It is a popular place for sailing and windsurfing, and rarely overcrowded. At the northern end of the promenade is a slipway where fishing boats known as cobles are launched or towed out to sea. These are flat bottom high bow boats designed to to be launched from and landed on shallow sandy beaches, and peculiar to Britains north east coast. The southern end of the beach is often deserted and the more energetic can walk onto the cliffs and, via the Headland Way, round Flamborough Head and on as fas as Bridlington.

The Cleveland Way

Filey marks the coastal end of this long distance footpath from Helmsley (see page 17). Its route follows the cliff tops to Scarborough and beyond. An easy days walk to Scarborough on the cliffs, returning by bus (service 118/121) is a popular choice.

Filey Brigg

The Brigg is one of the most distinctive geological features of Britain's east coast. Flat-topped, and projecting straight from the headland of Carr Naze for about a mile, it creates a natural breakwater which helps make Filey Bay the safe tranquil area it is, although it can be hazardous to unwary passing ships. It is said that the shelter of the Brigg would allow the entire British navy to ride safely at anchor even in force 10 gales; indeed there have been suggestions that the Bay could be the best spot for a national harbour on the east coast- fortunately that has not come to pass, as Filey would no longer be the

place it is. Towards the end of the Brigg is a rock formation called The Spittals - apparently man made - running at right angles to the Brigg, and some theories claim it could well have been one side of a small harbour built in Roman times. The Brigg is easily accessible at low tide and is a favourite stroll of about a mile for many visitors. There are plenty of rockpools, rich in specimens of fossil seaweed, and home to a variety of living forms. The chalk cliffs of Speeton, and Flamborough Head, are plainly visible from here. Northwards, the seascape can be more rugged as the sea storms lash the rocky coast up to the southern edge of Scarborough; the town itself can be seen, nestling under the shelter of its castle. In 1779, a sea battle involving the famous American seafarer, Admiral Paul Jones, and two British gunships was fought off the Brigg and an anchor, the size and pattern used by the King's ships of that period, was later recovered. It can now be seen in the garden of Scarborough's Grand Hotel.

—A Visitor Guide To Yorkshire—

Restaurants (see map page 324)

£

English **Corner Café and Bar** 6 Belle Vue Crescent 01723 512 261 ①

££

English **Leys Restaurant** 7-10 The Beach, 01723 513392 ②

Fish **Inghams** 40 Belle Vue St 01723 513 320 ③

English **Victoria** The Avenue 01723 513 23 ④

£££

Italian **San Marco** 13 Murray St 01723 515457 ⑤

English **Downcliffe Ho** The Beach 01723 513310 www.downcliffehouse.com ⑥

Italian **Bella Italia** 20-22 Mitford St 01723 516001 ⑦

Hotels (see map page 324)

★★

Downcliffe House The Beach 12 bedrooms ⑧
01723 513310 www.downcliffehouse.com

★★★

The White Lodge Hotel The Crescent 21 bedrooms ⑨
01723 514771 www.whitelodgehotelfiley.co.uk

★★★★(GA)

All Seasons Guest House 11 Rutland St 6 bedrooms ⑩
01723 515321 www.allseasonsfiley.co.uk

The Forge 23 Rutland Street 5 bedrooms ⑪
01723 514646 www.theforgefiley.com

Sea Brink Guest House The Beach 7 Bedrooms 01723 513257 ⑫

Parking Ⓟ

① Station Avenue 100 spaces ② Filey Country park 300 spaces

③ West Avenue 1000 spaces

Filey Visitor Information Centre
John Street
01763 383636
www.discoveryorkshirecoast.com

BRIDLINGTON

BRIDLINGTON

A well known destination on the county's east coast, Bridlington is both resort and fishing port. For many years, one of Yorkshires most popular holiday destinations, it has much to offer for all. Its wide sandy beaches - North Beach and South Beach - both enjoy blue flag status and are sufficiently extensive never to become too cramped or uncomfortable in peak season. Beyond the beach and seafront there is much more for the visitor to explore and enjoy in and around the town, and a weeks' holiday here can be spent in different ways every day.

History

Bridlington consists of two settlements which were separate until the mid 19thC. The northern one is older, stretching back to Roman times and possibly earlier. The Quays - around the harbour - developed later, and the two coalesced in rapid growth which followed the arrival of the railway in 1846. Roman coins have been found in the town, and there is some evidence of the existence of a roman road. The town is listed in the Domesday book as "*Bretlinton*" and was given to Gilbert de Gant, Earl of Lincoln, in 1072. Walter de Gant, probably Gilberts son, was responsible for the founding of the Priory in 1114. This was a place for Augustinian Canons, and rapidly grew to become one of the wealthiest monastic houses in the county. (Canons are unlike monks, as their life is entwined with serving the needs of the community in which they live). The priory survives as Bridlingtons parish church but there is only limited trace of the original building - re-erected in a different part of the present building- with the earliest structures dating from the13thC. The old town was a prosperous commercial centre from the early Middle Ages; trading in grain and malt, which was exported through the harbour at the Quay. The merchants in this trade had their homes along the High street and Westgate, and plenty of the houses built from the late 17thC onwards survive today.

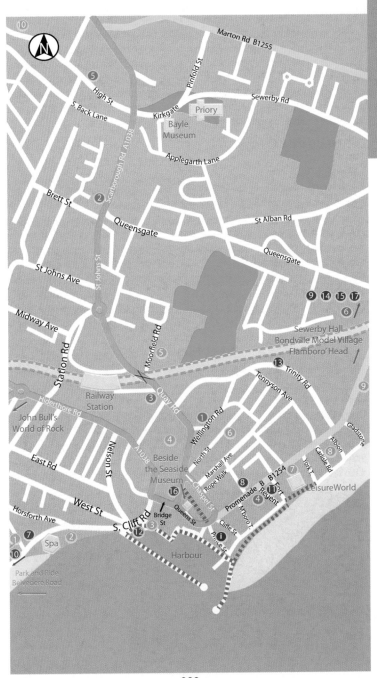

The Quay area began to develop in the 18thC becoming a fashionable bathing resort; and an alternative to the then rapidly rising popularity of Scarborough. The arrival of the railway linking the town with Hull and Scarborough, brought with it large volumes of visitors, and further development to accommodate a burgeoning population. Testimony to this are the large imposing stuccoed terraces which dominate the seafront. The late 19thC witnessed the building of the spa and associated promenade and theatre. Today the town relies substantially on the visitor for its living, although it continues to sustain a small fishing industry.

Getting Here

Rail the station is near the Harbour with regular services to Hull and Scarborough.

Road the town lies at the end of the A614 from York, and the A165 from Scarborough. Leeds is 90 min; London 4½ hours.

Bus all bus services arrive at and depart from the bus station on Marshall Avenue by the Promenade shopping centre.

destination	service(s)	frequency
Hull	121	hourly
Filey	121	hourly
Scarborough	121	hourly
York	744/845	5x per day/4x per day
Leeds	845	4x per day

Things to See and Do

The town, as a place to stay, offers much to the visitor, whether family or adult, and other coastal resorts such as Scarborough are within easy travelling distance for a days outing. The Old Town is worth a visit. Its gently curving High Street still fronted by an array of Georgian and earlier facades which lend an air of a graceful past, an ambience which continues into Westgate. The Quay and harbour area, although of more recent construction, has some 18thC buildings fronting onto the harbour, and a walk along the Promenade with its grand stuccoed terrace houses is a reminder of the resort's Edwardian and Victorian heyday.

Priory

The Priory is the towns parish church and features prominently in the towns history. It lies in an open area at the end of Kirkgate in the Old Town. The site had been occupied by a Saxon church and 11thC as a building for Augustinian canons, although little remains of that first building, being confined to two sections of the cloister arcade, re-erected in the north aisle in 1913.The nave of the church, and the associated priory gatehouse – the Bayle - is 13thC, although building works continued until the 15thC.   The priory became wealthy and powerful; the Augustinians owning land across Yorkshire, and taking duties from ship movements in the harbour.   The remains of a previous prior, John of Thwing, who was later beatified as St John of Bridlington, were buried in the church, and his shrine became the centre for pilgrimage, being visited by both Henry IV and Henry V.   Henry VIII's dissolution of the monasteries resulted in the demolition of much of the priory, leaving only the aisled nave of the church and the Bayle. The demolished buildings would have been attached to the church on its south side. Stone from the demolition was used to build the harbour and piers.   The two west towers do not match; the north west tower dating from the 13thC; the south west tower from the15thC. The interior is spacious, with a very long nave, and has some similarities with York Minster. Many fittings are elegant and richly decorated, with the stained glass dating mainly from the 19thC. The church is open to view although times vary. 01262 601938   www.bridlingtonpriory.co.uk

Bayle Museum

The 13thC Bayle, on Kirkgate, which "guards" the entry to the church on the south west side, is the former gatehouse to the Priory and the only surviving part of more extensive fortifications. The word Bayle derives from the French "baille" which means enclosure or ward. In the 14thC, a porter lived inside the Bayle to control visitors into the Priory. An Almoner also lived in the Bayle whose job it was to distribute food and ale to the poor of Bridlington. Today the building is a Museum focussing on the buildings history and aspects of historical life in the town. It is open Mon to Fri between April and September. There is an admission fee.   01262 674308 www.bayle.bridlington.net

Sewerby Hall

Set in 50 acres of well maintained gardens,18thC Sewerby Hall lies 2 miles north of the town.   The interior is elegantly and lavishly decorated. On the ground floor, the Halifax Room, Swinton Room and Orangery all deserve a visit. The magnificent grand oak staircase leads to the Amy Johnson room with its collection of mementoes tracing her life and achievements (see Hull p.365). Extensive grounds include a small zoo, gardens, a woodland walk, areas for picnicking, and a small golf course. A landtrain plies between the Leisure World complex, Limekiln Lane and the Hall.   The gardens are open year round; the Hall is open April to September. There is an admission fee.   01262 673769   www.eastriding.gov.uk/sewerby

the grounds of Sewerby Hall

Harbour and Seafront

Bridlington possesses two long stretches of safe sandy beaches which have gained European Blue Flag designations, and a working harbour which separates the two.   The north beach runs from the harbour for about 1½ miles to Sewerby; it has donkey rides and there are rockpools near the harbour; the south beach is wider and runs south of the harbour for about the same distance. Activities on the beach feature sea fishing, kitesurfing and windsurfing, and donkey rides. A landtrain operates on the promenade from Easter to September.

Bridlington Spa

The Spa is prominently located on South Marine Drive near the harbour. The recently restored complex is a premier entertainment venue with a host of top line concerts and other shows.   The Spa and gardens were built in 1896 to provide entertainment for the growing numbers of visitors to the town. After paying at the turnstile visitors could enjoy the extensive floral displays, walks and grassed areas, eat in the refreshment rooms, go to the theatre or a concert, or simply sit and listen to the band playing in the glass domed bandstand. The lake was kept filled by the iron rich water of a nearby chalybeate spring. The facilities comprised a theatre, concert hall, bandstand and refreshment rooms. In 1906 the original theatre was destroyed by fire, and the current Spa Theatre and Opera House opened in 1907 and was one of the earlier venues to show a new invention, the cinematograph.   In 1925 the last of the 1890's Spa was replaced with a new Spa Royal Hall which has been a feature of the British rock music circuit now for over 30 years with many famous artists playing here.

01266 78258   www.eastriding.gov.uk/leisure/tourism/spa

Leisureworld

On the Promenade near the seafront, this modern leisure complex provides a leisure pool, gym, sauna, indoor bowls, and café.

01262 606715   www.bridlingtonleisureworld.co.uk

Beside the seaside museum

On Queen Street just north of the harbour, this small venue gives a humourous insight into Bridlington's past as a traditional British seaside resort, with photo graphs, and quirky exhibitions featuring life size model folk in string vests, and fetching seaside garb as well re-creations of the famous stars who have in the past trod the boards at Bridlington.   01262 674308 www.eastriding.gov.uk

John Bulls World of Rock

Rock has long been a traditional British seaside sweet. One of the UK's main manufacturers is south of the town, on the Carnaby Industrial Estate. The company organise factory tours to show how rock is made and even allow you to try your hand at making it!! 01262 678525   www.john-bull-confectioners.co.uk

Bondville Model village

In the village of Sewerby, not far from the Hall is Bondville. This is a model village here ranking amongst the best in the country with over 200 buildings including a Castle, ruined Abbey and Harbour. Enjoy watching the villagers going about their everyday lives. There is also a model railway with trains pulling its carriages around the village and across the river where fishing boats and cruisers are moored.   01262 401736

Bempton Cliffs

Bempton Cliffs are 3 miles north of the town, on the north side of Flamborough Head. The towering 300 ft high cliffs, with their sheer drop into the North Sea contain a bird sanctuary managed by the RSPB. Over 200,000 birds nest on the cliffs during the spring and summer months; species include gannet, kittiwake and puffin. Visitors can walk along the clifftop path and see the cliffs and birds from a number of viewing points. Access is by car along a narrow lane. The nearest buses are services 501,504,510 from Bridlington. The cliffs are open all year, except in extreme weather. There is an admission fee for non RSPB members.   01262 851179   www.rspb.co.uk

Flamborough Head

The cliffs, four miles north east of Bridlington, are widely acknowledged as one of Britain's most spectacular headlands, thrusting out into the sea "like a great whale".   Flamborough's origins as a settlement are a little hazy. Arrow heads and flints found in the area suggest that the headland was a settlement in the Bronze age or even in the Stone age. There is some evidence of the Romans occupation, calling it "Ocelli Prom" and to have built a road to it from York. The name Flamborough is said to derive from the Anglo-Saxon word "Flaen" (meaning arrow head) to reflect the thrusting promontory into the sea. The lighthouse, nearly 100ft high, has a beacon visible 21miles out to sea. An earlier structure, from 1674, is thought to be the earliest surviving lighthouse in Britain. There are two landings on the headland- North Landing which gives access to the pebbled beach and some caves, and South Landing which is accessed through a small wooded ravine. It is where the Flamborough lifeboat is located. Here there is also a short circular nature-cum-sculpture trail.   The access roads are narrow but generally lightly trafficked, although the car park capacity is limited.   Flamborough village is known for its hand knitted fishermans jerseys and there is an annual "Danish sword dance" performance on Boxing Day.   Access by bus is to Flamborough village services 501,504,510.

chalk cliffs of Flamborough Head

Danes Dyke

Associated with Flamborough is Danes Dyke. Of uncertain origin, the dyke links cuts through the chalk uplands from Bempton Cliffs to Danes Dyke farm east of Sewerby Hall, and is thought to be a defensive ditch. Much of it is on private land, but a section between the Flamborough village road and Danes Dyke Farm is a small nature reserve and open to the public and has a car park.

Headland Way

Linking Bridlington with Sewerby Hall, Danes Dyke, Flamborough Head and Bempton cliffs is the Headland Way. This is a coastal path that links Bridlington and Filey. It follows the coastline round as far as Reighton Gap on Filey Bay.

Restaurants (see map page 329)

££

Vegetarian **Bean There** 10 Wellington Road 01262 679800 ①

Indian **Saffron** St John's Street 01262 677088 www.saffronbrid.co.uk ②

£££

Thai **Supattra Thai** Quay Road 01262 678565 www.supattrathairestaurant.com ③

Tex-Mex **Buffalo's** Regent Terrace 01262 400090 www.buffalosrestaurant.com ④

English **Burlington Restaurant** 91 High street Old Town ⑤
01262 400383 www.burlingtonsrestaurant.net

££££

English **Sewerby Grange** 441 Sewerby Road ⑥
01262 673439 www.sewerbygrange.co.uk

Hotels (see map page 329)

★★

Monarch Hotel South Marine Drive 28 bedrooms 01262 674447 ⑦

BRIDLINGTON

★★★(GA)

Brentwood House 42 Princess Street 01262 608739 **8**

★★★

Expanse Hotel North Marine Drive 44 bedrooms **9**
01262 675347 www.expanse.co.uk

★★★★(GA)

Royal Hotel Shaftesbury Road 18 bedrooms **10**
01262 672433 www.royalhotelbrid.co.uk

Balmoral Hotel 3-6 Fort terrace 01262 676432 www.thebalmoralhotel.net **11**

Rags Hotel South Pier 7 bedrooms 01262 400355 www.ragshotel.co.uk **12**

Mont Millais Hotel 64 Trinity Road 9 bedrooms **13**
01262 601890 www.montmillaishotel.co.uk

Revelstoke Hotel 1-3 Flamborough Road 26 bedrooms **14**
01262 672362 www.revelstokehotel.co.uk

★★★★★(GA)

Marton Grange Marton-cum-Sewerby 11 bedrooms **15**
01262 602034 www.marton-grange.co.uk

not rated

Brunswick Hotel 13 Manor Street 10 bedrooms **16**
01262 672186 www.bridlingtonhotel.co.uk

Sewerby Grange Hotel 441 Sewerby Road 8 bedrooms **17**
01262 673439 www.sewerbygrange.co.uk

Parking **P**

1 South Marine Drive	140 spaces	**6** North Street	50 spaces
2 Spa Slipway	23 spaces	**7** Leisureworld	49 spaces
3 Langdale Wharf	82 spaces	**8** Carlisle Road	189 spaces
4 Springfield Avenue	218 spaces	**9** Flamborough Road	85 spaces
5 Moorfield Road	597 spaces	**10** Stepney Grove	39 spaces

**Bridlington Visitor Information Centre
Prince Street
01262 673474
www.visithullandeastyorkshire.com**

HORNSEA

HORNSEA

Hornsea is a small traditional resort on the east coast 20 miles north east of Hull and 10 miles south of the much larger resort of Bridlington and best known for Hornsea Pottery whose tea sets and jugs are now considered highly collectable.

History

The middle ages saw Hornsea as a flourishing port. A medieval market cross survives in Southgate, just below the Market Place. Coastal erosion had destroyed the port by the 16thC, but its fortunes revived in the 18thC as the improvements to roads brought regular visitors from the rapidly expanding town of Hull to bathe in the sea. A number of Hull merchants built villas here, some of which survive such as the Old Hall in the Market Place, and The Pillars in Westgate. In the 19thC, following advent of the railway, this trend accelerated and a large number of seaside villas were constructed. By the turn of the 20thC, Hornsea was a thriving resort; indeed its fortunes continued - Lawrence of Arabia was a regular visitor, as was Winston Churchill - until the closure of the railway in 1964. The development of the Hornsea Pottery in the aftermath of the second world war provided the town with a further claim to fame as the brand gained in reputation, and a factory shop became a must see for most visitors to Yorkshire coast resorts. The pottery and shop closed in 2000, but the pottery ware itself is highly sought after, fetching premium prices on the open market. A popular retail park known as Hornsea Freeport has been developed on part of the site occupied by the old factory. Today, the town is an attractive small seaside resort with a safe beach and a sea front with all the trappings of amusement arcades and other commercial attractions found in such resorts.

Getting Here

Rail the nearest railway station is Bridlington (12 miles), where there are services to and from Hull and from Scarborough.

Road access is from the B1244 which comes from the Beverley direction, or the B1242 which comes from Bridlington direction. Leeds is 90min; Hull 40 min.

Bus all bus services pass through the centre.

destination	service(s)	frequency
Beverley	246	hourly
Bridlington	130	4x per day
Hull	240/246	hourly

The town lies at one end of the Transpennine trail, a route for walkers and cyclists crossing north of England between here and Southport in Lancashire.

www.transpenninetrail.org.uk

Things to see and do

Hornsea's charm lies as much in its genteel character away from the seafront, as much as the seafront, with its amusements arcades and safe sandy beach, provides an entertaining day out for families. The Market Place is worth visiting and Newbigin, one of the towns older streets provides a route to the seafront.

St Nicholas Church

Probably dating from the late 13thC, this cobble and ashlar building has an impressive interior. In the front of the churchyard, is a medieval market cross.

Hornsea Museum   13-17 Newbigin

This presents a tour of local life from the 18thC. It includes the Hornsea Pottery story. Open most days April to September. There is an admission charge.   01964 533443   www.hornseamuseum.co.uk

Hornsey Freeport   Rolston Road

A factory outlet centre on the south side of the town with many major brands It is set in attractive informal surroundings, part of which were once the Hornsea Pottery factory. Open all year. 01964 534211   hornseafreeport.com

The Mere

On the west side of the town, Hornsea Mere is the largest freshwater lake in Yorkshire. A designated nature reserve, it offers ample opportunities for birdwatching with species such as canada geese, gadwalls, reed

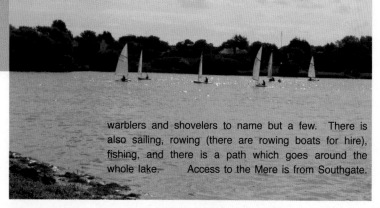

warblers and shovelers to name but a few. There is also sailing, rowing (there are rowing boats for hire), fishing, and there is a path which goes around the whole lake. Access to the Mere is from Southgate.

Bettinsons Folly

This early 19thC folly presents a distinct appearance to Newbigin. Built by William Bettison, a Hull brewer, in his garden so his manservant could ascend the tower when expecting his master to return from work, and when sighted to run back to ensure dinner could be served as he entered the house. The tower incorporates a cranked up flagpole, installed to convey private messages. During the second world war the tower was an air raid look out point and siren, (Hull was the most heavily bombed UK City after London). The siren was still in use until the late fifties/ sixties. The Folly is decorated with locally made 'treacle' bricks fired for durability. The tower can be seen from Willow Drive off Newbegin.

Seafront and Beach

Hornsea has long, wide, flat sandy beaches, and an extensive promenade. The beach and water are clean and safe and have attained Blue Flag status.

Restaurants (see map page 339)

££

English Dive into the Med 142 Newbigin 01964 536999 ①

English Swiss Cottage 49a New Road 01964 532458 ②

Hotels (see map page 339)

not rated

Earlham House 59a Eastgate 3 bedrooms 01964 537809 ③

Admiralty Guest House Marine Drive ④
01964 536414 www.admiraltyguesthouse.co.uk

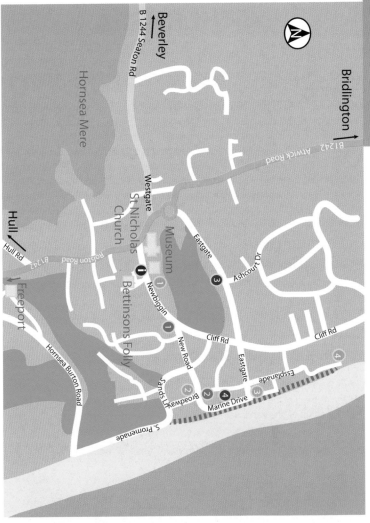

HORNSEA

Parking

① Newbegin	42 spaces	② Broadway	89 spaces
③ Eastgate	95 spaces	④ Morrow Avenue	50 spaces

Hornsea Visitor Information Centre
Newbiggin
0844 8112070
www.visithullandeastyorkshire.com

WITHERNSEA

WITHERNSEA

Withernsea is a small traditional resort of some 6000 people, 15 miles east of Hull. It has safe beaches and is a popular holiday destination for Yorkshire folk.

History

Withernsea, like many coastal resorts, is a creation of the railways. Until the arrival of the line from Hull in 1854, it was barely more than a hamlet. The town then grew rapidly, with ambitious plans for an elegant up-market resort based on a scheme drawn up by Hull architect Cuthbert Brodrick, but which never materialised.   A 1200ft long pier was built in 1877, although only the entrance towers still exist. The town became a late Victorian dormitory for Hull, as well as a place for weekend day trips. The railway closed in 1965.   Substantial sea defences have protected the town and the beaches from coastal erosion which is a recurring feature of this part of the coast.

Getting Here

Rail the nearest railway station is Hull.

Road the town lies at the end of the A1033 from Hull and is a 30 min drive.

Bus the town is served by routes 75,76,77 and 174, 175 providing a regular service to and from Hull together with a route 129 which goes to and from Hornsea.

Things to see and do

Pier Towers

All that remain of the original pier, these unusual edifices which are given the local nickname of "the sandcastles" are found at the south end of the promenade.

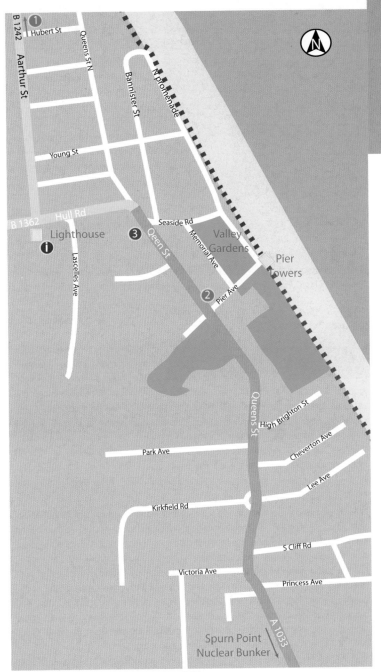

WITHERNSEA

B 1242

Hubert St

Arthur St

Queens St N

Bannister St

N promenade

Young St

B 1362

Hull Rd

Lighthouse

Lascelles Ave

Oeen St

Seaside Rd

Memorial Ave

Valley Gardens

Pier Towers

Pier Ave

Queens St

High Brighton St

Cheverton Ave

Park Ave

Lee Ave

Kirkfield Rd

S Cliff Rd

Victoria Ave

Princess Ave

A 1033

Spurn Point
Nuclear Bunker

341

Lighthouse

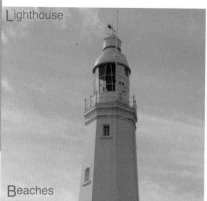

This late 19thC lighthouse is one of only a handful in the UK which stand inland and is now a museum. Visitors can climb the 144 steps to the top which, on a clear day, affords panoramic views over the sea and towards Hull. The museum is open most days. Opening times vary. There is an admission fee.   01964 614834
www.withernsealighthouse.co.uk

Beaches

With plenty of soft sand, the beach is ideal for walking. It does not get as crowded in the summer as some of the other resort beaches on this coast, is suitable for children, and has attained Blue Flag status.

Valley Gardens

Just behind the promenade on the sea front this is a small open garden area where entertainment and music shows are held during the summer months.

Nuclear Bunker

Two miles south of the town, Holmpton village has an unusual attraction, a nuclear bunker; one of a number built in the event of an invasion or a nuclear attack. It is in RAF Holmpton, originally an early warning radar station, and sometime a major hub in the UK's air defences. It became the national war HQ for RAF Support Command and then an experimental electronic warfare operations centre. The extensive command bunker which is nearly 100ft beneath the ground, and which is still operational, is open to visitors. Opening times vary. There is an admission fee.
01964 630342   www.rafholmpton.com

Spurn Point

A few miles to the south of the town is one of Britains' most distinctive coastal features. Spurn Point is a wilderness; a sand and shingle spit, as narrow as 50 metres in some places. Ravaged by the sea, it is a constantly shifting landscape- the point extends as material is washed down the coast from the north, but the spit is narrowing and is now sometimes cut off in bad weather. The area is ecologically delicate and a national nature reserve. There is road access except in adverse weather. Entry is controlled by the Yorkshire Wildlife Trust, and it is a popular destination for birdwatchers. Walking on the beaches is also possible in good weather, and a small heritage centre is open from Easter to October. There is a small admission fee by car and a regular bus service (route 73) from Withernsea to the point on Sundays during the Easter to October period.

Spurn Point

Restaurants (see map page 341)

£
English The Northfield   Waxholme Road, 01964 612551   1

££
English Victoria Tavern 193 Queen Street 0871 2078198   2

Hotels (see map page 341)
not rated
Alexandra Hotel   90 Queen Street 8 chalets and 5 bedrooms 01964 615688   3

DRIFFIELD

Known as the capital of the Yorkshire Wolds, Driffield is a market town of about 11,000 people. Connected to the outside world by road, rail, and canal and the place where the River Hull rises, it is a thriving commercial centre and home to a number of popular Yorkshire events.

History

The presence of prehistoric burial sites around the town strongly suggests a settlement with a very long history. The remains of a motte at Moot Hill is a reference to the existence of a castle in the area in about 13thC, although it is thought there may have been, in earlier times, a parliament for the Anglo Saxon kingdom of Deira, as well as a Roman settlement and possibly a Norman castle.   In the mid 18thC it was known as a centre for hunting and trout fishing for the gentry of the East Riding, but as the farms on the surrounding Yorkshire Wolds were improved to boost production of corn, the town became an important corn trading centre. The building of the Driffield Navigation Canal in 1770 helped what was a large village into a thriving town, processing and marketing agricultural produce. The arrival of the railway in 1846 strengthened the towns role as such a centre, although the railway also proved to be too great competitor to the canal, which fell into disrepair. Parts are now being restored.   Since the advent of the railways, the town has sustained its prosperity and currently remains an important market town in the east of the county.

Getting here

Rail the town is on the Hull-Bridlington line with regular each way service.

the end of the Driffield Canal

DRIFFIELD

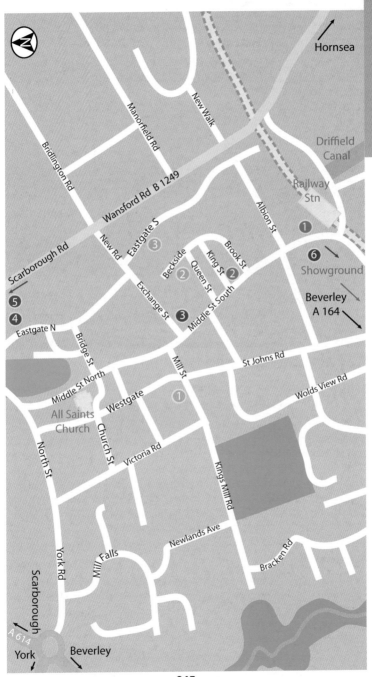

Road the town is on the A166 road between York and Bridlington 50 min from York and 20 min from Bridlington.

Bus there are regular services to:

destination	service	frequency
Scarborough	121	hourly
Bridlington	121	hourly
Hull	121	hourly
Beverley	121	hourly
York	744	4x per day

the wolds near driffield

Things to see and do

Driffield is compact with most points of interest centred around Middle Street which runs north- south through the town.

The Wolds

Driffield is the centre of the Yorkshire wolds, the elevated, gently rolling plateau, cut by numerous deep, steep-sided, flat-bottomed valleys and which extends from Garrowby Hill in the west all the way to the coast. These chalk hills provide exceptionally good drainage, so most valleys are dry which results in an "upside-down" farming system - livestock (mostly sheep and cows) graze the valleys, with the hills above used for crops. In the Wolds are small distinctive villages still untouched by commuting or other urbanizing trends, and which portray an accurate reflection of life as it always been lived in this part of the county

All Saints Church

A show piece stately 15thC west tower makes the church visible from a long distance, but much of the building is earlier. Some of the tower walls contain two large stones which predate the Norman conquest, although the much of the church is late12th/early13thC.

Market Place

The main street has a lively outdoor market is held every Thursday.

Driffield Canal

At Riverhead, on Riverhead Drive, just to the other side of the railway station, is the restored head of the Driffield Canal. It adjoined the River Hull for much of its length which ran past Beverley, and through Hull to the River Humber. This 18thC canal fell into disrepair but concerted efforts by volunteers has, over the last 30 years, borne fruit and the canal is now navigable up to Driffield. The riverhead and town lock form the head of the canal, and an attractive place to visit.

Festivals

For a small town, there are an unusually large number of regular annual events and which generally attract significant number of visitors.

Farmers markets	first Saturday of each month at the Showground	
May	Kite Festival Showground	
July	Annual Agricultural show	Showground
August	Traction engine and vintage vehicle Rally	Showground
	The Driffield Festival: Showground.	

Restaurants (see map page 345)

£

English **Buffers** Middle Street South 01377 250335 www.buffersrestaurant.co.uk ①

££

Italian **Marco Polo Pizzeria** Middle Street South 01377 257903 ②

Hotels (see map page 345)

★★★

Bell Hotel Market Place 16 bedrooms 01377 256661 www.bw-bellhotel.co.uk ③

★★★★★(GA)

Kilham Hall Driffield Rd Kilham 3 bedrooms 01262 420466 www.kilhamhall.co.uk ④

not rated

Old Mill Mill Lane Langtoft 9 bedrooms 01377 267284 www.old-mill-hotel.co.uk ⑤

The White Horse Inn Main St, Cranswick 10 bedrooms ⑥
01377 270383 www.whitehorse.me.uk

Parking Ⓟ

① Cross Hill 77 spaces ② Beckside 82 spaces ③ Eastgate S 102 spaces

347

BEVERLEY

BEVERLEY

the Minster

Beverley is a market town of 20,000 people lying quietly in the shadow of its much larger neighbour, Kingston on Hull. Often regarded as one of Britain's finest small country towns, it's largely intact historic core brims with character. Well worth a day or more for any visitor to explore its heritage, and experience its warm and civilised cultural environment.

History

There is some uncertainty as to Beverley's origins. The name Beverley is thought to derive from the presence of colonies of beavers in the nearby River Hull. Recent evidence shows it was probably a Roman settlement. It is certain there was a monastery here by 700AD; known as *Inderawuda*, an Angle name meaning the wood of the men of Deira, it was founded by John, Bishop of York, (who was beatified after his death) and is probably sited below the present Minster. Although the monastery suffered greatly at the hands of the Vikings, by the time of the Norman conquest, it was a place of pilgrimage to the tomb of St John, who had been canonized in 1037, and the steady stream of pilgrims created a settlement which provided for their needs. The shrine became one of the most important in England, and Beverley renowned as a place of sanctuary - this applied well beyond the Minster and covered the whole town. By 1377 Beverley was the 11th largest town in England and a prosperous commercial centre. Religious life was prevalent under the supervision of the Archbishopric of York. The River Hull was navigable and enabled the town to become a major centre in medieval times for the export of wool to the low countries. Flemingate is named for the Flemish merchants who regularly stayed here. High quality woollen cloth

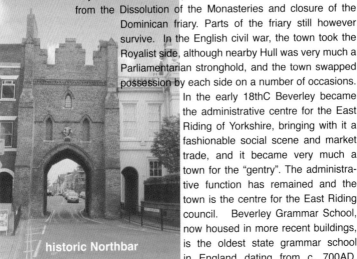

for export was being manufactured in the town by the mid 12thC, although this had died out by the 16thC. The importance of the town was dealt a blow from the Dissolution of the Monasteries and closure of the Dominican friary. Parts of the friary still however survive. In the English civil war, the town took the Royalist side, although nearby Hull was very much a Parliamentarian stronghold, and the town swapped possession by each side on a number of occasions. In the early 18thC Beverley became the administrative centre for the East Riding of Yorkshire, bringing with it a fashionable social scene and market trade, and it became very much a town for the "gentry". The administrative function has remained and the town is the centre for the East Riding council. Beverley Grammar School, now housed in more recent buildings, is the oldest state grammar school in England dating from c. 700AD.

historic Northbar

Getting here

Rail Beverley station is in the heart of the town with regular services to and from Hull and Bridlington.

Road The M62 is 15mins drive from the town via the A164. Once on the motorway, Leeds is 1h; Manchester 2hrs and London 4hrs. To the north and east, Bridlington is 45 mins.

Bus most services arrive at and depart from the bus station in Sow Hill Road.

destination	service(s)	frequency
Hull	121/746	30 min/hourly
Bridlington	121	30 mins
Driffield	121	30 mins
York	746	hourly
Scarborough	121	30 mins
London	562	1x per day

Things to See and Do

The core of the historic town, with a largely intact medieval street pattern, is defined by the two main religious buildings; the Minster to the south; St Mary's Church to the north, but also and unusually by the Bars; these are the "gates" through which travellers had to pass in order to get into the town, although there never any walls connecting them; instead there were ditches. Originally there were four bars: North Bar, South Bar, Newbiggin Bar and Norwood Bar.

Only **Northbar** survives, dating from 1409. This brick structure is squashed between two Georgian period houses; one of which was occupied by the well known artist F.W. Elwell (1870-1958). The medieval core contains much to interest and entertain the visitor. It is well worth starting any exploration of the centre either at the Minster and work through the streets as far as the North Bar, or the other way round.

Minster

Beverley Minster lies on the southern edge of the centre. Although a magnificent building, with the stature and proportions of a cathedral, it is a parish church. It was built between 1220 and 1425. It stands out from the surrounding countryside with its graceful slender twin west towers, and is one of the largest parish churches in the country; its 330ft length being longer than some cathedrals. It is constructed largely of magnesian limestone with extensive use of Purbeck marble in the interior. The east end, the older part, including the main transept, is largely Early English style with its lancet windows, pointed arches and dog tooth mouldings, but the east window is a later alteration; perpendicular in style it was replaced in 1416 to match the recently constructed west window. It has a cavernous, well lit nave with elaborate carvings - of particular note is the richly decorated canopy for the tomb of Percy (the tomb is also thought to contain the remains of Eleanor, the widow of Henry Percy, the first Earl of Alnwick who died c.1328). Between the choir stalls is the tomb of St John, the founder of the first Beverley minster. The west end is a later addition, completed in 1425 in the then prevailing Perpendicular style with large windows and vertical tracery to create the feeling of space. Whilst the Minster would have had much stained glass originally, little survives today and that which does is incorporated into the East window. The Minster is open most days. Admission is free.

01482 868540   www.beverleyminster.org.uk

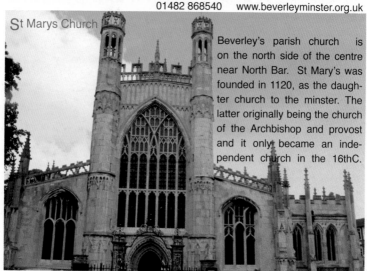

St Marys Church

Beverley's parish church is on the north side of the centre near North Bar. St Mary's was founded in 1120, as the daughter church to the minster. The latter originally being the church of the Archbishop and provost and it only became an independent church in the 16thC.

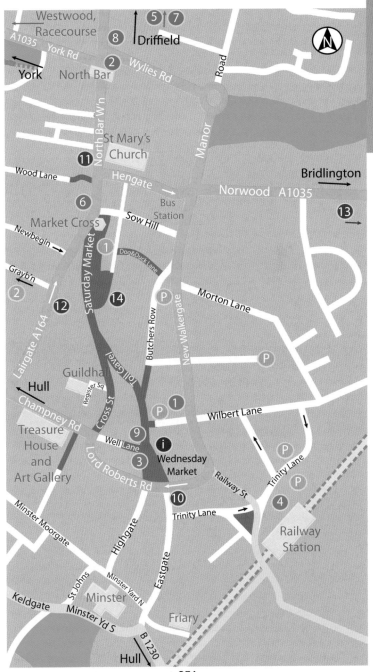

BEVERLEY

Westwood, Racecourse

A1035

5 7

8 Driffield

York Rd

York

2 North Bar

Wylies Rd

Manor Road

North Bar W'n

St Mary's Church

11

Wood Lane

Hengate

6

Bridlington

Norwood A1035

13

Market Cross

Newbegin

Sow Hill

Bus Station

1 Dog&Duck Lane

Grayb'n

2

Saturday Market

12 14

Morton Lane

P

New Walkergate

Butchers Row

Lairgate A164

Guildhall

Toll Gavel

Register Sq

Hull

Champney Rd

Cross St

P 1

Well Lane

9

Wilbert Lane

Treasure House and Art Gallery

Minster Moorgate

Lord Roberts Rd

i

3 Wednesday Market

10

Railway St

P Trinity Lane P

4

Railway Station

Highgate

Minster Moorgate

St Johns

Minster Yard N

Eastgate

Trinity Lane

Keldgate

Minster

Minster Yd S

B 1230

Friary

Hull

BEVERLEY

Said to be one of the most beautiful parish churches in England it is, like the Minster, constructed largely from magnesian limestone. Little is visible of the original Norman structure; this being confined to the plinth of one of the buttresses in the chancel. Most of the building dates from the 13thC with some later additions and alterations; the prominent central tower dating from the 16thC. The west front is Perpendicular style, late 14thC and its design possibly influenced that of Kings College Cambridge, built 100 years later. The interior includes interesting panelling and inscriptions; some relating to minstrels - Beverley was renowned as a meeting place for the northern guild of minstrels. The priests room is worth visiting with its displays of 18thC stocks and other local artefacts. The church is open most days.

Saturday and Wednesday Markets

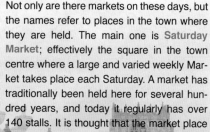

Not only are there markets on these days, but the names refer to places in the town where they are held. The main one is **Saturday Market**; effectively the square in the town centre where a large and varied weekly Market takes place each Saturday. A market has traditionally been held here for several hundred years, and today it regularly has over 140 stalls. It is thought that the market place may have been more extensive in medieval times, extending all the way back to Ladygate and possibly to Lairgate. The buildings fronting onto Saturday Market are an attractive medley of 17thC to 19thC construction, and together form an unspoilt historic townscape. In the centre is the **Market Cross**, dating from 1714, an open shelter with Doric columns and an interesting ornate roof style. The **Wednesday Market** is much smaller and takes place on a small open area of that name at the junction of Railway Street and Highgate.

Beverley Friary   Friars Lane

Remains of the 13thC friary take the form of a youth hostel in Friary Lane. Surviving Dominican friary buildings are not common in England, and Beverley was important from its other religious connections. The Friary would have been wealthy and the surviving buildings are thought to be the dormitory and library. After the1539 dissolution,the building was a private house until late 19thC, and after lying derelict it was restored as a youth hostel in 1984.

Treasure House   Champney Road

This modern building houses archives on the history of the East Riding, as well as providing a venue for local exhibitions and history lectures. The facility is open Monday to Friday; admission is free.   www.eastriding.gov.uk

Library and Art Gallery   Champney Road

Adjoining the Treasure House, the Art Gallery is a much older building- built in the Edwardian period of red brick in Queen Anne style - the gallery contains works of F.W. Elwell, many of which capture the life of the town. Admission is free, and opening times are as per the Treasure House.

Guildhall Register Square

Parts of the building date from the early 16thC, although the exterior is late Georgian. The Guildhall has been the centre of civic governance in Beverley for over 500 years. The restored courtroom dates from 1760 and has a distinctive and impressive rococo style ceiling and coat of arms. There is a large collection of 17thC civic furniture.The guildhall has a regular programme of exhibitions. Admission is free. The building is open on Fridays.

Westwood

This common pasture land has long been under the guardianship of the Pasture Masters, alongside the other common lands of Swinemoor and Figham Pasture. This pleasant open area of grassland is accessible to all residents and visitors. Within the confines of the pasture is Burton Bushes, a boggy remnant of the medieval wood pasture. There is a path which winds through the wooded area and then out on to the pasture where there are good views of the town.

Racecourse

To the immediate north of Westwood, on the north side of the A1035 road is the racecourse. Horseracing has been a constant feature of Beverley's social and sporting activity since the late 17thC. The race calendar features some 16 meets a year between April to October.   www.beverley-racecourse.co.uk

Restaurants (see map page 351)

££

Italian La Scala 22 New Walker Gate 01482 882277   ①

Thai Siam Lion 4 North Bar Without 01482 679797 www.siamlion.co.uk   ②

Italian Emilios 11 Wednesday Market 01482 882 028   ③

£££

European Cerutti 2 Station Square 01482 866700 www.ceruttis.co.uk   ④

English Westwood New Walk 01482 881999 www.thewestwood.co.uk   ⑤

Turkish Seraglio 5 North Bar Within 01482 887 878   ⑥

££££

English Pipe and Glass Inn West End, South Dalton   ⑦
01430 810426 www.pipeandglass.co.uk

English White's Restaurant 12a North Bar Without   ⑧
01482 866121 www.whitesrestaurant.co.uk

English Dine-on-the-Row 12 Butcher Row   ⑨
01482 502269 www.dineontherowe.com

Hotels (see map page 351)

★★

Tudor Rose 11 Wednesday Market   10 bed rooms   ⑩
 01482 882028   www.thetudorrosehotelbeverley.co.uk

BEVERLEY

***

Beverley Arms 25 North Bar Within 56 bedrooms 01482 869241 ⑪

The Lairgate 30 - 32 Lairgate, 25 bedrooms
01482 882141 http://www.bestwestern.co.uk/Hotels/Lairgate-Hotel-Beverley/ ⑫

Tickton Grange Tickton 20 bedrooms 01964 543666 www.ticktongrange.co.uk ⑬

not rated

Kings Head 38 Saturday Market 12 bed rooms ⑭
01482 868103 www.kingsheadpubbeverley.co.uk

Parking

① Saturday Market	141 spaces	⑤ Butcher Row	78 spaces
② Grayburn Lane	230 spaces	⑥ George Street	74 spaces
③ Spencer Street	37 spaces	⑦ Trinity Lane	166 spaces
④ School Lane	291 spaces		

**i Beverley Visitor Information Centre
Butcher Row
01482 391672
www.visithullandeastyorkshire.com**

saturday market around the Buttercross

HULL

the princes quay shopping centre

Kingston on Hull, to give it its full title, is probably one of Britain's most underrated cities. It takes its name from the River Hull which flows through it, although its waterfront and main maritime trade is on the Humber estuary. It is, by far, the largest settlement in the old Yorkshire East Riding, and one of only a handful of English cities to have sustained a leading role as a main population and industry centre from the middle ages to the present day. The city is best known for its ongoing relationship with the sea – its port having been active for several hundred years, and still one of the largest ports in Britain with a variety of marine related industries. The Old Town, much still surviving, has been largely restored. Recent investments in the form of The Deep, an innovative sea aquarium and retail therapy in the form of the Princes Quay and St Stephens shopping centres have helped sustain the city as one the county's key centres. Hull has, over the years, produced a large number of well known personalities whose achievements have influenced the direction of British life; a short bio of some of these appears in these pages. The city is also famous for the Humber Bridge, one of the longest suspension bridges in the world, and for its white telephone boxes, as it was the only British city to have its own telephone service until the mid 1990's, distinguished by white instead of red phone boxes. Although the mobile phone has rendered many phone boxes redundant, some can still be seen on the city streets.

History

Kingston is the name originally given to the small settlement of Wyke when acquired from the Abbey of Meaux by Edward 1 in 1293. Wyke at that time

HULL

was a small but prosperous port sited on the west side of the River Hull at its confluence with the Humber. Edward's purpose was to establish a supply base for his Scottish campaigns (known as the Hammer of the Scots, he spent much of the latter part of his reign in Scotland). As a consequence, the newly named Kingston grew quickly; Edward granting it a charter in 1299. The charter document itself is preserved and lies in the Guildhall archives. In the mid 14thC a defensive ditch was dug and a crenellated wall erected around the town. This was, unusually, constructed of local bricks. There were four gates, the most important being Beverley gate, as this was the main entrance into the town from Beverley and York, then both amongst Yorkshire's most important settlements. A small section of Beverley gate and wall are visible at the western end of Whitefriargate. The line of the wall – sadly demolished in the mid 19thC - is marked in dark brick along one side of the Princes Dock and Marina. Humber Street is laid out on the line on the old wall. The brickwalls and street pattern would be similar to such towns found in the Low Countries in that period and simply reinforced Hulls innate linkages with the Continent. The port became a member of the Hanseatic League as most of its trade - the export of wool and woollen cloth - was to the continent, particularly Northern Europe. Hull prospered and became a county in its own right. Henry VIII invested in more defensive works on the east side of the River Hull, and a century later the refusal by Sir John Hotham, the towns governor, to admit Charles 1st was the first act of the ensuing English Civil War. The 16th and 17thC saw Hull's continued prosperity, and the High Street witnessed the construction of gentleman's residences for wealthy merchants who had made their money from the port and whose businesses were nearby. One such is the Maister House (see page 358). The first dock was built in the late 18thC. Known as the Queens Dock, it was filled in in 1930 and is now Queens Gardens. The construction of further docks followed as the River Hull failed to accommodate the volume of boat traffic that had developed, particularly with the rise of the whaling industry. Much of Princes Dock, built 1829, and following the line of the town walls which were demolished to make way for it, is now part of the Princes Quay shopping scheme. The arrival of the railway in 1840, linking Hull to the West Riding and, a few years later, the rapid development of the trawler industry, merely served to enhance its continued growth and prosperity. The later 19thC and first half of the 20thC saw continuing success; city status was achieved in 1897, and a new city centre built a few years later based around Queen Victoria Square, King Edward Street, Jameson Street and Alfred Gelder Street. This grand scheme was followed in short order by a new city hall in 1903 and then a new guildhall. Such development typified Hull's prosperity which continued unabated until the post war period and the decline of the fishing industry - which formed a significant element in the ports activities. The city has had to look for further economic activities to replace it. Nevertheless the last twenty years has seen the renaissance of the character and attractiveness of the old town and much of the resplendent city centre.

Getting Here

Rail   Hull has direct intercity services to London (2½ hrs), and regular services to Manchester and Leeds. Local services also serve Bridlington, Goole, York and Sheffield.

Road   Hull lies at the eastern end of the M62, the cross Pennine route linking Liverpool Manchester and Leeds, and which is a section of the more ambitious European trunk route (E20) from Shannon in Ireland to St Petersburg in Russia. Locally, the city is within 40 min of the main east coast resorts, including those in Lincolnshire, via the Humber Bridge.

Sea   Hull enjoys regular ferry services with the Continent. Overnight services go to Rotterdam and Zeebrugge.   08716 642020 www.poferries.com

Bus   both local and national services serve the city. Most bus routes arrive and depart at the Paragon Interchange adjoining the main railway station.

destination	service(s)	frequency
Leeds	390/X62	1x per day/4x per day
York	746/534	hourly/1x per day
Beverley	121/562	hourly/1x per day
Bridlington	121	hourly
Driffield	121	hourly
Scarborough	121	hourly
Doncaster	562	1x per day
Hornsea	220/246	2x per day/hourly
Withernsea	75	hourly
London	562	1x per day

Things to see and do

The Deep   Sammy's Point
One of the city's newest attractions, opened in 2002, the Deep is proving to be a national icon visitor attraction having had over 2 million visitors from all over the world since opening. The extensive underwater tanks contain over 2500 species of fish and sea mammals, including a variety of species of shark. The centre is also a marine research facility. Displays are interactive and a visit will take between two and three hours. The Deep is open daily. There is an admission charge.   01482 381000 www.thedeep.co.uk

Spurn Lightship   Hull Marina   Castle Street
The Spurn lightship was anchored in the Humber estuary for nearly 50 years east of Spurn Point, guiding shipping safely into the Humber estuary. It is now a museum of life on a lightship in the first half of the 20thC. Open on weekends April to September. Admission is free.   01482 30030 www.hullcc.gov.uk

Guildhall   Lowgate and Alfred Gelder Street
Completed in 1911, this is perhaps the grandest Edwardian building in a city which prided itself on grand Edwardian buildings. Its importance was such to

HULL

The Deep, one of the most popular attractions

the city fathers that Cuthbert Brodrick's town hall, built only 40 years previously was demolished to make way for it. The stone faced elevation fronting on Alfred Gelder Street is 35 bays long and would not look out of place in Rome or other Italian historic cities. Behind its imposing facades, the lavish interior houses law courts, council chamber, a sumptuous banqueting hall and a collection of civic artefacts - from fine art, to silverware.   The building is open for guided tours Mons/Tues. Admission is free.   01482 300300 www.hullcc.gov.uk

Maister House 🏠   High Street
A grand 18thC house built for a wealthy Hull merchant, the building's sober facade hides a fascinating interior with a story of wealth, tragedy and high art. Owned by the National Trust, the building reflects the lifestyle of 18th century Hull merchants. It is used as offices but the grand staircase is open during office hours.   01733 87990 www.nationaltrust.org.uk

City Hall   Queen Victoria Square
Built in halcyon Edwardian times to provide the city with a venue fit for public meetings and concerts. The concert hall on the first floor was originally planned to seat 3,000 and Frank Matcham, the illustrious Victorian theatre architect, was commissioned to advise on the style and decoration of the interior, and his influence can clearly be seen throughout. The ground floor has shops facing onto the street, including the visitor information centre and a grand entrance up to the concert hall.The venue still provides a regular programme of concerts, public exhibitions and other entertainment.   01482 226655   www.hullcc.gov.uk/hullcityhall

Queens Gardens
Created from the former Queens Dock.   The gardens extend from Queen Victoria Square to Hull College; the latter being defined by a column with a statue of William Wilberforce. On the north side is a plaque commemorating Robinson Crusoe, Daniel Defoe's fictional character who sailed from Hull in 1651 on the voyage that ended with him being a castaway on a desert island. The plaque includes the quote, "*Had I the sense to return to Hull, I had been happy.*"

William Wilberforce Museum   High Street

William Wilberforce was born and bred in the city and his birthplace is now a testament to his life's achievement in the abolition of slavery.   The museum relates the story of the trans-Atlantic slave trade and its abolition, as well as covering contemporary slavery. The 17thC building was originally the official residence of the Governor of the city. It is open daily. Admission is free.

01482 300300   www.hullcc.gov.uk

William Wilberforce
Political Reformer   1759-1833

A leading British politician, and the driving force behind abolition of the slave trade. Born to a wealthy family of merchants in Hull (his grandfather had been a Lord Mayor), he became an MP, first for Hull then for Yorkshire. He sat as an independent, to avoid voting along party lines. He was a close companion to William Pitt, later Prime Minister.   Known as sociable and witty, his early adult years were spent gambling and drinking. He underwent a conversion to evangelical Christianity and rapidly became the main proponent behind parliamentary legislation to abolish the slave trade, a task that took him nearly 30 years and that only saw fruition finally through the Abolition of Slavery Act just after his death.   He is commemorated in Hull through the William Wilberforce Museum in High Street, housed in the property in which he was born and by the Wilberforce Monument at the eastern end of Queens Gardens.

Streetlife Museum   High Street

This museum, close to others in this part of the old town, contains exhibits and displays of transport of past eras; by sight sound and smell. The museum is open daily. Admission is free.   01482 300300 www.hullcc.gov.uk

Arctic Corsair

The Arctic corsair was the last deep sea trawler and now tells the story of trawlerman and Hulls fishing community. It is moored on the River Hull behind the Hull and East Riding Museum. Access is by guided tours most days between March and October. Admission is free.   01482 300300 www.hullcc.gov.uk

Hull and East Riding Museum   High Street

This museum provides comprehensive displays of natural and archeological history and features replicas of an Iron Age village and a Roman Bath house, as well as dinosaur bones and a collection of Viking treasures. The museum is open daily. Admission is free.   01482 300300 www.hullcc.gov.uk

Ferens Art Gallery   Queen Victoria Square

The gallery contains a substantial collection of paintings and sculptures stretching back to medieval times, and include works by Frans Hals, Antonio Canaletto and David Hockney. It was opened in 1927 as a result of a substantial donation by Thomas Ferens and reflects another era of city pride and patronage.   The museum is open daily. Admission is free.   01482 300300   www.hullcc.gov.uk

Maritime Museum   Queen Victoria Square

Focusing on Hull's extensive maritime history, the museum is located in the former town dock's office building, a magnificent richly decorated Victorian building of 1872.   Galleries are devoted to the whaling industry and the North Sea fishing industry, both of which underpinned Hulls economic prosperity in the 19th and 20thC respectively.   The museum is open daily. Admission is free.   01482 300300   www.hullcc.gov.uk

Hands on History Museum   Trinity Square

Aimed at children, the Hands on History Museum occupies the 426 year old former Hull Grammar School building. William Wilberforce attended this school, and it was also the site for Hull merchants guilds meetings. Today the museum offers a ground floor dedicated to Victorian Britain, with plenty of hands-on exhibits. The Second Floor plays host to 'The Story of Hull and its People' exhibit focusing on the city's social history alongside an ancient Egypt display.   The museum is open daily. Admission is free.   01482 300300 www.hullcc.gov.uk

Hull Truck Theatre   Ferensway

An increasingly well known and innovative theatre, the organisation is housed in a new 440 seat building which opened in 2009 and puts on a comprehensive programme, including works by Yorkshire playwright and former teacher John Godber.   01482 323638 www.hulltruck.co.uk

Thomas Ferens Businessman Philanthropist 1847-1930

Hailing from a Durham family, Thomas Ferens journeyed to Hull in 1868 to work for the well known Hull company Reckitt and Sons. He progressed rapidly through the company and was Chairman at the time of his death in 1930. He was a Liberal MP, representing Hull from 1906 to 1918, championing womens rights and advocating improvements in the lot of child orphans. His generous philanthropy enabled the city to enjoy an art gallery (the Ferens Art Gallery), and he was instrumental -with others- in establishing Hull University; he funded the creation of almshouses in the city and he bequeathed the family home- Holderness House - on the east side of the city, to be used after his death as a rest home for poor gentlewomen - for which it is still used.

New Theatre   Kingston Square

A performing venue since 1939, the theatre puts on a wide ranging diet of plays, ballet, musicals and children's shows including an annual pantomime.   01482 226655 www.hullcc.gov.uk/hullnewtheatre

Albermarle Music Centre   Ferensway

This is a music venue with seating for 250 and provides facilities for a variety of musical genres, from youth orchestras and brass bands to jazz groups and choirs.   Hull Philharmonic Orchestra uses the centre for rehearsals and provides a facility for young musicians across the Yorkshire region. 01482 300300

Holy Trinity Church   Market Place

One of the largest English parish churches, and built on a spot where a church has been standing since the 13thC. The current building dates from between the early14thC (the transepts), and the16thC (the tower). The size can best be appreciated by looking down the long nave. The stained glass is a more recent installation, dating from the 19thC.

Fort Paull Battery Rd Paull

Just to the East of the city, Fort Paull is a former gun battery built in 1864, although there has been a gun battery on this site since Henry VIII's time.   The present building was one of a number built around the British coast on the instructions of Lord Palmerston, the then Prime Minister who was concerned about the rising strength of the French navy, and feared that France could become a threat; a fear that never materialised. The Fort was decommissioned in 1960, and now houses a waxwork museum, a collection of armour and regularly stages military re-enactments. Bus services 78/79/80 from the city centre run regularly as far as Paull village.   01482 896236 www.fortpaull.com

Walk 1   The Old Town (inc Trinity House) ● ● ● ●

The core of Hull's history is to be found in the old town. Whilst little remains of the medieval city wall, there are other surviving buildings to interest the visitor, and a tour of the old town area is a must for any serious traveller to the city. The start is the south end of **High Street**, a narrow lane running parallel to the west of the River Hull with a number of little lanes linking it with the river. These are called staithes, the local name for a landing place. High Street was the heart of the town from its establishment in the13thC until the mid Victorian era. Here, the prosperous merchants had their houses, their warehouses and wharfs. At Scale Lane (No 5) there is a timber framed building, probably dating from the 15thC, and the only surviving such building in the city.

HULL

Humber Bridge

The fifth largest suspension bridge in the world, the towers of the bridge are visible over a wide area. The bridge, opened in 1982, replaced a ferry that had been operating for over 100 years, and was the final chapter in a long saga as to the best way to provide a permanent crossing of the River Humber. In the late19thC proposals were developed to provide a railway cross-

ing, and a bridge for road traffic was first put forward in the 1930's, but it was not until 1971 that construction started. At the time it was the longest single span suspension bridge in the world and held that distinction for 16 years; its total length is 7215ft, with the span between the towers being 4580ft. It carries 120,000 vehicles per week between Hull and East Yorkshire, on the north side, and Barton on Humber in Lincolnshire on the south side.

WALK 1 ▼

The walk along the High Street is full of buildings of 17th-19thC, such as No 41, Crowle House and No160 **Maister House**, as well as a number of museums including the **William Wilberforce Museum**. When High Street crosses Alfred Gelder Street, it is worth briefly continuing north to see **Blaydes House**, an 18thC house built for a merchant of that name.   For

● those visitors keen on the river, a riverside walk links Alfred Gelder Street just to the south west of the Drypool Bridge as far as the tidal surge barrier

● south of Castle Street.   Return to Alfred Gelder Street, and head west toward the main retail centre. The view is dominated by the **Guildhall**, on

● the right, and the General Post Office, a grand Edwardian building at the junction with Lowgate. Here, on the north side is a statue of Charles Wilson,

● a former Liberal MP for the city and a Lord Lieutenant of the East Riding.

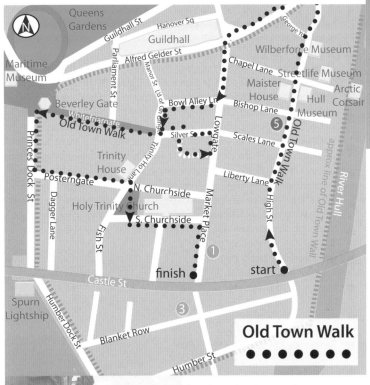

HULL

Queens Gardens
Guildhall St
Hanover Sq
Guildhall
Parliament St
Alfred Gelder St
Wilberforce Museum
Chapel Lane
Streetlife Museum
Maritime Museum
Maister House
Arctic Corsair
Beverley Gate
Manor St
Ld of Gr Ginger
Bowl Alley Ln
Bishop Lane
Hull Museum
Whitefriargate
Old Town Walk
Silver St
Lowgate
Scales Lane
Old Town Walk
5
Princes Dock St
Trinity Ho Lane
Trinity House
Liberty Lane
approx line of Old Town Walk
River Hull
Posterngate
N. Churchside
Market Place
High St
Dagger Lane
Holy Trinity Church
S. Churchside
1
Fish St
finish
start
Spurn Lightship
Castle St
3
Humber Dock St
Blanket Row
Old Town Walk
Humber St

Turning south along Lowgate, the modern imposing law courts are on the left, next to St Mary's Church. The church, originally built 14thC, was substantially restored in the 19thC by Sir George Gilbert Scott. Its spacious interior contains 15thC stained glass and other richly decorated fittings. Continue along Lowgate, past elegant facades of 19th offices, and turn into Bowlalley Lane where there are more Victorian buildings. Turn briefly into Exchange Alley to get a feel of what Victorian Hull would have been like. Another alley on the south side of the street leads to the Olde White Harte pub. At the end of Bowlalley Lane is the quaintly named Land of Green Ginger, a small narrow street the origin of whose name is unclear. In the Land of Green Ginger is, allegedly, the smallest window in the world, created for the George Hotel (now a pub) to look out discretely for arriving stage coaches.

WALK 1 ▼

363

WALK 1 ▼

HULL

From here turn south towards Silver Street along Trinity House Lane, and head east on Silver Street, effectively the eastern end of the shopping area, and turn into Hepworth's Arcade. This is a small 19thC ornately decorated shopping mall built for Leeds tailor Joseph Hepworth, and where Marks and Spencer opened their first Hull shop in 1899. Exiting onto Market Place, turn left and left again back into Silver Street; continue west past Trinity House Lane and the street becomes Whitefriargate, a main shopping street. Of note is the property occupied by Boots, which was formerly the Neptune Inn of 1795, and the Hull Customs office for a while. Opposite is Parliament Street, probably the most complete Georgian street in the city, created in 1795 to link Whitefriargate with the Queens Dock. At the western end of Whitefriargate, where the excavated remains of Beverley Gate – the western bar into the original medieval walled town- can be seen, turn left (south) on the east side of the Princes dock. Princes Quay shopping centre is on the far side, and turn left again (east) into Posterngate. On the north side of the street at the far end is Trinity House. The current buildings stand on the site of a Carmelite friary (the Whitefriars- hence the name for the nearby Whitefriargate), dissolved by Henry VIII. Trinity House was the home of a Hull seafarers guild from the mid 15thC, and one of the oldest institutions in the city, having previously been granted a charter by Henry VI in 1456. The guild probably existed before then as it is mentioned by Chaucer in his Canterbury Tales. The complex is centred around a courtyard - with a school, almshouses, a chapel, courtroom and council chamber. Much of the building and land bounded by Posterngate and Whitefriargate is owned by the Trinity House corporation. Trinity house itself, which fronts onto Trinity House Lane dates from 1753, replacing an earlier building. It consists of four sides surrounding a spacious court- yard. Three sides consist of single apartments for younger brethren or their widows, whilst the west side contains the hall, elegant dining and council rooms, reading-room, a museum, and the offices of the secretary. The stuccoed front is Tuscan in style. The interior includes many historic artefacts including a boat from Greenland in 1613, together with the dress and oars of the man found in it. There is a fine collection of portraits, antique plates, and many maritime curiosities. Adjoining the north side of Trinity House is a chapel, rebuilt in 1839-40 in a Grecian style. It is paved with marble, and the columns and pilasters are of the same material. On the opposite corner to Trinity house is Holy Trinity Church, and on King street, is an arched entrance on the west side leading to Prince Street.

Tucked away behind the buildings on King Street, is a gently curving row of restored Georgian townhouses. King Street opens onto the west elevation of Holy Trinity Church creating a small square where a weekly market is held. On the south side, known as South Church side, is the Old Grammar School, which currently houses the Hands On History Museum. The building dates from c.1585, and occupied by the school (founded 1330) until 1878. The walk finishes at the eastern end of Trinity Church in Market Place by the gilded statue of King William III, known to locals as King Billy, erected in 1734.

Walk 2 retail therapy

Hulls retail offers a wide choice within a compact area. Start at the Market Place end of Hepworths Arcade where there is a range of independent businesses, from joke shops to jewellers, and then along Silver Street into Whitefriargate, where the big name brands abound; ahead can be seen City Hall Queen Victoria Square and Princes Dock. Here is the bustling centre of the modern city, and there are opportunities to sit and watch the world go by. The ground floor to city hall contains a number of independent shops as well as the Visitor Information Centre. Also in the Square is the Maritime Museum and the monument to Queen Victoria, erected in 1903. Continue along King Edward Street. At the junction with Jameson Street is the entrance to the British Home Stores, which is notable for the giant curved mosaic mural above the entrance that dates from 1963 and is a representation of three ships - a testament to the Hull fishing fleet. Further along King Edward Street is the Prospect shopping centre, with a statue of Amy Johnson, Hull's female pilot pioneer. Go through the centre out to Ferensway, and cross into the city's most recent shopping complex, the award winning St Stephens Centre. Opened in 2007,and identified by a number of "toad statues", the scheme features a curved covered central street with shops - including many well known brands - on the ground floor, a food court on the first floor, and a cinema

Amy Johnson Aviator 1903-1941

The pioneering British woman pilot was Hull born and bred. After obtaining a pilots licence in 1929, she embarked on a series of record breaking flights, becoming the first woman to fly solo to Australia in 1930, then breaking further records in flights to Tokyo and to Cape town. Inthe second world war she was instrumental in the formation of the Air Transport Auxiliary, whose role was to ferry aircraft to places where they were needed for the war effort. During one of these flights she crashed into the River Thames and was killed. The museum at Sewerby Hall in Bridlington contains a collection of Amy Johnson memorabilia.

HULL

WALK 2 ▼

and leisure complex above.   Return to Ferensway and continue past the railway station, and the statue of Hull poet Philip Larkin, and Paragon Square on the eastern side of the street, where there is the Boer war memorial and Cenotaph to the fallen of the first world war.   Turn along Paragon Street back towards Queen Victoria Square, and about half way along turn right into **Paragon Arcade**. This is a short Victorian arcade with independent shops covered with a fine cast iron and glazed roof. At the far end, turn left onto Carr lane, the walk finishes by the **Ferens Art Gallery** at **Princes Quay shopping centre.** Built on stilts over the former Princes Dock, this is a modern shopping centre with most major shopping chains represented. On four levels, called decks, there is a cinema complex on the top deck. The centre south elevation looks out over the waterfront with the Marina and Spurn lightship directly in front.

Andrew Marvell *Poet* *1621-1678*

Andrew Marvell is a 17thC metaphysical poet and sometime Member of Parliament. He was born the son of a clergyman near Hull and educated at Hull Grammar School, and Trinity College Cambridge. He was MP for Hull from 1659 to his death, and a strong supporter of Cromwell. After the restoration of Charles II, he became cynical and dismissive of what he saw as a corrupt court, and satirised the court in verse which was published anonymously. He remained connected to Hull by also serving as the Trinity house agent in Hull.   There is a statue of him in Trinity Square. He is buried in St Giles in the Fields in London.

Sporting Life

The city's key sporting activities focus around football, and rugby. The city has a top line class football team, and three rugby teams, all strongly supported.

Football Hull boast a team which is a consistent performer in the top english leagues, with games regularly attracting gates over 15,000. **Hull City FC's** home matches are played in the new KC stadium

Hull's KC Stadium

in the west of the city off Anlaby Road. With an all seat capacity of 25,500, fans can watch top class games in comfort. The stadium is shared with Hull FC Rugby League club. Many bus services go to the stadium from the city centre.　　　　　01482 504600　www.hullcityafc.net

Rugby League Hull has two top class rugby league clubs, both well supported across the city.　Hull FC play at the KC stadium, and consistently play in the Super League.　　　01482 505600　www.hullfc.com
Hull Kingston Rovers, nicknamed The Robins,　play at a ground on the other side of the city at Preston Road. Like Hull FC, they are a top line Super League club and draw crowds of over 10,000 to home games. The stadium is served by buses 10F and 43.　　0844 2490105　www.hullkr.co.uk

Rugby Union is also played in the city. Although not as popular as　League, Hull have a team in national Rugby Union league, who play at a ground in the north of the city close to the cemetery.　The nearest bus service is 102/105 to Cottingham Road.　　　　01482 802119　www.hullrugbyunion.co.uk

Festivals

June	Humbermouth Literature Festival	various venues
July	Jazz Festival　Hull Truck Theatre	
	Maritime Festival　various venues	
September	Freedom Festival (every other year)　various　venues	
October	Hull Fair West Park	

Restaurants　(see map page 363 368 369)

££

English/Greek The Omelette 11/12 Albion Street　01482 328603　①

Turkish Mimosa Restaurant 406 Beverley Road　②
01482 474748　www.mimosahull.com

Chinese Mr Chu St Andrews Quay　01482 222288　www.mrchu.co.uk　③

£££

Italian Luciano's 2 Ferriby Road Hessle　01482 641109　④

Vegan Hitchcock's 1, Bishop Lane High St　⑤
01482 320233　www.hitchcocksrestaurant.co.uk

English Fudge 93 Princes Avenue　01482 441019　www.fudgefood.com　⑥

££££

English Boars Nest 22 Princes Avenue 01482 445577 www.theboarsnesthull.com ⑦

£££££

English Artisan 22　The Weir Hessle 01482　644906　www.artisanrestaurant.com　⑧

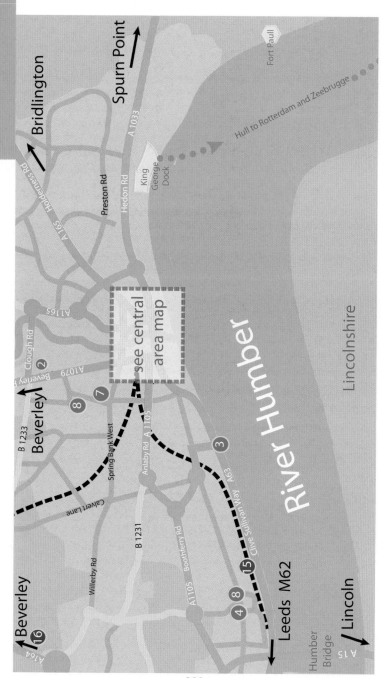

HULL

Bridlington

Spurn Point

Fort Paull

A 1033

Hull to Rotterdam and Zeebrugge

Preston Rd

Hedon Rd

King George Dock

Holderness Rd

A 165

Lincolnshire

A 1165

River Humber

Clough Rd

Beverley Rd

A 1079

B 1233

Beverley

② ⑧ ⑦

Spring Bank West A 1105

Anlaby Rd A 1105

A 63

③

Clive Sullivan Way

Calvert Lane

Willerby Rd

B 1231

Boothferry Rd

A 1105

⑮

④ ⑧

Leeds M62

Beverley

A 164

⑯

Humber Bridge

Lincoln

A 15

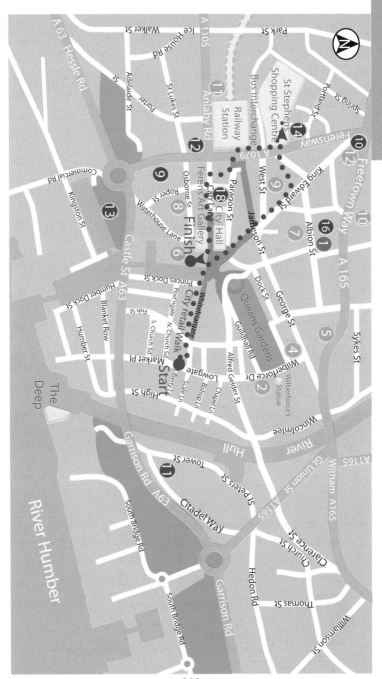

HULL

Hotels (see map page 363 368 369)

★★

Ibis Osbourne Street Ferensway 106 bedrooms 01482 387500 www.ibishotel.com ⑨

Campanile Beverley Road Freetown Way 48 bedrooms ⑩
01482 3225530 www.campanile-hull-city-centre.co.uk

★★★

Premier Inn 99 Tower Street 132 bedrooms ⑪
0871 527 8534 www.premierinn.com

Royal Hotel 170 Ferensway 155 bedrooms ⑫
01482 325087 www.hotels-hull.co.uk

Holiday Inn Hull Marina Castle Street 100 bedrooms ⑬
0871 9029043 www.holidayinn.com

Holiday Inn Express 80 Ferensway 128 bedrooms ⑭
01482 485700 www.hiexpress.com

The Village Henry Boot Way, Priory Way 116 bedrooms ⑮
0844 8472974 www.village-hotels.co.uk

Kingston Theatre 1-2 Kingston Square 28 Bedrooms ⑯
01482 225828 www.kingstontheatrehotel.com

Mercure Hull West Grange Park Willerby 116 Bedrooms ⑰
0844 8159037 www.mercure.com

★★★★

Portland 1 Paragon St 126 bedrooms 01482 326462 www.portland-hotel.co.uk ⑱

Parking Ⓟ

① Market Place	560 spaces	⑦ Albion Street	336 spaces
② Lowgate	61 spaces	⑧ Osborne street	419 spaces
③ Blanket Row	130 spaces	⑨ Prospect Centre	200 spaces
④ George Street	549 spaces	⑩ Francis Street	182 spaces
⑤ Charlotte Street	65 spaces	⑪ Hull Station	200 spaces
⑥ Princes Quay	1000 spaces	⑫ Pryme Street	614 spaces

**Hull Visitor Information Centre
Paragon Street
01482 223559
www.visithullandeastyorkshire.com**

GOOLE

Not often regarded as a destination on the tourist trail, Goole and it's surrounding area situated strategically on the confluence of the rivers Don, Ouse and Aire, nevertheless has interest to the visitor which will make it a worthwhile journey.

History

The town, by comparison to most Yorkshire towns and cities, is of relatively recent origin. The word Goole is middle English for sewer or channel. In the 17thC, a Dutch engineer named Vermuyden diverted the river Don to make it flow into the Ouse rather than the Aire at the request of King Charles 1st (who wanted to go hunting nearby and was fed up with the land regularly flooding); this had the effect of making the land more habitable and of making the lower reaches of the River Don more navigable. With the industrial revolution, demand for coal magnified, prompting improvements to the Aire and Calder canal, by extension of the canal system below Knottingley to link it to the Ouse and so provide the ability to transfer loads efficiently to seagoing vessels, and vice versa. To achieve the transfer, the Aire and Calder Navigation company built eight transhipment docks and, to service the docks, it also built the town of Goole in 1826. Goole has looked towards both the coal industry and the sea for it's living ever since. Demise of the coal industry has forced the town to diversify the ports capability, and today it is probably the UK's most significant inland port.

Getting here

Rail Goole has a railway station in the centre, with regular half hourly services to Doncaster and to Hull - each destination being c. 30 min ride.

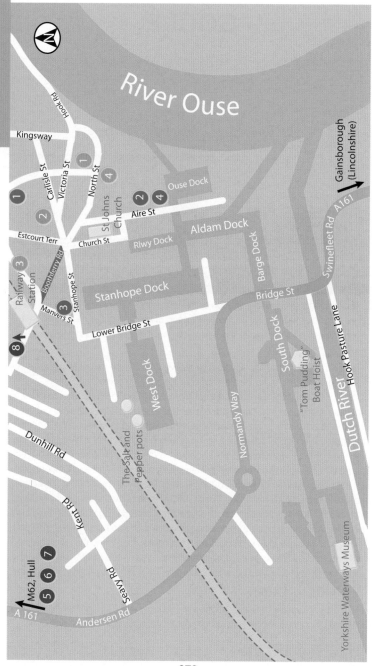

GOOLE

River Ouse

Hook Rd

Kingsway

Carlisle St

Victoria St

North St

St Johns Church

Aire St

Ouse Dock

Aldam Dock

Estcourt Terr

Church St

Rlwy Dock

Barge Dock

Boothferry Rd

Stanhope St

Stanhope Dock

Bridge St

Railway Station

Manvers St

Lower Bridge St

West Dock

South Dock

"Tom Pudding" Boat Hoist

Normandy Way

Dunhill Rd

The Salt and Pepper pots

Kent Rd

Seavy Rd

M62, Hull

A 161

Andersen Rd

Gainsborough (Lincolnshire)

A161

Swinefleet Rd

Hook Pasture Lane

Dutch River

Yorkshire Waterways Museum

Road The town is close to the UK motorway network- adjoining Junction 36 of the M62, and near the motorway junction with the M18. It is 25 min to Doncaster, 40 min to Hull; 50 min to Leeds.

Bus buses stop at North Street.

destination	service(s)	frequency
Leeds	X62	4x per day
Hull	X62	4x per day
Selby	8/400/401	hourly

Things to See and Do

The Docks

Goole docks are open to the public for informal viewing. They can be accessed from the end of Aire Street. There are 8 docks, two of which (Barge Dock and Ship Dock) date from the founding of the docks and town in 1826.

Yorkshire Waterways Museum

is situated on the Dutch river side, close to the docks and is accessed from Bridge Street. The Museum is based on the story of the Aire and Calder Navigation, but also has exhibits on barge families and the towns development as a port. It also includes the unique history of the coal carrying barges, the Tom Puddings. There are restored barges and other vessels to view. The museum is open daily. Admission is free. 01405 768730 www.waterwaymuseum.org.uk

The Boat Hoist and the Tom Pudding barges

The creation of the Docks in 1826 was accompanied by some ingenuity in finding ways to transfer coal from the barges onto sea going vessels. The navigation company's chief Engineer, William Bartholomew, devised a form of hoist and a barge which would allow laden barges to be lifted up and their loads discharged directly into the vessel. This operation proved efficient and worked well until the demise of the coal industry. Five hoists were built for this task and one hoist - no 5- has been preserved and can be seen in the South Dock. The barges that carried the coal from the coalfield to Goole were nicknamed Tom Puddings, because of their shape - they resemble a string of black puddings!! – but were effective; they could each carry up to 40 tons of coal and could be joined together into a train of 40 boats.

Salt and pepper pots

Rearing up from the flat landscape on the skyline are Goole's two water towers, named salt and pepper because they resemble such domestic cruet items. Standing on the north side of the docks off Bridge Street, they provide the town with water. The older brick tower which when completed in 1883 was the largest in the country was supplemented by the ferro concrete construction one in 1926.

Goole museum

There is a small museum above the library in the town centre and opposite the clocktower. It has information on Goole life primarily in the post war period.

A scale model of the late Malcolm Campbell's yacht, Bluebird which was built in the town is on display. The museum is open Mon to Sat. Admission is free.

St John's the Evangelist Parish Church

With its 200ft tall spire, this perpendicular style church of 1843 was built by the Aire and Calder Navigation company to serve the planned town. It is cruciform in shape and built of stone quarried near Wakefield in one of the quarries owned by the Navigation company and brought to Goole by their canal.

Howden

3 miles north east of the town is the rather older small town of Howden. Dating from at least the 10thC, the town was one of the larger in Yorkshire by the 14thC, but the combination of Henry VIII's dissolution of the Monasteries and the rise of Goole in the 19thC reduced its importance and size. However, it boasts a Minster whose towers stand out proudly amongst the flat lands of the Humberhead levels, visible from long distances. The Minster dates from the 13thC and is open most days. There is a small Market Place with a market cross whose base is medieval. To the south of the square is the Bishops Manor House, parts dating from the 14thC and originally used by the bishops of Durham to oversee the work of the Minster.

Restaurants (see map page 372)

£

Indian **Miah's** 2 Government Street 01405 761751 ①

£££

Fish **Mariani** Chapel Street 01405 761188 ②

French **The Goods Office** Railway Buildings Stanhope St 01405 769 555 ③

English **The Lowther Hotel** Aire Street 01405 767999 lowtherhotel.co.uk ④

Hotels (see map page 372)

★★★

Premier Inn Rawcliffe Road Howden 41 bedrooms ⑤
0871 527 8468 www.premierinn.com

not rated

Bowdens Hotel 35 Bridgegate Howden 11 bedrooms 01430 430805 ⑥

Minster View Hotel Corn Market Hill Howden 10 bedrooms 01430 430447 ⑦

Briarcroft 51 Clifton Gdns 8 bedrooms 01405 763024 www.briarcrofthotel.co.uk ⑧

Parking Ⓟ

① Burlington crescent ② Estcourt Street

③ Leisure Centre ④ Wesley Square

DONCASTER

It is easy to get to Doncaster as it sits astride the east coast main railway line and close to the A1 Great North Road. A town renowned for its railway engineering and race course, it first emerged as an important Roman fort, and for much of its history been one of the Yorkshire's wealthiest settlements. Its location equips it well for a night stop over when travelling north – south, and as a touring base for much of south and east Yorkshire, and in nearby Nottinghamshire and Derbyshire.

History

The first signs of settlement in Doncaster are from the period 79AD to 450AD when the Romans established a military presence here. Historians contend the reason for this was because the site of the town lay on the boundary between two powerful Celtic tribes; the warlike Brigantes to the north, and the more civilised Coritani to the south. *Danum* was the name given by the Romans to the town, which rapidly became an important fort on the alternative and safer, if longer, diversion of Ermine Street between Lincoln and York. It was the home to the Roman Crispinian horse garrison, named for Crispin, son of the Emperor Constantine. Original recruits to the garrison were thought to be from western Hungary, the eastern side of the Roman empire. It was sufficiently important to be recorded in the *Notitia Dignitatum*, a comprehensive record of Roman military locations across the empire (a 15thC copy is held in Oxford's Bodleian Library). There is little sign of Roman occupation now visible. Archaeologists consider the core of the roman fort was by the River Don, roughly along the boundaries of the present Minster grounds; excavations here have revealed defences and some internal buildings and a small stretch of fort wall can be seen in the Minster grounds. There is much archaeological interest in the St Sepulchre Gate area of the town centre, where extensive Roman remains are thought to lay below the road. After the departure of the Romans, the incoming Saxon tribes renamed the town *Donceaster* (ceaster was a name given by the Saxons to roman forts). The Domesday book refers to *Hexthorpe*, now a small suburb just to the west of the town centre but which then would have adjoined the roman fort, as having two mills and a church. The town was a prosperous trading centre by late medieval times. It was fortified, the walls being along the lines of the present streets of Market Road, Silver Street, and Printing Office Street. Charters were granted by Richard I in 1198, and in 1248 by Henry III; the market still operates today. By the 14thC the town was one of the wealthiest in the county, and by mid 15thC, had been granted the right to elect a Mayor. The gates into the medieval town have long since disappeared but are commemorated at Sunny Bar, and St Sepulchre Gate. The continuing wealth of the town in the 17th/18thC is amply demonstrated by the emergence of nearby stately homes, such as Brodsworth Hall and Cusworth Hall, and also by the lavish decorations, furniture and fittings to be found in the Mansion House on the High Street.

DONCASTER

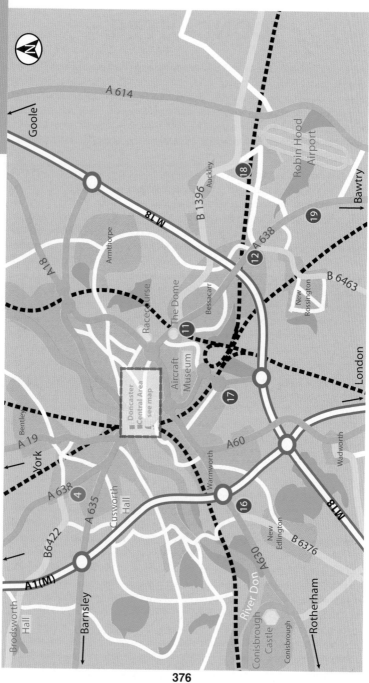

A 614
Goole
M 18
Robin Hood Airport
Bawtry
B 1396
Auckley
18
19
12 A 638
B 6463
Armthorpe
A18
New Rossington
Racecourse
The Dome
Besacarr
11
Aircraft Museum
London
Doncaster Central Area see map
17
A 19
Bentley
York
A60
A 638
4
Warmworth
Wadworth
Cusworth Hall
A 635
16
M 18
B6422
New Edlington
B 6376
A1(M)
River Don
A 630
Brodsworth Hall
Barnsley
Conisbrough Castle
Conisbrough
Rotherham

Doncaster's position on the Great North Road led it to become a coaching inn town, and spawned the emergence of the racecourse from stabling and exercise of horses used by travellers and carriage companies; a position greatly strengthened with the construction of the railway line in 1849. The town quickly became an important railway engineering centre; the Great Northern Railway establishing their engineering works here - works which would later famously build locomotives including The Mallard, which still holds the record for the fastest British steam locomotive, and the iconic Flying Scotsman. Other engineering industries also emerged in the late 19thC, including steel wire and rope making, tractor manufacturing and coal mining. Sadly, many of these industrial sectors have now ceased and today, Doncaster is reinventing itself as a major retail and educational centre. The development of Robin Hood airport at Finningley to the south offers exciting long term prospects for the towns future.

Getting Here

Rail   The railway station adjoins the Frenchgate shopping centre, with a park and ride facility for the train. There are frequent services to London, York, Edinburgh, Leeds, Manchester, Hull, and to Birmingham, as well as more local services to Sheffield, Cleethorpes and Wakefield.

Road Doncaster lies on the junction of the A1(M) London to Edinburgh Great North Road, and the M18, linking Sheffield and the M1 with Hull and East Yorkshire. London is 2.5 hrs; 1.5hrs to Manchester, 2hrs to Newcastle.

Bus most services arrive at and depart from the interchange at the railway station and under the Frenchgate shopping centre.

destination	service	frequency
Rotherham	220/221/X78	30 mins/10 mins
Sheffield	X78	10 mins
barnsley	219/222	30 mins
Wakefield	496	hourly
Pontefract	408/409/420/430	4x per day
London	426/562	1x per day
Newcastle	332	1x per day
Selby	405/407	hourly/3x per day
Worksop	22	30 mins
Scarborough	322	1x per day
Hull	322/562	1x per day

Things to see and do

The town is a mecca for shoppers from much of East Yorkshire and large areas of South Humberside and North Lincolnshire and as such has a vibrant and modern shopping centre, with most brands represented and plenty of opportunity to make a good day out. The market, centred around the former Corn Exchange, opposite the prominent Minster, is amongst the largest in the North of England with over 400 stalls, and has been the heart of the town centre for over 700 years.

All sections of the markets are open Tue, Fri and Sat. Wed is a specialist antique / secondhand market as well as a Farmers Market on the first and third Wed of the month. The Frenchgate shopping centre sits in the west of the centre adjoining the railway station and bus interchange. Completely rebuilt in 2000, it offers shoppers a wide variety of high street branded shops with over 100 stores. Further down the High Street lies the **Mansion House**. This is one of only three surviving mansion houses and has been in civic use since opening in 1749. Its lavish interior reflects the town's wealth during this period. Visits can be made by prior arrangement, and there are a number of annual open days. 01302 737600 www.doncaster.gov.uk

St Georges Minster

This is Doncaster's parish church, and most prominent landmark, visible from a wide expanse of the surrounding area. The present building on the site of previous such buildings, is Victorian, designed in Gothic style by the ubiquitous architect Sir George Gilbert Scott, following a fire which had destroyed the previous Norman building in 1853. Its richly decorated exterior, tower, and fine internal carvings show the level of determination that Doncaster citizens of that time had to not only to make good the loss of the church, but also their ability to contribute towards the cost, reflecting the towns wealth. The Minster is open Mon to Sat. Admission is free.

01302 323748

www.doncasterminster.org

Museum and Art Gallery   Chequers Road

The museum contains collections of art, archaeological artefacts and various aspects of natural and local history. It is open Mon to Sat. Admission is free.
01302 734293 www.doncaster.gov.uk

Doncaster Racecourse

One of the more prominent UK racecourses it hosts one of the horseracing seasons classic races, the St Leger. The course, 1 mile east of the town centre on the A638, is one of the oldest and largest in Britain, with a history of racing going back to the 16thC. The racing stemmed from the stabling of horses in the town by travellers and coaches using the Great North Road and has remained a well known feature ever since. There over 20 race meetings annually, both flat and national hunt.   01302 304200 www.doncaster-racecourse.co.uk

South Yorkshire Aircraft Museum

Otherwise known as Aeroventure, this is a small aeronautical museum located south of the town on what was once its original airfield. It contains a collection of military aircraft, together with a wide range of associated artefacts, and a flight simulator.   The museum is open Wed to Sun. There is an admission charge.
01302 761616 www.aeroventure.co.uk

Brodsworth Hall ✜

Just to the north of the town, this is one of the most complete Victorian country houses to be found in Britain. It was built by a wealthy London merchant banking family. The 30 or so rooms in the house retain their original furniture, fixtures and fittings and the story of the house for visitors can be recounted as a tale of how a once opulent mansion descended into genteel poverty. The house is open Tue to Sun afternoons from April to October. There is an admission charge. The adjoining gardens are open all year. There is no admission charge. Bus service 203 runs from the adjoining village into Doncaster 5 times daily.
01302 722598 www.english-heritage.org.uk

Cusworth Hall

Cusworth Hall

This is an 18thC country manor house, built by a local family, the Battie-Wrightson family, (many of whom were High Sheriffs of Yorkshire and MPs' during the 17th to 19thC) and set in extensive landscaped grounds. The Hall is classic Georgian in style, with a richly decorated Italianate chapel - a great status symbol in Georgian England - and which has some stunning ceiling paintings. It houses a museum whose collections give a deep insight into historic local life in this part of the county. The Hall is open Tues to Fri and afternoons on Sat and Sun. There is an admission charge. Bus services 42 and 219 pass near the Hall.   01302 782342 www.doncaster.gov.uk

DONCASTER

Conisbrough Castle ⊞

The remains of this medieval castle lie in the centre of the village of the same name and is a rare example of a circular stone keep castle, built by Henry II's half brother Hamelin Plantagenet in c.1180. It replaced an earlier motte and bailey earthworks and timber castle built shortly after the Norman Conquest by William de Warrenne. The castle was one of the centres of royalist and baronial intrigue and violent clashes during the 14thC, but was then neglected and by the mid 16thC its state of ruin had reached that which is evident today. One consequence of this was that it hardly featured in the English civil war and was not therefore subject to subsequent demolition ordered by Cromwell on so many other English castles. The castle features in Sir Walter Scott's famous novel Ivanhoe, but portrayed as a Saxon castle. It lies just north of the A630 roughly midway between Rotherham and Doncaster. It is open Sat to Wed for most of the year, and daily during July and August. There is an admission charge. Bus services X78 and 222 pass the site. Conisbrough village rail station is about half a mile away with regular services to Sheffield, Rotherham, Doncaster and Lincoln. 01709 863229 www.english-heritage.org.uk

Sporting life

The Keepmoat Stadium, a modern enclosed all seater ground, on the south side of the town is home to Doncaster Rovers Football club and to Doncaster Rugby League club. The football club play in the football league and have emerged as a powerful, ambitious side in recent years with home game attendance in excess of 10,000
01302 762576 www.doncaterroversfc.co.uk

Doncaster's lavish Mansion House

380

Restaurants (see map page 376 382)

££

Turkish **Turkuaz** 6 Nether Hall Road 013202 340069 www.turkuazbarandgrill.co.uk ①

Indian **Naaz** 2 Baldwin Ave 01302 788882 www.indianrestaurantdoncaster.co.uk ②

Italian **Fratellis** 11 Nether Hall Road   013202 343454 ③

Indian **Aagrah** Great North Road Woodlands 01302 728888 www.aagrah.com ④

Indian **Taj Mahal** 32 Hall Gate 0800 2949239 www.tajmahaldoncaster.co.uk ⑤

Italian **Santinis** 8C Nether Hall Road 01302 768878 ⑥

Italian **Carlo's** 5 Nether hall Road 01302 363447 ⑦

Italian **Quintus** 20 Hallgate 01302 238045 ⑧

Tex-Mex **Cactus Jack** 18 Hallgate 01302 321500 ⑨

£££

Mediterranean **Zest Bar Grill** 19-20 High St ⑩
01302 365005 www.zestbarandgrill.com

Hotels (see map page 376 382)

★★

Campanile Bawtry Road 50 Bedrooms ⑪
01302370770   www.campanile-doncaster.co.uk

Innkeepers Lodge Bawtry Road Bessacarr 25 Bedrooms ⑫
0845 1126032   www.innkeeperslodge.com

★★★

Grand St Leger Bennethorpe 20 Bedrooms 01302 364111 www.grandstleger.com ⑬

The Regent Regent Sq 52 Bedrooms 01302 364180 www.theregenthotel.co.uk ⑭

The Danum High Street 64 Bedrooms 01302 342261 www.danumhotel.com ⑮

Holiday Inn High Road Warmsworth 102 Bedrooms ⑯
0871 9429061 www.holidayinn.com

Holiday Inn Express Woodfield Way 94 Bedrooms ⑰
01302 314100 www.hiexpressdoncaster.co.uk

Ramada Encore First Avenue Auckley 102 Bedrooms ⑱
01302 718520 www.encoredoncaster.co.uk

★★★★

Mount Pleasant Great North Road 56 Bedrooms ⑲
01302 868696 www.mountpleasant.co.uk

not rated

Earl of Doncaster Bennethorpe 89 Bedrooms 01302 361371 www.theearl.co.uk ⑳

DONCASTER

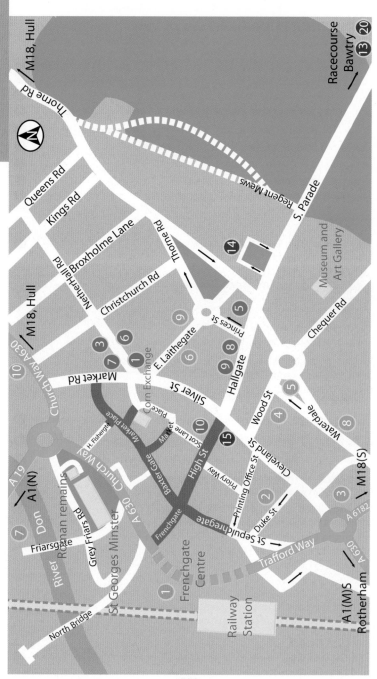

Parking (P)

(1) Frenchgate	1400 spaces	(2) Colonnades	95 spaces
(3) Southern	200 spaces	(4) Waterdale	850 spaces
(5) Waterdale central	440 spaces	(6) Frances St (Odeon)	114 spaces
(7) Friarsgate	360 spaces	(8) Waterdale Shopping	450 spaces
(9) East Laith Gate	102 spaces	(10) Chappell Drive	550 spaces

modern shopping malls in Frenchgate

ABBEYS CASTLES

YORKSHIRES ABBEYS CASTLES AND STATELY HOMES

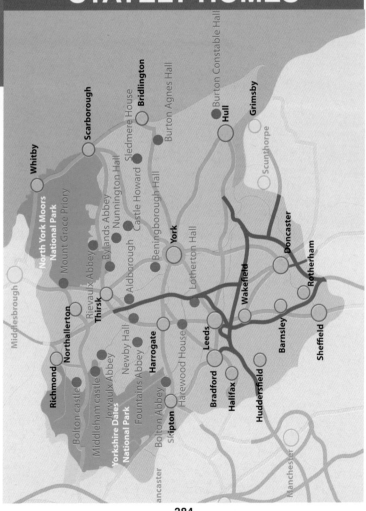

Burton Constable Hall

Bridlington

Burton Agnes Hall

Grimsby

Sledmere House

Scarborough

Hull

Scunthorpe

Whitby

North York Moors National Park

Mount Grace Priory

Nunnington Hall

Castle Howard

Doncaster

Bylands Abbey

Rievaulx Abbey

Beningborough Hall

York

Rotherham

Aldborough

Lotherton Hall

Thirsk

Wakefield

Northallerton

Newby Hall

Barnsley

Richmond

Harewood House

Leeds

Sheffield

Bolton castle

Jervaulx Abbey

Newby Abbey

Harrogate

Middleham castle

Yorkshire Dales National Park

Fountains Abbey

Bradford

Huddersfield

Halifax

Bolton Abbey

Skipton

Middlesbrough

Doncaster

Manchester

ALDBOROUGH

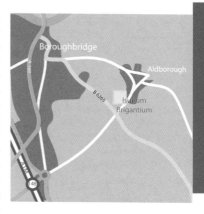

Near Boroughbridge, a small town on the A1 near Ripon, the former roman fort, *Isurium Brigantum* is the Roman name for this military outpost in the attractive village of Aldborough. It may well have marked the crossing of the River Ure by Dere Street, the Roman road running from York northwards into Scotland. Latterly, it became the capital of the Romanised Brigantes tribe as the Romans gradually withdrew from occupation. The museum contains a collection of artefacts recovered from excavations on the site. There is only limited surviving evidence of the Roman town save for a small area in the south-western quarter where several low sections of wall can be seen, as well as the foundations of two of the interval towers. At the far end of the site, concealed within protective buildings, are two mosaics that are believed to have been laid in the second or third century. Although now housed separately, they would originally have been contained in the same dwelling. The first mosaic depicts a lion sitting under a tree; the second, is an image of an eight sided star in the centre of the mosaic. A third mosaic is now displayed in the museum.

Opening times weekends and bank holidays from April to October. There is an admission charge. The site is close to a bus route with services 55,56,57,58 to Knaresborough and Harrogate, and 142/143 Ripon to York.

01423 322768   www.english-heritage.org.uk

LOTHERTON HALL

A country house to the north east of Leeds and some 5 miles south of Wetherby, whose history stretches back nearly 1000 years. the current house dates from 1895, although this was essentially a remodelling of a building which had stood, in various forms, on this site since the 13thC when the hall was inhabited by the Neville family, amongst whose number was Warwick the Kingmaker. The Gascoigne family acquired the house and estate in the 16thC together with nearby Parlington Hall (now demolished) and occupied it until 1970. The house and estate was gifted to the city of Leeds and has been developed as an historic attraction. the house itself contains artefacts which trace the history of a long established Yorkshire family as well as an extensive collection far eastern art, mainly assembled by Sir Alvary Gascoigne who was the British Ambassador to Russia and Japan and last of the Gascoigne line. The grounds contain a range of endangered bird species as well as herds of red deer, llamas and widespread wild flowers. There is an adventure playground and woodland play area. House and grounds are open daily. There is an admission charge.

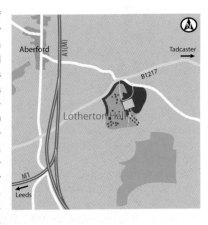

Bus services 64/64A between Leeds and Aberford pass the site.

www.leeds.gov.uk/lothertonhall

HAREWOOD HOUSE

Harewood House and estate, including the village, is an 18thC development, on land previously occupied by a country house and castle. There is a house, formal gardens, parkland, a church (built 1410), a ruined castle (built 1360), and the model village laid out and built between 1755 and 1800. The Harewood estate was originally two estates; that of the now ruined castle, built by Sir William Aldeburgh, and Gawthorpe Hall (not to be confused with the present Gawthorpe Hall near Burnley in Lancashire) which dated from 1260 but was demolished to make way for the present house in 1770. The current house was built by the Lascelles family, who acquired the Gawthorpe estate having made their fortune from West Indian sugar plantations. The house was built to a design by John Carr of York, and modified by Robert Adam. It is a gracious and finely balanced structure overlooking formal gardens and a lake, and is still the home of the Lascelles family (now the Earls of Harewood). The finely decorated interior is wholly the work of Robert Adam, who commissioned the finest artists of the Georgian era to create lavish panel paintings, stucco plasterwork and richly decorated wood carvings. The Otley born cabinet maker, Thomas Chippendale, was commissioned to make much of the furniture, some remaining in the house today. Of particular note is the Gallery, with its caryatid adorned chimneypiece, and Chippendale pier glasses, tables and window pelmets. The formal gardens sit below the terrace (a 19thC addition), with a layout strongly resembling parts of Versailles. Below the house is the stable block, now a tearoom and café and, in the woodland adjoining, is the bird garden housing one of England's best avian collections, and which can be visited separately to the house. Between the house and the ruined castle is the 15thC church of all Saints, built by the Aldeburgh family for their own use. Restored in the mid 19thC, the interior contains a 13thC font bowl. The landscaped parkland is the work of landscape designers of the late 18thC including Capability Brown and Humphrey Repton, and criss-crossed with footpaths and bridleways enabling visitors to see the spectacular setting of house and grounds. The whole estate is actively managed with regular guided tours and walks, an adventure playground, cafes and shops as well as a full programme of outdoor events, such as classic car shows and pop concerts in the parkland through the spring and summer months. The house, grounds, bird

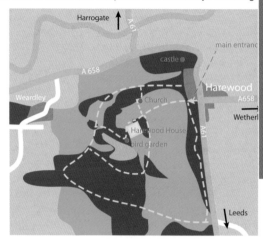

HAREWOOD HOUSE

garden and adventure playground are open daily April to October. There is an admission charge. The house and grounds are entered through Harewood village, at the junction of the A61 and A659. Bus services 36 and 923 stop in the village.   0113 2181010   www.harewood.org

NEWBY HALL

Newby Hall with its extensive attractive gardens lie in the open countryside of the Vale of York 5 miles east of Ripon and close to the River Ure. The house has been described as "the finest house I saw in Yorkshire" by early 18thC traveller Celia Fiennes and dates from 1693. It was built by the coal magnate and later MP for Ripon, Sir Edward Blackett, and although the architect is unknown, records point to involvement by Sir Christopher Wren. The

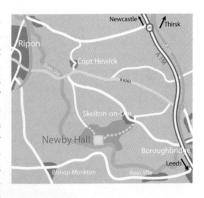

house was acquired by the Weddell family in the mid 18thC and descendants still live in a wing of the house. William Weddell inherited the estate in 1762. He had previously completed a Grand Tour of Italy and accumulated a vast collection of antique sculpture requiring substantial alterations to the house. These were carried out by Robert Adam and John Carr. Adam designed much of the interior to provide a sequence for the visitor to pass from the entrance hall to the sculpture gallery, where much of Weddell's collection remains today. The gardens were laid out in the early 20thC, and the central walk, with its herbaceous borders, provides a spectacular approach to the house from the river's edge. The gardens are a feature of the estate with differing kinds of displays from roses to tropical species and a number of formal displays. There is also a miniature railway and adventure playground in the grounds. The house and grounds are open April to September. There is an admission charge. Bus service 142 (Ripon to York) passes through the nearby village of Skelton-on-Ure.

0845 4504068   www.newbyhallandgardens.com

BOLTON ABBEY

Bolton Abbey lies off the A59 between Skipton and Harrogate at the point where the River Wharfe flows out of the Yorkshire Dales. Although the tiny village is of the same name, the title" abbey" is a misnomer; the religious building is and always has been a Priory. It dates from about 1170, and was founded by the order of the Augustinian Canons, whose monks and friars lived a mixed life alternating between quiet contemplation and apostolic ministry. The priory was broken up with the Dissolution of the Monasteries in the 16thC, and much fell into ruin. The western part of the main church however remained and still functions as the village's parish church. The building has been adapted over time, but the interior, unlike many churches in Yorkshire, is largely devoid of decorative enrichment.   The eastern part and the surrounding living quarters now stand as a dramatic picturesque ruin.   To the west, adjacent to the road, is Bolton Hall; one of the homes of the landowners, the Duke of Devonshire and part of which was originally the gatehouse to the priory.

Access to the priory is from the village where there is a car park. The Priory grounds extend down to the river where there is a small beach. A path leads across the river and along the east bank for about 1km, before re-crossing to the Cavendish pavilion where there is a café and restaurant, an extensive car park and room to picnic on the riverside.

BOLTON ABBEY

North of the pavilion is The Strid, a fastflowing narrow stretch of the River Wharfe tumbling furiously over rocks and ledges as it rushes down towards Ilkley.

A woodland walk has been created which takes visitors through the Strid Woods on the west bank of the river; the more hardy might well find themselves continuing on to Barden Bridge - a 17thC structure over the river adjacent to Barden Tower. This is now a romantic ruin, but was built about 1500 for Henry Clifford of Skipton Castle.   The Cavendish pavilion site also marks the start of the well trodden 3 mile footpath, through the aptly named Valley of Desolation, up to one of the Pennines higher tops, Simons Seat at 1500ft above sea level.   Access to the Priory is year round, and during the spring and summer months, guides are available for the church. There is no admission charge.

01756 718009   www.boltonabbey.com

FOUNTAINS ABBEY

FOUNTAINS ABBEY

A designated World Heritage Site (one of only 25 in the UK) and reputed to be the best preserved Cistercian Monastery in Britain, Fountains Abbey and its landscaped parkland of Studley Royal, lie in the small secluded valley of the River Skell as it drops down from the moors towards the River Ure at Ripon. The Abbey is 3 miles south west of the city, reached from the B6265 Pateley Bridge road. There is also an Elizabethan hall and a carefully designed and laid out deer park. Prior to the Dissolution, the Abbey was reputedly the richest of all Cistercian Abbeys in the country. It owed its roots to a group of dissident monks who broke away from the Benedictine St Mary's Abbey in York in about 1136. Most of the present buildings date from about 1160. The precisely cut masonry uses stone quarried from the cliff that forms the north bank of the Skell valley here. The Abbey grew in stature and size over the next 400 years, becoming one of the most influential establishments whose Abbott carried considerable weight in the Church and who sat in the Parliament of the day. A walk around the abbey gives a good feel for its size and stature. All of this came to an abrupt halt with Henry VIII's marital difficulties and the consequent Dissolution of the Monasteries. Acquisition of such Abbeys provided rich pickings for Henry's wealthy merchant class supporters and the Fountains Estate was acquired by Sir Richard Gresham, one such London merchant. Despite the Dissolution, the buildings although now merely unroofed shells, are in remarkably good condition and the full layout and operation of the Monastery as it would have been in the 16thC is easily discernible. Of particular note are the north entrance; the Huby tower, built in about 1500 by an Abbott of that name; the vast 300 ft long presbytery and nave, and the cellarium and lay brothers refectory adjoining the nave at right angles. The vaulted ceiling of the lower floor of the lay brothers dormitory is also an impressive sight. The abbey buildings are set in attractive well maintained grounds with opportunities for walking and picnicking.

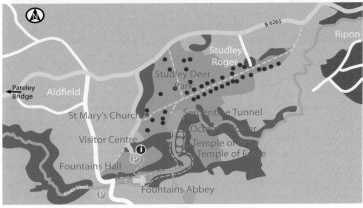

At the west entrance to the grounds is Fountains Hall. This is Elizabethan, built 1604. It uses stone from the then recently defunct abbey and the unusual height of the house stems from its proximity to the cliff behind. It was built by Sir Stephen Proctor, who had purchased the Abbey estate from Sir Richard Gresham. Proctor inherited his wealth from his ironmaster father, and was a fervent Puritan and persecutor of Catholics. Since many of his neighbours in the area remained Catholics, he was much resented and vilified locally. To the east of the Abbey is Studley Royal water garden and deer park. The park and the Abbey were acquired by William Aislabie, then Ripon's MP, who laid it out as a landscaped water garden. It is one of few surviving water gardens from the Georgian period. It consists of a series of linked ornamental lakes, canals and cascades with follies and temples positioned to create a range of eye catching dramatic vistas. The water garden leads to the Deer park, a landscaped parkland in the midst of which is the 19thC church of St Mary, commissioned by the Marquis and Marchioness of Ripon to commemorate a relative killed in unfortunate circumstances. To the north of the Abbey is the visitor centre with a café and restaurant. Visitor centre, abbey and gardens are open Sat to Thu in the winter months, and daily from February to October. There is an admission charge. Bus service 139 links the Abbey with Ripon bus station.

01765 608888   www.fountainsabbey.org.uk

⌗ RIEVAULX ABBEY

The name Rievaulx is more properly *Rye Vallis*, meaning the abbey in Ryedale. A Cistercian Abbey, it was founded by Walter L'Espec (see p.287) for the French Clairvaulx monks prior to the establishment of Fountains Abbey and only the latter, of all the English abbeys, remains more complete today. Set in a small wooded valley, Rievaulx's ruins exude a romantic, somewhat mysterious atmosphere. The size of the abbey needs to be appreciated.

At its peak, probably a few years after its foundation, records show there were 140 monks and 600 lay brothers at the Abbey. It would have filled that part of the Rye Valley. Much of the land was given by Walter L'Espec of nearby Helmsley castle. Abbeys of this size became economic entities of their own right, and during its heyday, Rievaulx, like Fountains and others, were large commercial undertakings, engaged in farming, forestry, and the woollen trade. After the Dissolution, Rievaulx was purchased by the Earl of Rutland, one of Henry's eager advisers and later sold to the Duncombe family who, in the 18thC, landscaped the eastern escarpment to cre-

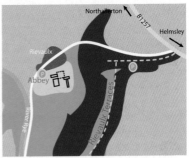

ate terraces and built two Grecian style temples; one to resemble the Temple of Fortuna Virilis in Rome; one to reflect a Tuscan temple. The Abbey is open daily April to October, with more limited opening in winter months. There is an admission charge. There are limited   seasonal bus services from Helmsley and Scarborough (service Moorsbus M18 and M91).

01439 798228 (Abbey) 01439 798340(Terrace)

www.english-heritage.org www.nationaltrust.org.uk

⊞ BYLANDS ABBEY

Another of Yorkshire's fine collection of monastic ruins, Bylands sits under the escarpment marking the edge of the North Yorks Moors, close to the village of Wass.   It is a 12thC Cistercian abbey and one of "the three shining lights of the north" (along with Rievaulx and Fountains).   Founded as a Savigniac Abbey in c.1137, it quickly became subject to the Cistercian order, and although never as prominent, it became a centre for sheep rearing and wool exports.   The Abbey's church, parts of which survive, is notable for having a rose window in the west elevation similar to York minster's famous south transept window.   It was reputed to be the largest and most magnificent church in the country when built, although subsequently surpassed by both Rievaulx and Fountains, its design and architectural features were widely copied in other churches across the country.   The floor of the nave has been excavated to reveal richly decorated green and yellow mosaics.   The abbey met its fate with the Dissolution of the Monasteries, but it is possible today to see, from the surviving foundations, the layout of the Abbey, and to explore the site. It is open daily April to September; more limited opening hours apply in the winter. There is an admission charge. Bus service 31X between Helmsley and York passes the site every two hours.

01347 868614 www.englishheritage.org.uk

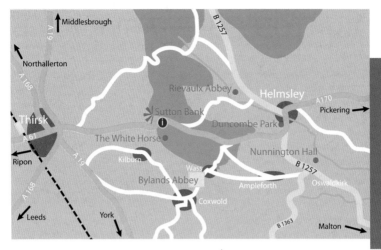

JERVAULX ABBEY

Situated on the southern banks of the River Ure in the Yorkshire Dales between Leyburn and Masham, Jervaulx is a Cistercian abbey, and the daughter house of Bylands. At its peak, the Abbey owned much of the upper Ure valley(Wensleydale) and became a centre for breeding horses - a practice which has continued today with the existence of a large number of stables for race hors-

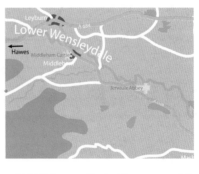

es in and around the nearby village of Middleham. Part of its commercial undertaking was the production of cheeses, and where the original Wensleydale cheese was created. As with all abbeys in this part of Yorkshire, Henry VIII's dissolution of the Monasteries in 1538 quickly created decline and ruin, with the estate being sold a number of times, including to the Cunliffe-Listers, the Bradford textile magnate family. The Abbey stands in the grounds of Jervaulx Hall on the A6108 and is open daily. There is an admission charge. Bus service 159 between Ripon and Richmond passes the site.

01677 460391   www.jervaulxabbey.com

393

BURTON CONSTABLE HALL

Burton Constable Hall lies 6 miles east of Hull just north of Sproatley village. It is an Elizabethan manor, built originally in 1560 for the Constable dynasty, who still occupy the house. Although substantial 17th and 18thC alterations were carried out, the house, from its exterior, is patently

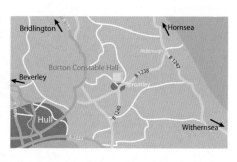

Elizabethan with its extensive use of large mullioned oriel windows and ornate cupolas on the north and south towers. Parts of the north wing are estimated to have formed part of an earlier hall, dating from the medieval era. The interior is generally more recent. The great hall, a spacious room whose height stretched from floor to roof, typical of Elizabethan manor houses, was modified in 1767 with the insertion of floors to create attic rooms in its upper part, and assumed a distinctly Jacobean appearance. There are many other rooms of note in this historic restored building. The Long Gallery, accessed from an impressive cantilevered staircase, runs along much of the west front at upper level, and is notable for its wood panelling, marble fireplace and intricately decorated bookcases. The decorations and fittings in the Chinese room, on the ground floor, with its pagodas, ceiling mounted dragons and extensive use of Chinese wallpaper is thought to have been influenced by George IV's flamboyant decoration and fittings in the Brighton Pavilion.

The house contains substantial collections of furniture and works of art, together with a renowned "cabinet of curiosities" which is an eclectic collection of scientific instruments, shells, rocks and minerals dating from William Constable's grand tours in the18thC. The surrounding parkland was laid out and landscaped by Capability Brown in the late 18thC. The Hall is open Sat to Thu between Easter and the end of October. There is an admission charge. Bus service 124/220/277 from Hull pass through nearby Sproatley village.

01964562400 www.burtonconstable.com

NUNNINGTON HALL

Nunnington Hall is a late 17thC manor house, nestling quietly on the banks of the river Rye about 7 miles from Malton. There was a manor house on the site in Tudor times, probably built by William Parr, 1st Earl of Essex and the sometime brother-in-law of Henry VIII. There are some surviving parts of this, although Sir Richard Graham, 1st Viscount Preston, built the majority of the present house. Charles II awarded him a baronetcy, in about 1662, for his services in securing the restoration of the Stuart Monarchy. The hall subsequently

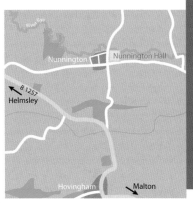

has been owned by a range of minor aristocratic and other well to do and military families, with artefacts of their occupation on display throughout the house. The interior contains a stone entrance hall with an original 16thC fireplace, together with many hunting trophies. The panelled oak hall has a large cartouche above the fireplace depicting the Preston family coat of arms. The various bedrooms provide a history of what life may have been like in the 19th and early 20thC. The hall stands in 8 acres of managed grounds including a walled garden and an organic meadow. It is open from March to October on Tue to Sun, and other times of the year on weekends only. There is an admission charge. Bus service 194 (Malton to Helmsley) serves the adjoining village (4x per day). 01439 748283 www.nationaltrust.org.uk

NUNNINGTON HALL

MOUNT GRACE PRIORY

MT GRACE PRIORY

The priory is a small but historically significant collection of buildings hiding amongst woodlands on the escarpment, overlooking the eastern side of the Vale of York 5 miles east of Northallerton and accessed from the A19. It was founded by the Earl of Kent, Richard II's half brother, in 1398 and was probably the last monastery established in Britain prior to the 1538 reformation. It is a monastery of the Carthusian order (translated as charterhouse); one of ten such mon-asteries in medieval England, where monks lived as hermits, each in their own little self contained set of rooms and small garden, coming together only on a small number of occasions

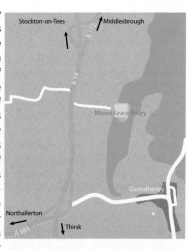

each week. The surviving buildings include the later guest accommodation, rebuilt in the 18thC, as well as a reconstructed monk's cell to replicate how the brothers lived in the priory. The foundations and some walls of the church can still be seen and visitors can access the entire site. The Priory is open Thu to Mon, March to October. More limited hours apply in the winter. There is an admission charge. Bus services 80 and 89 between Northallerton and Stokesley pass nearby on the A19. 01609 883494
www.english-heritage.org.uk

CASTLE HOWARD

One of the county's grandest houses, and made famous from the filming of the TV series Brideshead Revisited, Castle Howard is an early 18thC baroque palace of a size and grandeur to rival the best the European houses of that era. It was built by the Howard family, who still own and occupy it. The house and its extensive landscaped parkland lie in the Howardian Hills 4 miles west of Malton. The main house was constructed between 1699 and 1712, al-though the west wing was a later construction finished in the early 19thC. The design had been commissioned by the Charles Howard, 3rd Earl of Carlisle, then a very young (30yrs) First Lord of the Treasury – the post which soon after became known as that of the Prime Minister. There is uncertainty as to who really designed it. It is generally accredited to Sir John Vanbrugh, then better known as a playwright and well connected Whig activist. He, however, was not a trained architect, and this was his first commission. By all accounts he was engaging, charming and persuasive and these qualities plus his political connections may have landed him the job. It is likely that if Vanbrugh were the frontman, the bulk of the real design and detail would have been carried out by another. This was Nicholas Hawksmoor, sometime protégé of Sir Christopher Wren, and with whom Vanbrugh would go on to design Blenheim Palace.

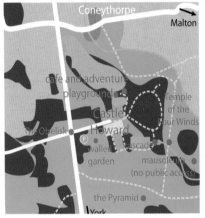

CASTLE HOWARD

Castle Howard was probably the first major building in the country to reflect the Baroque style of architecture then gaining rapid popularity in Europe. The house sits on a ridge. The north front, more severe in style, looks down over the Great Lake, whilst the more festive and wider south front looks down over formal landscaped gardens. The central decorative dome dominates both facades. The ornate interior contains many features of great interest. The spectacular palatial great hall in the centre of the house, reaches up through two storeys into the dome, with imposing staircases and balconies, although the eye is drawn overwhelmingly to the paintings in the dome, in the Venetian style by the Italian artist Antonio Pelligrini and depicting the Four elements, the figures of the Zodiac, and the tale of Phaeton. The Long Gallery, on the first floor, is 170 ft long and contains a number of tapestries and paintings. Some of the main bedrooms are open to view, and have been faithfully restored and furnished to their 18thC appearance. The house contains many paintings by well known artists such as Canaletto, Gainsborough and Reynolds, as well as sculptures, porcelain, furniture and tapestries. The family avidly collected works of art over the years. It was once estimated that there were 274 paintings in the house by well known English and Italian artists. The Music Room has a late 18thC piano and harp, as well as an extensive collection of sheet music dating from the period. The surrounding gardens and parkland are extensive and peppered with buildings and monuments designed and built just after the completion of the house. The Avenue forms the main road running north south to the west of the house. It is ramrod straight, lined with beech and lime trees for five miles and contains the Pyramid Gatehouse, (the original formal entrance to the estate and initially built simply as an arch), and an obelisk, unusually set in the middle of the road, and commemorating the successful completion of the main house. Carrmire Gate, marks the southern limit of the estate with its mock wall fortifications projecting either side. Travelling along The Avenue gives glimpses of the house as well as other features of the estate.

BENINGBROUGH HALL

The Pyramid, the Temple and the Mausoleum are all visible from the Avenue. The Mausoleum, designed by Hawksmoor, is south east of the house and of a size to match many 18thC London churches. It can probably be regarded as one of the finest mausolea in Europe. It was, and still is, the burial place for the Howard family.   The Temple of the Four Winds lies east of the house, beyond the south lake. It dates from 1726 and the last of Vanbrugh's designs for the house and estate (he died that year aged 63). It is based on the Villa Rotunda in Vicenza. A retreat for reading and refreshment it enjoys long distance views over the parkland.   The Pyramid, to the east of the pyramid gatehouse, dates from 1728 and its hollow inside, contains a large bust of the founder of the Castle Howard branch of the family, Lord William Howard.   There are many other features and attractions in these extensive parklands, including fountains, lakes and waterways which can be accessed along the comprehensive network of pathways.   A visit to the estate would not be complete without a tour round the walled garden with its ornate trellises and wide collection of roses of all kinds. The house is open daily between March and October. The gardens and parkland are open daily. There is an admission charge for both.

Bus services 180,181, serve the house from York (3x daily) and 182,183 link the house with Malton (5x daily).   01653 648333   www.castlehoward.co.uk

BENINGBROUGH HALL

Beningbrough Hall is 6 miles north west of York on the banks of the River Ouse. The Hall is an early 18thC red brick country house built by Sir John Bourchier, a wealthy merchant and sometime High Sheriff of Yorkshire, whose lineage can be traced back to the 13thC and who were closely related to the Plantagenets. Bourchier had acquired the Beningbrough estate in the mid 16thC.   It has an imposing but relatively plain exterior, belying a more delicate and intricate interior. The entrance hall runs through both storeys with giant Corinthian pilasters supporting the delicately wrought iron edged balconies, and a distinctive cantilevered staircase. There is much high quality panelling and decorated friezes evident, and the house is notable for its comprehensive collection of 18thC portraits, displayed and maintained in conjunction with the National Portrait Gallery. There is a walled garden and extensive surrounding parkland. The house is open most days between March and October. Bus service 58, York to Northallerton (4x daily) comes through the village of Shipton, two miles to the east.   01904 472027   www.nationaltrust.org.uk

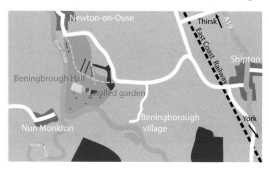

SLEDMERE HOUSE

The Sykes family built Sledmere House and village in the 18thC. They were a Leeds and Hull based family who had made their fortune from the cloth and shipping trades in the 17thC and early 18thC. The building of the Hall and the estate village represented the apotheosis of their rise to fame and fortune. There had long been a house on the site, but Sir Christopher Sykes, the 2nd baronet, bought the estate and created the present house. He enclosed large areas for cultivation, and moved the entire village to its present position. A fire in

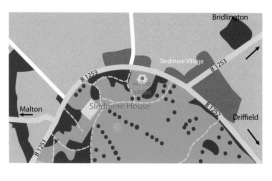

1911 gutted the house, but it was faithfully rebuilt, in stone (unusual for this part of Yorkshire), with Robert Adam designed interiors replicated, as the original drawings designs had survived. The interior rooms can be viewed and include music room, entrance hall with its rather imposing imperial staircase, and the long gallery or library which runs the length of the south front.

The house is set in extensive grounds, landscaped on the advice of Capability Brown, and the village is a near perfect example of the estate village of earlier times. House and gardens are open from Easter to September on Tue to Fri and Sun. There is an admission charge. Bus service 135 from Driffield to Sledmere runs Monday to Friday three times a day.

01377 236637 www.sledmerehouse.com

Burton Agnes Hall   Sledmere House

BURTON AGNES HALL

4 miles west of Bridlington, Burton Agnes is a village dominated by the Hall and estate. Built in the early 1600's for Sir Henry Griffith, it is still in the family's ownership - the descending line extending to the current occupants, the Cunliffe-Listers of Bradford and Swinton Park. The house adjoining is an earlier Norman house of which limited remains are visible as part of an outbuilding between the main house and the village church. The main structure, designed by Queen Elizabeth I's master mason, Robert Smythson, was commissioned by Sir Henry after his appointment by Elizabeth to the Council of the North. The house is approached through the Jacobean style gatehouse on the south side, with its imposing arch and bas relief of the family arms. It bears remarkable similarity to the well known great houses of Audley End in Essex and Hatfield in Hertfordshire. It fully reflects classic Elizabethan architecture with its warm red brick and mullioned window exterior, and a splendid interior with a great hall and a long gallery. The great hall is notable not only for its space, but also for its screen and highly decorative chimneypiece. The long Gallery which runs the entire length of the first floor above the great hall, contains a number of distinctive fittings, some obtained from other great Yorkshire manors, such as the fireplace from the former Methley Hall, and at either end are large venetian windows. Fine art and furniture are much in evidence; the product of over four centuries of collecting such pieces by the family, and include Impressionist paintings, Georgian furniture and porcelain. The gardens are open to visit -the walled garden contains the national collection of campanulas -and the grounds include a woodland sculpture walk.

House and gardens are open daily between April and October. There is an admission charge. Bus services 121, Hull to Scarborough route (hourly) and 744 Bridlington to York (4x per day) pass through the village

01262 490324

www.burtonagnes.com

BOLTON CASTLE

The majestic ruins of Bolton castle dominate the small village of Castle Bolton in Wensleydale, 12 miles west of Richmond. Of comparatively late construction, the castle, built for military purposes, is 14thC. Its promoter and owner was Richard le Scrope (1327-1403) and is still owned by his descendants. He was a prominent English baron and, as English Chancellor, one of the main protectors of the infant King Richard II. As the king grew up he became increasingly extravagant, and Le Scrope's efforts to contain this were met with his dismissal in 1382. He was restored to favour under Henry IV, and when he died was buried in Easby Abbey near Richmond (p.142). The castle has been witness to much of the turbulence of English history. Its scars are testament to its involvement in the Pilgrimage of Grace - the attempt by number of northern senior public and religious figures to prevent dissolution of the Monasteries by Henry VIII, where the 8th Baron le Scrope, gave sanctuary to some Abbots who were prominent in this cause. Mary Queen of Scots was imprisoned here for a year in 1568 prior to being moved to Tutbury Castle and then Sheffield.The English civil war saw the castle staunchly royalist, and was besieged by parliamentary forces

MIDDLEHAM CASTLE

for over a year in 1644-5, before surrendering. Following this parts were de-molished on Cromwell's orders but today, although not roofed, much of the orig-inal remains intact and accessible for the visitor.There are a range of original

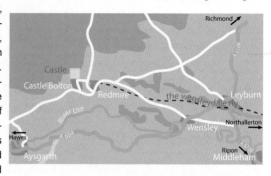

rooms to discover, including the kitch-ens, the armoury, and Mary Queen of Scots bedroom. Outside, the medi-eval gardens have been the subject of archaeological ex-cavation and parts have been restored including two walled areas and a maze.The castle is open daily February to October. There is an admission charge. Bus service 157 between Bedale and Hawes runs 3x per day to Castle Bolton.   01969 623981 www.boltoncastle.co.uk

⊞ MIDDLEHAM CASTLE

There has been a castle in the village of Middleham in Wensleydale since the Norman conquest. The ruins of the present structure date from the late 12thC when Robert Fitzrandolph took steps to protect Upper Wensleydale and Cover-dale. The castle passed into the hands of the Warwick family, and Richard, 16th Earl (known as Warwick the Kingmaker)

who was a leading figure in the Wars of the Roses, used the castle to imprison King Ed-ward IV for a short time during this period. After Warwick's death, his cousin (also called Richard) ascended to the throne as Richard III, to be killed two years later at the Battle of Bosworth in 1485.   The castle remained in the hands of the royal family of the day, although it had fallen into disuse by the time of James I when it was sold. The castle itself has a massive Norman keep, surrounded by

curtain walling, and extensive palatial residential quarters, probably added in the 15thC by the Earls of Warwick, as was the gatehouse. The castle provides the visitor with an excellent journey through a medieval fortified palace, and the viewing platforms give panoramic views out over Wensleydale. The imposing structure sits above the village centre, and is open daily April to September with more restricted opening in the winter months. There is an admission charge. Bus service 159 between Ripon and Richmond passes through Middleham 4 times per day.   01969 623899 www.englishheritage.org.uk

USEFUL CONTACTS

Visitor Information Websites

www.yorkshire.com covers the region as a whole and provides a wealth of information on the county for visitors. An excellent starting point for deciding where to go where to stay and what to do.

www.yorkshirenet.co.uk 01756 794488 covers the region as a whole providing information primarily on attractions accommodation and restaurants.

www.yorkshiredales.org.uk 0300 456 0030. website of the national park authority. Provides a comprehensive range of information about the national park.

www.northyorkmoors.org.uk 01439 770657 website of the national park authority. Provides a comprehensive range of information about the national park.

www.visithullandeastyorkshire.co.uk 01482 486600 provides detailed information for visitors to Hull, Beverley Bridlington, The Wolds, Driffield Withernsea and Hornsea.

www.discoveryorkshirecoast.com covers Scarborough, Whitby, Filey the east coast and the North York Moors area.

www.visityork.org 01904 550099 comprehensive site for the city and immediate surroundings.

www.enjoyharrogate.com covers Harrogate Ripon Knaresborough Masham and Nidderdale.

www.skiptonweb.co.uk provides information on the town.

www.visitbradford.com 01274 433678 comprehensive site for the city as well as Keighley Howarth and Ilkley.

www.visitleeds.co.uk 0113 242 5242 covers the city together with Otley and Wetherby.

www.experiencewakefield.co.uk 0845 601 8353 comprehensive information on the city as well as Castleford and Pontefract.

Travel Information

⋆Train services

www.nationalrail.co.uk 08457 484950

www.wymetro.com/TrainTravel 0113 245 7676 covers the west yorkshire area.

www.northernrail.org train company whose services cover most of the county.

www.thetrainline.com national rail ticket purchase site.

www.eastcoast.co.uk provides mainline services from London and Edinburgh to York Leeds Doncaster and other towns in the Vale of York.

www.eastmidlandstrains.co.uk 08457 125 678 provides information on services mainly into Sheffield and Doncaster.

www.hulltrains.co.uk 08450 710. 222 provides information on trains between Hull Doncaster and London

*Bus and Coach Information

www.wymetro.com/BusTravel 0113 245 7676 information on bus services in the West Yorkshire area.

www.dalesbus.org provides information on services in the dales and Moors, many of which are seasonal and aimed at visitor needs.

www.nationalexpress.com 08717 818178 national coach operator with comprehensive service network.

www.travelsouthyorkshire.com 01709 515151 information on bus services in the South Yorkshire area.

www.eyms.co.uk information on bus services in east yorkshire from Whitby down to Hull.

*Airport information

Leeds and Bradford airport 0871 288 2288   www.lbia.co.uk

Robin Hood A'pt(Doncaster) 0871 2202210   www.robinhoodairport.com

Humberside A'pt (Kirmington) 0844 8877747 www.humbersideairport.com

Teesside Airport 08712 242426   www.durhamteesvalleyairport.com

Manchester airport 08712 710711   www.manchesterairport.co.uk

*Airline Information

Jet2 www.jet2.com 0871 2261737 budget airline serving many european destinations.

Ryanair www.ryanair.com 0871 2460000 budget airline serving many european destinations.

British Airways www.ba.com 0844 4930787 provides services to a wide range of destinations from Manchester and to Heathrow from Leeds.

FlyBe www.flybe.com 0871 7002000 services to UK destinations and some European cities.

Thomas Cook www.thomascook.com services to holiday spots in the Mediterranean.

Eastern Airways www.easternairways.com 08703 669100 regular services to Scotland and Norway.

KLM www.klm.com 0871 2310000 regular services to Amsterdam.

BMI www.flybmi.com 0844 8484888 regular services to Brussels.

PIA www.piac.com.pk 0800 5871023 twice weeky flights between Leeds/Bradford and Islamabad.

Manx 2 www.manx2.com 0871 2000440 regular flights to the Isle of Man from Leeds/Bradford.

Wizzair www.wizzair.com 0906 9590002 regular flights between Doncaster airport and Polish destinations.

USEFUL CONTACTS

—A Visitor Guide To Yorkshire—

*Road Information

motorists
www.highways.gov.uk 0300 1235000 gives useful realtime information on traffic conditions on motorways and trunk roads.
www.viamichelin.co.uk provides information on road conditions.

cyclists
www.sustrans.org.uk   0117 926 8893   provides detailed information on safe cycling routes across the county.

*Ferry Information

www.poferries.com provides details of ferries between Hull and Rotterdam/ Zeebrugge as well as an online booking capability.

Weather forecasts
www.bbc.co.uk/weather
www.metoffice.gov.uk

Admission Charges
The guide indicates, as far as possible, where an attraction charges for entry. Since these are bound to vary widely and are inevitably subect to regular change, then it would be impossible to always give accurate information. As a guide, English Heritage and the National Trust charge between £3 and £9 for one adult ticket.   However, both offer annual and lifetime memberships in various categories. For more information visit :

www.english-heritage.org.uk/support-us/
www.nationaltrust.org.uk/membership/

Overseas Consulates in the County
Belgian Consulate Hull 01482 642304
Cyprus honorary consul Leeds 0113 2680308
Honorary Consul for Finland Leeds 0113 2306038
Greek Honorary Consul Leeds 0113 2262672
Consulate of Netherlands Hull   01482 224911
Consulate of Pakistan Bradford   01274 661114

USEFUL CONTACTS

INDEX

The index has been colour coded as far as practical to help make it easier to identify particular categories of attractions or features. Not all entries are colour coded; this would be far too confusing.

Abbeys and Priories ■ Beaches ■ Castles and Stately Homes ■ Chapter headings ■ Churches Cathedrals and Minsters ■ Museums and Art Galleries ■ Parks Gardens and Outdoor spaces ■ Retail ■ Walks ■

INDEX

INDEX

INDEX

INDEX

INDEX

INDEX

INDEX

Acknowledgements

photographs: the following photographs appear in the book courtesy of the specified authors or copyright holders :

Thornborough Henge page 10 Tony Newbould
Richmond Castle   page 12 Phil Smith
Boulby High Cliffs page 22 Helen Wilkinson Geograph project
York Railway museum page 33 Chris Mckenna
York minster page 35 Ian Cardinal Geograph project
York Mystery Plays page 52 York Mystery plays and York Evening Press
Ribblehead Viaduct page 78 VisitCumbria
Tan Hill page 94 Dave Dunford
Harrogate's Turkish Baths page 115 Harrogate International Centre
Harlow Carr Gardens page 116 Harrogate International Centre
Studley Water Garden page 134 Harrogate International Centre
Georgian Theatre Royal Richmond page 142 Cloud9 Photography
Granary Wharf at night   page 165 Steve Fareham Geograph Project
Pontefract Races page 204 Pontefract Park Race Company Ltd
Sutton Bank page 278 Mick Garratt
Helmsley Church page 284 David Dixon Geograph project
Chalk cliffs at Flamborough Head page 334 Pauline Eccles Geograph project
The Wolds nr Warter page 346 Keiuth Laverack Geograph project
The Deep at night page 359 Skyrider 2688
KC Stadium page 366 Yorkshire Forward
Burton constable Hall page 394 J Thomas Geograph project
Sledmere House page 400 Neil Oakes Geograph Project

Whitby

Manchester

Yorkshire Dales National Park

Richmond

Skipton

A65

Keighley

Huddersfield

Halifax

Bradford

A62

M62

A58

Leeds

Harrogate

A59

A660

Ripon

A61

A684

A1M

Sheffield

M1

A61

Wakefield

A1

Thirsk

A19

North York Moors National Park

Doncaster

A63

Selby

York

A64

A170

M18

M62

A1079

Beverley

Scarborough

A171

Hull

Bridlington

YORKSHIRE

ENGLANDS BIGGEST COUNTY